The Struggle for Development and Democracy: New Approaches
Volume 1

Studies in Critical Social Sciences Book Series

Haymarket Books is proud to be working with Brill Academic Publishers (www.brill.nl) to republish the *Studies in Critical Social Sciences* book series in paperback editions. This peer-reviewed book series offers insights into our current reality by exploring the content and consequences of power relationships under capitalism, and by considering the spaces of opposition and resistance to these changes that have been defining our new age. Our full catalog of *SCSS* volumes can be viewed at https://www.haymarketbooks.org/series_collections/4-studies-in-critical-social-sciences.

The Struggle for Development and Democracy

New Approaches

Volume 1

Alessandro Olsaretti

Haymarket Books
Chicago, IL

First published in 2021 by Brill Academic Publishers, The Netherlands

Published in paperback in 2023 by
Haymarket Books
P.O. Box 180165
Chicago, IL 60618
773-583-7884
www.haymarketbooks.org

ISBN: 978-1-64259-809-4

Distributed to the trade in the US through Consortium Book Sales and Distribution (www.cbsd.com) and internationally through Ingram Publisher Services International (www.ingramcontent.com).

This book was published with the generous support of Lannan Foundation and Wallace Action Fund.

Special discounts are available for bulk purchases by organizations and institutions. Please call 773-583-7884 or email info@haymarketbooks.org for more information.

Cover design by Jamie Kerry and Ragina Johnson.

Printed in the United States.

10 9 8 7 6 5 4 3 2 1

Library of Congress Cataloging-in-Publication data is available.

In memory of my father

∵

Contents

Acknowledgements

This book is part of a project that took shape during the course of a long and difficult intellectual journey that lasted thirty years. It is simply impossible for me to recall all those who influenced my work in one way or another during these thirty years, whether through teaching, stimulating conversations, friendly advice, or support of one type or another. Moreover, this book, including these acknowledgments, were written in the time of COVID, under time constraints made worse by financial constraints, with no time to sit down and carefully try to remember the names of all those I should acknowledge. Therefore, I limit myself here to acknowledging only those who just cannot be left out. Flora Dura, my mother, just cannot be left out. As a mother, she was my Prime Mover, as it were, the beginning of all things, because a child is borne by his mother and first socialized by his mother. Moreover, while I was growing up, and later as I tried to build my own nest, she had an uncanny and unfailing ability to be there, at important times, especially all difficult times, in my intellectual journey. It was only later in life that I understood the level of commitment, single-mindedness, and intelligence, that it takes to be such a presence in the life of a son. I also cannot leave out Renato Olsaretti, my godfather, who died as I was a child, and Renzo Olsaretti, my number one fan, and the real godfather, who helped me financially while I was finishing my PhD and later as I searched for a new career, despite the fact that he often jokingly described himself as a Pantalone, after the character in Italian popular theater known for his stinginess, similar in some ways to Moliere's character Harpagon.

I had to go my own way to pursue my principles and ideals, and this required cutting some bridges and devoting myself to research rather than family. It was not because of lack of appreciation, nor because my mother was the embodiment of tough love while I was growing up. To the contrary, I have learned my lessons, and put them to good use, although it is not the use that she expected, since my education ended up being so different than hers. It is true that I have wondered, tongue in cheek of course, about the meaning of the Latin phrase *nomen est omen*, which suggests that one's name presages one's future, since dura in Latin and in Italian means 'hard'. But it is also true that I gained through her an appreciation of Latin and the subtleties of grammar, which she instilled in me as a child by teaching me clever oracle pronouncements like the sibylline phrase *ibis redibis, nunquam per bella peribis*, which means 'you will go and return, never die in war', and which completely changes meaning if only one shifts the comma to *ibis redibis nunquam, per bella peribis*, which then means 'you will go to never return, and die in war'. Most importantly, it is also true that later in life she proved to be a perfect 'nonna' or grandmother, and she went out of her way to be listening and understanding, to the point of showing interest in my research in social history, social theory, and even sociology, which is so far from her classical education. For years, both her and Renzo lent a sympathetic hear to, and seemed bemused by, my efforts to formulate a theory, and my efforts to make sense of contemporary Italian history, periodically rocked by government scandals such as Tangentopoli or the SISMI scandal, bigger than any CIA, DIA, or NSA scandals, and yet which never led to a reform of the Italian state.

I had to go my own way to pursue my principles and ideals, simply because there are turning points in life after which, without any drama or doubt on my part, it is better to be independent than not to be independent. One such turning point for me was my research trip to Italy in 2010, other turning points came while I was writing up my dissertation and searching for a new career. In 2010 Maurilio Buffone, a school friend of mine who had been in touch with me, died after a long fight with cancer. As a youth I had been struck by the irony in another sibylline phrase I had been taught, 'he whom the gods love dies young', but this marked for me the beginning of maturity. We all act recklessly when we are young, to a greater or lesser extent, because we feel invulnerable, or because we think we have such a long time ahead of us. Maturity brings the realization that it is important to make the most of the time we have and not waste any of it. In my 2010 trip to Italy my mother and Renzo showed me hospitality, also through my mother's childhood friends Claudia and Salvatore Esposito and their children Luciana and Luca Esposito, both bright professionals, and through Silvia Olsaretti and Egidio Podda, all of whom bemusedly put up with my efforts to formulate a theory, which must have seemed so distant from their concerns, or even foreign. There is one other person not tied to me by institutional ties and who just cannot be left out, Fabio Frosini, an Italian philosopher I met by chance, who is a leading expert on Gramsci, and who was very generous with his time while I was a graduate student and influenced everything I have written on Gramsci, except this book. This book is outside his area of expertise, as I have ventured to extend Gramsci's theory introducing concepts from contemporary sociology, and in the index I refer to Gramscian concepts, rather than to Gramsci, in order to avoid entering into a debate as to whether the interpretation that I provide is really supported by Gramsci's text. I believe it is, but I argue this elsewhere. Fabio and Dolores Frosini also showed me hospitality in Bilbao.

Other persons who just cannot be left out are the scholars who taught me at McGill University. Most importantly, these scholars are John Anthony Hall, Axel van den Berg, Steven Rytina, and also Matthew Lange, Suzanne

Staggenborg, Rodney Nelson, Alberto Cambrosio, and Lucia Benacquisto, who supervised my dissertation or the readings and research that contributed to my dissertation. These scholars are also Uner Turgay, and Wael Hallaq, who were once at the Institute of Islamic Studies, and Elizabeth Elbourne, and Daviken Studnicki-Gizbert in the department of history, and also other historians at McGill University who showed an interest in my work, most importantly, James Delbourgo and Nicholas Dew, Malek Abisaab and Rula Abisaab Jordi. I also want to mention Peter Ghosh, who supervised my first research on Gramsci at Oxford University, for a degree I never completed, and yet which greatly influenced my later research. I have added references to these and to other persons and explained what I learned from them in the text and in the footnotes below, where I also discuss my experience as a graduate student and what I have learned through informal observation during my graduate studies and in all different walks of life. This is much more than anecdotal knowledge, and not just because the personal is political, which is true at least some of the time. I sought to make the theory that I propose as clear and relevant to people's lives as I possibly could, and good case studies are one way to do so. I also seek to convey how research is actually done, which is never always formal, especially if one researches culture. Culture does not exist just in books or datasets, but is part of lived experience, an understanding of which can start as informal observation in the most disparate walks of life, which can be subjected to formal scientific scrutiny in order to produce a scientific theory.

This book was written in the time of COVID and under many constraints, one of which was that I did not have access to libraries and books. Another one is that I am working under strict time constraints. Wikipedia pages contain a remarkable amount of information condensed in easily accessible form, sometimes with details that I was surprised to find online. But I also found inconsistencies in Wikipedia. I refer to many of the books that I have read without having been able to look them up recently. I have also referred to more recent scholarship that I could find online and that I knew it was important to cite, lest I be thought to have failed to cite authors who work in my field. For some of these references I was only able to consult online copies or publicly available online reviews. But I know they are all important and it was necessary to cite them. Some of the references might have small mistakes in them. Google Books is a very useful tool but has many such small mistakes. For example, Google cites the publisher of a book as the parent company, Knopf, rather than the actual publisher, Vintage. Other times a book was stated to have been published by Wiley, when it was published by Polity. Other times yet the titles of the books were slightly different than I remembered. It is also possible that I simply forgot to reference some books. I have cited all the books I could find, and all the important concepts conveyed to me in conversation that I could remember, by Hall and by other scholars at McGill University of course, since I know their work well. However, during the past thirty years I have read very widely, and it is possible that I derived some concepts from a book that I have long forgotten. It is also possible that I arrived at these concepts independently. I have come across cases of authors, even very famous authors, who arrived at concepts very similar to Gramsci's, many years later, and yet did not acknowledge Gramsci. If anyone has a genuine case to have arrived at a key concept that I discuss in this book before me, I will gladly acknowledge them. In any case, the originality of this book lies not so much in a ground-breaking new concept, which is what makes an academic star or an eminent scholar, who can seize upon a new concept and fly with it, as it were. This book is first and foremost a work of analysis, critique, and synthesis, based on long and painstaking work on the existing literature, and on informal observation of culture in all different walks of life. This is humble work that does not make one an academic star, but can provide a very important synthesis. There are some original concepts and diagrams that I came up with, by combining sociology and engineering as part of a social engineering for democracy, but these are part of another book. I believe these concepts and diagrams constitute a significantly new approach to development and democracy, which I begin to define in this book, but I make the main argument regarding these concepts and diagrams elsewhere.

As it turned out, I was able to make this synthesis also because I was willing to learn from all different walks of life, and from popular culture as much as from high culture. Another friend of mine, Colin Goldin, classically trained but with an interest in film, introduced me many years ago to work by the Taviani brothers, especially The Night of the Shooting Stars, which uses imagery from Italian popular culture and from Italian history that I related to. The Italian title of the film refers to the night of Saint Lawrence, and the film uses a frame story whereby a mother narrates to her child memories from the Second World War, which constitute the main story. The narration of memories from one generation to another is an important part of popular culture, and the imagery of the night of Saint Lawrence is an integral part of Italian popular culture. Every child in Italy knows that if you are patient and look at the sky long enough and hard enough on that night you might see a shooting star, or even more than one. They might not make your wishes come true, but seeing those shooting stars might be a wish in itself. Such imagery and such timeless human wishes were also a source for Dante's Divine Comedy, which although considered today a canonical text, once challenged high culture because it was written in Italian, or the Tuscan dialect that is the source of Italian, rather than Latin. I had an opportunity to re-read passages from the Divine Comedy recently, including passages from the Inferno, after Setrag and Claudia Manoukian thoughtfully gave me a copy of it as a present at my graduation party. Dante follows the conventional Catholic wisdom of the Middle Ages, which I presume was sanctioned by Vatican doctrine, and frames his description of Odysseus as a condemnation of a fraudulent advisor who led his men away from ordained truth. But the form of the text and its poetic imagery tell a different story. In Dante's memorable phrase, 'O frati [...] considerate la vostra semenza: fatti non foste a viver come bruti, ma per seguir virtute e canoscenza'. This is hard to translate, but essentially constitutes a sympathetic depiction of Odysseus' thirst for knowledge. The true Odysseus in Dante's Inferno is not a fraudulent advisor, but a mortal who defied both the gods of Olympus and the conventional Catholic wisdom of the Middle Ages, and yet managed to speak words that break through the frame imposed upon him by the times.

Figures

Introduction

This book is part of a project that in the last decade or so was motivated, and made all the more urgent, by the need to understand a serious social problem facing Western countries today, and an alarming political phenomenon associated with it. *The social problem* is an uneven development within countries, whereby development benefits the elites far more than the masses, and thus leads to growing inequalities within society. It is arguably the product of decades of neoliberal policies emphasizing market deregulation, which have led in many Western countries to the massive relocation of industry and a number of social problems, including uneven development. *The alarming political phenomenon* is populism, and it both followed from the uneven development caused by neoliberalism and aggravated it, so much so that it is appropriate to speak of neoliberalism and a populist backlash, as two intimately related social phenomena that contribute to the problem we face in Western countries today. Populism followed from uneven development because the impoverishment of the working class, and in some cases also of sections of the middle class and of the petite bourgeoisie, has created a reservoir of discontent that has fueled the rise of populism. Populism also aggravated uneven development, because it further divided and further impoverished the masses, by leading parts of the masses to support drastic and inappropriate means to solve the problems affecting them. Far from solving their problems, these means are only further undermining their position in society. This is because economic competition from migrants and from the working classes of developing countries are the most visible part of the social problem that we face in Western countries today, but not the most important part. The root cause of this problem lies elsewhere.

This book proposes a theory that serves to understand the origins of neoliberalism and the populist backlash that followed it, and to identify the root cause of uneven development within Western countries. In particular, this book puts forward several theses that corroborate a key hypothesis regarding this root cause. It also points to ways in which this hypothesis can be tested. This hypothesis suggests that *the root cause of uneven development within Western countries are Western elites,* and especially those powerful parts of these elites that are characterized below as *an imperialist world-elite,* which is an imperialist elite that is active on a world stage. This imperialist world-elite arguably has ties to other imperialist elites and to the establishments of Western countries. It is this imperialist world-elite who have elaborated the faulty theories of development associated with neoliberalism, which sees market competition as the only factor that drives development, and even as a panacea for all sorts of social problems. Failing education, pollution, military costs, just to name a few, have all been addressed by market mechanisms. It is this imperialist world-elite who have implemented policies of market deregulation that have led to a massive relocation of industry, in the name of encouraging market competition. Lastly, it is this imperialist world-elite who have suggested faulty answers to the problems that they created by pointing to scapegoats at home and abroad, namely, migrants and the working classes of developing countries. An especially cynical part of this imperialist world-elite and the establishments associated with it has risen to power by blaming the poorest and most disenfranchised social groups, migrants or foreign workers, for the social problem created by the imperialist world-elite in its self-serving pursuit of power. In doing so, it has only drawn public attention away from the root cause of the social problem. This root cause is the imperialist world-elite itself and the establishments who cooperate with it.

1 Defending Theory and an Eclectic Methodology for Formulating It

This book is organized in a manner that reflects my approach to research. This approach involves *pursuing multiple lines of inquiry at the same time*, which are presented in the text below as multiple arguments formulated side-by-side, making points along the way as the arguments require, in such a manner that the points of the different arguments reinforce each other. In addition, *I practice philosophy together with theory*. I address in this book some arguments that are considered part of the philosophy of social science, like defining theory and providing arguments in support of case studies. I divided this book from other books that I am working on, namely, books on humanist theories of society and history, and on humanist political philosophy, for reasons of space, and because the academic audiences are different. However, this book contains a fair amount of philosophy and theory, and the other books contain a fair amount of sociology of development. Thus, throughout this book, I formulate side by side arguments about theory and methodology, which belong to the philosophy of social science, together with arguments about neoliberalism and the populist backlash, and about development and democracy, which belong to sociology. In many of the chapters below there are two groups of arguments alongside each other. The first group are philosophical arguments, which can be described as meta theory, that is, a theory about theory. The second group are sociological arguments about development and democracy, which constitute the theory itself.

Before delving into these sociological arguments, I want to explain my *reasons for including meta theory with the theory itself.* There are two important reasons for this combination. The first is that theory is considered marginal in much or even most contemporary social science, and general theory of the kind that I propose even more so. The second reason is that the methods that I used to formulate the theory are eclectic. The entire theory might be rejected simply because it is far from mainstream social science. Rather than pretending to be doing mainstream social science, I decided instead to emphasize my differences and justify them.

To clarify the first reason, I defend theory in order to *pre-empt the criticism that theory is not science and therefore is not useful.* Thus, the meta theory emphasizes the importance of theory, and in particular of general theory, providing a defense of theory that is part of the philosophy of social science. It includes also a methodology argument about the best methodology to be used to formulate general theory, and where and how to test the hypotheses generated by theory. It reinforces the general theory of development and democracy that I propose. Both the meta theory and the theory itself are necessary because, in my experience, theories are not judged exclusively on their own merits in explaining the phenomena that they seek to address, but are always subjected to other criteria too, or are even subjected first to these other criteria. A general theory, which is furthermore based upon an eclectic methodology to formulate theory, is likely to be rejected simply because it does not fit into an easily recognized mold that meets the criteria associated with mainstream social science. Therefore, the meta theory is necessary in order to pre-empt criticisms based on these other criteria, and here I want to delve into the meta theory arguments, to further clarify the first reason for including meta-theory.

The meta theory addresses criticisms that often reinforce each other regarding the *status of theory as a form of knowledge*. These are criticisms of the kind: general theory is not a valid form of knowledge, since it cannot be proven. Or: these are mere hypotheses, where is the empirical evidence? In a nutshell, the meta theory claims that general theory is a valid form of scientific knowledge and that it is an integral part of social science. This argument also addresses criticisms regarding the methodology to be used to formulate theory. These are criticisms of the kind: this is not how you formulate theory. Or: you presuppose the question you set out to prove, a criticism often based on a narrow view of theory and how to formulate it. This book is divided into two volumes, this volume and a second volume.[1] In this volume, I set out the new

---

1 The second volume, forthcoming with Brill, is tentatively titled: The Struggle for Development and Democracy: a General Theory.

approach to social science and to development and democracy that I propose. In the second volume, I set out the general theory. Had I followed the conventions of mainstream social science, I would have divided this book into two very different volumes that would have been effectively two separate books, one on meta theory, the other proposing the theory itself. However, this would have weakened the goal of defending the theory of development and democracy, since parts of the defense would have been in another book. It would also have completely defeated the goal of contributing to overcoming specialization in research, which was one of my goals from the beginning.

To clarify the second reason for including meta theory, namely, my eclectic methodology, I want to *preempt criticisms of this methodology,* which includes relying upon informal observation, using case studies, and pursuing detailed research goals, all of which can be mis-represented as bad science. My methodology for building theory relies largely, though not exclusively, upon three distinctive methods. One involves *informal observation*, which I then subject to formal scrutiny and integrate into theory using more formal methods. The second method involves *using case studies* to build theory. After doing a large amount of reading to understand a series of academic questions, and the state of knowledge concerning these questions, I start with a simple case and then build up the theory by adding factors that are necessary to explain this case more in detail, or that are necessary to explain other cases. I actually pursue several such case studies, each focusing upon one mechanism, or upon one or a few causal factors in a mechanism. Sometimes this involves shifting the focus from one case to another, if I find the other case is more important. Both of these methods will become clearer in the course of this book. The third distinctive method that I have used in this book was to focus upon a number of *detailed* research goals. This project took a new turn when I reached a key insight that my research focused upon from that point onwards. Here I want to delve into this last method and the key insight.

This third method for formulating theory, by pursuing detailed research goals, might raise the *criticism that one presupposes the answers that one sets out to prove,* which however misrepresents this method. I want to address this criticism here because this type of misrepresentation is part of a fairly widespread pseudo-scientific and pseudo-impartial approach to research that I believe damages both research and public debate. For example, it is true that this project took a new turn when I reached a key insight, namely, that imperialist elites are responsible for problems of uneven development within Western countries, and I then focused my theory upon explaining how these elites could affect development. Stating this from the outset is a matter of intellectual honesty, and is thus a virtue, not a flawed method. In this project, I pursue *a humanist approach to philosophy and theory*, which entails formulating philosophy and theory in close inter-relationship with the practical problems that one needs to address, in this book, uneven development and its relationship to neoliberalism and the populist backlash. This approach can be described in philosophical terms as promoting the unity of theory and practice. It also entails putting the human subject at the center of a quest for knowledge. Rather than pretending the philosopher or theorist or scientist has no influence over the scientific process, and thus try to make the human subject transparent or invisible, this approach draws attention to the human subject and any specific goals this subject has.

The above criticism might then take the form of the following objection: *knowing in advance that imperialist elites are responsible for uneven development shows that one is not scientifically impartial.* There are many problems with this criticism. Here I just want to discuss the two most glaring ones. The first problem with this criticism is that it *misrepresents focusing upon a promising line of research,* and makes this seem as if one was not impartial. This is based on a misunderstanding of what being impartial means, and of the role of impartiality in scientific research. *Being impartial* means that one puts scientific truth above the insights, so that, if one cannot prove the insight, then the insight is discarded, rather than stubbornly wasting time and resources attempting to prove something that cannot be proven. It also means that, if one comes across evidence that is against the insight, one includes this evidence in one's research. It does not mean, however, that we should renounce acting upon insights, which would be disastrous for research. For example, being impartial should not be interpreted to mean that a researcher investigates hundreds of different lines of inquiry instead of just one or a few. In research, the ability to narrow down large numbers of lines of inquiry, to focus on just a few most promising ones, is essential to research success. The second problem with the criticism is that it *misrepresents the role of impartiality in scientific research.* The criticism demands of researchers virtues that belong to other positions in culture, or to an entire intellectual community, as opposed to an individual researcher. Impartiality does not *equally* apply to all positions, and only some positions require *complete* impartiality.

The *domain of law provides us with a good analogy that helps us understand the two most glaring problems with the criticism.* In chapter 5 I actually borrow some concepts from the domain of law in order to elucidate my second method for formulating theory. Here I just want to show how this domain is relevant to understand the two problems in the criticism of the third method. As far as the first problem is concerned, *being impartial does not rule out acting upon insights.* An individual researcher who acts upon an insight is in a position *analogous* to that of an investigator who was near the scene of a crime and saw a person with a smoking gun. The investigator should entertain the possibility that the gun was planted, or that the person was acting in self-defense, but should certainly focus the investigation on this person, rather than investigating equally everyone who lives in the neighborhood. As far as the second problem is concerned, the virtue of *complete impartiality is not required of an investigator*, nor of a researcher. It is required instead of the judge and jury who evaluate the case brought by the investigator. In academic research, these are editors, publishers, and ultimately the intellectual academic community, who are not directly involved in the case study. It would be a problem if the UN International Court of Justice, the International Criminal Court, or the Supreme Courts of Western countries were all staffed by judges trying to prove a case, not if an investigator bringing a case to them was trying to prove this case. To the contrary, this is part of the investigator's job. Analogously, it would be a problem if leading universities, university presses, and publishers, were all staffed with intellectuals trying to prove a case, not if an individual researcher was doing so.

Before delving into the sociological arguments, I want to add some important qualifications. Firstly, I want to emphasize a *limitation regarding the analogy to the domain of law* that I have just used. It is very important to remember that this is *just an analogy*. A sociologist researches social groups. A social group, if it is a small social group, might be involved in crimes, but crimes are actually committed only by individuals or organizations, because it is only individuals or organizations who make choices and pursue these choices. This is why one cannot bring legal charges against social groups, only against individuals or organizations, who might be at the head of a social group and influence its behavior, but are not the social group itself. This is also why legal charges are not brought by sociologists, but by investigators, and prosecutors who are part of the judiciary. The most that a sociologist can do is to point to the social groups and institutions in which individual criminals and specific criminal organizations might be found, and possibly start a public debate, which like all public debates in a democracy should be measured, balanced, and non-partisan. Secondly, I want to emphasize a *limitation regarding the generalizations about social groups that I propose*. This book is critical of elites, particularly aristocratic-military elites, because of their actions, a claim that would have to be verified through empirical tests. This book is *not* critical of aristocratic-military elites because of some anti-aristocratic bias, or because of a populist-like inclination to blame scapegoats, in this case higher-up in the hierarchy of power. This book does *not* seek to extend this criticism of elites to large social groups or entire countries. Therefore, my criticism of northern

Italian elites in this book does not entail a criticism of the people of northern Italy, and my criticism of imperialist elites in Great Britain does not entail a criticism of the people of Great Britain. A central contention of this project is that the main struggle in the modern history of the West is between elites and masses, not between countries or civilizations.

2 The New Theories and the Main Hypotheses and Theses on Neoliberalism

This volume is divided into three parts, each consisting of two chapters. It contains three theories formulated alongside each other: first, a meta theory, which I addressed above; second, a theory about neoliberalism and the populist backlash; and third, a general theory about development and democracy. Here I want to focus upon the second and third theories. The theory about neoliberalism and the populist backlash, and how to move past their errors, provides the main narrative of this volume. This *main narrative is structured around three lines of inquiry, one in each part of the book*. The first line of inquiry concerns a humanist theory of society and history and the difficulties that I encountered in formulating such a theory. The second line of inquiry concerns the theory of society and history proposed by Antonio Gramsci, the anti-fascist political theorist, which served as a model for my theory. These two lines of inquiry converged, as they both contributed to the third line of inquiry, regarding the collective action advantage of imperialist elites, and their participation in neoliberalism. The third part of the book is entirely focused upon this third line of inquiry, which took shape after I reached the *key insight that imperialist elites are responsible for problems of uneven development within Western countries*, and not just for wars and bad political choices, and that this goes back at least to the time of the rise of fascism in Italy, which arguably foreshadowed populism. This third line of inquiry is entirely focused upon understanding the relationship between imperialism, uneven development, neoliberalism and the populist backlash. It starts from the insight, which I arrived at as part of the first and second lines of inquiry, and which I begin to justify in this volume, that neoliberalism is based upon partial pictures of society and history, which led to faulty scientific models, which in their turn led to faulty development policies, and industry relocation and uneven development, and ultimately to the populist backlash.

How the first two lines of inquiry led to the third is slightly more complex than just the above insight regarding imperialist elites and uneven development, but it can be easily summarized. I started the project with the goal to formulate a humanist social science that would provide broad pictures of society and history, and more complex and nuanced views of human beings than those associated with most social science models, including the economic theories behind neoliberalism. I ran into many difficulties and eventually reached the *additional insight that if it is so difficult to formulate broad pictures and nuanced views it is because we lack the social conditions for producing them.* This is due to a number of factors, academic specialization and elitism standing out as especially important factors, because the faulty scientific models behind neoliberalism came to be widely accepted not just because of intellectual failures of individual economists, but because of failures due to the way in which universities are organized, which leaves the formulation of broad pictures and nuanced views to elites. Together with other work, this led me to yet another *insight, namely, that imperialist elites are responsible for imperialism, uneven development, and also for neoliberalism and the populist backlash.* The project then focused upon understanding how any elite could influence such disparate social phenomena, and where one could find evidence of the existence of this elite and its responsibilities for social problems and faulty scientific theories alike.

Part 1, and chapters 1 and 2, detail the goals and the insights of the project. These chapters are part of the first line of inquiry. *Chapter 1* details the overarching goal that motivated what I refer to below as 'this project'. The goal was and still is to formulate a humanist social science. This is a multidisciplinary social science that produces broad pictures of society and history, using nuanced views of human beings, and conceptualizing human behavior in all its main domains: the economy, culture, politics, and the military. By contrast, most social science today is built starting from one-sided pictures that emphasize only one side of human behavior, typically the behavior found in just one of these domains. What is worse, an ever-increasing part of social science takes economic behavior, which is arguably conceived of too one-sidedly even just for the economy itself, and applies it to culture, politics, and the military, as if profit maximization was all that individuals are capable of, or should aspire to. This chapter suggests instead that we should seek an altogether new approach to development and democracy, based on a multidisciplinary social science that takes into consideration contributions to development from politics and culture, besides the economy, or to put it another way, from states and civil society, besides markets. This chapter thus introduces two key concepts: political-military development, and cultural development. It also emphasizes that democracy closely interacts with development. *Chapter 2* details the difficulties that this project ran into, which were due mostly to the organization of universities, and to the elitism that is creeping into them. In chapter 5, I begin to explore the negative effects of academic specialization, which follow in part from the organization of universities.

Part 2, and chapters 3 and 4, detail Gramsci's project, and explain how this project builds upon it. These chapters are part of the second line of inquiry. *Chapter 3* introduces my interpretation of Gramsci's work and the reasons why I think it is important to continue this work. Gramsci's project sought to contribute to a renewal of social science that has served as a model for my project. The chapter introduces and contrasts Gramsci's project with those of orthodox Marxists, emphasizing that democracy was central to Gramsci's work. It also proposes views of democracy and science that do not portray democracy and science as uniquely or specifically European inventions, taking into consideration Edward Said's criticism of European pseudo-scientific views of the orient. However, I also critique some of Said's views and the misuses of these views, suggesting that, although much of European social science might have been implicated in imperialism, and even complicit with it, not all science is necessarily eurocentric or in the service of imperialism. *Chapter 4* continues detailing my interpretation of Gramsci's theory, by focusing upon the concept of cultural democracy, which is arguably very important to democracy, and which includes learning from popular culture in a mutual or two-way exchange that is part of my eclectic methodology for formulating theory. I also suggest, in response to arguments by postcolonial and subaltern studies scholar Gayatri Chakravorty Spivak, that this cultural democracy is one way in which the subaltern can speak, by finding a voice in a mutual exchange with those social scientists who come from the masses and are close to the masses.

Part 3, and chapters 5 and 6, detail my interpretation of the collective action advantage of imperialist elites, which led to neoliberalism and the populist backlash. These chapters are part of the third line of inquiry, which emerged from the first two lines, as they converged to suggest the reasons for the success of neoliberalism, and the continuation of disastrous economic policies, even as it became increasingly clear that they lead to uneven development, which eventually resulted in the populist backlash. *Chapter 5* addresses problems raised by the first line of inquiry, asking how we can improve upon social science, which is too specialized and elitist, and make it closer to the needs of policymakers and citizens. It also seeks to understand a key point introduced in the first part of this volume, namely, the sources of the new imperialism that has come from the West in the wake of the 9/11 attacks, and whether this imperialism is really new. This chapter also introduces the *main hypotheses and theses* of the entire project. *The main hypotheses* can be summarized as suggesting that neoliberalism and the associated economic policies that led to uneven development were implemented by a bloc of national elites with an imperialist world-elite that coordinated activities amongst national elites, thanks also to its hegemony. *The theses* include theses that describe two tendencies in countries in the West, one arising from social conflict, the other from interstate conflict, which explain the imperial expansion in the past and the consequent buildup of power by imperialist elites, and thus ultimately explain the creation of imperialist world-elites. These theses also show the usefulness of theory to social science, because they are key to testing the hypotheses, by corroborating and refining the hypotheses.

These theses *corroborate the hypotheses* by suggesting a plausible mechanism that explains both past imperial expansion in the West, and how imperialist elites can emerge in the West. They also *refine the hypotheses* by suggesting that an imperialist world-elite emerged in the past and by pointing to where we can find evidence of this. The aristocratic-military elite that built the British empire, the largest empire in European history, became an early imperialist world-elite that dominated trade flows and an earlier globalization. *Chapter 6* focuses on two case studies, the British aristocratic-military elite that built the British empire, and the northern Italian elite that built the modern Italian state and became an early national elite. It suggests that the key to understand the sources of power of the British aristocratic-military elite is to be found in its cultural institutions responsible for hegemony, notably universities. The key to understand the sources of power of the northern Italian elite is its greater ability to engage in collective action compared to the masses, thanks to a collective action advantage it enjoyed and arguably still enjoys. Chapter 6 explains this collective action advantage in terms of basic constituents of social interaction, out of which the collective action advantage arises. It also explains the first tendency toward expansion, suggesting that, when the collective action advantage of elites is challenged within their countries, this leads elites to look for ways to expand their power abroad, and to become imperialist elites. In the long run, this expansion enables elites to fight back against the masses fighting for democracy within their countries. In particular, this expansion enables elites to impose models of development and democracy that favor the elites over and above the masses. Thus the elites' hegemony, or their collective action advantage, lead to the uneven development associated with neoliberalism and the populist backlash.

PART 1

The Project and the Need for New Approaches

The So-called Reality of the External World

Man knows objectively in that knowledge is real for the whole of humankind historically unified in a unitary cultural system; but this process of historical unification occurs with the disappearance of the internal contradictions that tear human society apart, contradictions that are the condition for the formation of [different social] groups and the birth of non-universal and concrete ideologies, which however are immediately rendered transient by the practical origin of their essence. *Therefore there is a struggle for objectivity (to free oneself from partial and erroneous ideologies) and this struggle is the same as the struggle for the cultural unification of humankind.*

Antonio Gramsci, *Prison Notebooks*, Notebook 11, Note 17, p. 1416. My emphasis.[1]

∵

1 Antonio Gramsci, *Quaderni del Carcere*, ed. Valentino Gerratana, 4 vols. (Torino: Einaudi, 2007). This and other passages where I cite Gramsci are my translations from the Italian original. They reflect my interpretation of Gramsci's work.

CHAPTER 1

The Project and Theories of Development and Democracy

This book is part of a project, and before proceeding with the arguments of this book, it is useful to explain the place of this book in the project and the arguments put forward by this and other books in the project. The hypotheses and theses that I sketched out in the introduction are a vast subject. In order to address this subject adequately, I had to split the theory that I propose into several books that are part of the same project, all focused on questions of development and democracy. This book is divided into two volumes, which propose respectively an overview of the project, and an outline of a general theory of development and democracy. The arguments that I sketch in this book are provided with stronger theoretical foundations in other books that propose a humanist social science, and a humanist theory of society and history. I am also working on books that propose a humanist political philosophy, a humanist theory of politics and the military, humanist theories of emancipatory and subaltern politics, and humanist theories of urban and regional planning. They are all based on a large amount of material and many observations gathered over decades of work. I mention these other books in order to pre-empt two types of criticism. The first type of criticism is of the kind: how do you justify this? what are the theoretical and philosophical foundations of your approach? The answers to these and similar questions are in the books on humanist theories of society and history, and in the book on humanist political philosophy. The second type of criticism is of the kind: you have not addressed this point, or you have not worked out the implications of this point, what does it all mean for politics and the military? what does it all mean for cities and regions and the communities and neighborhoods within them? The answers to these questions are in the books on humanist theories of politics and the military, and on humanist theories of urban and regional planning.

1.1 The Project and the Answers and Alternatives That It Proposes

I decided to complete this book first because I think it is important to define clearly the goals of the project and the problems I seek to address, and to show with concrete examples that it is possible to understand and move past the errors of neoliberalism and the populist backlash. The idea of a populist backlash is a concept addressed, amongst others, by political scientist Rawi Abdelal, at Harvard University. My difference from Abdelal is that I tie it in specific ways to neoliberalism and imperialism.[1] Moreover, besides contributing to understanding the problem posed by neoliberalism and the populist backlash, *this book begins to suggest answers and to formulate alternatives*. The answers and alternatives that I sketch in this book are part of an *outline of a theory*, which is all the more useful being an outline. My overarching theoretical goal is to contribute to valid and useful theories that are alternative to neoliberal theories and that can lead to the formulation of development policies that encourage growth and at the same time benefit the masses as much as the elites. Therefore, being *an outline* has the advantage that it can serve as the starting point for new directions in research that many different researchers can contribute to. Formulating in full valid and useful alternatives to neoliberalism takes many different contributors, not a single person. I sought therefore to provide the outline of a theory because an outline can serve to define the broad directions within which many different contributors can pursue research, while still contributing to the same overall project. Similarly, being an outline *of a theory* does not diminish the usefulness of the arguments of this book, because theories are an indispensable first step both towards finding answers regarding the origins of neoliberalism and the populist backlash, and also towards formulating alternatives to neoliberal theories.

Let us consider the *answers* proposed by this book. The *answers* that I propose, and how I provide these answers, makes this book very different than books by linguist Noam Chomsky that touch upon many of the same questions. These questions include: is there an imperialist world-elite? who are they? what are the responsibilities of intellectuals for social problems? They also include questions indirectly touched upon by Chomsky: what is neoliberalism, what is hegemony, what are the prospects for the American Dream? While addressing the same questions, I differ from Chomsky in three important ways. In the first way, I provide *clear and unequivocal answers* that are different

1 The idea of a populist backlash is discussed by several scholars, including in particular by Rawi Abdelal, in his forthcoming article: Rawi Abdelal, "Dignity, Inequality, and the Populist Backlash: Lessons from America and Europe for a Sustainable Globalization," in *Harvard Business School Working Paper 20–123* (2020). Abdelal's work closely parallels many of the themes that I explore in my project. I came to focus on these themes through my own readings, and through discussions with Malek Abisaab and Rula Abisaab Jordi, amongst others, whose work I address below. Harvard University, where Abdelal teaches, is one of the elite universities where economics is taught together with political science, a point that I address in chapter 5.

than Chomsky's. Chomsky puts the grand question in the title of a recent book *Who Rules the World?* and then pours cold water on his audience: 'The question cannot have a simple and definite answer'.[2] By contrast, this book begins to answer the similar but more academic questions: is there an imperialist world-elite? Where can we find evidence of its existence? The answer is simpler than Chomsky claims and can be empirically tested and verified. I also have a more optimistic view than Chomsky's of the prospects of the American Dream, which I think could be as bright as they once were if only the United States and other Western countries managed to free themselves from the burden of the imperialist world-elite, and to sever the tie between capitalism and imperialism.

In the second way, *my approach to answering these questions emphasizes theory,* and is thus different than Chomsky's approach. Unlike him, I propose a theory, albeit in outline form, rather than just a discussion of questions that are of public interest. The theory is useful because it serves to answer questions, but I also seek to make the theory itself available, nut just hand down answers to questions. Therefore, my approach seeks to make sure that *the theory is clear and comprehensible*. This applies to the arguments as well as the answers, so that all those involved in formulating policies, from policymakers who formulate and implement policies, to citizens who assess the policies, can decide for themselves whether the arguments are convincing and thus whether to accept the answers. This is in contrast to most social scientists today, whose theories are incomprehensible even to many graduate students in their field and to social scientists working in other fields, and who simply hand down an answer to policymakers and citizens, seemingly expecting that the answer will be accepted based on their prestige and the prestige of social science. Even Chomsky takes this elitist approach, by providing a watered down theory. I believe this is extremely damaging both to social science and also to social movements and political parties, because it is creating a gulf between, on the one hand, social science and, on the other hand, policymakers and citizens, including activists involved in social movements. I believe instead that social science should be made as clear and comprehensible as possible, in order to make it directly accessible to policymakers and all citizens.

As far as the third way in which I differ from Chomsky is concerned, I worked hard to *propose a theory that is useful*, as all theory can and should be.

---

2 Noam Chomsky, *Who Rules the World?* (New York: Henry Holt and Company, 2016), 1. Chomsky's pessimistic view of the prospects of the American Dream is set out in: *Requiem for the American Dream: the 10 Principles of Concentration of Wealth & Power* (New York: Seven Stories Press, 2017). I address other bookss by Chomsky below.

As I practice theory, which is in contrast to specialized social science, theory is directly relevant to understand the problems of uneven development within Western countries, and thus the prospects of the American Dream, which is not available to increasingly large numbers of citizens. Theory can also provide concrete answers. It is thanks to theory that I can provide answers to the question that Chomsky says cannot have a definitive answer. It is also thanks to theory that I can begin to suggest alternatives to neoliberalism. By contrast, most social science today is specialized and focused exclusively upon empirical research and proposes theory that has only limited applications. The theory that still exists today often uses obscure language, whether mathematical language or thick jargon, and is far from being accessible, even to other researchers.[3] This is arguably encouraging a rejection of social theory and a withdrawal into a social science based upon empirical research alone, thus producing theories whose applications are limited to a very specific time and place. I address the definition of theory below, and the differences between a *social theory* and a theory of society in the book on the humanist theory of society. Here a preliminary definition should suffice. In most contemporary literature, social theory refers to the theory that informs sociology. In this project, I propose that we define social theory as a particular type of theory of society that gives especial importance to society.

Let us now consider the *alternatives* proposed by this book. The alternatives that I propose *emphasize the importance of a theory of society and history, which makes this book very different than mainstream approaches to development*, which are dominated by economists. A key difference is that *I use a multidisciplinary approach to social science*, which includes also philosophy and theory. In particular, this book incorporates contributions from many other social sciences, while building upon sociological work on development and democracy. The other social sciences that I draw from are: anthropology, history, geography, cultural studies, and military science, which are often considered separately from mainstream social science. These are in addition to economics and political science, which are widely recognized as social sciences.

3 For a clear-cut example of obscure and very specialized language on matters of public concern, see: Steven Rytina, "Scaling the Intergenerational Continuity of Occupation: Is Occupational Inheritance Ascriptive after All?," *American Journal of Sociology* 97, no. 6 (1992); "Is Occupational Mobility Declining in the US?," *Social Forces* 78, no. 4 (2000). From these very specialized empirical studies, Rytina in his retirement formulated a theory: *Network Persistence and the Axis of Hierarchy: How Orderly Stratification Is Implicit in Sticky Struggles* (London and New York: Anthem Press, 2020). In chapter 5 I classify this type of theory as detailed theory. Elsewhere I criticize obscure language and propose a theory regarding its social origins.

I combine all these disparate contributions in a theory of society and history, which serves as the foundation to understand development and democracy, the latter being two very important phenomena in society and history, or even the two most important phenomena. Unlike mainstream approaches to development, based on economics, *I use sociology as the starting point or basis for a multidisciplinary approach to social science* that draws from all of the above disciplines or domains of knowledge.

Another key difference is that I *extend this multidisciplinary approach to incorporate philosophy and theory*, in order to begin to find alternatives. I believe that *theory is an indispensable first step to find alternatives to neoliberalism* at this stage in time, or moment in political processes, for two main reasons. I want to go into some detail into these two reasons because theory is central to this project. I address the second reason in the next section of this chapter. The first reason is that theory is necessary to formulate *broad strategies that are informed by what can be called a strategic vision*. A strategic vision suggests which policies to pursue first, for example. I address in detail the importance of theory in chapter 5 and in the second volume. Here I just want to introduce the main arguments that are relevant to a strategic vision. A theory provides a broad picture, which is analogous to a bird's eye view, or a map laying out the entire field, and thus provides also the strategic vision that is associated with this broad picture. Theories, broad pictures, and a strategic vision, are important to formulate *successful* policies and implement them *efficiently*. This is because policies, in order to be successful and efficient, have to be coherent, firstly across different domains, and secondly across time and space. Lack of coherence can be disastrous because incoherent policies can undermine each other. Coherence, in addition to avoiding the pitfalls of lack of coherence, can also ensure that policies reinforce each other and are thus more successful and efficient than they would be on their own.

An *example of coherence across domains* are cultural policies to raise the education and skills of the workforce, which can and should reinforce economic policies to increase the competitiveness of an economy. The lack of such cultural policies likely contributed to uneven development in the wake of neoliberal policies, because the working class was forced to compete mostly by lowering wages, rather than by raising skills. An *example of coherence across time* are economic policies that can and should make long-term plans. It seems to me that neoliberalism has failed terribly on this account. In the short term, industry relocation has created savings for the economy in the form of cheaper consumer goods, but in the long term, this came at the cost of massive job losses in the sectors of the economy of Western countries that produced these goods, which ultimately shrank the economic base of society and *will lead to slower long-term* growth, at least for the working class and those sections of the middle class and the petite bourgeoisie affected by industry relocation. This is leading to ever increasing uneven development, as the elites benefited from the relocation of industry, while labouring social groups, which draw their income entirely or largely from their labour, either lost out, or benefited considerably less. An *example of coherence across space* is that policies can have very different effects in different parts of a country, including different parts of a city, because these parts have different unemployment levels, different skill levels, and different levels of capital available for investment. Policies that are advantageous for one part of the country might be less advantageous, or bad, or even disastrous, for other parts. They can thus lead to *growing* uneven development. In this project I argue that imperialism can cause uneven development, which can undermine democracy and development for the entire country in the long run, even in countries like the United States, whose development and democracy are very advanced.

1.2 The Project and Its Importance to Achieve a Paradigm Shift

There is a second reason why theory is an indispensable first step in order to find alternatives to neoliberalism, and it is that *theory is important to reconceptualize development and democracy*. In this project I propose two significantly new theories, one concerning democracy and collective action, the other concerning development. These significantly new theories are needed because the faults of neoliberalism are very deep, and formulating alternatives requires what could be called a paradigm shift, a significantly new way to conceptualize development and democracy, compared to mainstream economics and neoliberalism. I believe this new theory should start from an altogether different way of looking at society, human beings, and our place in the world. Historian of economics Alessandro Roncaglia has taken a similar approach, but he suggests different answers. Roncaglia suggests that mainstream economics, heavily influenced by a paradigm associated with neoliberal theory, is undergoing disaggregation, and that the neoliberal paradigm has been weakened, but no new paradigm has emerged, because of the fragmentation of economics into many competing schools. He suggests that a dialogue amongst the different schools in economics today could serve to define a new paradigm.[4]

4 Alessandro Roncaglia, *The Age of Fragmentation: a History of Contemporary Economic Thought*, trans. Alessandro Roncaglia (Cambridge and New York: Cambridge University Press, 2019). The concept of paradigm shift was first proposed by Thomas Kuhn in a recently

I want to clarify here what I mean by *paradigm shift* and at the same time emphasize my differences from the paradigm shift that Roncaglia proposes. *Three features of my approach set my work apart from Roncaglia's,* and also from much of mainstream social science. Firstly, *the paradigm shift that I propose is more comprehensive.* As I mentioned above, the answers that I propose build upon sociology rather than economics, and the dialogue that I seek to encourage is between all social sciences and human sciences, rather than just between schools of economics. It amounts to proposing a unified multidisciplinary social science, a project central to sociology at its inception in the early twentieth century, rather than a unified theory of economics as Roncaglia proposes. I also propose a humanist social science as this unified multidisciplinary social science. I begin to define it in this book, and continue elaborating upon it in the books on humanist social science. Secondly, *the paradigm shift that I propose goes deeper*, and I draw heavily from philosophy, particularly the philosophy of social science, in order to scrutinize the assumptions to be used by this humanist social science. Thirdly, *I apply the theory reflexively*, that is, I apply it to itself, and reflect upon the conditions that are necessary in order to enable objectivity in social science. These include *social* conditions for dialogue amongst different disciplines, from all the main domains of research, namely, economics, cultural studies, political science, and military science. Advocacy, like the one practiced by Roncaglia, is necessary but not sufficient. We also need to secure the actual social conditions for objectivity in social science, without which it is impossible to provide alternatives. I address this third feature in the second volume, here I want to focus upon the first two. They serve respectively to avoid one-sided pictures of society, and to avoid reductive scientific models of society, both of which are necessary to avoid the failures of neoliberalism.

The first feature of my approach, seeking a comprehensive paradigm shift as part of the goal to formulate a unified multidisciplinary social science, serves also to avoid one-sidedness. Avoiding one-sidedness entails to *avoid one-sided pictures of society*, which are based on just the economy, or culture, or politics or the military. As explained above in discussing coherence across domains, development, which today is associated chiefly with the economy alone, can

reprinted book: Thomas S. Kuhn and Ian Hacking, *The Structure of Scientific Revolutions*, Fourth edition. ed. (Chicago: The University of Chicago Press, 2012). Derek Boothman argues that Gramsci's project, by seeking new philosophical foundations for social science, was seeking a paradigm shift: Derek Boothman, "Gramsci, Croce e la Scienza," in *Gramsci e L'italia. Atti del Convegno Internazionale di Urbino. 24 – 25 Gennaio 1992*, ed. Ruggero Giacomini, Domenico Losurdo, and Michele Martelli (Napoli: La Città del Sole, 1994).

be greatly affected by culture. Moreover, economist Amartya Sen and philosopher Martha Nussbaum have made a convincing argument that development should not be conceived of exclusively as growth in income, but it should include capabilities, an argument that I begin to address in the second volume.[5] I build upon my work and other sociologists' work to suggest that there are collective capabilities, in addition to individual capabilities. I also propose that there are economic, cultural, political, and military capabilities, and that all are part of development. These capabilities correspond to economic, cultural, and political-military development. I focus especially upon political-military development and the related capabilities, and upon cultural development and the related capabilities, since both are understudied and both are part of hegemony, which is important to democracy. I want to add a few words here about political-military development, and also exemplify the usefulness of multidisciplinary theories that provide broad, as opposed to one-sided, pictures of society and history, which go beyond studying the economy alone, and seek to incorporate politics and the military in the study of development.

The multidisciplinary approach to social science that I propose, and the concept of *political-military development,* seek to bring the study of politics and the military together, within a humanist social science that is especially useful to understand both social conflict and interstate conflict, as well as their interactions. This multidisciplinary approach seeks also to encourage an exchange between studies of politics and of the military. This exchange is useful to understand *key questions in politics*. I approach both politics and the military as types of collective action and I argue that there are important areas of overlap between the two, for example in countries where social conditions lead to large numbers of volunteers and sizeable *irregular forces*. These act at the interface between politics and the military, and they take part in social conflict and interstate conflict at one and the same time. I use the word *volunteers* in this project to refer to all persons who volunteer to work without pay, and I focus upon military volunteers, or volunteer fighters. Below I begin also to integrate within the study of collective action, including collective action by violent social movements, questions of Intelligence and Communications, and questions of Command and Control, respectively abbreviated as IC and C2 in military science.

5 This approach is set out in: Amartya Sen, *Development as Freedom* (Oxford and New York: Oxford University Press, 2001); Martha C. Nussbaum, *Women and Human Development: the Capabilities Approach*, The Seeley Lectures (Cambridge and New York: Cambridge University Press, 2000).

The multidisciplinary approach that I propose, and the exchange between studies of politics and of the military, is useful also to understand *key military questions*. Within military science the *concept of total war* is being revised from its Second World War origins. This is an important concept that I address in the book on humanist theories of politics and the military. In my interpretation, this revision suggests that it is not just necessary to protect a country's economy and infrastructure through air defenses, an important lesson from the Second World War, but also from industrial espionage and from being undermined in other ways during peacetime, for example by the spread of criminality, which is associated with the destruction of community. In some countries, the entire society, not just the economy, can be undermined by violent social movements. A multidisciplinary approach to defense is therefore necessary. The multidisciplinary approach that I propose, which looks at society and social interaction within it as the common foundations for economic, cultural, political, and military activities, is ideally suited as the starting point for understanding total war.

The second feature of my approach, a paradigm shift that goes deeper than Roncaglia's, drawing heavily from philosophy, serves also to avoid reductiveness. Avoiding reductiveness entails to *avoid reductive scientific models*. Reductive scientific models are based on one-sided philosophies. An example of the use that I make of philosophy is to scrutinize assumptions, and thus to go deeper than Roncaglia in the paradigm shift. The faults of neoliberalism are very deep in the sense that they are rooted in very basic views. Arguably, neoliberalism is based upon one-sided views of society and human beings, emphasizing only markets and *Homo Oeconomicus*, out of which reductive economic models were built that became part of faulty theories of development and democracy. Moreover, it seems that the acceptance of these faulty theories of development and democracy was encouraged by the previous acceptance of the reductive views of society and human beings, which are the assumptions or axioms, in other words the starting points, from which reductive economic models were built. Therefore, we need a thorough revision of the assumptions that are the starting point for theories of development and democracy, which contribute to a paradigm shift.

Ultimately, this paradigm shift involves reconceptualizing the very way we look at ourselves and our place in the world, and the related view regarding how society works, human beings, and what is the course of key social phenomena like development and democracy in history. In brief, we should recover the concept of human beings as motivated by things other than just competition and profit, of society as based on many different arenas and the associated different types of behavior, each with its own principles, not just markets and acquisitive individualism. We should also recover the insight that development and democracy are necessary to each other, and that the tradeoff of more development for less democracy is bad for development as well as for democracy, in the long run. An integral part of the paradigm shift, therefore, is a significantly new theory of democracy, which complements a significantly new theory of development and its interaction with democracy. This book begins to outline these significantly new theories.

1.3 The Significantly New Theory of Democracy Proposed

The *significantly new theory of democracy is based upon two key insights* that are present in Gramsci's work. These are the insight that *collective action is very important to democracy,* Gramsci emphasized especially deliberate and sustained collective action, and the insight that *democracy involves the distribution of power in society*. I develop these insights into a theory that claims democracy consists in a distribution of power that is favorable to the masses, and that the ability to engage in collective action is what decides whether the distribution of power is more in favor of the elites, or of the masses. I complement these insights by Gramsci and propose an outline of the significantly new theory of democracy, using *key concepts from contemporary sociology, rather than political science.* Sociology is little known within studies of democracy or development, yet it has contributed important concepts that are very useful to both of these fields of study. Furthermore, I argue that sociology can be useful to overcome problems of specialization within universities and could serve as the basis for a unified multidisciplinary social science that includes studies of the economy, culture, politics, and the military.

Political sociology proved especially useful for the significantly new theory of democracy that I propose. I derived from it one important insight, namely, the insight *that democracy and collective action are related through contention,* a particular type of social conflict that is routinized and repeated over time. Sociologists Sydney Tarrow and Charles Tilly suggested that in order to understand democracy we should focus upon studying *the democratization process whereby democracy was achieved,* which involved contention between states and social movements, in which collective action played a very important part.[6] Another important insight that I derived from political sociology is

6 On democracy understood as a process of democratization, and the contentious politics that are part of this process, see: Marco Giugni, Doug McAdam, and Charles Tilly, eds., *From Contention to Democracy*, G – Reference, Information and Interdisciplinary Subjects

that there are *different sources of power*. Contemporary political sociology is focused on the study of power, and sociologist Michael Mann has proposed a comprehensive study of power that seeks to understand all sources of power, whether economic, cultural, political, or military.[7] This complements my goal to contribute to a unified multidisciplinary social science that includes all these domains of human activity.

The theory of democracy that I propose is significantly new, and marks a departure from much of political science, and also from these works of political sociology, because of the *way in which I reconceptualize collective action*. This reconceptualization can be summarized as two groups of claims regarding collective action and democracy. The first is that *collective action depends upon basic constituents of social interaction that changed in modern times with capitalism*. The theory of democracy that I propose suggests that, in the long process of contention between states and social movements, which I reformulate as a contention between elites and masses, modern democracies in the West arose when the basic constituents of social interaction changed in such a way as to favor collective action by the masses. These basic constituents include culture and various types of organization, all of which are especially important to collective action, and thus to democracy. I break down these basic constituents into even more basic constituents and suggest that, with the introduction of capitalism, sustained mass political mobilization becomes possible for the first time in the modern history of the West because of shifting cultural and political boundaries, and that this led to a shift in the balance of power in society in favor of the masses.

The second group of claims regarding collective action and democracy suggests that there are *three levels at which we must study collective action, each involving different actors, namely, individuals, social groups, and states*, which

---

Series (Lanham, Boulder, New York, and Oxford: Rowman & Littlefield Publishers, 1998); Charles Tilly, *Democracy* (Cambridge and New York: Cambridge University Press, 2007); *Contentious Performances*, Cambridge Studies in Contentious Politics (Cambridge and New York: Cambridge University Press, 2008).

7 Mann set out much of his theory in a 4-volumes book on the sources of social power, which was published in 1986, and which has been republished in its entirety in 2012: Michael Mann, *The Sources of Social Power, Vol. 1: a History of Power from the Beginning to Ad 1760* (Cambridge and New York: Cambridge University Press, 2012); *The Sources of Social Power, Vol. 2: the Rise of Classes and Nation-States, 1760–1914*, The Sources of Social Power (Cambridge and New York: Cambridge University Press, 2012); *The Sources of Social Power, Vol. 3: Global Empires and Revolution, 1890–1945* (Cambridge and New York: Cambridge University Press, 2012); *The Sources of Social Power, Vol. 4: Globalizations, 1945–2011* (Cambridge and New York: Cambridge University Press, 2012). The first volume defines extensive and intensive power.

I refer to respectively as micro, meso, and macro collective action. Much of political science today focuses upon micro collective action. Political sociology includes micro and meso collective action, but the latter is under-theorized. Chapter 6 introduces the concept of meso collective action within the context of a discussion of Gramsci's theory, and in it, and in the second volume, I begin to *define and theorize meso collective action*, which is collective action by social groups that occurs on a meso scale. I suggest that meso collective action is affected by the number of social groups, their position in the social hierarchy of power, their internal cohesiveness, and their organization, which includes the number of organizations such as social movement organizations within any given social group. All can be explained using more basic constituents of social interaction that affect the number of social groups, for example.

I arrive at this definition of meso collective action, and begin to *theorize the interaction between meso and micro collective action, through an analysis of meso collective action problems.* This formalizes a number of insights by Gramsci into the manner in which the northern Italian elite that built the modern Italian state was able to dominate the masses during the Risorgimento, the process of national unification whereby the modern Italian state was built out of a number of different states in the Italian peninsula during the course of the nineteenth century and early twentieth century. The elite was able to steer the process of national unification in a direction that favored it over and above the masses, and that had enduring consequences for both development and democracy in Italy. The elite was able to do so because it enjoyed a *meso collective action advantage,* which I refer to simply as collective action advantage in most of the text below. This was due both to basic constituents of social interaction, and also to the elites' ability to compound collective action problems faced by the masses. These involved micro collective action problems and also meso collective action problems, both of which have to be taken into consideration in order to understand collective action. A better organized elite, compared to the masses, can compound micro collective action problems faced by the masses, like defection, through cooptation for example. It can also exploit distinctive meso collective action problems faced by the masses. I suggest that we should consider the cooptation of the leadership of a social group to be a meso collective action problem, since leadership is part of the organization of a social group. There are other, less obvious but nevertheless important, meso collective action problems.

I focus upon *two specific types of meso collective action problems that are central to Gramsci's work*, both of which can prevent a social group from engaging in deliberate and sustained collective action. The *problem of volunteers* arises when a social group loses cohesiveness and produces large numbers of volunteers who can be used by the better organized elites for their own purposes, including further undermining the social group that lost cohesiveness. The *problem of subaltern social groups* arises when a social group lacks subalterns, or when subalterns are completely dependent upon elites. As part of this argument, I propose in this project a new interpretation of the Gramscian concepts of subalterns and subaltern social groups that are alternative to the concepts proposed by postcolonial or subaltern studies scholars associated with the study of subaltern social groups, including Spivak. I propose that subalterns are individuals who occupy in society a position analogous to that of subaltern officers in armies. Subalterns include professional activists, or activists who can devote large parts of their time to political activity. The problem of subaltern social groups consists in this: without a sufficient number of subalterns who are independent of elites, a social group drawn from the masses cannot engage in deliberate and sustained collective action. To get around this problem, it has to ally itself to a subaltern social group.

Political sociology also studies *macro collective action*, although this is the preserve of historical sociology and in particular of World Systems Theory, but even in the latter it is under-theorized. In the second volume I begin to *define and theorize macro collective action*, which is collective action by states, and which occurs on a macro scale. I suggest that, similarly to meso collective action by social groups, macro collective action by states is affected by the number of states, their position in the interstate hierarchy of power, their internal cohesiveness, and their organization. I also begin to *theorize the interaction between macro and meso collective action, through an analysis of the impact of macro collective action upon meso collective action problems.* This enables me to address an important deviation from the theory proposed above. Some countries have been struggling with imperfect democracies, and falling back into dictatorship, despite the introduction of capitalism, or perhaps because of it and the manner in which it took place.

This enables me to *reformulate sociologist Barrington Moore Jr's theory of the social origins of dictatorship and democracy and the controversial concept of Islamofascism.*[8] In other books, I suggest that Italy and other countries in the Mediterranean, in particular countries in the Balkans and in the Middle East, have suffered enduring problems of development and democracy due to the fact that modern capitalism was introduced later than in north-western

8 Barrington Moore's book has been re-printed recently as: Barrington Jr Moore, *Social Origins of Dictatorship and Democracy: Lord and Peasant in the Making of the Modern World* (Boston: Beacon Press, 2015).

Europe, and after powerful states had emerged there, which had begun building large colonial empires, and were fighting each other for influence in the Mediterranean. In Italy, and in countries in the Balkans and the Middle East, macro collective action affected meso collective action problems and led to dictatorship. This is because capitalism initially leads to loss of cohesiveness of social groups lower down the social hierarchy of power, creating large numbers of volunteers. In the presence of interstate conflict, this can lead to two social problems, the rise of violent social movements, and the emergence of large irregular forces, the combination of which undermines democracy and can lead to dictatorship. These are the social origins of fascist dictatorships in Italy and Greece, which are tragically being repeated, with some differences, in the Middle East.

1.4 The Significantly New Theory of Development Proposed

This volume introduces a number of important arguments regarding development and its relationship to democracy. The second volume further elaborates upon these arguments and puts forward the outline of a general theory of development and democracy, contributing to a significantly new theory of development, supported by *key concepts from sociology, rather than economics.* In particular, I build upon two key arguments that have been put forward in the sociology of development and that complement arguments put forward in political sociology. Together, these two key arguments amount to *a re-evaluation of the positive role that states can play in development* and challenge neoliberalism, which claims that development is largely or even exclusively driven by unrestricted markets, and that the role of the state should be minimal and should be restricted to guaranteeing the functioning of markets. I want to emphasize that this is *not* a theory in favor of states running the economy. I simply seek to redress the balance after neoliberalism led to an excessive reaction against the state and suggest that we ought to find a balance between over-reliance on the state and over-reliance upon markets.

The two key arguments from the sociology of development that I elaborate upon can serve to find this balance. The first argument concerns the *positive role that states can play in development by ensuring a functioning society*, not just markets. Sociologist Matthew Lange has argued that states play an important role in development by providing peace and stability. Lange is an expert on the British Empire who has studied the role of states in furthering development and the role of violence in delaying it. He can aptly be described as a leading expert in ethnic violence and other forms of mass violence.[9] His arguments can be summarized as suggesting that states are indispensable to a functioning society, without which development is thoroughly undermined. He has focused especially on the negative effects of violence, which led to failed states and lasting underdevelopment. I extend this argument to criminal phenomena like the mafia, which have hindered the development of southern Italy, where they coexisted with violent social movements like fascism, one spilling into the other, and both being caused by impoverishment and loss of community amongst some social groups, which lead large numbers of individuals to fend for themselves, and to have recourse to employment that is criminal or that borders on criminality, including shifting military employment, or participation as volunteers in irregular forces. The second argument has been put forward by sociologist Carlo Trigilia, and it suggests that *development is due to the right combination of state, society, and markets*.[10] I elaborate upon this argument by suggesting that this combination includes a balance between state, society, and markets, such that each can expand the type of power that is distinctive to it, and contribute to the others, without however taking them over.

The theory of development that I propose is significantly new, and marks a departure from mainstream economics, because it is *part of a general theory focusing on power*, which enables *reconceptualizing the sources of development* in altogether new ways. This reconceptualization is laid out in the second volume, where I outline the general theory in the form of 15 theses about development and democracy. Simplifying somewhat, the general theory can be summarized as arguing that states produce political-military power, which includes defense and internal peace and stability, society produces cultural power, which includes knowledge and science, and markets produce economic power, which includes wealth. All three, namely, state, society, and markets, are necessary to development, because each is best at producing its own type of power, since each type of power is maximized by a different type

---

9 Lange's book on the British empire is: Matthew Lange, *Lineages of Despotism and Development: British Colonialism and State Power* (Chicago: University of Chicago Press, 2009). His more recent research on violence is contained in: *Killing Others: a Natural History of Ethnic Violence* (Ithaca, New York: Cornell University Press, 2017).

10 Carlo Trigilia, *Economic Sociology: State, Market, and Society in Modern Capitalism* (Oxford: Blackwell, 2008). Trigilia has worked also on local development, a concept that is being researched in English-speaking countries too: Colin Crouch et al., *Local Production Systems in Europe: Rise or Demise?* (Oxford and New York: Oxford University Press, 2001); Carlo Trigilia, *Sviluppo Locale: un Progetto per l'Italia*, Saggi Tascabili Laterza (Bari: Laterza, 2005).

of individual behavior, a different type of organization, and a different arena in which individuals and organizations interact.

The general theory can be summarized as proposing *three significantly new arguments regarding the sources of development*. The first argument revisits and combines the Smithian division of labour in a factory and the Durkheimian division of labour in society, and suggests that *the division of labour in society is an important component of productivity*. This argument proposes that the division of labour in society led to the emergence of three important arenas in Western societies today: the political-military, the cultural, and the economic arenas, which respectively overlap with the state, society, and markets, although only roughly. The second argument suggests ways in which political-military power and cultural power contribute to development. I begin to reformulate Sen's capability approach to development using concepts derived from sociology.[11] I *propose the concepts of political-military development and cultural development, and elaborate upon these under-theorized types of development*, suggesting for example that there are important collective capabilities like military capabilities, which contribute to other types of development and to overall societal development. The third significantly new argument regarding the sources of development involves the *interaction between democracy and development, and the argument that democracy contributes to development*. This is not in itself a new argument, what is new are the specific contributions that I suggest democracy can give to development. In a nutshell, there are two such contributions. The first is guaranteeing a certain balance between state, society, and markets, whereas the second is preventing uneven development and social rents.

The first contribution that democracy can give to development is by guaranteeing the conditions for development, which include a certain balance between state, society, and markets. This contribution requires *placing institutional considerations in a social context*. I argue that an important condition for development, especially for lasting development, is that there should be a functioning division of labour in society, and that each of the three arenas should be able to expand the type of power that is distinctive to it, and thus advance political-military development and cultural development, as well as economic development, while contributing to the other arenas, and yet remaining independent of the other arenas. To conceptualize this type of interaction, I use

11 In this project I specifically address: Sen, *Development as Freedom*. I complement Sen's work with sociological work on collective capabilities, for example Evans' work: Peter B. Evans, "Collective Capabilities, Culture, and Amartya Sen's Development as Freedom," *Studies in comparative international development* 37, no. 2 (2002).

sociologist Peter Evans' *concept of embedded autonomy between state and society,* which refers to the interaction between state and society that advances development.[12] I suggest that it is useful to reconceptualize embedded autonomy as a feature that describes some state-society interaction, in which there is exchange of information and coordination of activities between state and society, while state and society remain independent of each other. I generalize this concept and extend it to the interaction between state, society, and markets, and between the three arenas. I suggest that embedded autonomy between arenas, a particular type of balance between arenas, whereby each arena contributes to the other ones, without being taken over by them, is an important condition for development. Democracy contributes to embedded autonomy and it is therefore necessary to development.

The second contribution that democracy gives to development is by limiting uneven development within a country, which creates social rents understood as easy profits made at the expense of disadvantaged social groups. *Democracy is important to prevent uneven development*, which can undermine in the long run both democracy and development. In formulating this argument, I build upon Gramsci's argument in the essay on *The Southern Question,* a question concerning the political and cultural origins of uneven development within Italy, and the enduring underdevelopment of southern Italy compared to the north of the country.[13] This enables me to revisit political scientist Robert Putnam's argument, as laid out in *Making Democracy Work*, which claims that the differences in development between the north and south of Italy are due to the different development of civil society, which I suggest we should consider to be part of cultural development, and a key factor in democracy.[14] I argue at the end of the next chapter, and in the second volume, that the reasons for the smaller cultural development of southern Italy compared to the north of the country are to be found in social conditions and in organizational problems that have an international dimension. Elsewhere, I also emphasize that they have nothing to do with explanations that stereotype southern Italian culture and make it seem as if it encourages violence, from the mafia to fascism. I emphasize instead the organization of culture, for example the relationship between high intellectuals, universities, and the rest of society, and

---

12 Peter B. Evans, *Embedded Autonomy: States and Industrial Transformation* (Princeton and Oxford: Princeton University Press, 1995).

13 Antonio Gramsci, *La Questione Meridionale* (Roma: Editori Riuniti, 1974).

14 Robert D. Putnam, Robert Leonardi, and Raffaella Y. Nanetti, *Making Democracy Work: Civic Traditions in Modern Italy* (Princeton and Oxford: Princeton University Press, 1994). I address the controversies over Putnam's work in the next section.

organizational problems that arise in the transition from agrarian-artisanal society to capitalist society. Here I want to focus upon the details of the theories of development and democracy that I propose and how they build upon Putnam's work and yet deviate from it in significant ways.

1.5 Uneven Development, Civil Society and Engineering

The importance of the new theories of development and democracy stands out when we consider *enduring cases of uneven development like the Southern Question in Italy*, which has proven intractable to traditional development policies and the economics they are based on. Therefore, I want to give details of the theories of development and democracy that I propose, together with concrete examples of how they can contribute to address questions of uneven development that are especially important in the wake of the 9/11 attacks and the 2008 financial crisis, and to understand the rise of populism. The theories involve reconceptualizing the contribution of both civil society and of the state to development. Let us begin by focusing here upon the contribution of civil society. In my interpretation, Putnam's work, which focuses on civil society and democracy in Italy, holds the lesson that institutions are important. It is not enough to preach ethical behavior in order to ensure the adoption of sound policies, something the Catholic Church did throughout Italy, but one needs also favorable social institutions, and I add in this project social structures, something that was only found in northern Italy. Scholars in the department of political science at McGill University have taken part in the debate on Putnam's work, providing answers informed by the strategic vision I mentioned earlier.[15]

15 Filippo Sabetti, *The Search for Good Government: Understanding the Paradox of Italian Democracy* (Montreal & Kingston, London, Ithaca: McGill-Queen's University Press, 2000); *Village Politics and the Mafia in Sicily* (Montreal & Kingston, London, Ithaca: McGill-Queen's University Press, 2002). Sabetti's book on good government went through a second edition in 2002. Italian-American and Italian-Canadian scholars in the departments of sociology and political science at McGill University have been shattering through their work the stereotype that Italians, and particularly south Italians, are prone to crime, which is the unspoken bone of contention over Putnam's claims regarding the backwardness of southern Italy, an argument that dates back to Cesare Lombroso's day. Anthony Masi and Antonia Maioni have had distinguished careers and became respectively Provost and Dean of Arts at McGill University. Christopher P. Manfredi has had a similarly distinguished career. These examples show that when Italians have the opportunity to work in environments in which fair competition and meritocracy prevail, they can be very successful. I am afraid, however, that this success is limited to the elite, and

More in particular, Putnam's work and subsequent debates have given *two important contributions to our understanding of questions of development and democracy* that are central to this book. The first is *a contribution to our understanding of uneven development.* They have added a new factor, civil society, to the Southern Question. I further expand upon this point by including in the explanation of uneven development within Italy the historical availability of volunteers, especially in the south, which is associated with other social phenomena like brigandage, the mafia, and fascism, all of which undermined both development and democracy. The second is *a contribution to our understanding of the way in which civil society contributes to development*, which is arguably the main point made by Putnam. Questions of uneven development can be explained at least in part by the uneven development of civil society. In this project I argue that the development of civil society is an important component of cultural development, which contributes both to democracy, and also to other types of development and to overall societal development.

Putnam's work is important because, despite the controversies that it stirred, the main point that it made remains a valid point. This is the point that *a vibrant civil society and its institutions contribute both to democracy and to development.* I expand upon this point in two directions, emphasizing respectively social structures, and universities. I address the importance of universities in the next section. I want to begin here with the first direction, regarding social structures. I *expand upon Putnam's approach to the study of civil society and incorporate it into a social engineering for democracy.* The concept of a social engineering for democracy is the central subject of the book on the humanist theory of society. Here I just want to introduce those parts of this concept that are necessary to understand the approach to civil society that I propose. Putnam's measure of favorable social institutions for democracy was a simple aggregate measure, namely, a count of NGOs for a given area or size of population. This count was much higher for northern Italy than for southern Italy. The social engineering approach emphasizes that, in addition to this count, we have to study the structures that exist amongst NGOs, and between NGOs and institutions, and NGOs and the public. The social engineering that I propose draws from civil engineering, and the usefulness of key concepts that I borrow from civil engineering can be illustrated by reference to buildings and the concept of collapse.

---

that ordinary Italians, Italian-Americans, and Italian-Canadians do not benefit from it. Moreover, in popular culture Italians are still often associated with the mafia or thieves of various stripes.

The concept of collapse can usefully be applied to society. Geographer Jared Diamond has famously applied the concept of collapse to human societies in studying environmental impacts, amongst other challenges faced by societies.[16] In this project I provide an *interpretation of the collapse of societies that borrows from engineering*, and specifically from civil engineering, as part of a social engineering for democracy. This social engineering is useful to make civil society stronger, while guaranteeing democracy. This is a challenge that is especially important in the wake of the 9/11 attacks and the increasingly bitter culture wars in the United States and other countries in the West affected by populism. *The concepts of strength and resilience, borrowed from civil engineering, are especially important* to understand collapse, since strength refers to the maximum load that a structure can bear without collapsing, and resilience refers to the ability to bear a load without collapsing even after parts of a structure have been damaged. Here I focus on the concept of resilience because it is especially important for democracy.

Civil engineering definitions of these concepts are easier to understand than their social equivalents and can serve as the starting point for a theory of strength and resilience in social structures that is relevant to understand social conflict and democracy. *Valuable buildings that are resilient can have redundant structures, coupled with modern fire alarm and fire suppression systems*, which can delay collapse, warn occupants when a fire starts, and monitor temperatures. Modern construction is also such that some debris will not easily ignite material inside a building and start a major fire. However, *if there is failure at multiple points in a structure, the whole structure collapses.* Failure at points in a structure that are closer to the ground can bring collapse. Every building rests upon foundations that carry the weight of the entire structure above them and transmit it to the ground. If the joints at the lower floors of a building that are closer to the ground fail, or if the foundations fail, then the *entire* structure above them collapses. These concepts are directly useful to special operations units like the 1st Air Brigade and the COMSUBIN of the Italian Armed Forces, or the SEALs of the United States Armed Forces.[17]

16 Jared Diamond, *Collapse: How Societies Choose to Fail or Succeed: Revised Edition* (London: Penguin, 2011). This book by Diamond has been very successful and has been reprinted three times, in 2005, 2011, and 2013. Diamond is a writer who has began addressing big questions in books for a general public, and his success shows the need that there is for such an approach.

17 I derive these concepts both from my studies in civil engineering and from research into military operations and the transformation of the Italian Armed Forces in recent years. The Italian Air force, like many NATO air forces, has built specialized units for special operations. This has led to the creation of the 1st Air Brigade, which includes the 9th Wing, with a squadron of special operations helicopters, the 16th Wing, which is a force

Moreover, they are relevant also to understand the collapse of societies, and social structures within politics and the military that are important for IC.

The concept of resilience in buildings is useful, because analogies with building design concepts can clarify the concept of resilience in society, which is not as straight-forward as the concept of strength. Designing for resilience entails introducing redundancies in a structure that enable it to resist damage. An example of such redundancies is this simple account of civil engineering structures. Structures are made up of structural members, which include beams or columns. Beams are horizontal structural members in a building that support the weight of floors, with the occupants, furniture and equipment, and transmit the weight to columns. Columns are vertical structural members, which transmit the weight of the building, including the weight transmitted to them by beams, to the foundations. There can be columns in different parts of the building, all of which transmit the weight to the foundations. If there are more columns, and there are more joints that tie together all the columns and the beams, this can make a structure much stronger and stiffer, and also more resilient, because if some columns fail, the remaining ones are still sufficient to transmit the weight to the foundations. Collapse can eventually occur also in resilient structures, but more failures of columns have to occur for the entire structure to collapse, because the structure can resist failure in one or a few columns, or on one side. Demolition of resilient structures can only be initiated by destroying numerous columns around the building all at once, with explosives for example. Seismic events like earthquakes, which typically

---

protection unit for the protection of bases, and the 17th Wing, which is a raiders unit for attacking enemy bases. In Italian the expression 'incursore', or raider, is used also by Italian Navy Special Forces, the COMSUBIN, and refers to any direct-action unit that operates deep in enemy territory. The 17th Wing's operations include direct action against enemy air bases, like destroying air base buildings or control towers, for example, since today military airports share air strips with civilian airports with air control towers. The 16th Wing is specialized instead in protecting air bases, precisely from units like the 17th Wing. Both are part of the same Air Brigade, since some of the expertise they need is the same, and a specialized knowledge of air bases is essential to both the 16th and the 17th Wing. By contrast, older units like the US Navy SEALs, whose name emphasizes that they are trained in Sea, Air and Land operations, were historically not as specialized, nor is the 101st Division. Perhaps by now the SEALs include also experts in protecting bases like those of the 1st Air Brigade. Below I describe the importance of military technology and professional military units to IC. The 9th Wing and the 16th Wing are both located in southern Italy, respectively in Caserta, near Naples, and at Grottaglie, near Taranto, the location of a large Italian Navy base. These areas provide military labour but not technologies, nor commands. The only NATO Corps Headquarters provided by Italy, the NRDC – IT, is based in the north of the country. Two of the three Italian Army Corps headquarters are based in the north of the country.

include large shocks, sometimes followed by a series of tremors, can have a similar effect.[18]

The *usefulness of the concept of resilience for C3I* can be readily understood. A valuable building that is used for IC or C2 can be made more resilient by building redundancies into it, such that if part of this structure is destroyed, the rest can still stand and convey intelligence or orders. *The concept of resilience in social structures*, specifically structures in politics and the military, can be readily understood starting from the above observations. For example, the concept of resilience introduced above can be easily extended to centers of power. Once, the 10 Downing street residence and bunker was the one center of power and symbol of political life in Great Britain. Today, with devolution, similar centers have been set up for the governments of Northern Ireland, Scotland, and Wales, complete with very interesting and iconic buildings like the Scottish parliament building, for example. Arguably, this can lead to political structures that are both closer to local realities on the ground, and more resilient, provided there are suitable structures connecting the different centers of power. The social engineering for democracy that I propose in the book on the humanist theory of society includes the design of these structures, besides prescribing multiple centers of power.

The concept of resilience can be applied to intelligence agencies. Resilience arguably applies to the Five Eyes, an intelligence-sharing alliance that focuses upon signals intelligence or SIGINT and that includes agencies from all five

18 I gained much of my understanding of these concepts through two professors at University College London, Richard Bassett, a professor of geotechnical engineering, which includes designing foundations for buildings, and James G. A. Croll, a professor of structural engineering, which includes designing the structures that carry the weight in buildings. Croll is an expert in the esoteric field of thermal buckling, the deformation of structures due to temperatures, high temperatures induced by a fire for example, and could make even this very specialized field fascinating to students. Structural engineering is the branch of civil engineering that specializes in the design of structures, which includes for example choosing the number and size of columns and beams in a building, and the type of joints between a column and a beam, leaving to architects the design of the exterior of the building and of the interior decoration of the building. As a simple and hypothetical illustration of redundancy in structures, consider the following point. Fazlur Rahman Khan's tubular structure for skyscrapers involves placing load-bearing columns all around the sides of the building. Another type of structure for skyscrapers involves placing load-bearing elements around the core of the building. It is intuitive that if these two structures were combined, they would provide redundancy, because if one or more sides of the building were destroyed, the core would still carry the weight of the building and prevent collapse, at least for a time. This example only applies to skyscrapers. Other types of structures, like the Montreal Biosfere geodesic structure designed by Buckminster Fuller for Expo 67, behave very differently.

major English-speaking countries, namely, Great Britain and its former settler colonies Australia, Canada, New Zealand, and the United States. It is intuitive that multiple centers for monitoring communications provide redundancy and are thus resilient compared to a single center, especially if there are structures between the centers. Different structures can be built with modern means of communication, and with different alliances. The Five Eyes possibly reflected a White Anglo-Saxon and Protestant bias in their composition, in excluding Ireland. A different alliance based on different cultural politics and strategic alliances and the need to monitor local communications to and from Great Britain, as well as the crucially important maritime traffic through the English Channel, would include Ireland and its centers of power, and would be strenghtened by centers of power in France and in the Benelux countries. Another example of a different alliance would be an alliance that includes centers of power in countries in widely dispersed yet strategic locations, Italy in the middle of the Mediterranean, Mexico in the Gulf of Mexico and the Caribbean, Brazil in South America, Japan in East Asia, and Iran and today the UAE and Qatar in the Persian Gulf. The Five Eyes have apparently reached out to include other countries over time, perhaps reflecting changes in both cultural politics and strategic priorities. Such alliances are crucially important to provide information, and can be helpful, but also pose threats. The Axis, another alliance of widely dispersed countries, which included Italy, Germany, and Japan, when these countries were ruled by Fascists and Nazis, forced the United States to fight on two fronts during the Second World War, and created a domestic scare because of perceived threats by immigrants from these countries.

1.6 The Importance of Civil Society and Universities

The second direction in which I expand upon Putnam' work involves *including universities in Italy as key institutions within civil society that contribute to both democracy and development.* I argue in this project that universities and other institution of learning are an integral part of cultural development. Universities in Italy and other civil society NGOs contribute to development in two ways. In the first way, civil society including universities contributes to democracy, and through it to development, because it affects the *formulation of public policies, and subjecting public policies to scrutiny*, which is essential to avoid corruption and waste. The role of civil society in formulating policies and scrutinizing policies is an important point often encountered in the literature on development, as well as a central point in Putnam's work. Regions of Italy like Liguria, Emilia Romagna and Tuscany, all have historically had more favorable social institutions, recently including many civil society NGOs. Favorable social institutions have ensured a more vibrant democracy, which in its turn led to better policies and greater development, compared to southern Italy most strikingly, but also compared to central Italy to some extent. Liguria also played a leading role in the creation of the modern Italian state, being both the place where Giuseppe Garibaldi was born, in the province of Imperia, and the place where he set sail for the *expedition of the thousand* to conquer the south of the country and create the modern Italian state.[19]

Here I want to emphasize, compared to Putnam, *the importance of universities to civil society, and through it to democracy and development.* One reason why universities are important to development is that they contribute to cultural development, which includes the production and dissemination of knowledge. Universities are crucially important to research and education, producing and disseminating knowledge and skills amongst a population. The importance of universities can be illustrated by reference to Bologna, the regional capital of Emilia Romagna, an insight suggested to me by numerous discussions with professionals from Naples, including a Naples research group of the Consiglio Nazionale delle Ricerche, or CNR, the National Research Council of Italy. These professionals pointed out to me how much harder it is to pursue a career and to do research in their fields in southern Italy, despite the fact that their fields are leading fields for development. Italian universities are often centrally managed from Rome, and even private companies are not as meritocratic in their appointments as they should be. Naples still offers a location as beautiful as any in the Mediterranean, and related amenities like a famous rowers' club that a professional can go to during his spare time, but even these assets are being undermined by unscrupulous entrepreneurs and

19 There are classic Garibaldi biographies: Christopher Hibbert, *Garibaldi and His Enemies: the Clash of Arms and Personalities in the Making of Italy* (London: Longman, 1965); Denis Mack Smith, *Garibaldi: a Great Life in Brief*, Great Lives Observed (Englewood Cliffs, New Jersey: Prentice-Hall, 1969). The latter went through a second edition in 1982. In Chapter 6 I address Gramsci's views of Garibaldi, which started a historical revision of the flattering pictures of Garibaldi that prevailed earlier, even in the British press of Garibaldi's day, where he was lionized as a liberal hero. Garibaldi himself took part in constructing a flattering public image of himself as a hero: Lucy Riall, "Hero, Saint or Revolutionary? Nineteenth-Century Politics and the Cult of Garibaldi," *Modern Italy* 3, no. 2 (1998); "Travel, Migration, Exile: Garibaldi's Global Fame," *Modern Italy* 19, no. 1 (2014). This is similar to the self-promotion that general Custer undertook in the United States. The more recent biographies of Garibaldi reveal a complex individual: *Garibaldi: Invention of a Hero* (New Haven and London: Yale University Press, 2008).

urban sprawl, which destroys the beauty of the places and creates few jobs, or even reduces jobs by undermining tourism.[20]

The reasons for this are complex, but it is possible to summarize some of them in a few paragraphs. Here I want to sketch simply *the different social bases associated with different models of development that prevailed in different parts of Italy* and suggest ways to explain their different fortunes in the wake of the 9/11 attacks and the financial crisis of 2008. Arguably, the different models of development that prevailed in different parts of Italy were due to the different extent of democracy that existed in these areas, an insight that I develop at length in this project. They were also due to the different importance of universities and other research-intensive institutions and cultural institutions in different parts of Italy. I discuss the political importance of universities in chapter 6 below, which focuses on case studies in historical sociology that are important for understanding elites. Here I want to *emphasize the economic importance of universities in Italy, and of research institution like the CNR, and their effect upon different models of development.* I suggest that we should consider universities and research institutions to be non-profits and NGOs, or like non-profits and NGOs, which are part of civil society. This approach can help us understand the different fortunes of the different models of development that prevailed in Italy. It leads me to diverge from Putnam' work and emphasize different geographical divisions within Italy, not just between north and south, but between north-west, north-east and parts of the center, and the south of Italy. These different geographical divisions are based upon different social bases.

Uneven development within Italy has been attributed to *three different models of development that prevailed in different parts of the country*, which are also associated with different universities that have given different contributions to development. The least known outside of Italy is perhaps the *model referred to as the Third Italy*, which was very successful for a few decades and seems recently to have run into difficulties. It is associated with the north-east of the country and parts of the center, and has enjoyed less fortune than the model that prevails in the north-west. *The Third Italy* is a model of economic development that is based upon small and medium-sized companies that are part of industrial districts, within which many companies producing similar

20 The rowers' club in Naples has produced Olympic champions like the Abbagnale brothers, whose training surpasses that of COMSUBIN operatives, and is also open to professionals from Naples. One problem that follows from lack of a properly functioning civil society and state, is the mismanagement of cities, which sadly has affected Naples and undermined tourism and other parts of the economy.

products are located. This is a model that is arguably based upon a vibrant economic democracy that also encouraged development.[21] I want to suggest here that the reasons for the problems that this model has recently faced are not so much due to the model itself, nor just to the size of the companies, but are due to failures of civil society and its contribution to the economy, particularly failures in the contribution that universities give to development. Small and medium-sized companies are more reliant upon external sources of research than large companies, which alone can fund research internally. Italy unfortunately still suffers from a lack of universities that produce world-level research or that are capable of transforming world-level research and turn it into technologies that have business applications. This is true even of the north-east of the country, compared to the north-west. Bologna, the capital of a once economically thriving region, is the seat of the oldest university involved in uninterrupted teaching in the West, for more than a thousand years. This university is also famous for being the place where Avogadro contributed to the birth of modern chemistry. However, the most famous institutes of technology and the most famous business universities, a fame built both upon both research and the quality of education, are all located in the north-west.

This leads me to another difference from Putnam's work. *It is important not to bundle the whole of northern Italy into one category, as if it was one undifferentiated reality*. Nor do I intend to portray northern Italy as an undifferentiated 'other' opposed to southern Italy. There are many important differences within northern Italy between one social group and another, including in the culture of these social groups. There are also important differences between different regions in northern Italy. The difference that I am emphasizing here, between north-eastern and north-western Italy, roughly overlapping with the Third and First Italy, is one such important difference. It is a socio-economic difference, which has nevertheless important cultural aspects too. Moreover,

---

21 On the Third Italy see: Francesco Bartolini, *La Terza Italia: Reinventare la Nazione alla Fine del Novecento*, Studi Storici Carocci (Roma: Carocci editore, 2015). Szabolcs Kemeny, a Hungarian economic sociologist, introduced me to these questions in the early 1990s, when the topic was still relatively new, especially outside Italy, yet was beginning to draw attention from outside Italy. Recently, this model of development has gone through a crisis and there have been suggestions that it is not a viable model of development. I believe this is based upon a misconception. Similar models of development based upon industrial districts are still thriving in Germany. The Third Italy is arguably losing because of lack of suitable universities and research institutions, and because of the lack of ties between existing universities and companies. I describe this problem below and in the second volume as lack of embedded autonomy between different arenas, and more specifically between state, society, and markets.

for the purposes of this book, it is especially useful to contrast the north-east with the north-west, or the Third Italy with the First Italy, because they are based on very different models of development. Liguria, Emilia Romagna and Tuscany, are all economically successful regions. The last two regions belong to the Third Italy, whereas Liguria is more closely associated with a different model of development.

This is the *model of development known as the First Italy*, and Liguria has been the location also of a key naval base, La Spezia, which is as important as any other NATO naval base.[22] This model has always been economically successful and it continued to be economically successful in the wake of the 9/11 attacks and the financial crisis of 2008. It includes the traditional industrial regions of Piedmont and Lombardy, with their regional capitals Turin and Milan being known also as the seats of the two most famous institutes of technology in Italy, the Polytechnic of Turin and the Polytechnic of Milan, a different type of institution than the University of Bologna, and an institution that is especially important in modern economies in which technological innovation is essential to competitiveness. Milan is also the seat of the most famous business school in Italy, actually a university in its own right, Bocconi University. This is a private university and in Italy it has the same prestige and importance that the Wharton Business School of the University of Pennsylvania has in the United States.[23] Milan is also the seat

22 La Spezia was an important naval base already in the nineteenth century, arguably just as important in the Mediterranean as the French naval base in Toulon, and comparable in importance due to its strategic position to the French naval base in Brest and the British naval base in Devonport, both being near the mouth of the English Channel, which is a very busy shipping lane with large maritime traffic. La Spezia was important under Mussolini's regime, and is still today an important nerve-center, as it were, for the Italian Navy because it is near the Sarzana-Luni airport, which hosts an Italian Navy helicopter detachment, and near Porto Venere, which hosts the special forces of the Italian Navy, the COMSUBIN. It is also relatively near Livorno, which is the seat of the Italian Naval Academy, and an important port in use since the 1640s or shortly after, founded by the Medici House, as a base for its fleets and for the Holy Military Order of Saint Stephen, a crusading order that could aptly be described as Tuscan raiders.

23 To Gramsci scholars, Bocconi University is most closely associated with economist Piero Sraffa, whose father taught there and later became dean of this university. Bocconi University is famous in Italy both for its research and as a university that provides good education, both for lawyers and managers, so much so that despite being a private university with relatively high fees for Italy, where public universities offer affordable education, Bocconi still attracts large numbers of applicants. It is comparable to the University of Pennsylvania and the Wharton School of Business for this as well as for other reasons. The University of Pennsylvania is part of the Ivy League, the group of the most prestigious and important universities in the United States. Similar to these universities and their business schools, Bocconi educates the future managers of companies in Italy.

of another important private university devoted entirely to research in medicine and health sciences, the San Raffaele University. Both Turin and Milan are famous for having been the seats of large private industrial enterprises like car manufacturers FIAT and Alfa Romeo, both of which became part of Fiat Chrysler Automobiles, or FCA, now part of the Franco-Italian automotive group Stellantis. More recently, areas near Milan have become the seat of important NATO headquarters in southern Europe like the NATO Rapid Deployment Corps – Italy, the NRDC-IT.

By contrast, *the model of development known as the Second Italy,* which includes the whole of southern Italy, and the islands Sardinia and Sicily, was dependent for many years upon state investment in the form of large public industrial enterprises, or state investment to prop up large private industrial enterprises facing financial difficulties like steel manufacturer ILVA, which was also at the center of a scandal related to pollution. Many of the large public industrial enterprises where built in areas where there was little or no social base, and little or no further investment, so that there could be no lasting development, and these large enterprises were disparagingly known in Italian political discourse as 'cathedrals in the desert', an expression roughly equivalent to the expression 'white elephant' in English. I argue in this project that this is due in part to the fact that there was insufficient coordination and sharing of information between state and society. It was also due to lack of sufficient cultural development. Southern Italian universities are also less famous for their research and education, with the only exception of the Federico II University in Naples, which I have learned about also through professionals from Naples. Southern Italian universities are arguably even more burdened than universities in other parts of the country by patrimonial practices described in Italy as baronial power. These are practices whereby powerful professors known as barons threat university posts as if they were feudal appanages, to be awarded to the most loyal followers, rather than the most innovative scientists.

An important sign of the uneven development between southern and northern Italy is in *the different types of contributions they give to the national economy, labour instead of knowledge.* The Italian Army provides a striking example of this instance of uneven development. Southern Italy is still a provider of labour to the rest of the country, including military labour, so much so that after the demise of the Soviet Union, and the transformation of the Italian Army from what was largely a conscript army to an all-professional force, the Garibaldi brigade was relocated to the south of the country, and the Aosta brigade in Sicily was turned into an all-professional brigade, in order to make these army units closer to their recruitment bases, whereas many other brigades located in the north-east of the country, where the Warsaw Pact might have attacked, were disbanded. However, high-technology army units and especially industry are still mostly located in the north of the country, or around Rome, because it is the national capital, with only some recent exceptions like the Pinerolo brigade, which I address below. For example, the Tactical Intelligence Brigade of the Italian Army, which provides eyes, electronic devices, and electronic warfare systems, all of which are an integral part of IC and are indispensable to direct any military operation today, has its dependent units in the center of the country, near Rome, or in the north-east.[24]

I argue in this project that *the roots of underdevelopment of southern Italy are to be found also in political-military causes*. The north-east, and parts of the center based on the Third Italy, might have more recently suffered from similar causes, which have undermined this model of development. The north-east, parts of the center, and southern Italy, have also been devasted by seismic events, through much of the past century, and strikingly and dramatically even in our times. This points to the importance of a functioning and efficient state, for example in enforcing adequate building codes, and in providing investment in building technology, which can ensure the safety of the population, and also prevent setbacks for development that follow major earthquakes. This and other important functions of states are evident most clearly when imperfect states fail to fulfill these functions. Professionals from Naples have introduced me to a fatalistic resignation to these devastating seismic events and to the lack of a functioning state, which some social groups in southern Italy seem to share, whereas I don't. It is both necessary and possible to make states function well, in those functions that pertain to states. A vibrant civil society that holds the state accountable and that provides renewal amongst political parties is indispensable. This book begins to sketch how civil society and the state have to interact for this to be possible.

24 An interesting point that I hope to address elsewhere is that although some Italian Army units are located away from main urban centers, for example the Tactical Intelligence Brigade has a unit in Sora and one in Treviso, both relatively small towns, IT professionals who come from these areas can find it extremely difficult to pursue an IT career in these small urban centers, partly because of the risk-averseness of small businesses towards IT, and partly, I would add, because of lack of suitable state-society ties, or embedded autonomy. There seems to be no easy way in these areas to move from a career in the military to a career in the economy.

1.7 The Importance of the State and Defense

Recent studies have begun to provide an understanding of *what drives development in these different models of development, particularly the Third Italy*. They have suggested that, in addition to a vibrant civil society, *the right type of state intervention is also necessary* to ensure both development and democracy. Here I want to emphasize that to achieve the right type of state intervention there has to be *embedded autonomy* between state and society, and more in general between the political-military arena and other arenas. I focus especially upon the relationship between the state and civil society, and between political-military and cultural development. Florence University and Siena University have pioneered in Italy the contemporary study of the interactions between state, society and markets, and the study of technological innovation, with the work of Trigilia and of economic historian Michelangelo Vasta respectively.[25] An Italian academic journal, *Stato e Mercato*, or State and Market, is devoted to research on the mutual interaction between states and markets, without reducing one to the other, as neoliberalism did by attributing all development to markets and by reducing states to little more than institutions devoted to guaranteeing markets. I want to give here some examples of the way in which a properly functioning state can contribute to development that is market-driven, by focusing upon political-military development and military capabilities, which are understudied, and which are most widely considered to be necessary to provide public goods like defense that a state has to be involved in producing. These are all examples of modern Italian Army units and their technologies, which also illustrate how far Italian industry and the Italian Army have advanced, both financially and technologically, since the post-Second World War years, when they were heavily reliant upon United States loans and United States-made weapons.

Interestingly, key cities in the Third Italy, Pordenone, Bologna, Venice, and Florence are also the cities where the Italian state introduced important organizational and technological innovations. It would be very interesting to see if

25 Michelangelo Vasta and his collaborators work on patents, the history of technology, and the history of the firm: Renato Giannetti, ed. *Nel Mito di Prometeo. L'Innovazione Tecnologica dalla Rivoluzione Industriale ad Oggi. Temi, Inventori e Protagonisti dall'Ottocento al Duemila* (Firenze: Ponte alle Grazie, 1996); Renato Giannetti and Michelangelo Vasta, *Evolution of Italian Enterprises in the 20th Century*, Contributions to Economics (Heidelberg and New York: Physica-Verlag HD, 2009). More recently they have focused on the form of enterprises: Andrea Colli and Michelangelo Vasta, *Forms of Enterprise in 20th Century Italy: Boundaries, Structures and Strategies* (Cheltenham UK and Northampton USA: Edward Elgar, 2010).

this investment ever bears fruit for the economy, or if political-military considerations dictate that the development of these regions should be sacrificed to ensure the continued power of political-military elites. Pordenone is the location of the headquarters of the Ariete, or Ram, brigade of the Italian Army, equipped with Italian-designed and built tanks. Bologna is the location of the headquarters of the Friuli airmobile brigade of the Italian Army, equipped with Italian-designed and built attack helicopters.[26] Venice is the location of the Serenissima regiment of the Italian Army, for which the Iveco SuperAV amphibious vehicle was designed, the fruit of a close cooperation between the Italian Army and Italian industry. Florence is the location of the division headquarters in command of all these units, first named the Mantova Division, then the Friuli, and today the Vittorio Veneto Division.[27] These are some of the first all-professional brigades in the Italian Army. Interestingly, a variant of the SuperAV that is offered by the British company BAE Systems has now been

26 Esercito Italiano, "Brigata Aeromobile 'Friuli'," Italian Army website. Friuli, the region of Italy from which this brigade draws its name, is also the home of schools for advanced scientific studies and scientific research institutes, the Scuola Internazionale Superiore di Studi Avanzati, or SISSA, or the International School for Advanced Studies, and of reputable physics departments, at the University of Udine or the University of Trieste. However, contemporary Italy is seriously affected by brain drain, whereby skilled workers and researchers that Italian society and the Italian state have invested in training, move abroad in search of a more interesting career and greater rewards. Physicists, for example, move to more prestigious foreign institutions like CERN, EPFL, and Fermilab.

27 In the book on humanist social science I address the cultural significance of names, here I just want to point out that these changes in name are highly symbolic, as a unit is bestowed all the traditions of previous units that carried its name. There are references to these names and traditions in the following Wikipedia pages: Wikipedia, "Division "Vittorio Veneto.""; "Mechanized Brigade "Mantova."" Oddly, the Italian Army website does not refer to the name Mantova Division, although the magazine of the Italian Army does: Esercito Italiano, "Rapporto Esercito 2011," Italian Army website. There have also been name changes that reflect operational needs and changes in doctrine, including name changes in the wake of the 9/11 attacks and the new international climate that followed these attacks. The acronyms COMFOD, COMFOP, NRDC – IT, COMFOP NORD, all reflect these changes, some of which are described in: "Il Comando Forze Operative Nord (Comfop Nord). La Storia," Italian Army website. Interestingly, it seems that sometimes the abbreviation, these are not acronyms, but abbreviations like those used by the Italian Navy, stand for different expressions, involving a shift in the dot. For example, it seems that COMFOP once stood for COMando FOrze di Proiezione, but now stands for COMando Forze OPerative, or from COM.FO.P. to COM.F.OP. as suggested in the following Wikipedia pages: Wikipedia, "3rd Army Corps (Italy)."; "5th Army Corps (Italy)." One wonders if the Italian Army follows a standard nomenclature, or these changes were simply ad hoc. However, Wikipedia pages sometimes are not consistent, and on a number of Wikipedia pages that mention these name changes, there are inconsistent dates.

selected by the US Marine Corps as its amphibious vehicle for the Amphibious Combat Vehicle, or ACV, program. The Italian Army's investment in designing an amphibious vehicle is part of an expansion of amphibious capabilities of European countries that has seen the set-up of a joint Italian-Spanish amphibious force, the Spanish contribution including both a marine brigade, and the modern Galicia-class navy vessels, named after the region Galicia, which has also been seeking to attract economic investment, besides military bases.

These examples of state intervention in the economy through the military illustrate *one way in which states can contribute to markets, by creating a demand for high-tech products, and a skilled workforce* that can then contribute to the economy.[28] This type of intervention requires embedded autonomy to be successful in the long run. For example, the same company that produces attack helicopters for the Italian Army, AgustaWestland, now part of Leonardo Helicopters, also has a large and thriving civilian helicopters division. The United States pioneered this type of state-driven development. In the United States, Silicon Valley emerged thanks to state investment in the semiconductor industry, which was initially driven largely by military research and military contracts. The semiconductor industry then enabled the rise of the modern consumer electronics industry, and later of personal computers. Political scientist turned urban and regional planner AnnaLee Saxenian has suggested that an especially open culture and universities were essential to this ability of Silicon Valley to innovate and remain competitive across massive economic changes. So was the organization of the Silicon Valley economy, based on small and medium-sized companies and startups.[29]

28 This point was made to me at a company I worked for. Scheduling of investments is crucial in development plans to launch a local economy after initial state contracts, because development agencies have to start attracting further contracts after new facilities are built and start creating employment, but before state contracts start declining, so there is a window of opportunity for development to take off. On the SuperAV, see: Jen Judson, "Prototypes for Marine Corps' New Amphibious Combat Vehicle Coming Together," Marine Corps Times.

29 AnnaLee Saxenian, *Regional Advantage: Culture and Competition in Silicon Valley and Route 128*, with a New Preface by the Author (Cambridge, Massachusetts and London: Harvard University Press, 1996). Interestingly, Saxenian contrasts in this book two different implementations of the same approach that was pioneered by the United States, one implemented in Massachusetts, around MIT and route 128 near Boston, the other implemented in California, around San Francisco and Silicon Valley. Saxenian argues that the latter was more successful also because of the greater cultural openness of California compared to Massachusetts. This is an interesting reversal of perceptions. At least in some parts of Italy MIT is the more revered institution, and it provides the model of scientific research that certain economic agents look to with interest, while envying California for its products such as Apple computers.

Interestingly, this type of economic organization is similar to that of the Third Italy economic model, but it has better functioning universities, capable both of producing innovative research, and of finding applications for this research. It has led to a model of research universities that emphasizes universities should take part both in fundamental research, and also in developing and marketing business applications through startups. The École Polytechnique Fédérale de Lausanne, or EPFL, a Swiss federal institute of technology in Lausanne, was attempting in the 1990s to foster a start-up culture based on the model of American universities, best exemplified by Silicon Valley universities. Arguably, another major fault of Italian universities, besides baronial power, is that they are tightly and centrally controlled by the state and mostly lack embedded autonomy and the ability to exchange information and coordinate activities with local entrepreneurs and economic agents more in general.

This tight central control by the state of cultural institutions is an instance of lack of democracy. In reformulating Trigilia's argument that development is the product of the right combination of state, society and markets, I also argue that *there has to be some democracy in all three arenas, and that the three arenas have to remain separate in order to ensure both development and democracy.* In particular, I propose a full definition of democracy as a distribution of power in all three arenas that is favorable to the masses, and a distribution of power across arenas, which ensures that the arenas remain separate and that no one arena takes over the other ones. This is necessary to prevent the political-military arena from taking over the other arenas, as happened in Italy under fascism, in Germany under nazism, and in Russia at the time of the Soviet Union. It is also necessary to prevent the economic arena from taking over the other arenas and imposing its logic upon them, as happened in many Western countries in the aftermath of neoliberalism. The key to embedded autonomy is that there is embeddedness, through networks that cross from one arena to the other, but also autonomy to advance the type of development that is distinctive to each arena, cultural development for example.

This enables me also to *revisit the argument that where there is less democracy, there is also less development,* once an obvious argument at the time of the decline of Cuba and the Soviet Union, but which remarkably seems to have been forgotten.[30] This argument is instead very important to promote security in the wake of the 9/11 attacks and such moves as Barack Obama's

30 For recent arguments by a scholar close to the September Group, see: Adam Przeworski et al., *Democracy and Development: Political Institutions and Well-Being in the World, 1950–1990*, Cambridge Studies in the Theory of Democracy (Cambridge and New York: Cambridge University Press, 2000).

normalization of relations with Cuba. Arguably, this argument can be reformulated as stating that what promotes development the most is a democratic state that is responsive to pressures from civil society. There was throughout Latin America a series of democratic political and social experiments in recent years that raised high hopes but that invariably ended up badly.[31] Besides being interesting from a theoretical point of view, these experiments are also interesting from a security point of view, since a democratic and thriving Central America is important to United States and ultimately to NATO security, besides being important to NAFTA and to global trade flows through Panama. I think it is desirable to study the reasons for the failure of these experiments and also to propose new theories of development and democracy that would enable us to pursue both development and democracy in more successful and efficient ways. This requires a better theory and also a theory that directly answers the question of how to improve the conditions of the masses. Interestingly, now that Cuba has begun opening up, and it is no longer the target of CIA covert operations involving Fidel Castro, there are signs that both markets and a thriving culture are developing, as exemplified by the *Instituto Cubano de Investigación Cultural 'Juan Marinello'*, or ICIC, which cooperates with the Cuban Ministry of Culture and the Ministry of Science, Technology and the Environment.[32] I want to qualify here what such initiatives can achieve, which must be independent of the State, and suggest why an independent cultural arena is important to development and democracy.

31 Macarena Gomez-Barris, *Beyond the Pink Tide: Art and Political Undercurrents in the Americas*, American Studies Now: Critical Histories of the Present (Berkeley and Los Angeles: University of California Press, 2018). Hugo Chavez and the disastrous civil war that is destroying Venezuela stand as a clear example. I believe that Gomez-Barris attributes these setbacks of democracy to the wrong sources of conflict, which are not just, or even not so much, internal to states like Venezuela. I also believe that, while culture is important, it is not sufficient for development, and that Gomez-Barris' exclusive focus on culture is as one-sided as the movements she criticizes. I also belong to a different generation than most readers of Gomez-Barris' work, and the main association with the concept of 'pink' for me is not with actresses who played girl roles, like Angelina Jolie in her memorable performance in the film *Girl, Interrupted*, but with the expression 'pinko', used to stereotype left-leaning intellectuals. I no longer find this expression funny.

32 Cuba was the target of many CIA covert operations involving Fidel Castro, including the disastrous Bay of Pigs invasion. A fellow student in my senior year of high school, who is from the United States, introduced in a history class an interesting perspective on military and covert operations, in which scheduling is crucial, an important point that I came to appreciate much later. The student suggested that the Bay of Pigs invasion was a fiasco because air support from Central America arrived too late due to a miscalculation of the time difference between Central America and Cuba. Scheduling is crucial to military planners and development agencies alike.

The ICIC is nowhere near as large and well-funded as cultural studies programs in the United States. For example, New York University, or NYU, has both a Department of Social and Cultural Analysis, and a Department of Media, Culture, and Communication. NYU is associated also with such cultural icons as Lady Gaga and Spike Lee, both of whom studied there, but it has also attracted established scholars from England like anthropologist Michael Gilsenan, who did pioneering work in the Middle East. It also has ties to Italian-American culture and to military traditions from Italy, represented by a statue to Garibaldi in Washington State Park, where NYU is located. Columbia University has similar ties, and a cultural studies program that is large, although not as large as the ones at NYU, but with a more prestigious past than NYU.[33] Yet the ICIC carries

33 There are also more humble traditions in Italian-American culture, represented for me by south Brooklyn and such restaurants as Joe's of Avenue U, or by the Bronx, once a thriving borough that produced musicians like Dion DiMucci and later like scholar Arthur Langer. There are also somewhat different Italian cultural traditions in North America than the Italian-American one, like those associated with Italian-Canadians. The Canadian policy of multiculturalism encourages different communities within Canada to retain their cultural identity, including their language. There are very large Italian-Canadian communities in Montreal and Toronto, which are striking precisely for their strong cultural identity, but which are still effectively part of the North-Eastern United States, the border between Canada and the United States being unguarded, and travel restrictions between the two countries being small or nearly non-existent. For a sociologist, this strong cultural identity stands out even from an occasional walk around Montreal's Little Italy. Italian is spoken commonly throughout Montreal's Little Italy to this day, although the Italian-Canadian community has largely moved to St Leonard, another neighborhood of Montreal. Many shops and the culture of the district are still closer to Italy than to Canada or the United States, as exemplified by Italian pastry shops Alati-Caserta and Motta, the many Italian restaurants and Italian ice cream parlours, some of which do not compromise with North American tastes. Most strikingly, the coffee culture is closer to the Italian than the North American coffee culture, and includes soccer, the national sport of Italy. The thriving Little Italy in Montreal also hosts cafes like Bar Sportivo, Conca d'Oro and Caffè Italia, a cafe which is a mix of old-fashioned Italian cafes and North American bars like the one depicted in the TV series Cheers. These cafes regularly show soccer matches, including matches in the Italian soccer league. The Little Italy in Montreal even hosts a sports store, Evangelista, which specializes in soccer gear. Evangelista is encouraged by the presence of the Impact Montreal soccer team, which plays in the Saputo soccer stadium built by Saputo Inc, a large dairy company founded by Italian-Canadian entrepreneur Lino Saputo. It is tragic that this thriving community life is overshadowed by the presence of the mafia, the Rizzuto mafia family of Montreal having at one point risen to prominence in North America, and with fascism, the Little Italy of Montreal hosting a Catholic Church called Madonna della Difesa, or Our Lady of Defence. This church was built and decorated between the 1920s and 1930s and has frescoes that in one corner of the church depict Benito Mussolini on horseback, surrounded by blackshirts, the Fascist death squads. This is not to deny the many positive aspects of Italian-Canadian culture.

out research on many topics that are central to contemporary cultural studies, and they even cultivate their image and reach to a wider public, having a fairly large website that is also stylishly designed, with tasteful frames in light yellow, or pastel and other hues of yellow.

However, behind these appearances, the question to ask is whether the ICIC is truly independent from the ministry and can pursue formulating a theory for the masses. The opening up of Cuba after Fidel Castro's death has produced also cultural initiatives that re-launched traditional Cuban music, which was accomplished most successfully by the Buena Vista Social Club, which toured the United States led by its lead singer Compay Segundo.[34] Cuba has had even older cultural ties to European countries, including Italy. But it is questionable whether these ties on their own, and whether the promotion of culture on its own, is sufficient to advance development and democracy.[35] Culture contributes to development and democracy through its contribution to civil society and to social movements that fight for democracy and a more equitable development. Culture and social movements are essential to development and democracy because social movements put pressure on states and prevent them from creating rents, or easy profits, for elites that do not contribute to the development of the whole of society.

At McGill University, Anahi Morales Hudon and sociologist Marcos Ancelovici had begun applying the study of culture to the study of social movements, including social movements like the one in Chiapas, Mexico, and the Occupy movement in Western countries.[36] There seems also to be *a growing*

Canadian Prime Ministers, who are weary of being associated with fascists, also because fascists were and still are racists, periodically pass by Montreal's Little Italy when they want to reach to the Italian-Canadian community. Bar Sportivo proudly displayed pictures of Canadian Prime Ministers who stopped there.

34 I developed an appreciation of the richness of Cuban culture, and of the revival of Cuban music, including the Buena Vista Social Club, through Amanda Hartman.

35 Italian-Cuban actor Thomas Milian, who had great success in Italy representing in a number of movies characters drawn from Roman popular culture, moved from Cuba to Italy. These characters included a policeman in Rome, and a character who is a small-time thief nicknamed 'er monnezza', Roman slang for 'garbage' or 'thrash', a type of character sometimes referred to as 'er sorcio', or 'the mouse' or 'rat'. Cuba had ties to Italy despite the United States embargo, and Cuba was recognized by the Vatican before Barack Obama normalized United States-Cuba relations. Of course, Cuba and Ernesto 'Che' Guevara figured largely in the Italian counterculture movement, and singer-songwriter Francesco Guccini singled out Che Guevara as one of his idols in several songs, including 'Stagioni', or 'Seasons', celebrating Che Guevara's death, in the 2000 album with the same name, and 'Canzone per il Che', or 'Song for the Che', in the 2004 album 'Ritratti', or 'Portraits'.

36 Stephanie Rousseau and Anahi Morales Hudon, *Indigenous Women's Movements in Latin America: Gender and Ethnicity in Peru, Mexico, and Bolivia*, Crossing Boundaries of Gender and Politics in the Global South (London and New York: Palgrave Macmillan, 2016).

interest in Gramsci amongst political sociologists like Hudon and Ancelovici, who work on social movements, because *empirical research is confirming the importance of culture to collective action*, a point highlighted by Gramsci.[37] Hudon is drawing attention also to the role of women and of gender identity questions in social movements, in a sense following in the footsteps of Malek Abisaab, who has researched women tobacco workers in Lebanon and their economic struggles, and who is now researching questions of female identity in the Middle East as it relates to the veil and politics.[38] It is therefore clear why the field of social movements studies is developing an interest in Gramscian studies, as exemplified by the success of anthropologist Kate Crehan's recent

---

Chiapas of course is known for 'Subcomandante Marcos', a man and not a 'Comandanta', but Hudon's work is drawing attention to the great importance of women for social movements, including revolutionary movements. I do not know Hudon's views on CIA covert operations in Cuba and Central America, but perhaps a more important role for women is becoming possible thanks to the shift from hard military power to cultural power.

37 Hudon and political theorist Philippe Dufort came to my dissertation defense on Gramsci, motivated by the growing recognition of the importance of culture, and the consequent growing interest in Gramsci, amongst social movement researchers. I also worked with Ancelovici on carrying out an interesting study of the Occupy movement in Montreal, or the 99/1 protest movement, in which a number of students, myself included, surveyed the occupiers claiming to represent the 99% percent of the population who were opposed to the increasingly wealthy 1%. The survey we carried out focused on the occupiers' motivations for participating in the movement. Ancelovici's published work on these topics includes: Marcos Ancelovici, "Occupy Montreal and the Politics of Horizontalism," in *Street Politics in the Age of Austerity: from the Indignados to Occupy*, ed. Marcos Ancelovici, Pascale Dufour, and Heloise Nez (Amsterdam: Amsterdam University Press, 2016); "In Search of Lost Radicalism: the Hot Autumn of 2010 and the Transformation of Labor Contention in France," *French Politics, Culture & Society* 29, no. 3 (2011); "Organizing against Globalization: the Case of Attac in France," *Politics & Society* 30, no. 3 (2002). This kind of empirical research is drawing attention to the importance of culture and to the usefulness of Gramsci's theory for the study of collective action.

38 Malek Abisaab, *Militant Women of a Fragile Nation*, Middle East Studies Beyond Dominant Paradigms (Syracuse: Syracuse University Press, 2010); "'Unruly' Factory Women in Lebanon: Contesting French Colonialism and the National State, 1940–1946," *Journal of Women's History* 16, no. 3 (2004). I gained through Abisaab many insights regarding questions of women's identity in the Middle East, the veil, and a return to traditional culture, which is the latest focus of Abisaab's research. Abisaab has recently started working also on democracy in the Arab world: "The So-Called Arab Spring, Islamism and the Dilemma of the Arab Left: 1970–2012," *R/evolutions: Global Trends & Regional Issues* 4, no. 1 (2016). I derive from my reading of Abisaab's work the view that the Arab Spring was a tame movement, and that it was incapable of bringing about any real change. I believe democracy requires considerable social change, and it is not therefore the work of just one movement and one spring, but a very long process. This applies to Quebec and the West as much as to Arab countries.

books on Gramsci's theory of culture.[39] These books have attracted attention precisely because of the relevance of Gramsci's theory to understand social movements from the Occupy movement to the Arab Spring, and the social movement in Quebec known as *Le Printemps Erable*, or the Maple Spring.[40] There also seems to be a growing academic interest in understanding Latin American social movements and Latin American culture, which is increasingly important after the rise of populism. This interest is fueled by work from such scholars as Renzo Llorente, who has written on Che Guevara's political theory, now that the dust has settled on CIA operations to target Che Guevara, and by work from such scholars as María Elena Martínez-López, who have studied the cultural construction of racial identities.[41]

---

39 Kate Crehan, *Gramsci, Culture and Anthropology* (Berkeley and Los Angeles: University of California Press, 2002); *Gramsci's Common Sense: Inequality and Its Narratives* (Durham and London: Duke University Press, 2016). Reviewers of Crehan's latest work have highlighted its relevance to understand contemporary social movements: Lindsay DuBois, "Gramsci's Common Sense: Inequality and Its Narratives by Kate Crehan," *Anthropologica* 62, no. 1 (2020); Claudio Sopranzetti, "Gramsci's Common Sense: Inequality and Its Narratives by Kate Crehan," *Anthropological Quarterly* 90, no. 4 (2017).

40 Ancelovici has written on the Maple Spring and so has philosopher Daniel Weinstock, at McGill University and Universite de Montreal: Daniel Weinstock, "The Political Philosophy of the "Printemps Érable,"" *Theory & Event* 15, no. 3 (2012); "Occupy, Indignados, et Le Printemps Érable: Vers un Agenda de Recherche," *McGill Law Journal/Revue de droit de McGill* 58, no. 2 (2012). I am not sure what political philosophy Weinstock is referring to in his article, since the participants in the Montreal Occupy movement that I surveyed often lacked theoretical reasons and were mostly emotionally opposed to elites, or driven to participation in the movement by the dire circumstances that they lived in. High intellectuals like Weinstock provided the ideology for the movement through interventions in the press, and ties to leading activists, but the survey highlighted for me the lack of ties between these high intellectuals and leading activists and the bulk of the occupiers.

41 Renzo Llorente, *The Political Theory of Che Guevara* (Lanham, Boulder, New York, and Oxford: Rowman & Littlefield International, 2018). Maria Elena Martínez, *Genealogical Fictions: Limpieza de Sangre, Religion, and Gender in Colonial Mexico*, Cultural Memory in the Present Series (Stanford, California: Stanford University Press, 2008). Interestingly, other authors are applying these concepts to Arab Americans: Sarah Gualtieri, *Between Arab and White: Race and Ethnicity in the Early Syrian American Diaspora*, American Crossroads (Berkeley and Los Angeles: University of California Press, 2009); *Arab Routes: Pathways to Syrian California*, Stanford Studies in Comparative Race and Ethnicity (Stanford, California: Stanford University Press, 2019). Gualtieri suggested to me that similar studies are being carried out of Italian-American racial identities, and Julia Gualtieri drew my attention to Richard Gambino's book on the lynching of Italian immigrants in the United States: Richard Gambino, *Vendetta: a True Story of the Worst Lynching in America, the Mass Murder of Italian-Americans in New Orleans in 1891, the Vicious Motivations Behind It, and the Tragic Repercussions That Linger to This Day* (Garden City, New York: Doubleday, 1977). This book has been reprinted in 1998 and in 2000. One of the signs that racial identities are to some extent culturally constructed is in the boundaries

In this book and in other parts of this project I expand upon their insights and propose a *general theory that can serve to understand ways in which social movements can use culture*, including identity and organization, to build their own alternative hegemony, which should enable previously marginalized social groups to pursue a more equitable development. This contributes to democracy, which contributes to development by denying elites what can be called *social rents*, easy profits that come from the ability to exploit marginalized social groups. Greater democracy, from social movements that successfully engage in collective action in order to defend their interests, can result in very different models of development, and also arguably in greater development. This book formulates this and related theses at great length, proposing that we reconceptualize the sources of development and that we focus on the interrelationship between development and democracy as being necessary to each other, the tradeoff of more development for less democracy, which is implicit in neoliberalism, and also in populism and Donald Trump's rhetoric, being bad for development as well as for democracy. This book seeks to explain why.

---

of these identities and who is considered to be part of one race or another, which changes over time.

CHAPTER 2

An Intellectual Journey, the Struggle for Objectivity, and Elitism

This book is the product of a long and difficult intellectual journey that lasted thirty years. An important goal of this intellectual journey that I was able to pursue only in the last fifteen years, and even then, only against mounting difficulties, was to formulate a theory that would provide a broad picture of society and history, which I believe is necessary to advance both development and democracy. In this chapter I want to explain what I mean by a broad picture of society and history, how it relates to a humanist social science, and my experience of the difficulties in formulating such a theory, some of which stem from the view that theory does not constitute valid or useful knowledge. Knowledge should be assessed on its own merits, regardless of who produced it and how, but *who produces knowledge and how is a very important question in its own right*. One reason for this is that some ways of producing knowledge are especially fruitful and it is therefore useful to describe them and share them. Much of the theory that I propose in this project started as informal observations that I subjected to formal scrutiny. This eclectic methodology was very fruitful and in chapter 4 I clarify what it entails and explain why it was useful. Another reason to share how knowledge was produced is that some knowledge is very hard to produce, and this might shed light on the contested nature of this knowledge and on faults in the organizations that produce knowledge. I suggest below that we ought to work on securing the social conditions for objectivity in social science and that this entails working against elitism. I place these claims within a broader socio-political context defined by Gramsci. Gramsci made a *very important claim that 'there is a struggle for objectivity'*, which I interpret to mean, amongst other things, that objectivity should not be taken for granted, because it is always contested and not easily achieved. Gramsci also added that this is a struggle 'to free oneself from partial and erroneous ideologies', which I understand to include ideologies that provide a partial, and thus incomplete, picture of reality.[1] The struggle for objectivity therefore includes producing broad pictures of society and history. One-sided ideologies, which I address at length in this book, are a particular type of partial ideologies.

---

1 Gramsci, *Quaderni del Carcere*, 1416.

2.1 Humanism, Synthesis, and Political-Military Development

My intellectual journey was unusual. During these thirty years, for reasons that are difficult to explain, I have ended up pursuing knowledge in a number of different fields ranging from history, to civil and environmental engineering, to computer studies and sociology. My academic areas of expertise are in sociology, the discipline of my doctoral studies, and they are focused on the sociology of development and political sociology. I have also gained some understanding of the sociology of culture and the sociology of knowledge. I approached all these sub-fields from an historical perspective associated with historical sociology. The focus of my past research in sociology was the history of social and political theory, and my specialty within it was Gramsci's social and political thought. My dissertation was on Gramsci's contribution to humanism and the philosophy of social science. I argued there, and in some articles, that Gramsci provided an original approach to social science that can be characterized as a humanist social science, and that he attempted to provide a broad picture of society and history that is useful to conceptualize, in significantly new ways, both how society works, and also the course of development and democracy in history. In this and in other books that are part of this project, I seek to complete the theory that Gramsci began to formulate, and to sketch a broad picture of society and history based largely upon Gramsci's pioneering work. In this task, I seek to combine knowledge from all my academic areas of expertise with insights gained from my professional knowledge of engineering and computer studies, and from informal observation in all different walks of life. I believe this broad picture is especially important today for anyone interested in furthering both development and democracy.

Despite being unusual, my intellectual journey is still very relevant to others. There is a *growing interest in combining theories from social science with theories that belong to engineering.*[2] In addition, the way that I combined these

2 There are scholars, and even entire sub-fields, which combine these different studies. Lars Skyttner is one such example. His work closely parallels many of the themes that I explore in this project: Lars Skyttner, *General Systems Theory: an Introduction*, Information Systems Series (Basingstoke: Macmillan, 1996); *General Systems Theory: Ideas & Applications* (Singapore and London: World Scientific, 2001). Skyttner's later book has gone through at least one reprinting, showing that this mix of fields is attracting attention. There is also an entire sub-field of ergonomics and management studies that is called socio-technical systems and that focuses on the same combination of social science and technical studies that I have pursued. For an overview of this sub-field, see: Guy H. Walker et al., "A Review of Sociotechnical Systems Theory: a Classic Concept for New Command and Control Paradigms," *Theoretical issues in ergonomics science* 9, no. 6 (2008).

diverse subjects makes my synthesis especially relevant to others. For example, the reasons why I ended up pursuing such diverse studies are peculiar to my background and to my long and difficult intellectual journey, yet some of these reasons are common to others who share parts of my predicament. Humanistic studies are being sidelined by the need to find a job in the modern economy, in such disciplines as engineering and computer studies, and even in universities the humanist ideal of an all-round education is being sidelined by specialization. Moreover, the theory that I propose below might be relevant to others also because I have sought to make virtue out of necessity, and I have found important concepts for my understanding of society and history in engineering disciplines that are apparently distant from the domains of knowledge traditionally associated with studies of society and history. At more than one point in my intellectual journey, I found myself sympathizing with Gramsci and developing what Gramsci called, following a popular Italian saying, the ability 'to draw blood from a turnip', which means to find something useful even in the most unlikely places. In Gramsci's case, and in my case, this has meant finding something useful in the most diverse and unlikely readings and observations.

In retrospect, I have found that it is possible to give a rationale to the diverse studies that I have pursued and the diverse readings that I have gone through. The rationale is that they enabled me to provide a *synthesis of humanistic education and technical education* that differs significantly from other syntheses. Whereas other syntheses apply an entire technical paradigm to society, I do the opposite, and apply a humanist paradigm to understand technology, which still involves however incorporating key concepts from technology in a humanist philosophy and social science. An especially clear example of the usefulness of this approach can be seen in parts of this project where I propose the concept of political-military development. The latter includes the key military *capabilities* of Command, Control, Communications and Intelligence, or C3I, which can usefully be divided into Intelligence and Communications, or IC, and Command and Control, or C2, capabilities.[3] These are the capabilities, including the organizational means, which enable exercising the *functions* of

3 Treatments of C3I are provided by: Thomas P. Coakley, *C3I: Issues of Command and Control* (Washington, DC: National Defense Uniiversity, 1991); George E. Orr, *Combat Operations C3I: Fundamentals and Interactions* (Montgomery, Alabama: Airpower Research Institute, Air University Press, 1983). Both these monographs emphasize the importance of C3I to military operations. Today the more common acronym is C4ISR, which includes also computers, surveillance and reconnaissance. For the sake of simplicity, and for the purposes of the argument of this book, it is sufficient to focus on C3I.

command, control, communications and intelligence, and I place them within a theory of development that emphasizes diverse capabilities, including political and military capabilities. I propose to call the advancement of these and other political and military capabilities political-military development.

IC lines are perhaps more readily associated with technologically sophisticated and high-profile means of communication. The first thing that might come to mind when one thinks of political-military IC lines is the direct line of communication from 10 Downing street, or the 10 Downing street bunker, to the White House, which enables direct communication from the Prime Minister of Great Britain to the President of the United States, and which is very important to handle national emergencies, whether before, as the threat is perceived, or during a national emergency, as the threat unfolds. Strong political working relationships like the Blair-Bush relationship rely also upon such communication lines. The wide diffusion of the internet is making sophisticated communication lines reach far and wide and lower down into the hierarchy of power.[4] For example, islands like Iceland, in the middle of the Atlantic, are connected to the internet via lines to Greenland and Canada, Great Britain and Norway, and are in fact very advanced in terms of local internet use. Even very remote islands like the Svalbard archipelago, near the Arctic Circle, can be served by fast internet connections, in the Svalbard's case thanks also to the research that is carried out there, and the space center located there.[5] The concept of political-military development that I propose draws attention to the fact that political-military elites of the past had lines of communication that reached to other elites, and also lower down the social hierarchy of power, into subaltern social groups, and into communities that are part of the masses. Although now the internet has replaced most mail, these communication lines could be as

4 For reports on internet connectivity and usage throughout the world, see: Silja Baller, Soumitra Dutta, and Bruno Lanvin, "The Global Information Technology Report, 2016," World Economic Forum in collaboration with INSEAD and the Cornell University Johnson School of Management; Soumitra Dutta and Irene Mia, "The Global Information Technology Report, 2010–2011," World Economic Forum in collaboration with INSEAD. For a report on the next stage of internet connectivity, which involves connecting all sorts of different electronic devices to the internet, a technology known as the Internet of Things, see: World Economic Forum, Global Internet of Things Council, and Pricewaterhouse Coopers, "State of the Connected World: Insight Report."

5 For internet connectivity in Iceland, see: Landsvirkjun, "International Data Connectivity in Iceland: A White Paper," Landsvirkjun, the National Power Company of Iceland. For internet connectivity in Svalbard, see: Rolf Skar, "Why and How Svalbard Got the Fibre," *Telektronikk* 3 (2004). A summary of internet connectivity to Svalbard is provided by: Wikipedia, "Svalbard Undersea Cable System."

low-tech as traditional mail. MI5 famously used a mail address, Po Box 500, for some of its communications.

Most importantly, IC lines could be as simple as networks of individuals that existed even in agrarian-artisanal societies. How these lines interact with social boundaries and social groups more in general is crucially important, and can greatly affect political-military development. Chapter 6 addresses collective action. This is key to political-military development, which emphasizes the interaction between politics and the military, within a theory that accounts for the emergence of the modern political-military arena. This account can be especially useful to understand the rise of violent social movements and the creation of large irregular forces, which can thoroughly undermine both development and democracy, an important point that I take up in the second volume. The account is therefore relevant to understand social phenomena ranging from fascism and nazism to Muslin fundamentalism. I want to emphasize here that I reject all stereotyping of Italians, or Muslims, or any other ethnic or religious groups, as inherently prone to violence, and I am instead seeking to understand the common socio-economic and international causes of violent social movements. All of this leads me to a significantly new theory of development and democracy, which could lead to a paradigm shift. I introduce key arguments of this significantly new theory at the end of this chapter and in the next two chapters. Here I want to begin by focusing upon the difficulties that I ran into as I sought to sketch a broad picture of society and history, and an important insight that I arrived at, namely, that broad pictures and theory, which is closely related to broad pictures, are so hard to formulate because of the social conditions that prevail in universities and also because of elitism. I also relate elitism to the culture of past elites and their humanistic education.

2.2 Broad Pictures and a Humanist Social Science

Gramsci's project for a humanist social science is important, amongst other reasons, because it first introduced the claim that 'there is a struggle for objectivity', began articulating what this struggle is about, and proposed a humanist philosophy and social science and a humanistic education as the best answers to the challenges of this struggle, and I add in this book also as the answers to problems of development and democracy. In particular, a humanist social science is especially relevant to policymakers and citizens involved in formulating and assessing development policies and in protecting democracy, besides social scientists working on development and democracy, because the policymakers and citizens need to be able to assess diverse policies in different domains, in politics and the military, and in culture, as well as the economy. A humanistic education is also directly relevant to my personal experience of a very long and difficult intellectual journey. There is another popular Italian saying that I found myself relating to after all these years, and it encourages one to 'learn the art and set it aside'. I now understand that this can be positively interpreted to mean that an art will always be useful sooner or later. What I do not accept, to this day, is that learning an art, or acquiring any skills and knowledge more in general, should be difficult. Yet an all-round humanistic education and the related knowledge are made very hard to acquire.

I have recently come across an interesting reworking of a Latin saying that states *dura ars, sed ars*, which can be translated as 'art is tough, but it is art'. It is a re-working of the famous saying *dura lex, sed lex,* 'the law is tough, but it is the law'. The latter can be interpreted to mean that the law can be tough, but it has to be obeyed because it is indispensable to social life. I believe that this is a reasonable starting point. However, I also believe that the law should be continuously improved and made more just and closer to the life and needs of the people who are affected by it, which is equally true of art. Unfortunately, we are still very far from achieving this goal today. In universities it is still fairly common to come across professors who are leading experts in their field and yet, despite their understanding of the field, they make it forbiddingly hard for others to understand this field, even for graduate students in the field, and university professors who work in other fields, let alone for policymakers or citizens. This behavior by leading experts is at least in part caused by the *increasing specialization in universities*, one aspect of which is the use of specialist languages that are very different than ordinary language.

Gramsci sought to start a project that would address this issue and that has served as a model for this project. There are several *reasons why I decided to pursue a project that is a continuation of Gramsci's project.* I had read Gramsci's work when I was still very young and had been fascinated by his attempt to formulate a *humanist philosophy and social science that considered all domains of human behavior*, not just the behavior encountered in one's academic field of expertise. I later read work by sociologist Max Weber, and found a similar effort to overcome specialization through a *multidisciplinary approach to social science.* Weber's project is very different than Gramsci's project, because Weber was committed to advancing German imperial grandeur in the Europe of his time, whereas Gramsci was committed to advancing the conditions of the masses. Weber was also dangerously close to totalitarian authors. Amongst the circle of intellectuals who gathered around Weber, there were Robert Michels, an admirer of Mussolini's who moved to Italy and was made a professor there after Mussolini's seizure of power, and Gyorgy Lukacs, the Hungarian Marxist, who moved to Soviet Russia and held important positions under Stalin. My interest in Weber's work is exclusively because of its multidisciplinary and historicist approach, and its use of philosophy to lay solid foundations for social science. Weber's work complements theoretically Gramsci's work because the need for a multidisciplinary social science was felt by both. Both of these authors also included a space or geographical dimension, and a time or historical dimension, in their multidisciplinary approach. Lastly, I also came to appreciate that both Gramsci and Weber were trying to combine philosophy with social science, in order to produce a widely accessible synthesis of the knowledge of society and history available in their times in the form of a general theory of society and history.

I define in detail what I mean by general theory in chapter 5, which is devoted to defining theory. Here I just want to introduce a *preliminary definition of general theory* as a theory that contributes to a broad picture of society and history, which is complementary to a worldview or conception of the world. Gramsci, building upon a tradition of German philosophy, saw philosophy chiefly as a worldview, which Gramsci referred to as a conception of the world. A conception of the world includes both a picture of the world, and concepts that describe how the world works, which include social mechanisms, in other words, a general theory. Gramsci also sought to make this conception of the world into a humanist philosophy, complemented by a humanist social science. *This humanist philosophy* would have included all domains of human activity: the economy, culture, politics and the military. It would also have included both dimensions of human activity: a time dimension associated with historical studies, and a space dimension associated with geographical studies. This was in contrast to the very narrow pictures of society and history that are, now as then, the product of specialized social science. Most economists, for example, specialize in studying a specific part of the economy, and neglect change over time and space.

A humanist social science is a science that shares this multidisciplinary approach involving multiple domains and dimensions of human activity, *as well as* a number of other views distinctive of the humanist philosophy. These views include a view of human beings as capable of behavior in all the above domains. They also include a humanist view of philosophy itself, which sees philosophy as existing in an exchange or dialogue with common sense or everyday philosophy, and ultimately with popular culture as a whole. I address this view in chapter 4, because it is important to the concept of cultural democracy. Lastly, a humanist philosophy includes views of art, engineering, and science, and also humanist views of politics and history, all of which are closely related to the humanist view of human beings. I address these views in the book on the humanist theory of society. The simpler definition of a humanist social science as a science that addresses multiple domains of human activity is sufficient for the arguments in this book. It is important instead to differentiate from the start between a humanistic education and a humanist one. A *humanistic education* is also based on multiple domains and is often inspired also by the ideals and sources of humanism, especially classics, or ancient Greek and Roman authors, but it is not explicitly based on a humanist philosophy. By contrast, a *humanist education* is a humanistic education complemented by a humanist philosophy.

Of course, with the expansion of knowledge in our day, it is impossible for a single person to formulate a general theory that is a synthesis of knowledge in *all* domains of human behavior, and provide a *complete* broad picture of society and history. However, this does not mean that we should give up formulating such a theory. Sociologist Dietrich Rueschemeyer has recently made a call for the formulation of a useful broad-ranging theory, and suggested how to achieve it, all of which met with a positive reception, showing there is a perceived need for such a theory.[6] This book pursues a similar goal, while being slightly more ambitious, however. In particular, I differ from Rueschemeyer and his *concept of 'theory frames'*, although I share many of his concerns.[7] The broad pictures that I refer to are more than just ways of framing questions, although using a broad picture effectively frames questions in a certain way, by creating associations. Broad pictures are actual pictures of society, which are part of a conception of the world. They are complemented by theories of society and history that propose actual social mechanisms to explain how society works, and not just how it looks. By actual social mechanisms I mean a specific type of explanation that is a mechanism because it uses structures and other components of society to explain social phenomena, in a manner analogous to

6 Dietrich Rueschemeyer, *Usable Theory: Analytic Tools for Social and Political Research* (Princeton and Oxford: Princeton University Press, 2009). Rueschemeyer has also addressed other very important concepts that are central to this project, namely, power and the division of labour: *Power and the Division of Labour*, Social and Political Theory from Polity Press (Cambridge, UK and Malden, Massachusetts: Polity, 1986). Matthew Lange, who completed his doctoral studies at Brown University, where Rueschemeyer taught, first drew my attention to Rueschemeyer's work and the interesting sociological work that is being done at Brown University. Rueschemeyer works in a German tradition of historical sociology that includes Ferdinand Tönnies, as well as Weber. I address both Tönnies' and Weber's views on community and society in the book on the humanist theory of society.

7 *Usable Theory*. I understand the concept of framing in the manner formulated by Lakoff: George Lakoff, *Don't Think of an Elephant!: Know Your Values and Frame the Debate*, Scribe Short Books (Melbourne and Carlton North, Australia: Scribe, 2005). Maurilio Buffone first drew my attention to Lakoff's work.

the manner in which the mechanism in a watch explains the movement of the lancets. Therefore, these social mechanisms are a subset of the mechanisms that Analytical Sociology focuses upon, and they are influenced by an engineering approach.[8]

2.3 The Difficulties Faced by Some Intellectual Projects

The goal to provide such a general theory and broad pictures is not beyond reach. For example, I propose here just a broad outline of a general theory, and elements out of which this theory can be built, and I emphasize the importance of collaborative projects as a way to address the difficulties that arise from the vastness of knowledge. What a single person can achieve in a lifetime is not sufficient to provide a synthesis of the vast knowledge available in modern societies. Yet we can go a long way towards it if we cooperate with others. Moreover, such efforts can be very rewarding. However, *collaborative projects in social science are very rare* compared to collaborative projects in natural science, where collaborative projects are the norm. What is worse, no collaborative project in social science that sought to produce broad pictures of society and history, and a truly multidisciplinary social science, has ever progressed much beyond the preliminary stages of collaborative projects. *It is important to understand the ultimate reasons behind these difficulties.* The Latin saying *ars longa, vita brevis* can be interpreted to mean either that art takes a long time to learn, while life is short, or that art can go a long way, in a short life, something that can be achieved also by cooperating with others, intergenerationally, as well as within the same generation. Both interpretations of this Latin saying apply to Gramsci's own intellectual journey, which seems to have been beset by the difficulties of learning a *dura ars*.

Gramsci sought to start a *collaborative project* in order to provide a multidisciplinary social science and a broad picture of society and history. For example, Gramsci sought to gather around the political periodical that he founded, the *Ordine Nuovo*, or New Order, a number of different activists who were specialists of politics, and later also specialists of economics, like Piero Sraffa.

8 On social mechanisms, see: Peter Hedstrom and Peter Bearman, *Social Mechanisms: an Analytical Approach to Social Theory* (Cambridge and New York: Cambridge University Press, 1998). I differ from Analytical Sociology in that the subset of social mechanisms that I focus upon include actual structures, approached through a structural-foundational view of social interaction, and an architectural-engineering analogy of society, both of which I define in the book on the humanist theory of society.

Gramsci seems to have had plans to start an institute for the study of economics that might have been headed by Sraffa and that would have complemented the work on politics carried out by Gramsci and the other contributors to the *Ordine Nuovo*.[9] Gramsci also encouraged the study of philosophy. His arrest by the Fascist government that had taken over Italy meant that this project never got off the ground. It is said that Benito Mussolini himself had requested that Gramsci's brain should be prevented from working for twenty years, and that Gramsci should therefore receive an especially long and harsh prison sentence, for subversive activities against fascism. However, in the isolation of a prison cell, with books and with occasional feedback provided by Sraffa, Gramsci began outlining what his project would have been like, in the hope of being able to restart it after his release from prison. Gramsci never got to restart his project. He died only a few weeks after being released from prison for deteriorating health, in 1937. He was only 46, but the prison notes that he wrote are some of the most original writings in modern political theory.[10]

Some of the difficulties encountered by Gramsci in providing a multidisciplinary social science and a broad picture of society and history also affected other projects. Weber too ran into difficulties and died before he could complete such a social science and pictures of society and history.[11] Other projects that attempted to reach similar goals, like G. A. Cohen's project that I address in chapter 3, ended up crashing and returning to the fold. It is remarkable that no other scholar got much further than Gramsci or Weber. Cesare Lombroso, a notorious anthropologist and criminologist, argued in nineteenth-century

9 On Gramsci and Sraffa's work, the projects they were engaged in, and the Turin cultural scene that they were both part of, see: Angelo D'Orsi, "Piero Sraffa e la 'Cultura Positiva': la Formazione Torinese," *Il Pensiero Economico Italiano* 8, no. 1 (2000).

10 There are many biographies on Gramsci, some of the best known are: Alastair Davidson, *Antonio Gramsci: Towards an Intellectual Biography* (Atlantic Highlands, N.J.: Humanities Press, 1977); Giuseppe Fiori and Tom Nairn, *Antonio Gramsci: Life of a Revolutionary*, Verso Modern Classics (London and New York: Verso, 1990); Dante Germino, *Antonio Gramsci: Architect of a New Politics*, Political Traditions in Foreign Policy Series (Baton Rouge and London: Lousiana State University Press, 1990); Antonio Santucci, *Antonio Gramsci, 1981–1937*, Tutto e Subito (Palermo: Sellerio, 2005).

11 Reinhard Bendix and Guenther Roth, *Max Weber: an Intellectual Portrait* (Berkeley and Los Angeles: University of California Press, 1977); Alan Sica, *Max Weber and the New Century* (New Brunswick USA, London: Transaction Publishers, 2004); Marianne Weber, *Max Weber: a Biography* (New York and London: Routledge, 2017). Peter Homans has suggested that there is a 'creative illness' that affected many intellectual figures, including Sigmund Freud and Max Weber, see Homan's contribution in: Peter Homans and James S. Hans, *Symbolic Loss: the Ambiguity of Mourning and Memory at Century's End*, Studies in Religion and Culture (Charlottesville, Virginia: University Press of Virginia, 2000).

Italy that intellectuals are prone to psychological disorders.[12] I do not think this is true. Much more simply, the answer might be that projects that seek to provide original and significantly new approaches to any field run into entrenched ways of thinking that can make it very hard to get by, and thus very stressful, for anyone straying from the fold. For example, finding a job in modern universities can be exceedingly difficult if one's research does not get immediate recognition, which requires fitting into a mold that is easily recognized.[13] These difficulties apply especially to general theory that seeks to provide a broad picture of society and history, and to new approaches to social science like a multidisciplinary social science. This is arguably because social science is a smaller field than natural science, and therefore has less funding and less room for experimentation, simply because, for example, 100 *scholars* can join forces and pursue collaborative projects in only two or three directions of research, whereas 1000 scholars can pursue many more projects. Fortunately, the expansion of research on social science topics within the economy is partly compensating for this.

Joseph Buttigieg's case might be an instance of this lack of resources, coupled however with perfectionism. Buttigieg was a professor of English, originally from Malta, at the University of Notre Dame, who undertook to translate into English Gramsci's complete and unabridged *Prison Notebooks*. The original Italian edition is more than 2300 pages long and it is divided into 29 notebooks.[14] It contains references to hundreds of Italian intellectuals, their works

12 Cesare Lombroso, "Genius and Insanity," in *The Man of Genius* (London: Charles Scribner's Sons, 1895); George Mora, "One Hundred Years from Lombroso's First Essay Genius and Insanity," *American Journal of Psychiatry* 121, no. 6 (1964). Much of Lombroso's work has been recently republished, for example: Cesare Lombroso and Guglielmo Ferrero, *Criminal Woman, the Prostitute, and the Normal Woman*, trans. Nicole Hahn Rafter and Mary Gibson (Durham and London: Duke University Press, 2004); Cesare Lombroso, *Criminal Man*, trans. Nicole Hahn Rafter and Mary Gibson (Durham and London: Duke University Press, 2006). This work claims that criminal traits are inborn.

13 Arguably, the 1960s included an effort to change the organization of universities. For the impact of 1960s movements on universities and social theory in particular, see: Alan Sica and Stephen Turner, eds., *The Disobedient Generation: Social Theorists in the Sixties* (Chicago: University of Chicago Press, 2005).

14 This is the edition curated by Valentino Gerratana: Gramsci, *Quaderni del Carcere*. This edition is essentially the same as the 1975 edition, which was reprinted in 2001 and 2007. This edition is very close to the original text, written by hand while Gramsci was in prison, although recently modifications have been suggested to it by the editors of the national edition of Gramsci's work, some of which could shed new light on important topics. An instance of these new light is provided by: Fabio Frosini, "Note sul Programma di Lavoro sugli "Intellettuali Italiani" Alla Luce della Nuova Edizione Critica," *Studi Storici* 52, no. 4 (2011). Frosini drew my attention to debates on Gerratana's work, and his military

and debates, who today are little known or unknown even in Italy. Buttigieg undertook the detailed job of providing research on each and every intellectual that Gramsci referred to.[15] Over the span of 15 years, Buttigieg translated and published only the first 8 Notebooks. A 2006 symposium hosted by the journal *Rethinking Marxism* hailed Buttigieg's detailed work as an achievement and pointed to the many important contributions that Buttigieg had given to translating Gramsci's work.[16] However, Buttigieg died in 2019 without having translated a single more notebook, and Gramsci's work is available in English chiefly in selections from the notebooks that make only small parts of Gramsci's work available, and only in much abridged editions heavily influenced by editorial choices.[17]

---

activities. The following are important points regarding Gerratana's activities that are relevant to a theory of intellectuals. Gerratana can be construed as an active type of intellectual, or *engagé* intellectual on the model of Jean-Paul Sartre and Simone De Beauvoir. However, these intellectuals' participation in military activities could be disastrous at times. Gerratana was in the Resistance during the Second World War and was involved in the via Rasella attack against Nazi occupation troops in Rome, which was very controversial because it triggered a brutal reprisal known as the Eccidio delle Fosse Ardeatine, or Ardeatine massacre, after the name of the place where the occupation troops buried the bodies of more than 300 Italians that they summarily executed in reprisal against the via Rasella attack, in an unmarked grave hard to reach. Herbert Kappler and the SS in Rome were amongst those directly responsible for the massacre, but Gerratana was arguably indirectly responsible, as he triggered the reprisals.

15 Antonio Gramsci, *Prison Notebooks*, trans. Joseph Buttigieg, 3 vols., vol. 1 (New York: Columbia University Press, 1992); *Prison Notebooks*, trans. Joseph Buttigieg, 3 vols., vol. 2 (New York: Columbia University Press, 1996); *Prison Notebooks*, trans. Joseph Buttigieg, 3 vols., vol. 3 (New York: Columbia University Press, 2007).

16 The symposium was in the first issue of 2006 and contained the following interesting contributions: Joseph Anthony Buttigieg, "The Prison Notebooks: Antonio Gramsci's Work in Progress," *Rethinking Marxism* 18, no. 1 (2006); Joseph W. Childers, "Of Prison Notebooks and the Restoration of an Archive," ibid. (2006/01/01); Peter Ives, "The Mammoth Task of Translating Gramsci," ibid.; David F. Ruccio, "Unfinished Business: Gramsci's Prison Notebooks," ibid.; William V. Spanos, "Cuvier's Little Bone: Joseph Buttigieg's English Edition of Antonio Gramsci's Prison Notebooks," ibid.

17 The Columbia University Press website makes no reference to this fact and does not even mention that the set of three volumes that they sell contains only a small portion of Gramsci's work. It is possible that between 2007, the date of publication of the third volume, and 2019, Columbia terminated the contract it had with Buttigieg, and decided not to hire anyone else because of the high expense involved. There are however a Spanish-language translation and a German-language translation, showing that despite the size of the notebooks it is possible to translate them. Columbia University did publish the complete letters from prison: Antonio Gramsci, *Letters from Prison, Vol. I*, ed. Frank Rosengarten, trans. Raymond Rosenthal (New York: Columbia University Press, 1994); *Letters from Prison, Vol. II*, ed. Frank Rosengarten, trans. Raymond Rosenthal,

The reason why no broad pictures were produced is that we lack the social conditions for producing such broad pictures, a claim that can be further extended to arrive at the more general claim that *we lack the social conditions for objectivity in social science*. Throughout this volume, and in the book on the humanist social science, I argue that one of the main failures of neoliberalism, and also of most mainstream social science, is that they rely upon partial or incomplete pictures that *over*-simplify human beings and society, leading to reductive and faulty scientific models. This widespread failure transcends the individual researcher, and is due to lack of social conditions. These conditions include the academic job market, and also the organization of intellectual work in universities today. Lastly, it might also be related to the political aspects of research, including the very political question of who funds which research and why. Addressing these social conditions is a big challenge that is related to Gramsci's claim that 'there is a struggle for objectivity', because in order to win this struggle we have to secure the social conditions for objectivity, and especially the social conditions for objectivity in social science. Put simply, without a valid and useful theory, it is impossible to formulate and achieve political goals. As it applies to the goals of this book, without a valid alternative to neoliberalism, it is impossible to formulate and implement alternative economic policies. Therefore, I want to suggest what the struggle for objectivity is about, and what are the challenges we face in the formulation of broad pictures of society and history, because this begins to explain both why the formulation of these broad pictures is so hard to achieve, and also what we can do to secure the social conditions for objectivity in social science.

2.4 McGill University and the Social Conditions for Objectivity

I obtained many insights regarding, first, the 'struggle for objectivity' and, second, the difficulties in formulating a theory that provides broad pictures of society and history, from informal observation into universities, which suggested to me that one of the main reasons for the difficulties in producing broad pictures is the *organization of universities, which deeply affects the social conditions for objectivity,* and especially the social conditions for objectivity in social science. They are best illustrated by reference to McGill University, where I studied for my PhD. I bring up the case of McGill University in part

The Complete and Definitive Edition of Gramsci's Prison Letters (New York: Columbia University Press, 1994).

because I know it well. I also bring up McGill University because important considerations suggest that, if a general theory providing a broad picture of society and history was going to be produced in our time, it would have been produced at an institution like McGill University. Here I want to delve first into the reasons why such a theory should have emerged at an institution like McGill University, and then propose explanations as to why such a theory was never produced.

McGill University is a leading institution in Canada, where it is often referred to as the Harvard of Canada, but I want to suggest that it is much more than that. It represents an approach to research that, in addition to being multidisciplinary, is still poised and emphasizes an all-round education, at a time when culture wars are compounding academic specialization and destroying these qualities.[18] McGill University has remarkably been spared being drawn into the culture wars that have engulfed the United States and also some parts of Canada. Perhaps this is comparable to the calm at the eye of the hurricane, where there is quiet and still air, while the winds around it destroy everything in their path. Significantly, this calm enables innovation, rather than stifling it. It also enables formulating a *strategic vision*, a broad way to look at society and history that is comparable to a bird's eye view and that can lead to broad pictures of society and history, as the two mutually help each other: a strategic vision helps sketch broad pictures of society and history and, conversely, these broad pictures contribute to the strategic vision, which needs something analogous to a large map showing all ongoing activities.

---

18 There is a vast literature on culture wars, for example: Jim George and Kim Huynh, *The Culture Wars: Australian and American Politics in the 21st Century* (London and New York: Palgrave Macmillan, 2009); James Davison Hunter, *Culture Wars: the Struggle to Control the Family, Art, Education, Law, and Politics in America* (New York: Basic Books, 1992); James L. Nolan, ed. *The American Culture Wars: Current Contests and Future Prospects* (Charlottesville, Virginia: University Press of Virginia, 1996); Ira Shor, *Culture Wars: School and Society in the Conservative Restoration* (Chicago: University of Chicago Press, 1992). I address only specific aspects of the culture wars that are relevant to the multidisciplinary approach that I propose, which includes history, and leads me to emphasize that culture wars are old and have affected Europe as well as the United States, as detailed in: Christopher Clark and Wolfram Kaiser, *Culture Wars: Secular-Catholic Conflict in Nineteenth-Century Europe* (Cambridge and New York: Cambridge University Press, 2003); Ronald J. Ross, *The Failure of Bismarck's Kulturkampf: Catholicism and State Power in Imperial Germany, 1871–1887* (Wshington, DC: Catholic University of America Press, 2000). Buttigieg has proposed an interesting perspective on Gramsci's legacy and how it is relevant to understand some aspects of culture wars, although without using the expression 'culture wars': Joseph Anthony Buttigieg, "After Gramsci," *The Journal of the Midwest Modern Language Association* 24, no. 1 (1991); "The Contemporary Discourse on Civil Society: A Gramscian Critique," *boundary 2* 32, no. 1 (2005).

Montreal, and McGill University within it, illustrate also that calm encourages social change, not just innovation. The strategic vision can complement social change, including revolutionary change, which does not necessarily entail mayhem and violence. Significantly, between 1960 and 1970 approximately, the entire province of Quebec, as well as its capital Montreal, where McGill University is located, went through a revolution in culture and government that is known as *La Révolution Tranquille*, or the Quiet Revolution, for having been low-key and yet having brought about profound social change. It also introduced profound changes in the built environment of Montreal and launched mass rapid transit in this city, which makes use of powerful computers. These have nothing to envy from the 500 top physics supercomputers, such is their power, and transportation planning for mass rapid transit is beginning to be modeled by sociology and sub-disciplines like computational sociology, whose models require as much, or even more, computing power as physics models. Sociologists, including José Ignacio Nazif Munoz, are also beginning to apply sociology to transportation planning in an effort aimed at reducing accidents, which are arguably a serious social problem.[19] This computing power can also be used to model social interaction and social stratification, which are arguably affected by the availability of means of transportation and communication. I emphasize the 500 top physics supercomputers because they are the embodiment of an approach to natural science that is set as a model for social science, a model that Gramsci sought to reject.

A scholar at McGill University produced the closest thing to a general theory providing a broad picture of society and history, based on a multidisciplinary social science that takes into consideration historical and geographical dimensions. Immanuel Wallerstein wrote a landmark work of contemporary historical sociology, *The Modern World System*, while at McGill University in the early to mid 1970s.[20] McGill University must have been a refuge from the turmoil

19 The Quiet Revolution is commonly characterized as the secularization of government and the demise of the influence of the Catholic Church of Quebec, which was once very powerful, as powerful as any Catholic Church in the Americas. José Ignacio Nazif Munoz, another graduate student at McGill University when I was there, introduced me to the use of sociology for transportation planning, his research focusing on traffic accidents and how to minimize them, a field of research that is becoming increasingly important and that I hope to address elsewhere.

20 The first volume, the one written at McGill University, is: Immanuel Maurice Wallerstein, *The Modern World-System: Capitalist Agriculture and the Origins of the European World-Economy in the Sixteeth Century*, Studies in Social Discontinuity (New York: Academic Press, 1976). All 4 volumes have been recently republished: *The Modern World-System, Vol. I: Capitalist Agriculture and the Origins of the European World-Economy in the Sixteenth Century*, (Berkeley and Los Angeles: University of California Press, 2011); *The*

of American politics, polarized by opposition to the Civil Rights Movement, efforts to continue the Vietnam War, and the assassinations of John Fitzgerald Kennedy and Robert Kennedy. Wallerstein's work is important to my argument because it is arguably the one contemporary attempt to provide a general theory and a broad picture of society and history that contribute to the strategic vision, which is necessary to set and achieve goals, and to formulate policies, including policies in political and military domains. It is also arguably the most famous sociological work produced in the department of sociology at McGill University. Wallerstein's work defined a new theoretical paradigm called World Systems Theory, relaunched the sub-field of historical sociology, and led to many other similar studies.[21] Yet by the early 2000s neither it, nor similar past works, were taught to graduate students at McGill University, except those like myself who specifically chose to study these works.

Modern World-System, Vol. II: Mercantilism and the Consolidation of the European World-Economy, 1600–1750; *The Modern World-System, Vol. III: the Second Era of Great Expansion of the Capitalist World-Economy, 1730s–1840s*; *The Modern World-System, Vol. IV: Centrist Liberalism Triumphant, 1789–1914*.

21 For a review of the vast literature that is part of the paradigm defined by Wallerstein, see: Christopher Chase-Dunn and Peter Grimes, "World-Systems Analysis," *Annual review of sociology* (1995). There was an institutional and organizational dimension to Wallerstein's project. Wallerstein returned to the United States where he started the Fernand Braudel Center at Binghamton University and an academic journal associated with this center, called simply *Review* of the Fernand Braudel Center. In his retirement, Wallerstein moved to Yale University, in what was arguably a belated recognition for his efforts in defining a new paradigm in sociology. Fernand Braudel's work on the Mediterranean and on Capitalism had defined a new approach that Wallerstein built upon, but Wallerstein's World Systems Theory went considerably beyond Braudel's approach. Braudel's most important work is in two multi-volume books. The first, on the Mediterranean, was published in the 1950s and translated into English in the 1970s: Fernand Braudel, *The Mediterranean and the Mediterranean World in the Age of Philip II, Vol. 1*, trans. Sian Reynolds (New York: Harper & Row, 1972); *The Mediterranean and the Mediterranean World in the Age of Philip II, Vol. 2*, trans. Sian Reynolds (New York: Harper & Row, 1973). The second book, on capitalism, was published in 1979 or 1981 in English, possibly in boxed sets, but the volumes I could find are: *The Structure of Everyday Life: Civilization and Capitalism, 15th-18th Century, Vol. 1*, trans. Sian Reynolds (New York: Harper & Row, 1981); *The Wheels of Commerce: Civilization & Capitalism 15th-18th Century, Vol. 2*, trans. Sian Reynolds (New York: Harper & Row, 1982); *The Perspective of the World: Civilization & Capitalism, 15th – 18th Century Vol. 3*, trans. Sian Reynolds (New York: Harper & Row, 1984). I elaborated upon some aspects of Braudel's work, specifically the concept of 'political enterprise of optimum dimension' and the idea that the Mediterranean constituted a system, in: Alessandro Olsaretti, "Political Dynamics in the Rise of Fakhr Al-Din, 1590–1633: Crusade, Trade, and State Formation Along the Levantine Coast," *The International History Review* 30, no. 4 (2008).

There also survives at McGill University, presumably thanks to the calm that prevails there, the *multidisciplinary approach to social science and the concern with multiple domains and dimensions of human activity* that distinguished sociology at its inception. In the department of sociology at McGill University there are scholars who work on studying all of the main domains of human activity. John Anthony Hall, my dissertation supervisor, is a leading scholar who made his name with a landmark work of historical sociology on the rise of the West, which shows remarkable insight into this process that complements and makes sense of important parts of Wallerstein's work.[22] He has since focused on political sociology and has studied, amongst other things, the role of the military and the effects of war on modern nationalism, as well as the interaction of culture and politics in nationalism more in general.[23] Axel van den Berg, whose seminar in social theory I was enrolled in, and who together with Hall supervised my area studies in political sociology, led the rediscovery in contemporary sociology of the role that states have in history.[24] Other scholars in this department whose courses I was enrolled in included Steven Rytina, a specialist in mathematical models of social stratification and inequality, whose work involved applying abstract modelling techniques to concrete social problems. Rytina works in the best tradition of British pragmatic thinking, embodied by naval commanders like Denys Rayner and by the inventors of new military technologies like the radar, which paved the way for radar detection and suppression technologies, and arguably also for modern SIGINT, or signals intelligence, the detection and classification of electronic signals.[25] Lange, for

22 John Anthony Hall, *Powers and Liberties: the Causes and Consequences of the Rise of the West* (Berkeley and Los Angeles: University of California Press, 1986).

23 Hall's work on nationalism includes his own interpretation of nationalism: "Nationalisms: Classified and Explained," *Daedalus* 122, no. 3 (1993); "Globalization and Nationalism," *Thesis Eleven* 63, no. 1 (2000). Hall's work also rekindled interest in Ernest Gellner's theory of nationalism: *The State of the Nation: Ernest Gellner and the Theory of Nationalism* (Cambridge and New York: Cambridge University Press, 1998). Recently, Hall has focused on nationalism in relation to military sociology and international relations: John Anthony Hall and Sinisa Malesevic, *Nationalism and War* (Cambridge and New York: Cambridge University Press, 2013).

24 Axel Van den Berg, *The Immanent Utopia: from Marxism on the State to the State of Marxism* (Princeton and Oxford: Princeton University Press, 1988). Van den Berg's book was recently republished with a new introduction: *The Immanent Utopia: from Marxism on the State to the State of Marxism* (London and New York: Routledge, 2018). Van den Berg also introduced to graduate students, myself included, the concept of meta theory.

25 William A. Gamson, Bruce Fireman, and Steven Rytina, *Encounters with Unjust Authority*, Dorsey Series in Sociology (Belmont, CA: Dorsey Press, 1982); Rytina, *Network Persistence and the Axis of Hierarchy*.

whose undergraduate class in political sociology I was a teaching assistant, and who supervised my area studies in the sociology of development, has done very important work in both the sociology of development and in the methodology of historical sociology, which I address in chapter 6, besides his work on the British empire, violence, and development.

Yet even at McGill University this multidisciplinary approach to social science and the concern with multiple domains and dimensions of human activity never produced another theory than Wallerstein's, or any further elaborations of Wallerstein's theory, nor were these studies encouraged amongst graduate students.[26] I believe there are *two reasons why a complete broad picture of society and history was never produced* at McGill University: mindless empiricism, and elitism. By *mindless empiricism* I mean an unreflecting attitude towards scientific research that reduces all science to empirical research alone. Mindless empiricism led to downplaying or even stigmatizing theory. Broad pictures of society and history need theory, because such broad pictures are only provided by theory, or with substantial contributions from theory. My experience of research in social theory is that it has been marginalized or even actively discouraged. Theory is portrayed as 'mere theory', little better than speculation, and contrasted with empirical research, which is seen as the only source of valid scientific knowledge. This always seemed to me a bizarre stance, because leading scholars often branch out into theory, or even have made their name by working on theory. It seems to me that this is due to *elitism*, whereby leading scholars can focus on theory, while everyone else should do empirical research.

This leads me to *one of the main goals of this project*, namely, to contribute towards a *greater emphasis on theory that provides broad pictures of society and history*. Theory is indispensable to sketch broad pictures of society and history. *Lack of theory and broad pictures are bad for politics*. This is because a strategic vision needs the broad pictures of society and history, and both a strategic vision and broad pictures are necessary, not just for leading scholars, but also for policymakers and citizens, who are, respectively, those who are supposed to set and approve development policies, neither of which should be left to the leading scholars alone. *Lack of theory and broad pictures is also bad for social science*. The contrast opposing theory to empirical research is a false

26 Wallerstein's book is the closest thing to such a broad picture, but it has taken the form of a very detailed synthesis of a huge amount of historical scholarship. Only more recently he has provided broad pictures, for example in: Immanuel Wallerstein, "World-Systems Analysis," in *Social Theory Today*, ed. Anthony Giddens and Jonathan H. Turner (Stanford: Stanford University Press, 1987); Immanuel Maurice Wallerstein, *Historical Capitalism with Capitalist Civilization* (London and New York: Verso, 1995).

dichotomy. Far from being opposed, theory and empirical research are complementary. I argue below that theory is the necessary prerequisite to empirical research and that without theory, or with bad theory, empirical research is doomed to fail. I believe that both theory and empirical research are necessary to social science, and that everyone working in social science should do at least some theory work, and some empirical work.

Mindless empiricism and elitism also lead to downplaying arts, and cultural studies more in general, and this is another reason why a theory providing a broad picture of society and history was never produced at McGill University. Culture, including arts such as painting, sculpture, literature, and music, is an essential domain of human activity, and any broad picture that neglects it is deeply flawed. There was at McGill University not a single graduate seminar on cultural sociology, nor on specialized sub-fields like the sociology of art, or the sociology of literature. Yet these are important fields. There is at McGill University a department of Art History and Communication Studies, founded by Christine Ross, a leading scholar in these fields, and a scholar as eminent as Hall. This department is based on the premise that art and related skills are central to communications, and thus to social life and ultimately to all human activities, since *a distinguishing feature of human beings is our capacity to communicate through complex symbols.*[27] Yet this has been lost on sociology. Leading scholars like Hall, who began his career with a work on the sociology of literature, or Rodney Nelson, another professor at McGill at the time when I was there, who built his career on the sociology of culture and the sociology of literature, have effectively ceased teaching these subjects.[28]

Moreover, *the social study of arts and related fields are neglected through much of sociology*, not just at McGill University. I believe that part of the reason for this neglect is that studies of arts and symbolism cannot be easily quantified,

27 Jurgen Habermas's entire theory emphasizes the importance of communication: Jurgen Habermas, *The Theory of Communicative Action, Vol. 1: Reason and the Rationalization of Society*, trans. Thomas McCarthy (Boston: Beacon Press, 1984); *The Theory of Communicative Action, Vol. 2: Lifeworld and System, a Critique of Functionalist Reason,* trans. Thomas McCarthy (Boston: Beacon Press, 1984). Hall worked on Habermas: John Anthony Hall, "Gellner and Habermas on Epistemology and Politics or Need We Feel Disenchanted?," *Philosophy of the Social Sciences* 12, no. 4 (1982). Hall mentioned Habermas to me in a cautiously positive manner, showing there are sociologists in North America who still value this kind of approach, despite the fact that Habermas' language is obscure.

28 Hall's book on literature is: *The Sociology of Literature* (London: Longman, 1979). Rodney Nelson has focused on teaching rather than research, possibly also because in his fields of interest it is difficult to publish.

and are thus not easily subjected to empirical research, which emphasizes quantitative methods. Some journals like *Poetics* have begun applying statistics to studies of arts. Some of these studies involve applying statistical analysis to individual responses to art, in order to find out about average tastes in one social group or another, for example. Some of these studies can lead to mathematical models of society, like the models of social stratification that Rytina worked on, since taste serves to define belonging to one social group or another, and thus becomes constitutive of social stratification. Sociologist Pierre Bourdieu's book *Distinction* laid the groundwork for this kind of study.[29] Quantitative studies are important, but our understanding of arts cannot be reduced exclusively to the understanding provided by these studies. The *crucially important study of symbols, including complex symbols, remains the preserve of semiotics and linguistics*, both of which are taught separately from social science. Studies of arts and symbolism are thought instead to be akin to matters of opinion, and thus not to be part of scientific knowledge. This too is associated with elitism. The implication is that those who want to study arts and complex symbolism can do so as part of their personal cultivation, if they have the time and money to do so. *The study of arts is therefore the preserve of elites*, who alone have the time and money to dedicate themselves to understanding these domains of human activity. This is arguably part of a broader trend today that sees an all-round humanistic education to be of little use, yet nothing could be more wrong.

The above discussion of arts leads me also to the *social conditions for objectivity in social science*. In order to secure the ability to produce theories that are both valid and useful, we need to act upon these *social conditions*, which in addition to the organization of universities, include such *social* considerations as which social group produces knowledge and how, the funding for different types of knowledge, and many other considerations regarding how knowledge is actually produced and disseminated, which always involves a social component. I address in chapter 5, which deals with specialization in universities, the insight that intellectual production has been hampered by an over-reliance upon empirical studies alone, and also by institutional compartmentalization, whereby culture comes to be taught in separate departments from other social sciences. Both of these points, regarding empiricism and compartmentalization, are related to the manner in which the profession is organized, which

29 Pierre Bourdieu, *Distinction: a Social Critique of the Judgement of Taste*, trans. Richard Nice (Cambridge, Massachusetts and London: Harvard University Press, 1984). I address other important works by Bourdieu in the book on humanist social science.

is another important aspect of the social conditions for objectivity in social science.

2.5 Aristocratic-military Elites and a Humanistic Education

In order to understand the importance of a humanistic education, and its current association with elitism, it is useful to consider *past elites who benefited from a humanistic education* and how these elites are changing. The elites of the past put a great premium on a humanistic and all-round education that included arts and literature. An integral part of the education of British elites in the past, and a coming of age ritual, used to be to travel to sites of ancient civilizations, ancient Roman and Greek civilizations in particular, or cities associated with the Italian Renaissance, to learn about the arts and history of these civilizations, in what came to be known as the Grand Tour.[30] One of the most prestigious and traditional degree courses at Oxford University, which educated British elites, is the *Literae humaniores* course, a name that can perhaps best be translated idiomatically as 'literature of human matters'.[31] This name implies a contrast with studies of theology, suggesting that humanism is closer to human concerns. The *Literae humaniores* course is essentially a humanistic degree course, that is, a course inspired by the ideals and sources of humanism, but not explicitly based on a humanist philosophy. It is a degree course focused on classics, which include language studies of ancient Greek and Latin, and studies of ancient Greek and Roman arts, history, and philosophy, which are the precursors of humanism.

This *humanistic education was thought to be useful also for individuals in critical decision-making positions*. George III and his son Prince Edward, respectively the British monarch and the commander of British forces in Canada at the time of the American Revolutionary War, had informal education by tutors. Later British aristocratic-military elites who can be considered the

30 There is a vast literature on this subject. I deal with the cultural phenomena that this early form of cultural tourism generated in: Alessandro Olsaretti, "Urban Culture, Curiosity and the Aesthetics of Distance: the Representation of Picturesque Carnivals in Early Victorian Travelogues to the Levant," *Social History* 32, no. 3 (2007). Valentina Bono pointed out to me the continuing importance of cultural tourism to sites of ancient civilizations like Rome, and the curiosity that still motivates visitors.

31 On social science studies and Classics at Oxford University, see: Norman Chester, *Economics, Politics and Social Studies in Oxford, 1900–85* (London and New York: Palgrave Macmillan, 1986); C. Stray, *Oxford Classics: Teaching and Learning 1800–2000* (London, Berlin, New York: Bloomsbury, 2013).

spiritual descendants of these leaders, and continued their politics by building the Second British Empire, had formal humanistic educations steeped in classics and arts. This was true even of men like Army General Douglas Haig and Prime Minister Winston Churchill, the most important British leaders at the time of the First World War and the Second World War respectively, who played a crucial role in the very costly British victories in both of these wars, and who had earlier played a role in expanding the British Empire. They were aristocrats with military training, or even with careers built entirely in the military, yet they benefited from a humanistic education. Haig seems to have studied Classics and Modern Languages at Oxford University, an interesting combination of arts subjects, and seems to have had an interest in social science. Churchill had a less formal education, but like many members of the British elites, he painted and wrote poetry.[32] Interestingly, even those members of the elites who presented themselves as anti-elite, had humanistic educations steeped in classics and arts, and benefited from them. Marx wrote poetry and a doctoral dissertation on ancient Greek philosophy. He was also influenced by Aristotle's ideal of the good life as involving an all-round cultivation of human faculties.[33] American leaders of the time had similar humanistic educations.

---

32 The details of Haig's education are not readily available, since he left Oxford before completing his degree. Haig might have had an interest in social science, possibly Political Economy. On Haig, see: John Terraine, *Douglas Haig: the Educated Soldier* (London: Cassell, 2005); J. Paul Harris, *Douglas Haig and the First World War*, Cambridge Military Histories (Cambridge and New York: Cambridge University Press, 2008). On Churchill, see: Andrew Roberts, *Churchill: Walking with Destiny* (London: Penguin, 2018). On the breadth of Churchill's knowledge of literature, see: Darrell Holley and Winston Churchill, *Churchill's Literary Allusions: an Index to the Education of a Soldier, Statesman, and Litterateur* (Jefferson, North Carolina: McFarland, 1987).

33 McLellan's biography of Marx is a classic, now in its 4th edition: David McLellan, *Karl Marx: A Biography*, 4th ed. (London and New York: Palgrave Macmillan, 2006). Gareth Steadman-Jones' biography comes from a historian who pioneered the study of language in social history: Gareth Stedman Jones, *Karl Marx: Greatness and Illusion* (London: Penguin, 2016). Alvin Ward Gouldner provided in the 1970s and 1980s an interesting perspective on the shortcomings of both sociology and Marxism, focusing on the role of intellectuals in this crisis and in Marxism: Alvin Ward Gouldner, *The Coming Crisis in Western Sociology* (New York: Basic Books, 1970); *The Future of Intellectuals and the Rise of the New Class*, Critical Social Studies (Basingstoke: Macmillan, 1979); *Against Fragmentation: the Origins of Marxism and the Sociology of Intellectuals* (Oxford and New York: Oxford University Press, 1985). On the recent renewal of interest in Marx, see: Marcello Musto, *The Marx Revival: Key Concepts and New Critical Interpretations* (Cambridge and New York: Cambridge University Press, 2020). This has led to new biographies of Marx: Werner Blumenberg and Gareth Stedman Jones, *Karl Marx: an Illustrated Biography*, trans. Douglas Scott (London and New York: Verso, 2000); Marcello Musto,

Thomas Jefferson and John Adams, respectively the third and second President of the United States after George Washington's withdrawal from politics and untimely death, had educations steeped in classics and modern languages.[34]

Classics and arts were thus deemed essential to the education of individuals in leadership positions whose task it was to make very important decisions. We are very far culturally from this world. However, as Gramsci argued, *the importance of culture has increased*, not decreased, in our times.[35] This has made an all-round humanistic education more, not less, important. One aspect of this concerns all citizens. We are required in modern societies to deal with diverse types of social situations. These include participation in politics thanks to the expansion of democracy, besides participation in the economy, which itself is expanding in directions that require more decision-making and management skills associated with the ability to assess and synthesize diverse information from different domains of human behavior. All of this requires an all-round humanistic education.

Gramsci also highlighted important *changes in the sources of elite power*. Whereas once military power was the predominant source of power in societies, and it was used with little or no regard for human life, today culture has taken its place. This is true of countries that are part of the West, but it is also arguably increasingly true of countries in other parts of the world that

---

The Last Years of Karl Marx: an Intellectual Biography, trans. Patrick Camiller (Stanford, California: Stanford University Press, 2020).

34 Both Adams and Jefferson studied Latin and Greek and modern languages. Recent biographies of Adams and Jefferson include: David McCullough, *John Adams* (New York: Simon & Schuster, 2001). John B. Boles, *Jefferson: Architect of American Liberty* (New York: Basic Books, 2017). For a critical view of Thomas Jefferson, who seems to have been perfectly at ease adapting to the times and even to contradictory positions, as the occasion demanded, see: Andrew Burstein, *Jefferson's Secrets: Death and Desire at Monticello* (New York: Basic Books, 2006); *Democracy's Muse: How Thomas Jefferson Became an FDR Liberal, a Reagan Republican, and a Tea Party Fanatic, All the While Being Dead* (Charlottesville, Virginia: University of Virginia Press, 2015). There is even a biography of Jefferson by a renowned and controversial popular literature author who is a vocal atheist: Christopher Hitchens, *Thomas Jefferson: Author of America*, Eminent Lives (New York, London, Toronto: Harper Perennial, 2009).

35 Gramsci is considered a precursor of modern cultural studies. On his contribution to the study of culture, see: Crehan, *Gramsci, Culture and Anthropology*; "Gramsci's Concept of Common Sense: a Useful Concept for Anthropologists?," *Journal of Modern Italian Studies* 16, no. 2 (2011). In English-speaking countries Gramsci is still associated chiefly with the study of culture, and this is the part of his work that has been translated the most, for example in: Antonio Gramsci, *Selections from Cultural Writings*, trans. William Boelhower (Cambridge, Massachusetts and London: Harvard University Press, 1991).

are rapidly industrializing.[36] *Gramsci's theory of intellectuals* drew attention to the growing importance of intellectuals in modern societies and to the more cautious stances on policy and intellectual matters alike that are associated with cultural elites, by contrast with military elites.[37] The modern counterpart of Haig would be politicians like Boris Johnson, the British Prime Minister. The modern counterpart of former British Prime Minister Churchill would be scholars like Andrew Dawson, a young sociologist at York University in Toronto, who as a student at McGill University pursued an interest in arts and in social theory, but wrote a thesis based largely on empirical work.[38]

The point that I am trying to make is that *contemporary leaders seem more cautious in resorting to war* and that high-ranking military officers seem more careful with soldiers' lives, while politicians have become more knowledgeable and use culture before resorting to violence. For example, a writer who was a vocal imperialist like Rudyard Kipling, active from before the First and Second World Wars, had he been alive today, would be a cautious general like Canadian General Romeo Dallaire, who commanded UN troops in Rwanda at the time of the Rwandan genocide, and who was far more cautious than Haig in committing troops to combat, perhaps too cautions, since the genocide continued despite the presence of UN troops, as if the UN troops had not been there.

36 Hall's work on consent deals with this social phenomenon, although he has his own distinctive interpretation of consent compared to Gramsci's: John Anthony Hall, *Coercion and Consent: Studies on the Modern State* (Cambridge, UK and Malden, Massachusetts: Polity Press, 1994).

37 Gramsci also contributed to the modern sociology of intellectuals. I address the literature on this point, and propose insights regarding Gramsci's contribution to it, in: Alessandro Olsaretti, "Beyond Class: the Many Facets of Gramsci's Theory of Intellectuals," *Journal of Classical Sociology* 14, no. 4 (2014). This field has been reviewed from a Hungarian or East European perspective in: Larry P. King and Ivan Szelényi, *Theories of the New Class: Intellectuals and Power*, Contradictions (Minneapolis, Minnesota: University of Minnesota Press, 2004).

38 Dawson has worked mostly on the interaction between law and development in Central America, building upon Matthew Lange's work: Andrew Dawson, "Political Violence in Consolidated Democracies: the Development and Institutionalization of Partisan Violence in Late Colonial Jamaica (1938–62)," *Social science history* 40, no. 2 (2016); "The Social Determinants of the Rule of Law: a Comparison of Jamaica and Barbados," *World Development* 45 (2013). Dawson's work is very interesting also because he managed somehow to combine empirical research with a strategic vision, as his earlier research dealt with the rule of law and violence in Central America, and his later research with similar questions in Afghanistan, two hot-spots and strategically important areas. I discussed Dawson's research on Afghanistan with him at a meeting we had at the Universite de Montreal. His approach to research is very interesting and his work on Afghanistan could provide very important insights.

There are exceptions to this of course. Former British Prime Minister Stanley Baldwin, who was in power shortly before the Second World War, was much criticized in Great Britain for his overly cautious attitude towards war with Hitler and failure to rearm, whereas contemporary social theorists like van den Berg share instead Marx's warlike attitude and firebrand rhetoric, even when they are critical of Marx. This over-reaction perhaps was due to the excesses of such military commanders as Herbert Kitchener, the military commander during the Boer War and the invasion of Sudan, who used scorched-earth policies, and who long before the Second World War introduced concentration camps, in a brutal twist to pragmatic thinking.

There is a social dimension to this change. These cautious generals and scholars show a *move from the hard military power of aristocratic-military elites to the soft power of cultural elites*, although, as Weber argued, violence is still central to modern states, more than most people realize.[39] There were such precedents in the focus on soft power amongst some cultural elites of the past, and not just during the Italian Renaissance. Jefferson, besides being a politician and in a sense a forerunner of contemporary political thought represented today by Hall, which is no small thing, was also a humanist of sorts and was arguably a far more perceptive strategist than Haig and Churchill, who were more focused on leadership.[40] The same could be said of Adams, and today of such perceptive cultural critics as Will Straw.[41] It is only figures like Jefferson or Hall, and Adams or Straw, and perhaps Kitchener or Rytina, who can provide the strategic vision, thanks to their vast and wide-ranging knowledge. *There has also been a change in the number and base of elite institutions.* Whereas between two hundred years ago and one hundred years ago Oxford University

39 See Weber's essay "Politics as a vocation" in: Max Weber et al., *From Max Weber: Essays in Sociology* (London and New York: Routledge, 1991). Max Weber famously described the state as an organization that holds the monopoly of legitimate violence over a territory. I believe this point is central to Hall's work too and it is very important to understand the history of the West to this day.

40 Burstein, *Democracy's Muse*; Karl Lehmann, *Thomas Jefferson, American Humanist* (Charlottesville, Virginia: University Press of Virginia, 1985); Merrill D. Peterson, *Thomas Jefferson and the New Nation: a Biography*, A Galaxy Book (Oxford and New York: Oxford University Press, USA, 1975).

41 Straw is a professor in the department of Art History and Communication Studies at McGill University, who is responsible, amongst other things, for very interesting research on urban culture in modern times, with a focus on multimedia, which is being explored also by Carlo Ratti at MIT. Straw has recently investigated the concept of cultural scene as it applies to urban studies: Will Straw, "Cultural Scenes," *Loisir et société/Society and Leisure* 27, no. 2 (2004); "Some Things a Scene Might Be: Postface," *Cultural studies* 29, no. 3 (2015).

and Cambridge University alone served to educate British aristocratic-military elites, today Commonwealth universities like McGill University, and American Ivy League universities, educate world-elites, including imperialist elites like G. W. Bush, who studied at Yale University.[42] Moreover, whereas a hundred years ago Haig and Churchill moved in exclusive circles and Old Boys' clubs, had they been alive today they would still move in exclusive circles, but they would also rub elbows with such common folk as construction company *impresarios*, or teachers and librarians, just to mention some other professions associated with soft power.

2.6 Broad Pictures of Society and History and Their Importance

One might object that a humanistic education, and broad pictures of society and history associated with it, are not relevant to anyone except the elites who make decisions. I disagree with this objection, and here I want to focus on explaining *why it is still important to provide such broad pictures today* and give concrete examples of their continued importance. Some of these reasons are related to the importance of broad pictures for policymakers and citizens, and to the need to intervene in public debates polarized by culture wars in order to provide answers that are better than the answers that pundits can provide, because they are informed by social science. In this project I draw attention to the fact that philosophy and social scienc can provide also a moderating influence upon public debate. My view regarding the relevance of broad pictures to policymakers and citizens can be summarized in a few sentences. *Broad pictures serve to answer big questions that we all need answers to.* These are not just existential questions, although the latter do play a part in the continued importance of broad pictures. Broad pictures that answer big questions are needed most of all for practical reasons, because answers to big questions set the broad parameters for policies, and also for important choices by citizens. These can be even more important at a time when democracies feel they are under threat, or at a time when public debate is polarized by culture wars. Most professors shun big questions today, but this is only because of the growing specialization of universities, which leads them to ask and answer

42 The McGill University website reports that the student body includes over 10,000 students, which is over 27% of the student body, who come from more than 150 countries other than Canada: International Student Services (ISS) at McGill, "International Student Body: Mcgill's International Student Body," Office of International Student Services, "About International Student Services (ISS)," ibid.

very specific questions, rather than big questions. Yet when the occasional academic study dares to ask these big questions, it has success, sometimes immediate, other times delayed. In many of the footnotes in this book I point to the different editions of the books that I cite in order both to emphasize the success of these books, and also to draw attention to questions regarding the immediate or delayed success of books, and the influence of the cultural climate prevailing at one point in time or another.

It is useful to *consider several studies that dared to ask big questions and that illustrate the continued importance of broad pictures of society and history*. In this project I make widespread use of *classics of social theory*, and of social science more in general, chiefly because it is these classics that address big questions. I also refer often to the *scholars who taught me at McGill University*, where I did all my postgraduate studies, because I found they have important lessons to teach, although I interpret these lessons very differently than they do, and I apply them to altogether different goals. An important lesson that I have learned from them regards their approach to big questions, which suggests that it is possible to contribute to debates in culture, as well as to academic debates, and even to take a stance on culture wars, while continuing to produce academic research. Another important lesson is that theory can address phenomena that span vast areas, or even the entire world, like globalization.[43] I differ radically from these scholars in the answers that I suggest to these big questions, a point that I address in chapter 3. However, I undoubtedly learned from their approach to big questions, and in this book I hope to show that it is both possible and desirable, even necessary, to provide a broad picture

43 This is what Wallerstein's World Systems Theory does. John Anthony Hall too approaches such wide area questions, for example in: Hall, "Globalization and Nationalism." Interestingly, the entire journal *Thesis Eleven* is devoted to addressing such big questions. It is named after the last thesis of Marx's *Theses on Feuerbach*, which is inscribed also on Marx's grave in Highgate Cemetery in London. Published in Australia, this journal is a venue for general social theory from around the world, as well as for Australian social theory, including theory by two Australian Gramsci experts: Peter D. Thomas, "Hegemony, Passive Revolution and the Modern Prince," *Thesis Eleven*, 117 (2013); Alastair Davidson, "The Uses and Abuses of Gramsci," ibid., no. 95 (2008). Australia seems however to have embarked on promoting an especially narrow view of academic research, while seeking to make it directly relevant to policy, an approach that involves emphasizing specialized empirical research, which is exactly the opposite of my approach. I believe that specialized empirical research often does not provide adequate answers for policy, not on its own. I gained the above insight into higher education in Australia through Renee Worringer, a historian who worked in Australia around the time that John Howard was Prime Minister.

of society and history that answers big questions, and that therefore this broad picture of society and history is very important.

It is useful to begin *by defining the big questions that are central to this project* and that I seek to answer. They all concern development and democracy. In particular, the broad picture of society and history that I propose seeks to answer such big questions as: what are development and democracy? how do they relate to the organization of society? How do they relate to struggle in history? and most importantly, what are the best ways to win this struggle for the masses? In the course of this project, I try to show that these are amongst the most important questions that can be asked. This is because of the following insight that is central to the view that 'there is a struggle for objectivity': without democracy it is impossible to answer adequately any question, and it is impossible to act upon any of the answers in such a manner that they benefit the masses, instead of just benefiting the elites. One reason for this is that *broad pictures, strategic vision, and big questions are all inter-related.* If the broad picture can provide what I referred to above as a strategic vision, then it can provide answers to big questions, and can help set the broad parameters within which to formulate and implement policies, for example. Here I want to discuss the importance of broad pictures for answering big questions in a number of domains, and give concrete examples of these big questions and the strategic vision.

Broad pictures can provide answers to *big questions that are important for the military and for security.* Hall's masterly and accessibly written book *Is America Breaking Apart?* which he co-wrote with Charles Lindholm, was first published in 1999 and went on to a second edition in 2001, only two years later, before, not after, the 9/11 attacks.[44] These have certainly increased the appeal

---

44 John Anthony Hall and Charles Lindholm, *Is America Breaking Apart?* (Princeton and Oxford: Princeton University Press, 2001). Robert Putnam was addressing similar issues at around the same time: Robert D. Putnam, *Bowling Alone: the Collapse and Revival of American Community*, A Touchstone Book (New York: Simon & Schuster, 2000). The story at the beginning of Putnam's book captures several aspects of American culture, including bowling. Putnam focused upon the loss of community in American life, but since community is important to democracy, its loss is a serious concern. The idea that the United States had a vibrant democracy thanks to a strong civil society, and thanks also to strong communal ties and volunteering in the community, is as old as Alexis de Tocqueville's classic on American democracy, which exists in several translations and was also reprinted around this time: Alexis de Tocqueville, John Stone, and Stephen Mennell, *Alexis de Tocqueville on Democracy, Revolution, and Society*, Heritage of Sociology Series (Chicago: University of Chicago Press, 1982); Alexis de Tocqueville and Sanford Kessler, *Democracy in America (Abridged)*, trans. Stephen D. Grant, Hackett Classics Series (Indianapolis and Cambridge: Hackett Publisher, 2001). Volunteering is being replaced by professional NGOs, which need financing, and a professional sector of services to NGOs.

of this book, but clearly the publisher must have perceived there was demand, and possibly a need, for a book on this topic, presumably because of ongoing culture wars in the United States. In this book, Hall, who is a sociologist with expertise in European history and the rise of the West, and Lindholm, who is an anthropologist with expertise in Middle Eastern cultures, joined forces to sketch the prospects for American society at a crucial time in American history. Both these scholars share a view of history as involving struggle and have provided broad pictures and addressed big questions other times. Hall has addressed big questions also in his more recent book *The Importance of Being Civil: the Struggle for Political Decency*, which alludes to the importance of such key topics for political life as sympathy and deceit, and such key topics for states as intelligence.[45]

Intelligence has come prominently to the fore in the wake of the 9/11 attacks, since these attacks were a major blow to American security and led to a drastic overhaul of the intelligence community of the United States and the controversial expansion in the powers and subsequent activities of the NSA, although national security questions were a concern already in the 1990s.[46] Hall's account is a high-level, or strategic, account of intelligence that differs from the tactical intelligence that is the main task of such units as the Tactical Intelligence Brigade of the Italian Army, or even of the Military Intelligence Brigades of the United States Army. This project proposes instead a single theory of intelligence that encompasses both levels, the strategic and the tactical. In order to understand challenges to security like the 9/11 attacks, it is necessary to take

---

There are professional fundraising organizations with their own call centers that raise funds on behalf of NGOs, who use part of these funds to pay the wages of professionals in their staff, and part for their activities on behalf of communities. The United States is today the country with the highest level of gifts in the world to NGOs as a percentage of GDP, and this means there is still a thriving NGO sector. I wonder, however, about the meaning of this change. Giving gifts is very important, but the professionalization of volunteering, if carried too far, can lead to loss of community.

45 John Anthony Hall, *The Importance of Being Civil: the Struggle for Political Decency* (Princeton and Oxford: Princeton University Press, 2013). Another example is Hall's intervention in the study of world orders, a topic that is also addressed by Chomsky: *International Orders* (Cambridge, UK and Malden, Massachusetts: Polity Press, 1996); Noam Chomsky, *World Orders, Old and New* (New York: Columbia University Press, 1996). I find that social science can contribute much to this study, which should not focus on sinister views of a new world order being imposed by mysterious powers, as conspiracy theories suggest, but should focus instead upon concrete problems that arise in social conflict and interstate conflict, and upon the need to regulate and limit this conflict, identifying the causes of this conflict, whether they are terrorists or imperialist elites.

46 Peter J. Katzenstein, ed. *The Culture of National Security: Norms and Identity in World Politics* (New York: Columbia University Press, 1996).

into consideration both levels. The 9/11 attacks raised also a number of other questions, as they triggered a series of events, from the invasion of Afghanistan to the invasion of Iraq, and led to other controversial decisions associated with the War on Terror. They arguably also contributed to the ongoing culture wars in the United States, raising a number of politicized yet important questions. These questions include cultural differences between the West and other parts of the world. Lindholm has addressed big questions other times too, with his book *The Struggle for the World: Liberation Movements for the 21st Century*.[47]

Broad pictures can also provide answers to *big questions that are important for culture and politics*. Interestingly, some specialists are beginning to feel the need to sketch broad pictures and ask big questions, precisely because they are important for culture and politics. Such is the case with scholars of Islamic studies and the Middle East who focus on *topics that are relevant to Christian-Muslim relations*. I was first introduced to these big questions while studying for an MA with a focus on Ottoman history at the Institute of Islamic Studies, or IIS, at McGill University. The work of Uner Turgay, my MA thesis supervisor, focused on the economic history of northern Turkey and on trade between different shores of the Black Sea, including the Crimea. Thi is a very specialized field, so specialized that Turgay's work is not widely available. This work was nevertheless informed by the questions, which must be central to many Turkish nationalists: why did the Ottoman empire fail to stand up to European empires? and why has secularism failed in Turkey and been replaced by political movements that emphasize religion?[48] Other scholars in Islamic Studies

47 Charles Lindholm and Jose Pedro Zuquete, *The Struggle for the World: Liberation Movements for the 21st Century* (Stanford, California: Stanford University Press, 2010). Lindholm makes an interesting choice of words in his title in characterizing movements as being 'for' the Twenty-First Century, implying that they are adequate to twenty-first century tasks, and possibly built for these tasks, given the increasing professionalization of civil society and also of social movement organizations. The same choice of words and a similar perspective is adopted by: David S. Meyer and Sidney Tarrow, eds., *The Social Movement Society: Contentious Politics for a New Century*, People, Passions, and Power (Lanham, Boulder, New York, and Oxford: Rowman & Littlefield Publishers, 1997).

48 The first question was central to Turgay, a scholar from an earlier generation that still looked up to Mustafa Kemal Ataturk, the founding father of modern Turkey. On these questions, Turgay introduced me to Kemal Karpat's work, whose approach is close to sociology: Kemal H. Karpat, "The Transformation of the Ottoman State, 1789–1908," *International Journal of Middle East Studies* 3, no. 3 (1972); *An Inquiry into the Social Foundations of Nationalism in the Ottoman State: from Social Estates to Classes, from Millets to Nations* (Center of International Studies, Princeton University, 1973). This sociological approach has been pursued also by one of Bernard Lewis's students: Fatma Muge Gocek, *Rise of the Bourgeoisie, Demise of Empire: Ottoman Westernization and Social Change* (Oxford and New York: Oxford University Press, 1996). More recently, Karpat has

have openly began asking big questions. Such is the case with Wael Hallaq, whose courses on Islamic law and legal institutions I followed while at the IIS. Hallaq is a leading scholar in Islamic law and a specialist in the legal and political thought of medieval Islamic thinkers, including Ibn Taymiyyah, a precursor of strict interpretations of Islam.[49] Hallaq has moved from these very specialized studies to ask big questions with his book *The Impossible State: Islam, Politics, and Modernity's Moral Predicament*, which relates Islam to the condition of modernity in general.[50] It is therefore directly relevant to understand the ideology behind modern terrorist organizations like the Islamic State of Iraq and Syria, or ISIS, better known as the Islamic State of Iraq and the Levant, or ISIL. In this book Hallaq also borrows from the thought of Nazi political theorist Carl Schmitt, in order to complement Islamic legal and political thought on the state. This unfortunately gives ideological justification to G. W. Bush's label 'Islamofascism' to describe the terrorists threatening the United States and possibly the ideologists behind them.[51] Both Turgay and Hallaq worked for many years at the McGill IIS, and I believe this institute and their work

begun addressing big questions relating to modernity: Kemal H. Karpat, *The Politicization of Islam: Reconstructing Identity, State, Faith, and Community in the Late Ottoman State*, Studies in Middle Eastern History (Oxford and New York: Oxford University Press, 2001).

49 Wael B. Hallaq, *A History of Islamic Legal Theories: an Introduction to Sunni Usul Al-Fiqh* (Cambridge and New York: Cambridge University Press, 1997); *Authority, Continuity and Change in Islamic Law* (Cambridge and New York: Cambridge University Press, 2001). Hallaq conveyed in a seminar that he considered Ibn Taymiyyah an important thinker, who might have informed Hallaq's later work, if I understood Hallaq correctly.

50 *The Impossible State: Islam, Politics, and Modernity's Moral Predicament* (New York: Columbia University Press, 2012). In this book Hallaq borrows explicitly from Carl Schmitt, ignoring Jan-Werner Muller's insights and criticisms of both Schmitt and populism: Jan-Werner Muller, *A Dangerous Mind: Carl Schmitt in Post-War European Thought* (New Haven and London: Yale University Press, 2003). Despite his insights into Schmitt's political theory, Muller stops short of comparing Nazi ideology and populist ideology. Muller is in a tradition of social science closely related to historical studies, and in his book on populism focuses chiefly on details and the insights that details can provide: *What Is Populism?* (Philadelphia: University of Pennsylvania Press, 2016). In this project I provide a broader picture and point to the structural similarities between, on the one hand, fascism and nazism and, on the other hand, populism and Muslim fundamentalism.

51 William Safire, "Islamofascism," *New York Times*, October 1st 2006. For a review of all uses of the word 'Islamofascism' and of the association between Islam and fascism, see: Tamir Bar-On, "'Islamofascism': Four Competing Discourses on the Islamism-Fascism Comparison," *Fascism* 7, no. 2 (2018). This article approaches the question from a history of ideas standpoint, tracing the uses of the expression in works by intellectuals. I approach it instead from a structural standpoint, highlighting that both populism and Muslim fundamentalism, which is *not* Islam, resemble fascism because of the way they fit within the modern state system. I make this argument in the second volume.

constitutes another reason why we should pay much more attention to scholarship produced at McGill University, including the IIS.

Providing answers to big questions is even more important at a time of culture wars. A clear example is historian Renee Worringer's recent introduction to the Ottoman empire that seeks to answer the question: who were the Ottomans? This is very important at a time when culture wars are portraying a misleading and sinister picture of the Muslim 'other'. This picture is in some ways a throwback to the worst times of Christian-Muslim conflict at the time of the clash between the Habsburg and Ottoman empires in the sixteenth and seventeenth centuries.[52] Answering big questions regarding Islam, Christianity and modernity can contribute to heightening culture wars, if the answers are in the wrong hands and are manipulated to stoke up these culture wars. Other answers can contribute to deflating culture wars, if only they were placed in the right hands, not the hands of journalists who are unscrupulous, and pursue big audiences more than they pursue truth. For example, I think it is very important *not* to conflate Islam with terrorism. This applies also to the strict interpretations of Islam that have become widespread in many Muslim countries, encouraging the return to the veil, for example. In this, I have learned from the approach of other scholars also at the McGill IIS, who have provided a nuanced view of Arab countries and Islam, highlighting the numerous cultural traditions within these countries, and within this world religion, which often go against the grain of mainstream views.

---

52 Renee Worringer, *A Short History of the Ottoman Empire* (Toronto: University of Toronto Press, 2020). I believe instead that the Habsburg-Ottoman conflict was mostly a clash between empires, not between cultures or religions. States around that time had begun using culture systematically to advance their political ends. A more nuanced view of Christian-Muslim conflict during the rise and decline of the Ottoman empire has been provided by historian Daniel Goffman, at DePaul University in Chicago: Daniel Goffman, *The Ottoman Empire and Early Modern Europe*, New Approaches to European History (Cambridge and New York: Cambridge University Press, 2002). Worringer is specialized in comparative history and has provided a very interesting comparative history of Turkey and Japan, two states that in their recent history struggled to deal with the West. Interestingly, the perspective that this provides has been used to suggest that there is an Asian modernity that is alternative to Western modernity: Renee Worringer, Andras Hamori, and Bernard Lewis, eds., *The Islamic Middle East and Japan: Perceptions, Aspirations, and the Birth of Intra-Asian Modernity* (Princeton: Markus Wiener Publishers, 2007). I am sceptical about this argument. I believe it might lead one to conflate all Asian cultures as if they all shared the same view of modernity, in some sort of new Orientalism. Asia is a huge continent that includes many different cultures, each with its own history, an obvious point this is all too often forgotten.

This can be seen in work by Laila Parsons, a leading scholar of Arab Nationalism and the Druze community, a Muslim heterodox community which is part of an old heterodox streak that is integral to Islam.[53] Parsons is someone in the British tradition of studies about Arab countries initiated by Lady Esther Stanhope, the female equivalent of Philhellenes like Lord Byron, who supported the bloody struggle for Greek independence. These authors perhaps took their task of understanding foreign cultures to extremes, as they began dressing up or camouflaging as native ethnic groups of the countries they visited.[54] But the need to understand foreign cultures is important, and Stanhope's daring in doing so is especially interesting. Literary theorist Marilyn Booth is an example of a scholar who has devoted her entire work to this task, providing studies of Arab women that defy stereotypes, as well as translating Arab novels to make them available to Western audiences.[55] Together with

53 Laila Parsons, *The Druze between Palestine and Israel 1947–49*, St Anthony's Series (London and New York: Palgrave Macmillan, 2000). More recently Parsons has written a study of an Arab nationalist military leader described by some as the Arab Garibaldi: *The Commander: Fawzi Al-Qawuqji and the Fight for Arab Independence 1914–1948* (London: Saqi, 2017).

54 I am thinking about the expression 'going native' used to describe what these early Orientalists did. Lady Esther Stanhope left her own voluminous memoirs: Charles Lewis Meryon and Hester Stanhope, *Memoirs of the Lady Hester Stanhope: As Related by Herself in Conversations with Her Physician*, Cambridge Library Collection – Travel, Middle East and Asia Minor (Cambridge and New York: Cambridge University Press, 2012); *The Additional Memoirs of Lady Hester Stanhope: an Unpublished Historical Account for the Years 1819–1820* (Sussex Academic Press, 2017). On Lord Byron and the Philhellenes, a 1972 book has recently been reprinted: William St Clair and Roderick Beaton, *That Greece Might Still Be Free: the Philhellenes in the War of Independence* (Cambridge: Open Book Publishers, 2008).

55 Booth has specialized in studying biographies of Arab women: Marilyn Booth, " 'May Her Likes Be Multiplied': 'Famous Women', Biography and Gendered Prescription in Egypt, 1892–1935," *Signs: Journal of Women in Culture and Society* 22, no. 4 (1997); *May Her Likes Be Multiplied: Biography and Gender Politics in Egypt* (Berkeley and Los Angeles: University of California Press, 2001); *Classes of Ladies of Cloistered Spaces: Writing Feminist History through Biography in Fin-de-Siecle Egypt* (Edinburgh: Edinburgh University Press, 2015). Booth has also translated from Arabic into English several novels, for example: Rajaa Alsanea, *Girls of Riyadh*, trans. Rajaa Alsanea and Marilyn Booth (London: Penguin, 2007); Alia Mamdouh, *The Loved Ones: A Modern Arabic Novel*, trans. Marilyn Booth, Women Writing the Middle East (Cairo: The American University in Cairo Press, 2006). Riyadh is unfortunately associated in Western political discourse with Usama Bin Laden, since it was his birthplace. However, this novel shows a very different place than the one that Western audiences might think of first. The novel was very controversial, and so was Booth's translation, as Booth added her very own view of Riyadh and its now famous inhabitants, four girls negotiating their place in society between tradition and modernity. Booth has also worked on an important approach to contemporary studies of literature,

translation expert Derek Boothman, Booth and Boothman represent a British academic tradition of, and interest in, translation studies that is especially important to promote mutual understanding across cultural and linguistic divisions. Malek Abisaab and Rula Abisaab Jordi have also provided, similarly to Parsons, nuanced views of Lebanon and a remarkable study of Hezbollah as a complex organization making a sophisticated use of culture, rather than *just* a terrorist organization devoted to violence.[56] I argue, however, that there

for example the circulation of texts from a world literature perspective compatible with World Systems Theory, an approach pioneered by Columbia University scholar Franco Moretti: Marilyn Booth, *Migrating Texts: Circulating Translations around the Ottoman Mediterranean*, Edinburgh Studies on the Ottoman Empire (Edinburgh: Edinburgh University Press, 2019). Booth however does not refrain from touching upon controversial and less flattering topics: "Un/Safe/Ly at Home: Narratives of Sexual Coercion in 1920s Egypt," *Gender & History* 16, no. 3 (2004). Booth has worked also on another important topic, the theory of translation and cultural exchange: "'The Muslim Woman' as Celebrity Author and the Politics of Translating Arabic: Girls of Riyadh Go on the Road," *Journal of Middle East Women's Studies* 6, no. 3 (2010); "On Translation and Madness," *Translation Review* 65, no. 1 (2003); "Three's a Crowd: the Translator-Author-Publisher and the Engineering of Girls of Riyadh for an Anglophone Readership," in *Translating Women: Different Voices and New Horizons*, ed. Luise von Flotow and Farzaneh Farahzad (London and New York: Routledge, 2017); "Translator V. Author (2007) Girls of Riyadh Go to New York," *Translation Studies* 1, no. 2 (2008); "The World of Obituaries: Gender across Cultures and over Time," *Biography* 26, no. 3 (2003). I address the theory of translation, in conjunction with the concept of cultural intermediary, in other parts of this project. Here I just want to point out that there is a growing recognition that translation theory was important to Gramsci: Derek Boothman, *Traducibilità e Processi Traduttivi: un Caso: A. Gramsci Linguista*, S.T.A.R.: Studi sulla Traduzione (Perugia: Guerra Edizioni, 2004). I also want to draw attention to a remarkable similarity. Although Booth works at Oxford University, a bastion of tradition, and she is the Khalid bin Abdullah Al Saud Professor for the Study of the Contemporary Arab World, her work is remarkably similar to that of North American scholars like Michelle Hartman, who works however within a completely different intellectual tradition. Both cover issues of feminism and gender in the Middle East, both have undertaken many translations of contemporary novels from Arabic into English, and both have looked at social issues in the Arab world through the prism of literature. Clearly, even Oxford University, associated with the British aristocratic-military elite and empire-building, is feeling the need to focus upon these contemporary issues, while at the same time targeting stereotypes of Arabs in Western countries by presenting Arab culture through a different lens.

56 Rula Jordi Abisaab and Malek Abisaab, *The Shi'ites of Lebanon: Modernism, Communism, and Hizbullah's Islamists*, Middle East Studies Beyond Dominant Paradigms (Syracuse: Syracuse University Press, 2014). I differ from their view because, from a different perspective associated with World Systems Theory, Hezbollah seems to me to be participating in Israel's violent efforts to ensure its security, rather than providing alternatives to these efforts and bring peace to the Middle East, whereas Abisaab and Abisaab Jordi presented to me Hezbollah as a resistance force and even drew parallels with Gramsci, citing my work on Lebanese nationalist elites: Michelle Hartman and

are *structural similarities between, on the one hand, fascism and nazism and, on the other hand, contemporary political phenomena like populism and fundamentalism*, including Muslim fundamentalism, because they are all *systemic movements*, that is, movements that reinforce a skewed balance of power in the world system, rather than undermining it, and thus ultimately help imperialist elites.[57] The label 'Islamofascism' is an appropriate description, although the explanation for this is complex. In the second volume I argue that both fascism and Muslim fundamentalism are caused by a combination of heightened social conflict and interstate conflict that make use of irregular forces, and that both are tied to imperialism. Perhaps G.W. Bush, despite appearances of being clueless, had much greater understanding of the terrorists whose operations he was handling than he is thought to have had.

Answering big questions can be important in its own right, besides being important because it can provide a strategic vision. There are *existential questions* that are central to all of us as human beings, and that we all strive to some extent to find answers to. Identity questions, such as: who am I? what is my place in the world? are an example of important existential questions, since such identity questions affect how we conceive of community and how

---

Alessandro Olsaretti, "'The First Boat and the First Oar': Inventions of Lebanon in the Writings of Michel Chiha.," *Radical History Review*, no. 86 (2003). My interpretation of Gramsci, and Abisaab's and Abisaab Jordi's interpretation of Gramsci, ended up diverging greatly.

57 In other words, they are *not antisystemic*. On the concept of antisystemic movements, see: Giovanni Arrighi, Terence K. Hopkins, and Immanuel Maurice Wallerstein, *Antisystemic Movements* (London and New York: Verso, 2012). Abisaab and Abisaab Jordi have suggested to me that Hezbollah is an antisystemic movement. I want to anticipate here an argument that I elaborate upon in the second volume in order to avoid misunderstandings. Pointing to the structural similarities between, on the one hand, Muslim fundamentalism and populism and, on the other hand, fascism and nazism, does not mean that I equate Islam with fascism. Firstly, I am referring to Muslim *fundamentalism*, which is *not* Islam. Secondly, I am referring to structural similarities. For example, Italy was rocked by terrorism, which has now disappeared thanks to good policing, during the Years of Led, and I do not believe Italians are fascists or terrorists. These phases in which blind or indiscriminate violence flares up are phases in the expansion of the state system, which come and go in conjunction with social and interstate conflict. I argue in this project that fundamentalists of various stripes and terrorists could all be tied to imperialist elites. I also do not think that fundamentalism is limited to Muslim cultures or the Arab world. For example, below I address Joseph Stiglitz' view that neoliberalism is a form of 'market fundamentalism'. I also point to what is arguably a form of Christian fundamentalism, represented by Ann Coulter and more recently by Steve Bannon and the Alt-right. Here too I am referring to Christian *fundamentalism*, which is *not* Christianity.

we participate in collective action and make choices related to it.[58] The importance of existential questions was confirmed to me by many discussions with other graduate students at McGill University. Some of these discussions also illustrate another point, namely, that *the broad picture of society and history and the strategic vision have to be accompanied by ethics*. This view was shared by other graduate students at McGill University, who organized a book club in which we discussed classics of social thought and also classics of philosophy, including Aristotle's *Nicomachean Ethics*. Interestingly, Nussbaum has recently promoted Aristotle's work and shown its relevance to the philosophy of social science and to social theory. Anna-Liisa Aunio, the student who hosted the book club, introduced interesting questions from her research into environmental issues. She also introduced more ethical dilemmas like the following conundrum, presumably from her readings in history. In the book on the humanist theory of society I address the importance of the concept of ethical-political behavior for these reasons.

For the purposes of the discussion in this volume, it is enough *to illustrate the concept of ethical-political behavior* through the ethical conundrum we debated. Churchill might have known in advance, from an intelligence agent, that Nazis were going to destroy Coventry, but might have decided not to act upon this information in order not to expose the agent. Was Churchill right? Several of the students had a rosy picture of Churchill and his own intelligence agents, some of them basing it on a rosy picture of politicians that seemed to me to have been drawn with an entire palette of pastel colors, whereas other students were weary of Churchill's motives, all of which made for a very interesting discussion. Dawson was present at this and other book club meetings, where he made many interesting points, and we began an occasional exchange of views that proved useful to me and my work on the theory of society and

58 Philosopher G. A. Cohen pointed out that identity, which is part of existential questions, plays an important role in our lives and in our motivations. Cohen states this clearly in the second edition of his book on the theory of history, which contains earlier essays that take this criticism into account: Gerald Allan Cohen, *Karl Marx's Theory of History: a Defence*, Princeton Paperbacks (Princeton and Oxford: Princeton University Press, 2001); *History, Labour, and Freedom: Themes from Marx* (Oxford: Clarendon Press, 1988). In this second edition and in the earlier essays Cohen explains that he had stopped believing in Marx's theory of history because identity questions are as important as, or even more important than, economic questions, which were the focus of Marx's theory. In the second volume I propose to deal with this point by incorporating culture in studying society and history, and I draw attention to the importance of modern sociological theories of nationalism, which was arguably more successful than Marxism precisely by addressing identity questions, a point made by Gellner.

history.[59] Churchill's decision is an instance of a political decision that should be subjected to both ethical and political considerations. In order to make such decisions, politicians and the citizens who have to assess politicians' decisions have to act upon a combination of ethics and politics, and there has to be freedom of opinion, not just staged disagreements. I have benefited from similar discussions with political theorist Paul BouHabib, who studied international relations and then went on to complete a doctorate in political theory focusing on Locke's philosophy. The important point that I have learned from these discussions is a point that is common amongst philosophers, but that is rarely touched upon in social science, namely, that one cannot make political decisions based upon social science alone, because these decisions have an ethical component and, conversely, that one cannot make political decisions based upon ethics alone, because one needs an understanding of social science in order to anticipate the impacts that the decisions have on society.

2.7 Implications for Cultural Studies and International Relations

The new theories of development and democracy that I propose have important implications for studies of culture and international relations, which lead me to a very different approach to the big questions sketched out above than mainstream approaches. This is because the new theories lead me to a *thorough reconceptualization of culture and how it interacts with other domains of human behavior, including politics and the military.* We cannot understand social conflict or interstate conflict without at least some understanding of culture. This is because culture, together with organization, is a basic factor that greatly affects collective action, whether by social groups or states. This book begins to expand upon Gramsci's theory of hegemony, understood as political-military power supported by cultural power, by extending this theory from social groups to states, as suggested by Giovanni Arrighi, a theorist in World Systems Theory who cooperated with the neogramscians at York University in Toronto, Stephen Gill and Robert W. Cox.[60] Although the University of Toronto

59 For example, Dawson introduced to me Hendrick Spruyt's work, which is important for some of the arguments of this project: Hendrik Spruyt, *The Sovereign State and Its Competitors: an Analysis of Systems Change*, Princeton Studies in International History and Politics (Princeton and Oxford: Princeton University Press, 1994).

60 This suggestion was made by Arrighi in a work on international relations that is associated with the school of international relations sometimes called 'neogramscians', whose founders Cox and Gill are at York University in Toronto: Giovanni Arrighi, "The Three Hegemonies of Historical Capitalism," in *Gramsci, Historical Materialism and*

is the larger and more famous university, York University in Toronto has a large and unique graduate program in Social and Political Thought, and Canadian scholarship on Gramsci has been produced mostly at this university. This book's goal is to contribute to a theory of power that takes into consideration social conflict, interstate conflict, and their interactions, conceptualized as the interaction between meso and macro collective action introduced in the previous chapter. The general theory sketched in the second volume begins contributing to this theory of power. This theory enables me to revisit and extend Gramsci's interpretation of the Southern Question, and relate it to the Oriental Question, which in Gramsci's notes referred to the combination of social and interstate conflict in the Balkans and the Middle East.[61] Boothman, who is a Gramsci scholar, as well as translation expert, at the University of Bologna, has first drawn attention to Gramsci's interest in questions relating to Islam, which is an important point, although Boothman's approach did not include the comparative perspective that I use in this project.

The Southern Question and the Oriental Question, besides sharing similar social origins, and I argue similar origins in international relations, shared also an *impact upon cultural perceptions of conflict,* as conflict led in both cases to views of other cultures that are little better than stereotypes, which distorted culture and stoked up conflict. In modern times culture has been increasingly used, and often manipulated and distorted, in both social and interstate conflict. For example, in the long struggle for Greek independence during the nineteenth century, the perception emerged of this struggle as an *age-old* ethno-religious struggle pitting Greeks against Turks, Eastern Christianity against Islam, which is not supported by previous historical records. Similar distortions of culture led in our times to the *dangerously misleading perception that there is a clash of civilizations*, put forward most clearly by political scientist Samuel Huntington.[62] In some formulations, like the one put forward by historian Bernard Lewis, Western intervention in the Middle East led to a

International Relations, ed. Stephen Gill (Cambridge and New York: Cambridge University Press, 1993).

61 Derek Boothman, "Islam in Gramsci's Journalism and the Prison Notebooks: The Shifting Patterns of Hegemony," *Historical Materialism* 20, no. 4 (2012). See also Boothman's entry for 'islamismo' in: Guido Liguori and Pasquale Voza, eds., *Dizionario Gramsciano: 1926–1937* (Roma: Carocci, 2009).

62 Samuel P. Huntington, *The Clash of Civilizations and the Remaking of World Order* (London: Penguin, 1997). A similar approach to Huntington's can be found in Gellner's latest work on nationalism: Ernest Gellner, *Nationalism*, Master Minds Series (London: Phoenix, 1998).

violent reaction, and thus to a clash of civilizations.[63] This perception is based on an essentialization of Muslim culture that associates Islam with violence and terrorism and that is very similar to the of perception of the West as violent that is common amongst Muslim fundamentalists themselves. In general, the manipulation of culture associated with the ideology of violent social movements is closely related to the ideology of Western politicians who are all too ready to resort to war, thus playing into the hand of violent social movements and their equally violent leaders. The argument regarding embedded autonomy introduced in chapter 1 emphasizes that we have to guarantee that culture remains autonomous from politics and is not distorted by it.

This book also begins to propose *a way to reconceptualize culture that avoids essentializing culture*, and that is squarely against a disembodied view of culture that sees culture exclusively as expressed values. Culture is instead part of social interaction and is affected by organization and by social structures. This serves to *reconceptualize the laden concept of civilization*, by suggesting that civilization itself is affected by organization and by social structures, and also that there are different types of civilizations than just civilizations defined by ethno-religious cultures, and in which structures play an even more important role, as in historian Fernand Braudel's argument that there existed in early modern times a Mediterranean civilization despite ethno-religious divisions.[64] This has important implications for the way we perceive of the interaction between culture and international relations. Civilizations do not clash, states do. When states or other organizations specialized in violence encourage diffuse violence or blind violence, this can help create the perception that there is a clash of civilizations, especially if some intellectuals are willing to contribute to this perception.

What makes this diffuse or blind violence possible are not so much essential features of a civilization, or of a culture, but social conditions that include the

---

63 Bernard Lewis, *What Went Wrong?: Western Impact and Middle Eastern Response* (Oxford and New York: Oxford University Press, 2002). Lewis was one of the observers who realized the danger posed by Bin Laden already well before the 9/11 attacks: "License to Kill-Usama Bin Ladin's Declaration of Jihad," *Foreign Affairs* 77 (1998). Lewis' use of the expression 'license to kill' seems to me an inappropriately light-hearted parallel between actual terrorists and entertainment characters, as the expression is used in James Bond films. Or did Lewis, who apparently was in British military intelligence, actually mean to identify terrorists who happen to be Muslims with British military intelligence? There is a cultural link between the two, because the terrorists create the pretext used by some Western politicians to invade countries, which gives the terrorists a 'license to kill'.

64 This is the perspective proposed by Braudel in: Braudel, *The Mediterranean, Vol. 1*; *The Mediterranean, Vol. 2*.

existence of specific types of society, and transitional organizational problems in moving from one type of society to another. Building upon an argument put forward by anthropologist Ernest Gellner, I suggest that these problems arise in the transition from agrarian-artisanal society to capitalist society, and that in capitalist society collective action by the masses is enabled on a larger scale, and it can be manipulated to encourage diffuse violence or blind violence, by volunteers and irregular forces, for example.[65] The second volume and the book on the humanist theory of society are largely devoted to this reconceptualization of culture, without essentializing these types of society either. The challenge that I take up in these other books is to make models of these types of society that can be extended and adapted to different cases, and that can become as complex as local conditions require, avoiding reductionism. The book on the humanist theory of society proposes models tailored to Italy and to countries in the Middle East that depict important aspects of the Southern Question and the Oriental Question. In this book I simply begin to apply the theories of development and democracy that I propose to these two important questions.

Understanding the social origins of these questions is relevant beyond Italy, the Balkans, and the Middle East. It is especially relevant to *understand the problem posed by neoliberalism and the populist backlash,* and the threat they pose to development and democracy. Together, the combination of imperialism with uneven development, manipulation of culture, and instability due to transition organizational problems and in particular due to the presence of large numbers of volunteers and irregular forces, can undermine development and democracy even in countries where development and democracy are advanced. Neoliberalism and the populist backlash can exploit the uneven development across countries to introduce or reinforce uneven development within a country, as neoliberalism and industry relocation did in many countries in the West, including the United States. They can exploit instability in foreign countries to create threats or perceived threats that justify drastic measures, which polarize public opinion and undermine freedoms and ultimately democracy, as populism did and arguably is still doing. *The problem posed by*

65 In this project I address both of Gellner's books on nationalism, which argued that nationalism was associated with industrial society. One is the book that laid out Gellner's theory of nationalism: Ernest Gellner, *Nations and Nationalism*, Cornell Paperbacks (Ithaca, New York: Cornell University Press, 1983). The other is the later book, published in 1998, which is closer to Lewis' perspective: *Nationalism*. In this project I modify Gellner's argument to suggest that nationalism is associated, not with industrial society, but with capitalist society and capitalism, which led equally to capitalist agriculture, a concept introduced by Wallerstein in historical sociology, and to capitalist industry, or capitalism in manufacturing. In many countries capitalist agriculture preceded capitalist industry.

neoliberalism and the populist backlash is a serious problem for the long-term prospects of development that could spell the end of the American Dream, which is increasingly out of reach for large parts of the population that do not benefit from the model of development proposed by neoliberalism. Worse still, if an imperialist world-elite should arise that is active on a truly global scale, and that can exploit this problem to its advantage, it could put an end to development and democracy in the United States and throughout the West. For all these reasons, we must address the problem posed by neoliberalism and the populist backlash before it gets out of hand. Identifying the sources of the problem is the necessary first step, formulating valid alternatives is the next step. I believe that both are within reach.

PART 2

Continuing Gramsci's Project through a Humanist Social Science

Some Problems for the Study of the Evolution of the Philosophy of Praxis [to Address]

In G. De Ruggiero's book, *Renaissance and Reformation*, one can see the attitude of many [high] intellectuals, starting with Erasmus: to fold when faced with persecution and burning at the stake. The bearer of the Protestant Reformation was the German people as a whole, not the intellectuals. Precisely this desertion of intellectuals when faced with the enemy explains the [initial] "barrenness" of the Reformation in producing a high culture, until from the masses of the population a new group of intellectuals was selected [in a process that] culminated with [German] classical philosophy. *Something similar has happened until now with the philosophy of praxis; the high intellectuals who arose on its terrain, besides being few in numbers, were not tied to the people, they did not arise from the people, but were the expression of traditional intermediate classes, to which they returned at the time of great historical "turning points"*; others remained, but to subject the new worldview to a systematic revision, not to promote its independent evolution.

Antonio Gramsci, *Prison Notebooks*, Notebook 16, Note 9, p. 1862. My emphasis.

∵

CHAPTER 3

Gramsci's Project and a Significantly New Theory of Democracy

This project is largely a continuation of Gramsci's project. In this chapter, I focus on explaining a number of concepts that are central both to Gramsci's project and to this project. All these concepts pertain to the definition of democracy and to the definition of science. At the same time, I also differentiate Gramsci's project and this project from other projects. I emphasize that Gramsci's project included a humanist social science, which makes Gramsci's project very different than recent projects by contemporary Italian authors. I also emphasize the differences between Gramsci's project and the projects of contemporary Marxist authors whose projects resemble Gramsci's project, particularly those who can be described as orthodox Marxists. I differentiate Gramsci's project firstly from the orthodox Marxism associated with Structural Marxism and the misconception that the economy is all there is to development. I propose instead that politics and collective action are central human activities that have to take their place alongside the economy in a theory of history. I then differentiate Gramsci's project from Analytical Marxism, which is arguably still an orthodox Marxism, by emphasizing both the different assumptions regarding human beings that inform these two projects, and the fact that humanism rejects the use of evolutionary mechanisms to explain modern history, emphasizing instead that we are capable of deliberate and sustained collective action, an especially important type of goal-oriented human activity, which enables us to escape the grip of evolutionary mechanisms. Lastly, I also emphasize my differences from the scholars at McGill University who taught me, all of which ultimately stem from the view that Gramsci's project for a humanist social science included a theory of democracy, understood not just as a theory of democratic institutions, but also as a theory of the social origins of democracy, which are based on the ability to engage in collective action and change the distribution of power in society in favor of the masses.

3.1 Gramsci and His Legacy and Approach to Philosophy

Because of the length of my intellectual journey, and because both Gramsci and contemporary humanism are little known, or are presented in an

 | DOI:10.1163/9789004470521_007

oversimplified way in social science today, I want to take all the space that is necessary at the beginning of this project in order to *explain my reading of Gramsci and why I believe Gramsci's project for a humanist social science is still important today*. My reading of Gramsci is that he was first and foremost an anti-fascist political theorist committed to improving the conditions of the masses. I believe that this, anti-fascist political theorist, is the most accurate characterization of Gramsci, not so much as a Marxist theoretician, not even as a Western Marxist, a label often attached to Gramsci in English-speaking countries.[1] It is necessary therefore to explain how I see Gramsci, what I think is Gramsci's most important legacy, and why it is important to take up this legacy. In this chapter and the next I specifically address my interpretation of Gramsci's project, focusing on the parts of this project that I seek to continue through a significantly new theory of democracy. My reading of Gramsci's project is that it was a project aimed at formulating a humanist social science based upon a humanist philosophy best described as a philosophy of praxis.[2] In this chapter and the next I address *Gramsci's multidisciplinary approach to social science*, which includes a specific view of philosophy that served as the foundation for his humanist social science. Before delving into these points, I want to distance myself from politicized debates regarding Gramsci, which I believe are drawing attention away from a very interesting approach to science and knowledge more in general.

Gramsci has been portrayed by some authors as a controversial figure, because of his ties to the Italian Communist Party, and because of alleged ties to spy rings in Great Britain and the Soviet Union. Both portrayals led to *highly*

1 The concept of Western Marxism as a tradition markedly different than soviet Marxism, and Gramsci's location within it, was proposed by: Perry Anderson, *Considerations on Western Marxism* (London: New Left Books, 1976). Interestingly, this was around the same time when the Italian Communist Party broke from the Soviet Union and actively tried to promote a Eurocommunism strategy. The concept of Western Marxism has been recently re-proposed by: Joseph V. Femia, "Western Marxism," in *Twentieth-Century Marxism: a Global Introduction*, ed. Daryl Glaser and David M. Walker (London and New York: Routledge, 2007). Recently, Cospito has provided a detailed reading of Gramsci's analysis and critique of Marxism and has suggested that Gramsci was moving away from Marxism and trying to start an altogether new philosophy: Giuseppe Cospito, *Il Ritmo del Pensiero: per una Lettura Diacronica dei 'Quaderni del Carcere' di Gramsci* (Napoli: Bibliopolis, 2011).

2 I set out this argument in: Alessandro Olsaretti, "From the Return to Labriola to the Anti-Croce: Philosophy, Praxis and Human Nature in Gramsci's *Prison Notebooks*," *Historical Materialism* 24, no. 4 (2016); "Croce, Philosophy and Intellectuals: Three Aspects of Gramsci's Theory of Hegemony," *Critical Sociology* 42, no. 3 (2016). This argument, and my reading of Gramsci's project as being focused on philosophy, as well as social science, was influenced by Fabio Frosini, whose work I address below.

politicized debates. The first debate involves chiefly the responsibilities of Italian Communist Party leaders for Gramsci's arrest and death. Gramsci was one of the founders of the Italian Communist Party and had left for the Soviet Union after Mussolini's seizure of power. He returned to Italy to participate in parliamentary politics and build up an opposition to the Fascist regime, but was arrested shortly after being elected to parliament, despite his parliamentary immunity. Events in the trial that followed, and subsequent attempts to get him out of jail, all of which failed, suggest that he might have been set up by other Italian Communist Party leaders, because of his opposition to the totalitarian turn in Russia, and possibly because of his opposition to these other leaders.[3] Recently, another highly politicized debate has started in Italy, after the suggestion was made that Gramsci was caught in spy rings active between Great Britain, Italy and the Soviet Union. There has been talk of a missing notebook that he wrote in prison that contained important information, and that Piero Sraffa, an Italian economist at Cambridge University who corresponded with Gramsci while he was in jail, constituted a bridge from Italy, through Great Britain, to the Soviet Union and Italian political exiles there. There has also been talk that Gramsci's conditions in jail were not as severe as once taught.[4]

I am not interested in either one of these politicized debates for two reasons. The first is that I do not have access to archives and these are hypotheses that only archives can give answers to. The second reason is that I am a sociologist whose expertise includes social and political theory, and the contribution that I can give to democracy today is through my own reading of Gramsci's work, and by proposing a theory that contributes to democracy, rather than to erudite debates over missing notebooks, or thrilling stories of intrigue in the Italian Communist Party. I believe that *today what matters the most is Gramsci's work*, not his persona, and that this work is very interesting in its own right. In the United States established theorists, both on the right and the left of the

3 There have been several interventions in this debate, for example: Marco Palla, "Il Gramsci Abbandonato," *Belfagor* 41, no. 5 (1986); Aldo Natoli, "Gramsci in Carcere, il Partito, il Comintern," ibid. 43, no. 2 (1988); Claudio Natoli, "Gramsci in Carcere: le Campagne per la Liberazione, il Partito, l'Internazionale (1932–1933)," *Studi storici* 36, no. 2 (1995). More recent interventions in this debate include: Silvio Pons, "L''Affare Gramsci-Togliatti' a Mosca (1938–1941)," ibid. 45, no. 1 (2004).

4 Luciano Canfora, *Spie, Urss, Antifascismo: Gramsci, 1926–1937* (Roma: Salerno, 2012). Franco Lo Piparo, *I Due Carceri di Gramsci: la Prigione Fascista e il Labirinto Comunista*, Saggine (Roma: Donzelli, 2012). Earlier books that are relevant to this debate, as well as to the other debate, are: Angelo Rossi, *Gramsci da Eretico a Icona: Storia di 'un Cazzotto nell'Occhio,'* Prima Pagina (Napoli: Guida, 2010); Angelo Rossi and Giuseppe Vacca, *Gramsci Tra Mussolini e Stalin*, Le Terre (Roma: Fazi, 2007).

political spectrum, have emphasized that Gramsci's work is relevant beyond right and left divisions, and that in the United States the right has made more use of Gramsci's work than the left.[5] In Italy Gramsci is considered by most authorities today to be a canonical author, and his complete works are being prepared as part of an initiative by the Institute of the Italian Encyclopedia of the Treccani publishing house, an established and highly regarded publisher. This initiative is sponsored by the President of the Republic and supported by the Ministry of Culture.[6] Gramsci wrote many notes for his project while he was in jail, using books purchased thanks to Sraffa, and on a few occasions suggested to him by Sraffa. These notes have been collected into the *Prison Notebooks*, an unabridged collection of the notebooks that Gramsci wrote while in prison, which contain *numerous very important insights*, some of which are very specific to the Italy of Gramsci's time, while others are more broad-ranging. I focus in this book on some of the insights that were specific to Italy, but especially on the more broad-ranging insights, and I propose a new theory that builds upon Gramsci's work, using my expertise in social and political theory and in contemporary sociology.

I have no political affiliation.[7] However, I share Gramsci's *ideal that it is important to advance progressive causes and to improve the conditions of the*

---

5 Maurice A. Finocchiaro, *Beyond Right and Left: Democratic Elitism in Mosca and Gramsci* (New Haven and London: Yale University Press, 1999); Joseph Anthony Buttigieg, "Reading Gramsci Now," in *Perspectives on Gramsci: Politics, Culture and Social Theory*, ed. Joseph Francese (London and New York: Routledge, 2009); "Gramsci on Civil Society," *boundary 2* 22, no. 3 (March 1, 2005 1995). "The Contemporary Discourse on Civil Society: A Gramscian Critique." However, I completely disagree with Finocchiaro in equating as democratic elitists Gramsci and Gaetano Mosca, whose theory arguably presaged both fascism and the rise of establishments. I believe that Gramsci was committed to democracy more than Finocchiaro suggests. I address these points in chapter 6.

6 See the webpage: Fondazione Gramsci, "Edizione Nazionale Scritti Antonio Gramsci."

7 I have devoted most of my life to intellectual work of one type or another, even while working on and off as an analyst. I volunteered on a couple of occasions for the New Democratic Party of Canada, and attended a couple of NDP meetings, signing up for NDP leaflets and briefly joining the NDP. I did not pursue this or any other political participation for several reasons, related to my opposition to establishments, which are arguably very old in many countries in the West. When I was young, I attended a few mass meetings of the Italian Communist Party, and did research at the Fondazione Gramsci, which used to have ties to the party, but is now independent of any political or other official affiliations. My position when I was younger is perhaps best described by an expression common at that time in Italy, 'compagni di strada' or 'fellow travellers'. In my case, this involved sharing the ultimate goal of achieving a better life for all working people, and the conviction that intellectuals and cultural work are indispensable to this goal. Being a fellow traveller also meant that I led the life of a peripatetic intellectual, always on the road from one country to another, and from one university or company to another.

masses, including the working class, and also the middle class and petite bourgeoisie, whose conditions seemed to be improving since Gramsci's time, but have now deteriorated in many Western countries in a manner that seems to have set us back decades or even longer. I also share Gramsci's ideal that modern social movements and political parties, and ultimately *all citizens, should have a theory of their choice that helps guide decisions* and that they should understand and contribute to this theory. Gramsci used soviet theorist Nikolai Bukharin's introduction to materialist theories of history, which Gramsci referred to as the *Popular Handbook of Sociology*, in the courses that he taught to party officials, and was committed to the idea that every activist should understand the theory, as well as the means and the ends, to be used in politics. In this project I seek, amongst other things, to provide a synthesis of contemporary sociology, which is little known and under-appreciated amongst activists and politicians, development professionals, and even amongst graduate students in other social sciences, like political science.

However, this project, and Gramsci's project that I build upon, deviate from Bukharin and soviet Marxism by putting great emphasis on a democratic approach to philosophy, and to knowledge more in general, that I believe is especially important. Gramsci sought to *contribute to a philosophy of praxis*, or practical activity, which included Renaissance humanism, and pragmatism, as well as Marxism in its earlier formulation before *Capital*.[8] This led Gramsci, as he grew weary of Bukharin's shortcomings, to attempt to write first and foremost a critique of prevailing philosophies in the Italy of his time, together with an introduction to philosophy that was also a critique of Bukharin's work.[9]

8 I address Gramsci's project for a philosophy of praxis and its relation to the young Marx who wrote the *Theses on Feuerbach* in: Olsaretti, "From the Return to Labriola to the Anti-Croce." Gramsci's project and its ties to both Marx and Renaissance humanism are addressed by Frosini in a number of articles: Fabio Frosini, "Il 'Ritorno a Marx' nei *Quaderni del Carcere* (1930)," in *Marx e Gramsci: Memoria e Attualità*, ed. Giuseppe Prestipino and Marina Paladini Musitelli (Roma: Manifestolibri, 2001); "Riforma e Rinascimento," in *Le Parole di Gramsci: Per un Lessico Dei Quaderni del Carcere* ed. Fabio Frosini and Guido Liguori (Roma: Carocci, 2004); "Filosofia della Praxis," in *Le Parole di Gramsci: per un Lessico Dei Quaderni del Carcere*, ed. Fabio Frosini and Guido Liguori (Roma: Carocci, 2004); "Il Neoidealismo Italiano e L'elaborazione della Filosofia della Praxis," in *Gramsci nel Suo Tempo*, ed. Francesco Giasi (Roma: Carocci, 2008). Gramsci's ties to pragmatism are addressed by: Nadia Urbinati, "L'individuo Democratico Tra Tocqueville, Gramsci e Dewey," in *Gramsci e il Novecento*, ed. Giuseppe Vacca (Roma: Carocci, 1999).

9 These two critiques are the critique of Croce's philosophy and related idealist concepts in Notebook 10, and the critique of Bukharin's sociology and related materialist concepts in Notebook 11. On the importance of these two notebooks, which are entirely organized around these two topics, see: Gianni Francioni, "Gramsci Tra Croce e Bukharin: sulla Struttura Dei *Quaderni* 10 e 11," *Critica Marxista* 25, no. 6 (1987).

This reflects Gramsci's *democratic approach to philosophy*, because these critiques and the introduction to philosophy would contribute to explaining the assumptions and the thinking behind the theory proposed by Gramsci, and would provide activists with the means to assess independently all theories they were exposed to, whether Gramsci's, Bukharin's, or others'. Only by understanding the theory can policymakers and citizens, including activists and development professionals, make informed decisions about whether to accept the answers and alternatives that the theory proposes.

An important but often overlooked aspect of Gramsci's work that shows his *democratic approach to knowledge* is that he looked up to the Protestant Reformation as an ideal of a popular cultural movement because of its wide appeal and its democratic approach to scriptures. Gramsci compared the Reformation to the Enlightenment. He saw the French Enlightenment as a movement making modern science widely available, and thus contributing to political participation by the masses, who would have access to the same intellectual tools and understanding that the elites had access to.[10] This attitude towards intellectual tools and understanding, present both in the Reformation and the Enlightenment, is an important precondition for democracy. The Reformation fought to make even a sacred text like the Bible accessible to all members of the community, who were encouraged to read it, discuss it, and interpret it. By contrast, much of social science today produces specialized research that is *not* a sacred text and yet is obscure and inaccessible except to the initiated few, even when it addresses questions of pressing public concern, like growing inequalities within society. This is a remarkable fact calling for an explanation. The goal of social science is *not* to produce sacred texts, but texts that directly address human affairs only, yet much of the social science produced today is as obscure as the Latin Bible. Culturally, and possibly in other ways too, this is a step back to the Middle Ages, before the Enlightenment, before the Reformation.

---

10 The comparison that Gramsci drew between the Reformation and the Renaissance has been reviewed in: Frosini, "Riforma e Rinascimento." There is less work on Gramsci's views on the Enlightenment. Interestingly, some of the same themes regarding the Reformation and the Enlightenment and their relation to socialism have been addressed by sociologist Robert Wuthnow in: Robert Wuthnow, *Communities of Discourse: Ideology and Social Structure in the Reformation, the Enlightenment, and European Socialism* (Cambridge, Massachusetts and London: Harvard University Press, 1989). This book has been reprinted in 1993 and in 2009.

3.2 Gramsci's Project and His Theory of Democracy

Gramsci arguably also sought *to contribute to democracy*, not just a democratic approach to knowledge. There are important parts of his work that address key questions for democracy and that this project builds upon. These are Gramsci's theory of hegemony, and his concept of a humanist social science. *Gramsci's theory of hegemony* contributed to the significantly new theory of democracy that this project proposes. The reintroduction of the concept of hegemony is Gramsci's most famous contribution to contemporary political theory. Gramsci is arguably the thinker who started the modern study of hegemony, a concept first formulated in ancient Greece, where it was associated with the cultural, political and military influence of Athenian democracy over other Greek cities.[11] Historian Peter Ghosh, an expert on Weber, and on British Prime Minister Benjamin Disraeli, a politician who was close to the British aristocratic-military elite, has also provided his own interpretation of Gramsci.[12] Ghosh has suggested that Gramsci's concept of hegemony was simply a shorthand for a political strategy, advising activists to build up cultural power first. This is a misrepresentation of Gramsci's theory, due at least in part to the fact that Ghosh does not read Italian and did not have access to the whole of Gramsci's work. I subscribe instead to the view that Gramsci's concept of hegemony was part of a whole theory of power that Gramsci was working on.[13] Gramsci's

11 The ties between Gramsci and ancient Greek and Roman thought have been highlighted and investigated by Benedetto Fontana in: Benedetto Fontana, "Logos and Kratos: Gramsci and the Ancients on Hegemony," *Journal of the History of Ideas* 61, no. 2 (2000); "Gramsci on Politics and State," *Journal of Classical Sociology* 2, no. 2 (2002). In modern usage, the concept of hegemony is associated with Lenin, but Lenin just introduced the word in modern political discourse, and used it for political purposes.

12 Ghosh wrote on Weber taking a history of ideas approach: Peter Ghosh, *Max Weber and the Protestant Ethic: Twin Histories*, paperback ed. (Oxford and New York: Oxford University Press, 2017). This book is very similar in approach to Frosini's work on Gramsci, as it combines philological work with the history of ideas. I began reading Weber's work while a student in Ghosh's tutorials, and I ended up diverging from Ghosh's approach for the same reasons why I diverged from Frosini's, and ultimately Croce's, approach.

13 Ghosh has suggested that Gramsci used the concept of hegemony in the same manner as Lenin, simply as a shorthand for a political tactics: "Gramscian Hegemony: an Absolutely Historicist Approach," *History of European Ideas* 27 (2001). Ghosh supervised my undergraduate dissertation in the early 1990s at Oxford University, on Gramsci and Machiavelli, and we had many instructive disagreements. I believe that Gramsci instead sought to formulate a whole theory of power and included hegemony as an important type of power. This point is made by several Italian authors who work on Gramsci. This view was proposed already in the 1980s by: Leonardo Paggi, *Le Strategie del Potere in Gramsci* (Roma: Editori Riuniti, 1984). More recently, the same view was proposed by a number of different authors whose work was brought together by Angelo D'Orsi in the edited volume: Angelo

theory of hegemony studied power by focusing on both its political-military and its cultural components, an approach that is very important to understand power in modern societies.

In my interpretation, Gramsci's theory of hegemony is distinguished by *two complementary claims,* both of which relate to the importance of politics and in particular of collective action. The first is that hegemonic power is defined by various *combinations of political-military power with cultural power*. It therefore entails the ability to formulate and disseminate concepts and entire theories that support political and military decisions. The second claim is that *cultural power always has two components, namely, a cultural component and an organizational component.* Drawing attention to the organizational component is especially important. In this project I argue that this enables us to formulate a new way to conceptualize culture that does not see culture as if it were disembodied, but as something that is always part of actual social groups and social structures. The organizational component can be either *social organization,* which includes the number and relative position of social groups in a society, or *organization proper*, for example a university or a media company, which are affected by organizational questions such as the number of personnel, their hierarchy, and the rules that they are subject to within this organization. Both claims are very important to understand collective action.

What is less known about Gramsci's work, including his theory of hegemony, is that it was motivated by a *guiding concern with democracy* that sets Gramsci's work apart from that of most or even all Marxist or Marxian thinkers. Some Gramsci scholars have pointed to the importance that Gramsci attached to participation in free and fair parliamentary elections, which guaranteed to the working class the ability to get a voice in the process whereby policies were formulated and adopted. This was a view that Gramsci shared with Sraffa, despite other disagreements between them.[14] Moreover, Gramsci went further, and began to lay the groundwork for a significantly new theory of democracy. I derive from my reading of Gramsci the view that democracy involves the ability to engage in collective action, and the criticism that without a distribution

D'Orsi, *Egemonie* (Napoli: Libreria Dante & Descartes, 2008). Fontana has recently made a similar point in English-language articles: Benedetto Fontana, "State and Society: the Concept of Hegemony in Gramsci," in *Hegemony and Power: Consensus and Coercion in Contemporary Politics*, ed. Mark Haugaard and Howard H. Lentner (Lanham: Lexington Books, 2006); "Hegemony and Power in Gramsci," in *Hegemony: Studies in Consensus and Coercion*, ed. Richard Howson and Kylie Smith (London and New York: Routledge, 2008).

14 Jean-Pierre Potier, *Piero Sraffa: Unorthodox Economist (1898–1983)* (London and New York: Routledge, 1991).

of power favourable to the masses, democratic institutions remain an empty letter devoid of effect. Other thinkers were formulating similar views, but Gramsci is one of the few who saw this criticism to be complementary to democratic institutions, and sought to build a better democracy, instead of rejecting democratic institutions because of an unfavourable distribution of power. All of this leads me to radically different views of democracy than those of McGill University scholars, including a non-eurocentric view that has nothing to do with the view that associates democracy with Europe, and praises it or rejects it according to the perception of the role of Europe in modern history. My differences from these scholars are addressed in the last two sections of this chapter.

Gramsci's *multidisciplinary approach to social science* also greatly contributed to the significantly new theory of democracy that this project proposes. The foundations for this theory are provided by a social science that includes all the main sources of power: political-military and cultural power, besides economic power. The significantly new theory of democracy thus takes into consideration all the different types of democracy. It suggests *there are political-military democracy, and also cultural, and economic democracy.* I focus in this chapter upon political-military democracy, understood as the distribution of power in politics and the military, which is closely related to the traditional concept of democracy. In the next chapter I focus upon cultural democracy, understood as the distribution of power within culture. The latter is a very important aspect of democracy, and I want to qualify here my argument regarding cultural democracy, and the second point regarding hegemony that I introduced above, namely, that culture is affected by organization. In the aftermath of twentieth century totalitarian regimes, the *association of culture with organization should raise concerns*, which should not however lead us to reject it wholesale. It is indispensable to consider organization when dealing with culture. As argued in chapter 2, if the social conditions for objectivity in social science are missing, it is extremely difficult to formulate any scientific theories, and these social conditions are related to the organization of universities. Moreover, *even the best concepts and theories will not go very far unless they are supported by an organization.* With the emergence of a few massive media conglomerates, reaching policymakers and the public can be as daunting a task, or even more daunting a task, as gaining an audience within universities. In brief, it is necessary for culture to be supported by organization, both social organization and organization proper. Therefore, I argue throughout this project that the main problem we face today is not how to make culture separate from organization, but *how to make the organization of culture accountable and how to ensure that it works for democracy.* Put another way, we need to encourage cultural democracy.

3.3 Gramsci's Project and Related Projects in Italy

Gramsci based his project upon a precedent set by Benedetto Croce, an idealist philosopher who had a huge influence upon Italian culture, including upon the young Gramsci. Gramsci grew up intellectually under Croce's shadow, a tough burden to bear because of Croce's stature, both as an intellectual and as a cultural entrepreneur. Historian Edmund Jacobitti, in his *Revolutionary Humanism and Historicism in Modern Italy*, and in a number of articles, has drawn attention to the fact that Italian historicism was born out of the close collaboration between Croce and Giovanni Gentile, another philosopher who later became the highest intellectual exponent of fascism.[15] Jacobitti also drew attention to the fact that *Croce and Gentile's collaboration could be characterized as a sophisticated cultural enterprise*, resembling in some ways the cultural activities of the Catholic Church, albeit on a much smaller scale.[16] It also presaged some aspects of intellectual production, including organizational questions, all of which are central to universities today, with the notable addition that Croce benefited from the fact that he was independently wealthy and could have considerable freedom in his research. Croce's intellectual leadership was exercised not just through the many influential books that he published, but also through a prestigious journal that he edited, *La Critica*, and an important publisher that he worked with and whose book series he edited, Laterza. In later life Croce also founded and directed the influential Istituto Italiano per gli Studi Storici, *or* IISS, the Italian Institute for Historical Studies, which remains today an influential higher learning institution in Italy and especially southern Italy.[17]

15 Edmund E. Jacobitti, *Revolutionary Humanism and Historicism in Modern Italy* (New Haven and London: Yale University Press, 1981). I address Gentile's work and his collaboration with Croce in the book on the humanist social science.

16 "Hegemony before Gramsci: The Case of Benedetto Croce," *Journal of Modern History* 52 (March 1980 1980); "The Religious Vision of Antonio Gramsci or the Italian Origins of Hegemony as Found in Croce, Cuoco, Machiavelli, and the Church," *Italian Quarterly*, no. 97–98 (1984).

17 I gained an appreciation of the importance of organizational questions in universities also through Marialetizia Pizzuti and her husband Dario. In particular, I realized the importance of including a perspective on organizational questions based on the viewpoint of administrators and professors, a view from above, as it were, and combine it with my view from below, based largely upon my experience as a student.

Croce's philosophy was problematic for several reasons. I address in the book on humanist social science a crucial problem of Croce's philosophy highlighted by Gramsci, namely, that it was divisive and arguably contributed to the rise of fascism. Here I want to draw attention to another criticism raised by Gramsci, who pointed to Croce's failure to formulate a humanist social science. As far as humanism is concerned, Croce's philosophy gave important contributions to it, but it remained essentially an idealist philosophy that emphasized cultural work and the formulation of ideas as the main human activity, acknowledging economics, but largely neglecting politics and the military. As far as social science in Italy is concerned, Croce made progress towards formulating a philosophy of social science, but never formulated a social science itself, focusing on historical studies instead. This might have had an enduring negative impact upon sociology in Italy, where the only notable department of sociology today is at the university of Trento, in northern Italy, and the only sociologist there who can be said to approach Croce's stature is Gianfranco Poggi, at least in my fields of expertise.[18] Remarkably, *the Gramsci Foundation in Rome has made no progress on these fronts either*, despite being devoted to preserving and advancing Gramsci's work. After the Second World War, it was under the shadow of Palmiro Togliatti, a former contributor to the *Ordine Nuovo*, and leader of the Italian Communist Party, who took over Gramsci's project and published Gramsci's *Prison Notebooks* in a much abridged form, completely re-organizing them and changing the order of many notes, an operation the main goal of which was to claim Gramsci as an orthodox Marxist, and thus to associate him with a paradigm that few support, and thus also diminishing the originality of Gramsci's work.[19] In the two decades that followed, many debates over Gramsci's work in Italy were heavily politicized and simply sought to claim Gramsci for one orthodoxy or another.[20] They therefore effectively hijacked and crashed Gramsci's project.

---

18 Examples of Poggi's work that have been translated into English include: Gianfranco Poggi, *The State: Its Nature, Development and Prospects* (Cambridge, UK and Malden, Massachusetts: Polity Press, 1990). This book was reprinted in 2004 and 2007. Poggi has also contributed to contemporary theories of power: *Forms of Power* (Cambridge, UK and Malden, Massachusetts: Polity Press, 2001).

19 Despite his ties to Russia and soviet communism, Togliatti closely cooperated with other Italian political leaders like Alcide De Gasperi to make democracy possible in Italy. However, Togliatti seems to have been as controlling, in the cultural initiatives of the Italian Communist Party, including the publication of Gramsci's work, as Buttigieg was perfectionist in the translation of Gramsci's work. Andrea Valassi drew my attention to De Gasperi's role in re-establishing democracy in Italy.

20 These Italian debates have been reviewed in: Guido Liguori, *Gramsci Conteso: Storia di un Dibattito, 1922–1996* (Roma: Editori riuniti, 1996). There have also been debates in the

In the 1990s, philosopher *Fabio Frosini, at the University of Urbino, started a rediscovery of Gramsci's work in Italy* that freed it from these politicized interpretations. Frosini works within Croce's historicist tradition of philosophy, which is still very influential in Italy, and studies philosophy together with the history of philosophy, an approach that I take in this project, where I study philosophy and social science together with the history of these disciplines. Frosini has worked with other Gramsci scholars like Giuseppe Cospito at the University of Pavia and more recently with Michele Filippini at the University of Bologna. An important achievement of Frosini's and Cospito's work has been to initiate a philological approach to Gramsci's work that is based on techniques borrowed from linguistics. This consists in a detailed study of Gramsci's language in the *Prison Notebooks*, to establish what exactly Gramsci meant by each word that he used, and how he organized his notes using headers and thematic notebooks.[21] My doctoral dissertation on Gramsci's humanism and his philosophy of social science was in part a philological study that built upon Frosini's and Cospito's pioneering example, and in part a preliminary assessment of the continued relevance of Gramsci's thought by relating it to contemporary scholarship. Another important achievement of Frosini's and Cospito's philological approach has been to recover Gramsci's true concerns, philosophy and politics, and the originality of his work. This is a first step linking Gramsci to such precursors of humanism as Aristotle, whose philosophy emphasized that human beings are a *Zoon Politikon*, or political being.

My *difference from Croce's historicist approach to philosophy and the philological approach to Gramsci's work* is that I start with these approaches, but then move on to another approach, aiming for different goals than theirs. In this respect, my approach is similar to Roncaglia's, who works on the history of economics in order to suggest new directions of research for economics.[22] The main progress of the philological approach beyond linguistics was only in the

English-speaking world, reviewed by Alastair Davidson in a 1972 essay, which was recently republished, together with many other articles discussing or exemplifying Gramsci's reception in the English-speaking world, in: James Martin, *Antonio Gramsci: Contemporary Applications* (London and New York: Routledge, 2002).

21 Fabio Frosini, *Gramsci e la Filosofia: Saggio sui Quaderni del Carcere* (Roma: Carocci, 2003); Cospito, *Il Ritmo del Pensiero*.

22 Roncaglia's approach is remarkably similar to mine and incorporates many of the same concerns that I began exploring in my doctoral dissertation: Alessandro Roncaglia, *The Wealth of Ideas: a History of Economic Thought*, trans. R. N. Lebow (Cambridge and New York: Cambridge University Press, 2005); *The Age of Fragmentation*. This is no doubt because in Italy there survives a historicist approach to economics, part of a history of ideas approach to all social sciences that was influenced by Croce, a point that I address elsewhere. La Sapienza University in Rome, where Roncaglia teaches, is also an Italian university with a truly international reputation and presence, drawing upon influences

history of ideas, which is concerned with studying the evolution of concepts in an author's life, not just one work, and relating these concepts to similar concepts by other authors, in order to establish, amongst other things, the originality of an author's ideas. Because of this focus, *the philological approach never produced a social science*, let alone a humanist social science. Despite its fundamental achievements, the philological approach never moved beyond the intellectual boundaries set by Croce to social science in Italy, whereas Gramsci aimed precisely to move beyond these boundaries. This is true even of studies like Filippini's book comparing Gramsci to founding figures of sociology, or like the recent international conference organized by Frosini on Gramsci's concept of hegemony, and how it has been reworked by contemporary theorists.[23] These studies are effectively a type of comparative history of ideas. They identify key concepts in an author's work and compare and contrast them with similar concepts produced by other authors. I believe that this kind of study is part of the necessary theoretical groundwork for formulating theory. But after this groundwork, one has to formulate the theory, something that the philological approach never did. Moreover, Filippini's recent book *Using Gramsci*, while pointing to the relevance of Gramsci's work today, frames the goal of reviving Gramsci's project in terms that I find are negative. As some Gramsci scholars have pointed out, Gramsci's work has long been used and abused by authors of various ideological persuasions.[24] It was never brought back on the research agenda of a school or a group of researchers committed to recovering the letter and the spirit of Gramsci's work, and also to continue his project.

---

from many parts of the world, and pioneering new approaches to the management and organization of universities. La Sapienza is also were economist Federico Caffè taught.

23 Michele Filippini, *Una Politica di Massa: Antonio Gramsci e la Rivoluzione della Società* (Roma: Carocci, 2015). Frosini organized at the University of Urbino an international conference titled 'Hegemony after Gramsci', which focused upon further elaborations of the concept of hegemony after Gramsci's death. The papers presented at this conference were published in a special issue of the online journal *Materialismo Storico*, with an introduction by Frosini: Fabio Frosini, "Egemonia Dopo Gramsci," *Materialismo Storico* 2, no. 1 (2017). There was also a second number on the topic: "L'egemonia Dopo Gramsci# 2: Storia, Politica e Teoria (Urbino 2018)," *Materialismo Storico* VII, no. 2 (2019). Lastly, Frosini has also recently published on Gramsci's concept of hegemony outside of these conferences: "¿ Qué Es la 'Crisis de Hegemonía' ?: Apuntes Sobre Historia, Revolución Y Visibilidad en Gramsci," *Las Torres de Lucca: revista internacional de filosofía política* 6, no. 11 (2017); "Gramsci in Translation: Egemonia e Rivoluzione Passiva nell'Europa di Oggi," *Materialismo Storico*, no. 1 (2019). The main focus of these articles is linguistic analysis and the comparative history of ideas.

24 Michele Filippini, *Using Gramsci: a New Approach*, trans. Patrick J. Barr (London: Pluto, 2017). Davidson pointed out the abuses of Gramsci's work in: Davidson, "The Uses and Abuses of Gramsci."

I have always been puzzled by this tendency, in a number of projects I have come across and that became successful, to get off to a promising start, but to end up crashing and leading nowhere. In Frosini's case I was also puzzled by a complete change of language and style. Frosini's first book, *Gramsci e la Filosofia*, or *Gramsci and Philosophy*, was notable amongst other things also for a concise and clear prose in writing about politics that reminds one of Emilio Lussu, a politician in Italy with ties to Sardinian separatist movements, who as a military officer had fought in costly battles during the First World War and wrote a clear and concise account of these battles shorn of rhetoric, yet showing the madness of the First World War and of frontal assaults against fortified positions heavily defended by machine guns and artillery.[25] Lussu was an officer in the Sassari brigade, which fought on mountains, although mountain fighting in the Italian Army is the competence of an army specialty, today the Alpine Troops Command, and the Tridentina Division. By contrast, Frosini's second book, *La Religione dell'Uomo Moderno*, or *The Religion of Modern Man*, focuses on philosophy seen as a modern religion and is distinguished instead by a very technical and obscure language, reminiscent of Chantal Mouffe and Ernesto Laclau's work on Gramsci, which I believe has served to discredit Gramsci's work amongst English-speaking audiences, in England at least, by associating Gramsci's work with that of his interpreters, which is obscure and inaccessible.[26] Frosini's second book is also based upon an equation of philosophy with religion that I do not subscribe to.[27]

25 Frosini, *Gramsci e la Filosofia*. Emilio Lussu, *Un Anno sull'Altipiano* (Torino: Einaudi, 2014).

26 Fabio Frosini, *La Religione dell'Uomo Moderno: Politica e Verità nei Quaderni del Carcere di Antonio Gramsci* (Roma: Carocci, 2010). Laclau and Mouffe's work that I am referring to is: Ernesto Laclau and Chantal Mouffe, *Hegemony and Socialist Strategy: Towards a Radical Democratic Politics* (London and New York: Verso, 2001). The first edition of this work was published in 1985.

27 I disagree with this entire approach. Philosophy is not a form of religion adopted by atheists and agnostics. I believe it is something other than religion. It can be in addition to religion. I address this argument in detail in other parts of this project, here I just want to emphasize my difference from Frosini. A similar point with regards to philosophy not being comparable to religion was made by Laborde in her discussion of liberal concepts of religion: Cecile Laborde, *Liberalism's Religion* (Cambridge, Massachusetts and London: Harvard University Press, 2017).

3.4 Gramsci's Project and the Projects of Structural Marxists

Gramsci's reception outside Italy has also been obstructed by projects that are similar to his project, and that have enjoyed far greater success, both intellectually and as cultural enterprises. In my interpretation, the main achievement of political theorist Peter Thomas, in *The Gramscian Moment*, is to have argued convincingly that a favorable reception of Gramsci's work in English-speaking countries has been delayed for decades by the fact that philosopher Luis Althusser and historical sociologist Perry Anderson had negative views of Gramsci's work, and to some extent over-criticized and mis-represented this work.[28] Althusser is best known as the founder of Structural Marxism, and Anderson as the defender and publicizer of Althusserianism in Great Britain. Thomas suggested that Gramsci would have his moment of fame in English-speaking countries after the passing of Althusser's and Anderson's moments. This is true to some extent because of the growing interest in Gramsci encouraged by such different journals as Historical Materialism, and Rethinking Marxism.[29] However, it seems unlikely to me that a true interest in Gramsci will develop as things stand. Anderson's initiatives are reminiscent of Croce's, because besides writing many books, Anderson has great and lasting influence

28 Peter D. Thomas, *The Gramscian Moment: Philosophy, Hegemony and Marxism* (Leiden and Boston: Brill, 2009). Thomas has also written on many other subjects on Gramsci, for example on Gramsci's project for a Modern Prince, a topic I began researching many years ago: "Toward the Modern Prince," in *Gramsci in the World*, ed. Roberto M. Dainotto and Fredric Jameson (Durham and London: Duke University Press, 2020). All contributions in this volume contain interesting new directions for research on Gramsci that I have been working on too, showing that there is a growing perceived need to address Gramsci's work even amongst established scholars. One of the difficulties that I ran into with my research on Gramsci is that Gramsci was considered until recently a marginal author in England, and to some extent in the United States too. In English-speaking countries Gramsci was revered in some quarters that Anderson described as sectarians, to describe small committed groups of activists that only preach to the converted, by analogy to small religious groups that are in contrast to established Churches like the Anglican Church and the Catholic Church. Thomas also translated from the German an important article on Gramsci's work on economics: Michael R. Kratke and Peter D. Thomas as translator, "Antonio Gramsci's Contribution to a Critical Economics," *Historical Materialism* 19, no. 3 (2011). Interestingly, this shows the importance to social science of the tradition of translation represented by Booth and Boothman, but in the context of social theory it raises the question that Gramsci described as 'the translatability of scientific languages', namely, how closely can one scientific text mirror or shadow another, and thus convey to some other audiences the original text?

29 John Anthony Hall, *Ernest Gellner: an Intellectual Biography* (London and New York: Verso, 2014).

on English Marxist scholars and historical sociologists also as the editor of the *New Left Review*, and as the publisher of Verso Books, which are respectively the premier journal and premier publisher of left-leaning scholars in England and to some extent also in other English-speaking countries, including the United States. Verso publishes works by many other leading scholars, not just left-leaning scholars, including right-leaning scholars like Hall, for example Hall's biography of Gellner. Gramsci is likely to be seen always through the lens of high intellectuals not interested in his politics, because of Anderson's enduring influence, and the inability of sectarian intellectuals, or small groups of dissenters, to provide alternatives.

An important part of Althusser's and Anderson's lasting influence is to have revived an *orthodox Marxism in the West* that is diametrically opposed to Gramsci's project and that is based on a completely different reading of Marx than Gramsci's. Althusser, in his book *For Marx*, made a back-handed compliment to Gramsci, asking who had ever tried to follow the explorations initiated by Marx and Engels, and concluding 'I can only think of Gramsci'.[30] This was a back-handed compliment because Althusser went on to launch a sustained attack against Gramsci for having attempted to formulate a humanist theory of history. Althusser's apparent paradox, praising Gramsci, yet rejecting his work, is resolved when we take a history of ideas approach to Marx's work. This work spanned decades and went through various phases. Scholars have often contrasted work by the young Marx with work by the later Marx, including *Capital*.[31] Gramsci sought to continue the approach of the young Marx, whereas Althusser sought to continue the approach of the later Marx. The first was a humanist approach, whereas the second, as set out in *Capital*, was a materialistic-economistic approach, by which I mean an approach entirely based upon the economy, and reducing history to the development of material factors that are part of the economy.

Interestingly, Althusser's criticism spawned a defence called *Per Gramsci*, or *For Gramsci*.[32] This is a book dedicated to defending Gramsci's work written

30 The French original is: Luis Althusser, *Pour Marx*, Collection Théorie (Paris: François Maspero, 1965). The first English translation was published in 1969. It has been reprinted at least twice by Verso, including the second time in the Radical Thinkers series: *For Marx*, Radical Thinkers (London and New York: Verso, 2010).

31 Althusser first introduced this distinction in *For Marx*. Other authors have touched upon it: Shlomo Avineri, *The Social and Political Thought of Karl Marx*, Cambridge Studies in the History and Theory of Politics (Cambridge and New York: Cambridge University Press, 1968); *Karl Marx: Philosophy and Revolution*, Jewish Lives (New Haven and London: Yale University Press, 2019).

32 Maria Antonietta Macciocchi, *Per Gramsci* (Bologna: Il Mulino, 1974).

by an Italian journalist and public intellectual, Maria Antonietta Macciocchi, with a personal history that in one way is remarkably similar to Gramsci's, who was characterized by political theorist Nadia Urbinati as someone 'from the periphery of modernity'.[33] Similarly to Gramsci, Macciocchi was originally from such a periphery, in Macciocchi's case a small town in central Italy called Isola del Liri, and went on to become a journalist. Unlike Gramsci, however, Macciocchi had the good fortune of rising high in her career, far above Isola del Liri, becoming a professor in France. I hope to address the details of this argument elsewhere. Here, I want to emphasize how Gramsci's project differs from orthodox Marxism, starting with Althusser's Structural Marxism, which arguably sought to revive orthodox Marxism. I argue throughout this project that *many intellectuals of various stripes, including Marx himself, have failed the masses*.[34] In Marx's case, one of the reasons for this failure is related to the shift in concerns from the young Marx to the later Marx, the latter's work being the work that is central to orthodox Marxism.

Marx's late work, *Capital* most notably, began a specific tradition in the theory of history, which gave credit to the *misconception that the economy is all there is to development*, and that all that states have to do is to foster the economy. In an odd way, neoliberalism, although ideologically opposed to Marxism, continues this misconception. Another reason for this failure is that Marx developed an anti-humanist view of history and a *politics emphasizing violent revolution in response to economic grievances*, which contained the seeds of the tragic misuses of Marx's thought that have marred the history of Marxism. Lastly, the failures of Marx's politics have contributed to a strong anti-intellectualism amongst the masses, which I believe contributes to the subordination of the masses to elites. There are times when philosophy and theory ought to be one of the first steps towards an emancipatory politics, because one ought to begin by freeing oneself from the misconceptions and faulty ideologies that have led to past mistakes, which include both Marxism and neoliberalism. The dangers of continuing to work with faulty assumptions are clearly exemplified by Thomas Piketty's book *Capital in the 21st Century*.[35] This book, despite being

33 Nadia Urbinati, "From the Periphery of Modernity: Antonio Gramsci's Theory of Subordination and Hegemony," *Political Theory* 26, no. 3 (1998).

34 This is my reading of: Gouldner, *Against Fragmentation: the Origins of Marxism and the Sociology of Intellectuals*.

35 Thomas Piketty, *Capital in the Twenty-First Century*, trans. Arthur Goldhammer (Cambridge, Massachusetts and London: Harvard University Press, 2017). The first edition was from 2013. This work generated a stir and had great success with the public, showing there is still an interest in historical theories of economics. The work of philosophers like Daniel Weinstock, who combine ethics with the study of public policy, seems to have

a thoroughly researched empirical work, shares the same misconception as Marx's *Capital*, namely, that the economy is all there is to development, and shows Piketty as a modern-day Marx still holding the same misconception, despite his research, and despite more than a century of failed and even tragic experiments.

Because of the seriousness of the failures of *these* important Marxist intellectuals, starting with Marx himself, I want to clarify exactly which points of the young Marx's project I believe are still important, and *how I differ from the orthodox Marxism associated with Althusser and Anderson*. I build upon two insights by Gramsci that place me at loggerheads with this orthodox Marxism. The first insight is the overall insight that the valuable approach of the young Marx was focused on *a humanist philosophy and the associated view of history emphasizing knowledge and understanding*, in order to promote collective action that is both deliberate and sustained. This is in contrast to the anti-humanist view of history emphasizing economics and violent revolution in response to economic grievances, which is what Marx ended up advocating in his later work. Knowledge and understanding are crucial to achieving goals. The book on humanist social science explores in greater detail this humanist approach, which Gramsci described by reference to the ancient Greek philosophical injunction 'know thyself'. In my interpretation, this injunction emphasizes that the first step in a quest for knowledge is reflecting upon the influences that one has been subjected to, and achieving an understanding of past mistakes, without which there can be no intellectual progress, and without which cultural development is stunted.

I believe the importance of knowledge and understanding in humanist philosophy follows from a view of history that emphasizes collective action, and in particular deliberate and sustained collective action. *Knowledge is important in order to be able to engage in deliberate and sustained collective action*. Collective action that seeks to achieve social change that is favorable to the masses has to have both of these features, namely, it has to be deliberate, and it has to be sustained. *Deliberate collective action* is crucially important to achieve favorable social change. Gramsci argued that any social group that intends to bring about social change in its favor needs to be able to engage in deliberate collective action that is clear about its goals and pursues them consistently. To do so, the social group needs a plan, and a plan

opened up new directions for research and also revived interest in normative theories of economics, which inform Piketty's work.

needs a theory. One has to have a theory of how society works, and where history is heading, in order to bring about social change that is advantageous to the social group, and not just haphazard efforts and unintended consequences.[36] Gramsci also argued that this social group would have to be able to engage in *sustained collective action*. This was in contrast to sporadic collective action in response to specific grievances, like mass strikes that followed sudden deteriorations in economic conditions. These strikes might come and go with temporary fluctuations in economic conditions, without altering the root causes of long-term trends in deteriorating economic conditions. Populism seems to be an instance of collective action that is neither deliberate nor sustained.

The second insight by Gramsci that I build upon is that *one or more cultural organizations, not just a few individuals, are necessary to formulate a theory* for the masses, in order to contribute to deliberate and sustained collective action by the masses. In other words, one needs to participate in a collaborative project. Gramsci also argued that a crucial first step towards building such an organization was that the masses ought to build first their own groups of 'organic intellectuals'. This is a crucial concept that I address in the book on humanist social science, contrasting organic and traditional intellectuals without, however, disparaging the work of traditional intellectuals. Organic intellectuals are intellectuals who are politically close to the masses, like journalists, or economically and functionally close to the masses, in the sense of being close to production, like engineers.[37] I argue that organic intellectuals are essential to any emancipatory politics, and to answer important questions related to development and democracy.

36 The concept of unintended consequences looms large in Perry Anderson's early work, including his criticism of E.P. Thompson. This criticism is contained in: Perry Anderson, *Arguments within English Marxism* (London: New Left Books, 1980). The many articles written by Anderson on the topic have been collected in one volume and translated into Spanish: Perry Anderson and E. Terrén, *Teoría, Política e Historia: un Debate con E. P. Thompson*, Teoria (Mexico City: Siglo XXI, 1985).

37 I address Gramsci's theory of intellectuals and the distinction between traditional and organic intellectuals in: Olsaretti, "Beyond Class." In this article I also propose another distinction that is central to this project, between high and low intellectuals, a distinction that I derive from my reading of Gramsci's work. This distinction is not addressed in any literature on Gramsci that I could find.

3.5 Gramsci's Project and the Projects of Analytical Marxists

The other notable contemporary project that is similar to Gramsci's project was started by G. A. Cohen with his book *Karl Marx's Theory of History*.[38] This book and later work by Cohen started Analytical Marxism. Despite their differences, there are also some *significant similarities between Cohen' and Gramsci's projects*. One similarity is that they were both collaborative projects. After publishing his book on Marx's theory of history, Cohen started a group of like-minded intellectuals, the September Group, devoted to formulating a modern theory of history that followed the example set by Marx. Cohen, a philosopher, was joined by economists, political scientists and social theorists, including Samuel Bowles and Herbert Gintis, forming an impressive roster of scholars. Another similarity between Cohen's and Gramsci's project was that they both sought to cover the same domains of human activity and the associated fields of scholarship: philosophy, politics, and economics. No one in the September Group worked on Gramsci or cited Gramsci as a source of inspiration for the project of this group, showing that there is a perceived need in English-speaking countries for the kind of project that Gramsci was trying to start, even amongst those who do not know Gramsci.

There are *three very valuable points made by Cohen that complement Gramsci's project*. The first point concerns *Althusser's style*. Cohen's work was driven in part by dissatisfaction with Althusser's Structural Marxism and its obscure language and unclear claims regarding social structures.[39] This is a very valuable

38 G. A. Cohen stands for Gerald Allan Cohen. I used his initials since Cohen, despite being Canadian, completed his graduate studies and pursued his whole career in Great Britain, and in his books used an old convention of British scholars, always to use initials rather than spelling one's full name. The first edition of Cohen's book on Marx's theory of history is: Gerald Allan Cohen, *Karl Marx's Theory of History: a Defence*, Princeton Paperbacks (Princeton and Oxford: Princeton University Press, 1978).

39 Some authors have suggested that Althusser's project and G. A. Cohen's project are important projects that were complementary and that it is worth to revive them: Andrew Levine, *A Future for Marxism?: Althusser, the Analytical Turn and the Revival of Socialist Theory* (London: Pluto, 2003). I find instead that the only commonality they have is that they both attempted to revive orthodox Marxism, Althusser by combining it with French structuralism, Cohen by combining it with Analytic Philosophy. I believe that orthodox Marxism should never be revived nor imitated, because it was a fundamentally flawed, one-sided theory. We should only rescue from Marx's, Althusser's and Cohen's projects important insights and concepts, but not the overarching framework they used. Cohen' project was an important step forward compared to Trotsky's work, which was either polemical, or extremely detailed and erudite history. But Cohen made his theory of history take one step forward and two steps backwards, as it were, for reasons that I explain next.

point, and in this project I seek to provide exact definitions of social structures and to make clear claims regarding the impact of these structures on collective action. The second point concerns the *need to build a theory of history systematically, from the ground up*, starting with clearly stated assumptions, from which one derives through logic statements that can be tested. These assumptions include assumptions regarding the behavior of individuals, which serves to explain social structures. Political theorist Jon Elster, another member of the September Group, studied these foundations extensively, although in using the metaphor 'nuts and bolts' for these foundations, he conflated two distinct points, namely, the need to define individual behavior clearly, and the need to define structures clearly. I think it is necessary instead to describe both individual's behavior and social structures as two distinct, yet closely inter-related concepts[40] The third point is that Cohen focused on *rebuilding Marx's theory of history by integrating it with contemporary concepts* and the latest theoretical advances in social sciences. Cohen thus represents a completely different approach than the approach adopted by Frosini, Cospito, and the philological school of Gramscian studies. I combined the two approaches by undertaking first, in my dissertation, a philological study to understand Gramsci's project, and then by taking, in this and other books in this project, the approach pioneered by Cohen. This entails that I take Gramsci's project one or a few steps further, reconstructing Gramsci's theory from the ground up, and integrating within it the latest advances in social science.

Cohen's project also differs from Gramsci's project in some important respects. Cohen ended up proposing a version of orthodox Marxism built upon concepts drawn from economics that describe human beings exclusively as *Homo Oeconomicus*, a concept which underpins much of economic theory, including neoliberalism. Cohen and others in the September Group used these concepts to attempt to justify the orthodox Marxist misconception that the economy is all there is to development. Thus, Cohen ended up building upon the worst of both worlds, that is, the worst of economic thinking, and the worst of Marxist thinking, which is orthodox Marxism. Cohen himself dropped several of these

40 The main books where Elster discusses the 'nuts and bolts' are: Jon Elster, *Nuts and Bolts for the Social Sciences* (Cambridge and New York: Cambridge University Press, 1989); *Explaining Social Behavior: More Nuts and Bolts for the Social Sciences*, Revised edition ed. (Cambridge and New York: Cambridge University Press, 2015). In the book on the humanist theory of society I propose a structural-foundational view of social interaction that uses concepts analogous to 'nuts and bolts', namely, foundations of society in individual behavior, and I extend these foundations beyond the 'nuts and bolts' to include structures and boundaries, in the second volume and the book on humanist social theory.

concepts in his later work. Others in the September Group *continued proposing flawed assumptions*, however. It is especially remarkable that, after Bowles and Gintis did work to provide new concepts in place of *Homo Oeconomicus*, they still ended up suggesting an anti-humanist theory. Bowles and Gintis and a number of other scholars did very important empirical work showing that the concept of *Homo Oeconomicus* is flawed, also because human beings are capable of cooperation and altruism, and not just of acquisitive individualism as posited by *Homo Oeconomicus*. They even explicitly called for a return to Aristotle's concept of *Zoon Politikon*, or political being, which is very close to some of Gramsci's goals.[41] However, they failed to draw the most important logical conclusion from all this work, which is that as human beings we are capable of deliberate and sustained collective action, which makes us capable of escaping the grip of evolutionary mechanisms.

By contrast, Bowles and Gintis still built *reductive models of social interaction based upon evolutionary mechanisms only*, which can be run on computers in order to predict the outcomes of many interactions. These are the mainstay of the work of the Santa Fe Institute that Bowles and Gintis cooperate with, building computer models of evolutionary processes that and are part of the growing field of computational sociology.[42] I am very sceptical of evolutionary models applied to *modern history*. One reason for my skepticism concerns the very status of these models. It seems to me that these models heavily reflect

---

41 Samuel Bowles and Herbert Gintis, "Social Preferences, Homo Oeconomicus and *Zoon Politikon*," in *The Oxford Handbook of Contextual Political Analysis*, ed. Robert E. Goodin and Charles Tilly (Oxford and New York: Oxford University Press, 2006).

42 The following books are clear examples of the use of evolutionary mechanisms and of Bowles and Gintis' anti-humanist approach: Herbert Gintis, *The Bounds of Reason: Game Theory and the Unification of the Behavioral Sciences – Revised Edition* (Princeton and Oxford: Princeton University Press, 2009). Samuel Bowles and Herbert Gintis, *A Cooperative Species: Human Reciprocity and Its Evolution* (Princeton and Oxford: Princeton University Press, 2011). The latter applies evolutionary mechanisms to early human societies that Bowles and Gintis refer to as built around 'an oddly cooperative animal', effectively comparable to 'hunting apes'. Moreover, Bowles and Gintis also argue that the whole of social science should be built on game-theory, an increasingly frequent claim that I address in this project. Bowles and Gintis' scientific language seems to be re-introducing racism through the back door. Interestingly, Gintis alludes to physics, specifically quantum mechanics, in his recent book: Herbert Gintis, *Individuality and Entanglement: the Moral and Material Bases of Social Life* (Princeton and Oxford: Princeton University Press, 2016). Another interesting point is that evolutionary mechanisms based upon game theory lend themselves to be modeled by computer systems and large social science labs are becoming a bit like large physics labs, or large physics bunkers like CERN in Geneva and the Gran Sasso physics laboratory in Italy, where the data gathered by sensors is put through large farms of powerful computers.

the assumptions of those who build them, and are thus more like plans than models. I therefore introduce in this project an important difference between scientific criteria and engineering criteria, the latter being more like plans, and explain how the humanist social science that I propose seeks to contribute to both. I also think that these models are based on a social science approach that is influenced by the approach of physics laboratories or bunkers that run models of physical interactions and that make use of supercomputers like the top 500 physics supercomputers in the world tracked by the TOP500 project. For all their power, these supercomputers model interactions of physical objects, not human beings. These models can be usefully extended to animals, not to human beings endowed with intelligence and knowledge.[43]

There is also another important difference between Gramsci's project and Cohen's project. The *September Group has done insufficient or flawed theoretical groundwork*, in particular, insufficient scrutiny of the assumptions they use. This is true even of Cohen, who is an Analytic philosopher, and who sees his work as including scrutinizing assumptions and providing clear definitions. Cohen had the intellectual honesty of openly admitting his theoretical errors. However, some of these errors are puzzling and call for an explanation. Amongst Cohen's more controversial claims in his book on Marx's theory of history, there was upholding functional explanation, which had been largely discredited in social science by the time he was writing, and which is essentially a modern reformulation of Aristotle's teleological explanation, which had been discredited by philosophers even earlier. Teleological explanation

---

43 The Santa Fe Institute cooperates with other centers like the Michigan Center for the Study of Complex Systems, and works like Holland's are indebted to both: John H. Holland, *Signals and Boundaries: Building Blocks for Complex Adaptive Systems* (Cambridge, Massachusetts: MIT Press, 2012). The emergence of Complex Adaptive Systems, which I touch upon in the book on humanist social science, has contributed to the rise of computational sociology, a discipline that applies computer models to society. I gained this insight through Angela Lu, who was applying network analysis and computer models to the study of Chinese bureaucracy and contacted me because she had an interest in my work on Gramsci's theory of intellectuals. Scholars in China seem to be developing an interest in combining social networks analysis, pioneered at Stanford University, with computational sociology. It would be interesting to compare Chinese bureaucrats and intellectuals to bureaucrats and intellectuals in other East Asian countries like Japan. It would also be interesting to compare computational sociology to analogous studies in physics. Physicist Vincenzo Savona pointed out to me the importance of supercomputers for physics, as the models provided by theoretical physicists are fed to supercomputers, which are widely employed. The TOP500 project tracks the top 500 supercomputers in the world and the main users of supercomputers. China and the United States are respectively the first and second users of supercomputers.

involves the claim that the *telos*, that is, the effect at the end of a causal chain, explains previous causes, as if a causal chain could work backwards, as it were, to explain previous causes. This might be a good way that we as human being can proceed to formulate theories, but it is not how the world works. I believe these controversial claims by Cohen are part of a *tendency by scholars to take over original projects that could change social science and then crash these projects and return to the fold*, as it were. Specialization, which is so ingrained in universities today, is at least partly responsible for this. It has confirmed to me the importance of Gramsci's idea that the masses should produce their own organic intellectuals, who will not return to the fold, and who will continue the work that is needed to produce significantly new theories of development and democracy that advance the conditions of the masses.

3.6 A View of Democracy That Rejects Eurocentrism

As much as I differ from orthodox Marxists, I also differ from socially conservative scholars close to communitarian ideologies, and from postcolonial scholars who have been seeking to provide answers to these socially conservative scholars. In this section I want to emphasize how my theory differs from the work of McGill University scholars who have addressed big questions, and whose work I reviewed in the previous chapter, including Hall, who is a sociologist, and Hallaq, who is an Islamist whose work includes social theory. Hall is amongst the theorists who share the view that democracy is a defining feature of the West and praise the West for it.[44] Hallaq is amongst the theorists who see tradition as a defining feature of Muslim culture, and by extension of other non-Western cultures, and praise these cultures for it. Hallaq made this point to me in a number of discussions. Hall and Hallaq are in some ways two sides of the same ideological coin, because they share the same underlying view that equates the West with democracy and modernity, and the rest of the world with non-democratic politics and tradition. This is a culturally specific view of democracy associated with eurocentrism, which sees Europe, and ultimately the West, as the cradle of democracy. This view is wrong and can be dangerous at a time of culture wars. Even worse, it can be reinforced by analogous views regarding the West as the cradle of modern science, and the rest of the world as mired in tradition and opposed to science. These are views that are implicit

44 This is implicit in early work by Hall, which tries to understand the different models that prevailed in other parts of the world: Hall, *Powers and Liberties*.

in the work of some postcolonial critics, which can be used to reinforce socially conservative positions. Therefore, in the next section, I address also my differences from postcolonial scholars like Said, whose work is at the crossroads between literary theory and cultural theory, and has been taken up by Hallaq. Said has also been influential amongst subaltern studies scholars, who can be considered to be a sub-group amongst postcolonial scholars. My differences from all these scholars can be summed up as differences over what constitutes democracy, and over what constitutes valid scientific knowledge. Here I begin by addressing the differences over what constitutes democracy.

I want to clarify these differences both because democracy is central to this project, and also because Weber's work that I build upon has been criticized as being eurocentric.[45] Therefore, I want to begin by emphasizing that this project is not a eurocentric project, because it is not a project about the unique virtues of Western democracies, nor about any alleged clash of civilizations based upon supposedly different stances over democracy between the West and other civilizations. These points entail that I have radically different views than Hall, Hallaq and Lindholm's about what constitutes the struggle for the world. While I share their view that struggle of one form or another is central to history, I profoundly disagree with them over what this struggle is about, and what is the place of democracy in this struggle. I believe that the struggle for the world is a struggle over development and democracy. I also believe that the masses in the West are losing this struggle, just like the masses in the developing world, although in manners that are not so visible and obvious. This means that I radically disagree with historians Victor Hanson and Niall Ferguson, because I find questions like 'why the West has won' to be deeply misleading, as they suggest that the struggle is between 'the West and the rest' and that the West is the depository of a more advanced culture.[46] This also

---

45 Hallaq considered Weber's work to be eurocentric. For a review of arguments regarding eurocentrism see chapter 1 in: Peter Gran, *Beyond Eurocentrism: a New View of Modern World History* (Syracuse: Syracuse University Press, 1996).

46 Thus I am diametrically opposed to: Victor David Hanson, *Why the West Has Won: Carnage and Culture from Salamis to Vietnam* (London: Faber & Faber, 2001); *The Father of Us All: War and History, Ancient and Modern*, The Group on Military History and Contemporary Conflict, the Hoover Institution, Stanford University (London, Berlin, New York: Bloomsbury, 2010). The phrase 'the west and the rest' was proposed by Niall Ferguson in: Niall Ferguson, *Civilization: the West and the Rest* (London: Penguin, 2011). Although below I point out that Ferguson's historical studies exemplify a very important concern with history, I find his conceptual apparatus misleading and not much of an improvement on Enoch Powell's views, and his reference to eunuchs part of a macho militarism that resembles populism, whereby high intellectuals who are part of the

means that I believe that knowledge about this struggle that is gained by the masses in any part of the world is very relevant to those engaged in this struggle in other parts of the world.

My *differences over what constitutes democracy*, compared to the above scholars, include three significant differences. The first concerns the very *definition of democracy and its alleged opposition to tradition*, as well as its historical and geographical specificity. It is important to address the claim that democracy is opposed to tradition and to respond to Hallaq's work, which is informed by the conviction that traditional societies with high moral standards are opposed to democracy because it brings about lax moral standards. This seems to be a feature of *strands of thought* that are equally anti-democratic within both Islam and Christianity. Arguably, there is a Christian fundamentalism that is defined by intolerant views of other cultures or ideologies, just like Muslim fundamentalism, and that is integral to culture wars within the United States and other Western countries.[47] One misconception in these strands of thought is to equate democracy with modernity, and with Western modernity in particular, and to suggest that modernity undermines tradition. This encourages *some* traditionalists outside the West to reject democracy as twice alien, because it is Western, and because it is modern.

In order to address this misconception, we have to consider the *historical and geographical specificity of democracy*. In brief, *democracy is neither a modern nor a Western invention*. Regarding the historical specificity, I argue in this project that the struggle for democracy in Western countries has been raging on and off for the past five hundred years. It built upon similar struggles in the ancient world that date back to more than two thousand years ago. Therefore, democracy is not a modern invention. Regarding the geographical specificity of democracy, I propose a broader view of democracy, which I argue includes a more egalitarian distribution of power than in other state types, specifically empires, and cannot be reduced just to the modern institutions associated with parliamentary democracy, which was pioneered in the West. From this viewpoint, the struggle for the world is a struggle for a more egalitarian

intellectual establishment use the same language as populist leaders and praise the martial virtues of the masses, especially when they have to justify costly wars.

47 The representatives of this Christian fundamentalism are pundits like Ann Coulter and Steve Bannon. There is also an Italian version of this intolerant strand, sometimes referred to as 'teocons'. I do *not* believe that Christianity is inherently intolerant, just like I do *not* believe that Islam is inherently intolerant. These intolerant *strands of thought* have been recently re-created in conjunction with culture wars, after a long period of decline, and seem to be politically, rather than culturally or religiously, driven and motivated.

distribution of power, and a more equitable distribution of the fruits of development, and it is a central feature of human history, which has surfaced at various times through most of human history and in most parts of the world. Therefore, democracy is not a Western invention. Hall and Hallaq's view that democracy is a modern invention of the West is incorrect.

The second difference between my view of democracy and those of the above scholars concerns the *components of democracy that are important in the struggle for the world*. The crucial factors that influence this struggle are *culture and organization*, the key ingredients of hegemony, and social structures, which set limits to what can be achieved using culture and organization. I argue below that, in order for democratic forces to win the struggle for the world, we ought to build upon culture and organization, which includes building upon community, not undermining it, as implicit in Marx's work, for example. *Tradition is part of the struggle for cultural democracy,* since tradition is based upon community, which is based upon culture. Cultural democracy includes the freedom to express and develop one's community, and thus one's culture. I argue below that cultural democracy is a key component of democracy, and that culture and organization, including community and tradition, and the associated cultural freedoms, ought to be defended and guaranteed. Therefore, Hallaq's implication that traditionalists are struggling to defend their communities and traditional ways of life against democracy is incorrect, because traditionalists are struggling for cultural democracy. The mistake of *some* traditionalists, which Hallaq seems to encourage, is to focus upon cultural democracy alone and neglect political democracy. This is the exact same mistake made in Western countries by fascists, nazis, and today by populists, which lends weight to the idea that there are similarities between, on the one hand, fascism and nazism and, on the other hand, populism and Christian and Muslim fundamentalisms, because all are systemic movements.

The third difference between my view of democracy and those of the above scholars concerns *the main actors in the struggle for the world*. The main actors in this struggle are not different nations, nor different civilizations or religions, but *empires and democracies*. The main social groups affected, who stand to win or lose the most in this struggle, are imperialist elites and the masses. In this project I also make another claim, and argue that the struggle between empires and democracies has power as its main bone of contention and is a struggle that profoundly affects all domains of human behavior: the economy, culture, politics and the military. This struggle in the West took a new turn with the expansion of parliamentary democracy, which on its own was not sufficient to guarantee democracy, however. To the contrary, *the struggle for democracy in the West generated a powerful reaction from elites at the beginning of the modern era*, after 1500, drastically altering the fate of European countries, and then of other countries in the world, where a new form of imperialism, colonialism, was exported at gunpoint by European elites. I argue in the second volume that imperialism has affected Western countries too, and is undermining democracy within them. Therefore, I differ radically from Hall and those who hold views that emphasize the uniqueness of the West, and who argue that the reasons for the rise of the West reside in its commitment to democracy and the strength of parliamentary democracy. I also differ from Hallaq, and the traditionalists in the West and outside the West who follow Hallaq's way of thinking. I believe that the liberation that people throughout the world can and should strive for is liberation from empires and imperialist elites, which should be the central goal of any emancipatory politics. It is *not* liberation from parliamentary democracy and the West, which are not a panacea, as Hall seems to believe, but are not a threat either, as Hallaq implies, except when they are manipulated by imperialist elites.

3.7 A View of Scientific Knowledge That Rejects Eurocentrism

The work of socially conservative scholars is paradoxically reinforced by the work of postcolonial scholars, who can be defined as scholars working on the challenges of emancipatory politics in countries that were freed from colonialism. One way in which work by one group reinforces work by the other group, is by reinforcing simplistic views of social science and objectivity. The first group tend to embrace all science produced in the West as objective. This is a culturally specific and triumphalist view of science associated with eurocentrism, which sees Europe, and ultimately the West, as the cradle of modern science. The second group tend to reject all science produced in the West as subjective and implicated in imperialism. I differ from both groups of scholars over what constitutes valid scientific knowledge, and ultimately over the very concept of objectivity, a point I address in the book on humanist social theory. I want to introduce here my interpretation of the concept of *subjectivity, which entails conforming to attributes of the subject, as a useful reconceptualization of the contribution from postcolonial scholars* that we should take into consideration. Subjectivity refers to attributes of the subject that are useful in order to achieve objectivity, which entails conforming to attributes of the object. The latter is a common definition of objectivity and of valid scientific knowledge, which is typically understood to be all there is to knowledge. By contrast, postcolonial scholars emphasize that attributes of the subject, like a scientist's geographical location and culture, can influence negatively the scientific knowledge that the subject produces. My point is that, while taking subjectivity into consideration, we should not see it as necessarily preventing all objective knowledge. To the contrary, as suggested in the introduction, stating clearly a subject's goals at the outset of a project is a matter of intellectual honesty, and a virtue that can contribute to achieving objectivity. Moreover, these goals are not fixed by our culture, whatever this culture might be. In the book on humanist social science I propose a socio-political version of the ancient Greek injunction 'know thyself' as a way to identify and overcome the influences that are due to one's geographical location and culture.

My goal in this section is also to *reject an unreflecting over-reaction, or knee-jerk reaction, against all social science produced in the West.* Said's book *Orientalism* rightly highlighted that European knowledge about Asia was not scientifically objective, but reflected a European viewpoint upon Asia that was deeply implicated in European imperialism.[48] Said's *Orientalism* undoubtedly initiated an important criticism of European knowledge about countries in Asia. This criticism has however been put to misleading uses that actually contribute to the imperialism that they claim to criticize.[49] Said himself might be partly responsible for this. The label orientalist has sometimes been used in such a way as to reject all knowledge about Asia that is acquired in Europe as orientalist, which is associated with a form of reverse-orientalism that has been called occidentalism.[50] This misleading use is accentuated in Hallaq's recent book *Restating Orientalism*, which arguably continues and amplifies a knee-jerk reaction already implicit in *Orientalism*, which considered only orientalist knowledge produced in Europe, and made it seem as if all knowledge

48 Edward W. Said, *Orientalism* (Vintage Books, 1994). The majority of books studied by Said was undoubtedly orientalist, but he did not consider other, non-orientalist books. Said focused on high culture. In popular travelogues a different perspective emerges. There was a condescending attitude and exoticist stereotyping of the oriental 'other', but this overlapped with a similar attitude towards the working classes in England: Olsaretti, "Urban Culture, Curiosity and the Aesthetics of Distance."

49 For a review of the reaction generated by Said and the many works that addressed his points, see: Lata Mani and Ruth Frankenberg, "The Challenge of Orientalism," *Economy and Society* 14, no. 2 (1985). Gellner also intervened in the debate.

50 Studies of occidentalism include: James G. Carrier, "Occidentalism: the World Turned Upside-Down," *American ethnologist* 19, no. 2 (1992); Wang Ning, "Orientalism Versus Occidentalism?," *New Literary History* 28, no. 1 (1997). An important book for this study is the collection: James G. Carrier, ed. *Occidentalism: Images of the West* (Oxford: Clarendon Press, 1995). An instance of contemporary studies of occidentalism that is focused on postcolonial theory and shares the obscure language of parts of postcolonial theory is: Couze Venn, *Occidentalism: Modernity and Subjectivity*, Published in Association with Theory, Culture & Society (London, Thousand Oaks, New Delhi: SAGE Publications, 2000).

produced in Europe is inadequate, or even pernicious, for cultures that are not part of Europe.[51] This is actually not so different from the views espoused by movements like Boko Haram, which reject all Western education as pernicious. This knee-jerk reaction, common to high intellectuals like Hallaq, and grass-root movements like Boko Haram, amounts to a dangerous ideological operation. This ideological operation favors imperialism by discouraging masses in the West and outside the West from learning important lessons from each other, which could help them deal with imperialist elites.

In order to help achieve the *goal of avoiding knee-jerk reactions against science, and to encourage an exchange of knowledge between the masses in Western and non-Western countries*, I want to sketch in this section the view of subjectivity that informs the rest of this book. It is useful to start with a clarification. In this section I *focus in upon eurocentrism, rather than orientalism, because eurocentrism is a more general criticism* of European social science than orientalism. All orientalist knowledge is eurocentric, but eurocentrism as a label can be applicable also to European knowledge of non-Asian cultures, and to a self-important view of European culture and science as being special compared to other cultures and sciences. Another important clarification regards the criticisms that I want to address. *This book can be criticized as eurocentric for two reasons: its focus and its location*. A focus on Europe is associated in some studies with the eurocentric view that European culture is more important than other cultures because it fostered democracy and science and brought modernity to the world. I do not share this view. The other reason why this book could be classified as eurocentric is that it was conceived of and researched entirely in Europe and North America, and this location in *some* studies leads to the biases just mentioned, sometimes in more subtle forms. But these biases are not necessarily present in all books produced in the West, and in the book on humanist social science I argue that it is possible to escape the ideological influences that one was subjected to and avoid past mistakes of intellectuals. In discussing the location of this book, I also want to show how the subjectivity of my argument can actually contribute to objectivity. Here I want to begin by discussing the focus of this book, and also show how subjectivity does not necessarily undermine the objectivity of the argument.

The *focus* of this book arises from attributes of the author who wrote it and is thus an aspect of its subjectivity. However, this focus on Europe does not necessarily make it eurocentric, or any less objective than it would otherwise be, if

---

51 Wael B. Hallaq, *Restating Orientalism: a Critique of Modern Knowledge* (New York: Columbia University Press, 2018).

the author was not European. I reject the eurocentric view that European culture is more important than other cultures, and therefore *this is not yet another book about the uniqueness of European culture and how it fostered democracy and science*, something implicitly or explicitly argued by the above scholars, either to praise or to deprecate Europe for having brought democracy, science and ultimately modernity to the world. By contrast, this book is simply focused on Europe. This focus is dictated by the simple fact that it is impossible for one person to acquire knowledge about the entire world. Even generalists have to specialize to some extent, and my knowledge is limited to countries in the West, particularly in Europe. Being focused upon Europe, without believing in the greater importance of European culture, has two important consequences for the theory that I propose. The first consequence is that *this work does not propose a theory about other parts of the world*, or the entire world, it simply suggests that the theory about Europe that it proposes might be of interest to researchers whose work focuses on other parts of the world. I especially point to the relevance of this theory to other countries in the West, Canada and the United States, but also to some extent to countries in the Middle East, and to China and India.

The second important consequence of this focus for the theory that I propose is that this theory is *informed by a completely different perspective* than the perspective associated with eurocentrism, which sees the world as divided into Europe, or the West, and the rest of world, and attributes these divisions to religion or culture more in general. By contrast, *I emphasize differences within Europe*. In particular, the theory that I propose is a theory about the different routes to development and democracy taken in modern history by some countries in Europe, comparing and contrasting these routes to the routes taken by other countries in Europe. The routes that I focus upon are the routes taken by north-western European countries, and those taken by south-central European countries. The first group consists of England, France, and Spain, the Netherlands and Portugal constituting an intermediate case. The second group consists of Italy, Germany, and Switzerland. I also address the important case of the Ottoman empire, which included all of south-eastern Europe, as well as North Africa and the Middle East. This is useful to provide an answer to orientalist and occidentalist views, both of which presuppose the entire West to be an undifferentiated entity. I emphasize instead important differences within Europe, where south-central European countries were sidelined, and in the case of some Italian states were conquered, by north-western European states. I also *emphasize commonalities across civilizations defined by religion*. The emphasis in this book is on state type and systems, not on civilizations conceived of as separate cultural entities. As argued by Braudel, most Mediterranean countries, especially countries in south-central Europe, south-eastern Europe, North Africa and the Middle East, were all part of one Mediterranean civilization defined by an economy tied together by numerous trading networks, which constituted a system. Beginning with the modern era, ca 1500, the entire Mediterranean system went into a period of decline and was replaced by an Atlantic system dominated by north-western European countries, which would form the core of the modern world system.[52]

This different perspective is still associated with the view that *north-western Europe was contingently, as opposed to inherently, superior in terms of sheer military power*, to other parts of Europe and to other Mediterranean countries for a certain historical period. I argue in this project that it is *important to understand the routes to development taken by north-western European countries* in modern history, because they are necessary to understand the world we live in today, particularly phenomena like globalization, and the challenges and threats that we face. The imperialist elites in these countries have had a disproportionate impact upon modern history and possibly continue doing so. *They all created within a relatively short time span large colonial* empires that have indisputably had an impact upon other parts of the world that they conquered. The imperialist elites *also initiated globalization* and drove it for a long time in a manner that benefited themselves at the expense of other social groups and other countries, both in Europe and outside Europe.

This is an important point both ethically and politically. If we want to create a more equitable world, we ought to start by studying the sources of past inequalities, since knowledge of these sources is indispensable to prevent such inequalities from arising again in the future. Because of their impact upon other parts of the world, and because of their role in globalization, it is especially important to study north-western European countries and the imperialist elites of these countries, in order to understand what made possible their disproportionate impact upon modern history. For example, this project seeks to bring out the importance of political-military power in the routes to development taken by these countries, and to draw attention to the role that intelligence plays in political-military power, which is neglected by political science and political sociology alike. This power is arguably very important, and ought to be taken into consideration alongside economic power. To ignore it and focus exclusively upon one's cultural freedoms, without taking imperialism and globalization into account, is irresponsible and dooms to failure the social

52 This is the perspective proposed by Braudel in: Braudel, *The Mediterranean, Vol. 1*; *The Mediterranean, Vol. 2*. The idea that the Atlantic was part of the modern world system is central to Wallerstein's work, which builds upon Braudel's work.

groups and countries that take this approach. As with the problem posed by neoliberalism and the populist backlash, so with imperialism, identifying the sources of the problem is the necessary first step, formulating valid alternatives is the next step.

The *location* where this book was conceived and first researched does not make this book eurocentric either. This *entails a different view of power, of the influence of power on knowledge, and also of the knowing subject*, than the views endorsed by key postcolonial theorists. The *different view of power*, which I detail in the book on the humanist social science, is that it is not all-encompassing and ubiquitous over a territory. The theoretical origins of Hallaq's error are in a different view of power that was implicit in Said's *Orientalism*, which mistakenly and misleadingly combined Gramsci's work on power with work by sociologist Michel Foucault. Gramsci's notion of hegemony, which is essentially political-military power reinforced by cultural power, always contained a criticism of the political uses of culture. However, by combining this approach with Foucault's account of power, which is at best mystifying, and which suggests that there are diffuse sources of power that affect all aspects of culture and that cannot be traced to specific sources, Said effectively implied that no work produced in the West could escape these diffuse sources of power and escape orientalism or eurocentrism. Both Foucault and Said, by suggesting that power works in mysterious ways, have effectively reintroduced the medieval idea of an 'inscrutable god' criticized by Gramsci.[53] This amounted to treating Gramsci's project in a manner very similar to that of Italian scholars like Togliatti, and thus crushing Gramsci's project. This project is devoted instead to showing that, as suggested by Gramsci and the tradition of Italian humanism that Gramsci sought to continue, power is a human construct, and it is something that can be known, understood, and traced to human sources.

This also entails a *different view of the influence of power over knowledge, and of the knowing subject*, which amounts to a different way of conceiving of subjectivity compared to key postcolonial thinkers. The ability to know and understand the power that one was subjected to can contribute to freeing oneself from this power. Furthermore, it is possible to formulate a theory that enables us to pursue an emancipatory politics together with others who share our goals. Said's *Orientalism* paved the way for other important studies

53 Gramsci borrowed from Croce the view that some materialists effectively saw material forces as if they were an 'inscrutable god', who would have been inherent in material forces: Gramsci, *Quaderni del Carcere*, 1225. I deliberately refer to 'god' with a small letter, both to reproduce correctly the text that I cite, and to emphasize that *this* 'god' is nothing but a human power, which has social sources that can be understood and identified.

that have questioned the objectivity of Western social science, like Johannes Fabian's and Gayatri Chakravorty Spivak's studies.[54] In my interpretation, Fabian's argument does not preclude the possibility of objective knowledge, it simply calls for the sensible approach that anthropologists should apply to themselves, reflexively, the same categories that they apply to the subjects they study, an approach which stems from a different view of the knowing subject as *capable of self-reflection* and ultimately of self-consciousness, compared to Hall and Hallaq's views. This view informs the book on humanist social science, where I apply the sociology of knowledge and the sociology of intellectuals to understand problems in modern social science in the West, including my own effort to formulate a humanist social science.

Similarly, in my interpretation, Spivak's question 'can the subaltern speak?', a question over which rivers of ink have been poured, does not preclude the possibility that subalterns can speak.[55] In the book on humanist social science I argue *that the question as to whether the subaltern can speak has clear answers*. This is in contrast to those critics who made this question seem to be very difficult to answer, also by using obscure language, all of which stems from a different view of the knowing subject compared to Gramsci's. The clear answers are based on *a dynamic view of the knowing subject, who can change, even if only in small steps*. Thus, to paraphrase Spivak, the subaltern can speak when they secure the social conditions for objectivity in social science, which would also enable the subaltern to express their views, and when they create their own organic intellectuals and eventually raise the whole of the masses, including themselves, to the intellectual level of the elites. The concept of 'know thyself' as a way to free oneself from cultural influences, is relevant also to the question as to whether the subaltern can speak. I elaborate upon these points in other books that are part of this project, including the book on emancipatory and

54 Fabian applied and extended Said's critique to anthropology, showing how the very conceptual categories used by Western anthropologists were biased and influenced by their social position: Johannes Fabian, *Time and the Other: How Anthropology Makes Its Object* (New York: Columbia University Press, 1983). This book was reprinted in 2002 and 2014. For commonalities between Fabian and Spivak, see: Maja Alexandra Nazaruk, "Coevalness and the Self-Immolating Woman: Anthropology's Objects," *Global Journal of Anthropology Research* 4 (2017).

55 Gayatri Chakravorty Spivak, "Can the Subaltern Speak?," in *Marxism and the Interpretation of Culture*, ed. Cary Nelson and Lawrence Grossberg (Basingstoke: Macmillan, 1988). This essay has generated many responses and, recently, at least two monographs devoted to this question and the responses it generated: Rosalind Morris, *Can the Subaltern Speak?: Reflections on the History of an Idea* (New York: Columbia University Press, 2010); Graham Riach, *An Analysis of Gayatri Chakravorty Spivak's Can the Subaltern Speak?*, The Macat Library (London and New York: Routledge, 2017).

subaltern politics. A subaltern politics that addresses how to recruit and train subalterns ought to be an integral part of any emancipatory politics. In particular, I suggest that a successful politics to emancipate the masses from the rule of elites ought to include the conditions whereby the masses can create their own intellectuals, and that these intellectuals ought to be part of an accountable, open and democratic elite that is drawn from the masses and works for the masses.

This emancipatory and subaltern politics might have wide application, especially if it is true that with the emergence of the modern world system, and with ongoing globalization, there is a single struggle for the world, which in science manifests itself as a single struggle for objectivity that affects all those opposed to imperialist elites. For example, a very important lesson that I propose in this project is that *imperialist elites have uniformly employed divide-and-rule tactics*, which benefited from an ideology that sees one country or region of the world, which is claimed to share just one viewpoint, to be opposed to another country or region of the world, which is claimed to share a single antagonistic viewpoint. Both Said and Hallaq's work is dependent upon this ideology. I propose instead that there are many social groups and many viewpoints in every country or region, and even more in each of the major world civilizations, including Christianity and Islam. It is true that at times one of these social groups and its viewpoint might become hegemonic. In the case of imperialist elites, this is achieved also by exploiting divide-and-rule tactics based on ideologies that make it seems like there is a clash of civilizations. Said, Hallaq, and Spivak, whether knowingly or unknowingly, end up contributing to the power of these imperialist elites. I also propose that *the most important conflict in modern history is between imperialist elites and the masses*, on a global scale. Therefore, all those who have been subjected to imperialism at one time or another can and should learn from each other. I believe that an exchange between generalists and specialists from the West who are opposed to imperialism, and generalists and specialists from other parts of the world who are also opposed to imperialism, could be an especially important way of learning from each other, and would help us deal with European imperialist elites. This book begins to suggest how.

CHAPTER 4

A Humanist Social Science That Promotes Cultural Democracy

Gramsci's guiding concern with democracy included also the view that democracy has a cultural component that can aptly be called cultural democracy, and the significantly new theory of democracy that I seek to contribute to includes a theory of cultural democracy. I integrate the concept of cultural democracy within a full definition of democracy in the second volume, where I argue that cultural democracy should reinforce political-military democracy, while remaining distinct from it. Here I want to emphasize that *cultural democracy is important because it ensures the participation of popular culture in the cultural life of a country,* and makes sure that popular culture is not simply manipulated from above in order to advance the power of elites. In this chapter I want to emphasize that the humanist social science that I propose is informed by cultural democracy and promotes it. As pointed out by Jacobitti, Gramsci worked within a tradition of Italian humanism that includes philosopher Giambattista Vico and that suggested philosophy exists in a mutual exchange with common sense or everyday philosophy. This is based on a specific view of philosophy as something common to all men, and below I formalize this view into an anthropological-sociological view of philosophy and science. I also discuss concrete instances of this mutual exchange, firstly, in the manner in which philosophy and science can learn from popular culture, and secondly, in the manner in which they can learn from popular art in particular. I then detail how this learning from popular culture and art is central to my eclectic methodology for formulating theory. Lastly, I consider the manner in which the resulting theory contributes to popular culture, both through substantive theories that contribute to the needs of all citizens, and also by exercising a moderating influence upon culture that is especially important at a time of culture wars and in the wake of neoliberalism and the populist backlash.

4.1 Gramsci's Humanist Social Science and Cultural Democracy

In this project I suggest that *the humanist social science proposed by Gramsci was an integral part of cultural democracy.* There was a close inter-relationship in Gramsci's work between, on the one hand, philosophy and science and, on the other hand, popular culture. This is clear when we consider *the goals of Gramsci's project.* Frosini pointed out that Gramsci's prison work coalesced after a certain point around a few directions of research, one focused upon philosophy and the theory of history, and I would add social science, the other focused upon intellectuals, popular culture, and popular creativity.[1] Other Gramsci scholars have pointed to the importance that Gramsci attached to engaging popular culture and contributing to it, in a manner showing respect for popular culture, and a desire to encourage it and build upon it, which stems from a democratic view of culture.[2] This is also clear when we consider *the manner in which these goals fit into Gramsci's theory*. In his theory, hegemony, social science and cultural democracy form a group of concepts that reinforce each other. In order to achieve democracy in full, the masses, including subaltern social groups, must be able to formulate a theory that contributes to an alternative hegemony. A humanist social science that engages popular culture can contribute to this alternative hegemony by *genuinely incorporating popular culture in the formulation of social science.* This is the kind of social science that is produced by intellectuals who are organic to the masses, and that is part of the process whereby subalterns speak their mind and raise themselves and the rest of the masses to the intellectual level of elites.

This humanist social science is very important, because it makes Gramsci's emphasis upon the organization of culture, which is associated with his theory of hegemony, and which I expand upon in this project, *very different from the emphasis of totalitarian regimes upon the organization of culture*, which consisted largely or even exclusively in manipulating of culture. For example, it is based on a completely different attitude than the attitude of Fascists, like Mussolini himself and Alessandro Pavolini, the head of the Ministry of Popular Culture set up by Mussolini, who simply sought to manipulate popular culture.[3] I address fascists' manipulation of culture elsewhere in this project. Here I just want to emphasize that this is not what I am advocating. I want to

---

1 Frosini, *Gramsci e la Filosofia*. For an overview of how Gramsci's project took shape, see: "Realtà, Scrittura, Metodo: Considerazioni Preliminari a una Nuova Lettura Dei "Quaderni del Carcere,"" in *Gramsci Tra Filologia e Storiografia*, ed. Giuseppe Cospito (Napoli: Bibliopolis, 2010); "Note sul Programma di Lavoro sugli "Intellettuali Italiani" Alla Luce della Nuova Edizione Critica."

2 Alessandro Carlucci, *Gramsci and Languages: Unification, Diversity, Hegemony* (Chicago: Haymarket Books, 2014).

3 The name of the Fascist Ministry of Popular Culture started by Mussolini, the *Ministero della Cultura Popolare*, was abbreviated as *Min. Cul. Pop.*, which in a terrible irony is spelled almost exactly like the Italian slang expression for 'I screw the people'. One wonders if Benito Mussolini, who started the ministry, realized this.

underline instead that fascism, including its manipulation of culture, should never be underestimated or taken lightly, not even today, when we seem to have moved beyond it.

An important goal of this project is to continue instead Gramsci's effort to formulate a humanist social science that contributes to cultural democracy. This is based on a *distinctively humanist view of philosophy and science*, which emphasizes that philosophy, and in this project I extend the argument to social science, exists in a mutual exchange or dialogue with popular culture, in particular that part of popular cultural that Vico and Gramsci called common sense, which can be defined as everyday philosophy, at least as a preliminary definition.[4] This exchange has a normative aspect, because philosophy and social science do not exist simply for the elites, but have to contribute to the whole of society, and thus to popular culture. It also has a methodological aspect, and below I define in greater detail what I mean by methodological eclecticism, emphasizing in particular that it includes drawing informal observations from culture, including especially popular culture. The next four sections in this chapter all emphasize that the study of popular culture, and popular art, far from being akin to matters of opinion, is an integral part of social science, and that to take popular culture seriously and to learn from it is both good science and a contribution to cultural democracy. Instead of manipulating popular culture, this chapter suggests ways to engage with it, as a contribution to cultural democracy.

In this chapter I emphasize that *the mutual exchange between, on the one hand, philosophy and social science and, on the other hand, popular culture, works both ways*, which means that philosophy and science should not simply hand down answers from a high pulpit, like the Catholic Church did in the Middle Ages, or positivists did in the nineteenth century.[5] I do not address

4 Edmund E. Jacobitti, "From Vico's Common Sense to Gramsci's Hegemony," in *Vico and Marx: Affinities and Contrasts*, ed. Giorgio Tagliacozzo (Basingstoke: Macmillan, 1983).

5 I am thinking of Comte's view of sociology as a positivist religion, or 'religion of humanity', as discussed in: Terence R. Wright, *The Religion of Humanity: the Impact of Comtean Positivism on Victorian Britain* (Cambridge and New York: Cambridge University Press, 2008). This is a reprint of the 1986 edition. I am also thinking of Frosini's view that Gramsci's philosophy provided the 'religion of modern man', which is laid out in: Frosini, *La Religione dell'Uomo Moderno*. It would be interesting to compare this view of humanism with Thomas Jefferson's view. In this project, I propose a view of humanism that is very different than Comte's. I also propose a different view of philosophy and religion than Comte's and Frosini's views. Philosophy is something different than religion. As Gramsci emphasized, building upon Croce's view of philosophy, philosophy makes it possible to live without religion, for those who choose to do so. This is thanks to the fact that it provides a worldview that is typically provided by religion and serves to answer big questions that are also typically answered by religion. But philosophy does not replace religion. It is something different.

the whole of philosophy and science but *focus only upon theory* for reasons of space. Theory is an important part of social science because, as I argue in the book on humanist political philosophy, theory is an integral part of both philosophy and social science. Therefore, in this chapter I focus on the mutual exchange between theory and popular culture. On the one hand, popular culture can contribute to theory. In the rest of this chapter I argue that theory can draw from popular culture, not only the questions that it is necessary to answer, but also insights and even some preliminary answers. These can be provided by informal observation drawn from popular culture, which one then subjects to formal scrutiny. On the other hand, theory can contribute to popular culture. The latter, by combining informal observation with formal scientific observation and formal scientific method, can provide a valid and useful theory and fully worked out answers to social problems, enriching culture and contributing to the formulation of effective and successful policies. The last two sections concern general theory and detail the contributions that theory can give to popular culture. These contributions are both substantive theories that enrich popular culture and help citizens make choices, and also a moderating influence that is equally important in making choices.

4.2 The Anthropological-Sociological View of Philosophy

The humanist view of philosophy as engaged in a mutual exchange with common sense or everyday philosophy presupposes a specific view of philosophy and science. This is the view of philosophy as something common to all men, which means that the exchange between philosophy and popular culture is simply an exchange between professional philosophers and non-professional philosophers, a view that can be extended to science. This view of philosophy and science, which I formulate in greater detail in the book on humanist social science, can be aptly characterized as an *anthropological-sociological view of philosophy and science*, and the exponents of this view that I draw from in this book are Gramsci and Gellner. It complements the answer to Fabian's criticism suggested at the end of the last chapter, by applying to Western philosophy and science the same concepts that are applied to non-Western philosophy and science. These concepts are part of a broader, non-culturally specific view of philosophy and science that avoids, for example, claims that philosophy and science are distinctively European domains of knowledge. This view of philosophy and science is defined by two features, relating respectively to anthropology and sociology. This view also applies to theory, including general theory, which is an integral part of the humanist social science that I propose.

The first feature involves emphasizing the *anthropological aspect* of philosophy and science. *Gramsci extended the view of philosophy by relating it to culture.* In particular, he extended the German concept of philosophy as worldview in an anthropological direction, arguing that philosophy includes a worldview as a crucially important *component*, and that we all have a philosophy, because a worldview is part of culture, and also of the manner in which we interact with the world. In extending the concept of philosophy in this manner, Gramsci was building upon Vico's view of philosophy as including common sense, or everyday philosophy, and thus as something that we all use. Vico in his turn built upon ancient Greek views of philosophy that first formulated philosophy precisely in the form of dialogues with common sense, in Socratic dialogues most famously. *Gramsci also extended the concept of both philosophy and science by relating them to basic faculties* that we all share, because they are part of the way that the human mind works. He wrote that 'every man is a philosopher' and also that 'every man is a scientist', which respectively mean that every human being has the capacity to form and act upon a worldview, and every human being has the capacity to observe nature and society.[6] These are basic human faculties, not Western inventions. This anthropological view of science was also supported by anthropologist Claude Levi-Strauss, who made a point similar to Gramsci's regarding science in populations throughout the world.[7]

The second feature involves emphasizing the *sociological aspect* of philosophy and science. This is only implicit in Gramsci's work, and it involves extending the concept of worldview in a sociological direction, by emphasizing that *philosophy exists in all human societies and in all social groups*, which engage in the same basic human activity of trying to make sense of the world we live in, by providing a picture of this world. The same can be said of science, which involves providing rigorous descriptions of the mechanisms that explain how the world works. *The forms of philosophy and of science change according to the society and the social groups* within which they are elaborated. They range from the most sophisticated to the most rudimentary, depending first and foremost upon the type of society, rather than upon alleged cultural differences, or innate differences of the human mind, between different civilizations or countries. The most sophisticated philosophy is found in large-scale societies with

6 Gramsci, *Quaderni del Carcere*, 1346.

7 See the discussion in: Claude Levi-Strauss, *The Savage Mind*, trans. D. Weightman and J. Weightman, Nature of Human Society (Chicago: University of Chicago Press, 1966). This point is addressed in chapter 1 of Levi-Strauss' book. I address Levi-Strauss' work in the second volume, and the concept of 'mind' in the book on humanist political philosophy.

an advanced division of labour and groups of intellectuals, philosophers and scientists, who are trained and devoted entirely to formulating philosophy and science, and who in modern times are equipped with libraries, computers, laboratories, and other capital-intensive and technologically advanced means of cultural production. The more rudimentary type is found in small-scale societies made up of few individuals, with little or no division of labour, and little or no capital, and no specialized means of cultural production. In this project I build upon anthropologists' and geographers' work emphasizing the importance of population density and the scale of social interaction, and I suggest that these two parameters set limits on the achievements that a society is capable of, regardless of the faculties of individuals.

This anthropological-sociological view of philosophy and science is *especially useful to cultural democracy*. The normative aspect mentioned above regarding the exchange between, on the one hand, philosophy and science and, on the other hand, popular culture, becomes much clearer when we frame it in sociological terms. Gellner suggested that with modern industrial society there is a tendency for a 'universal high culture' to emerge, by which he meant a high culture that is universally available in society, and which he exemplified with universal literacy, to which we should add universal compulsory education and increasingly widely available higher education.[8] I discuss this concept in the book on humanist social theory. Here I want to emphasize that contributing to a universal high culture is an integral part of Gramsci's politics, which emphasizes the importance of raising the masses to the same intellectual level as the elites, which is something that I argue ought to form the basis of any emancipatory politics. This is not something that happens overnight, but is the result of long processes whereby some subalterns start breaking away from the elite and start formulating theories that respond to the needs and aspirations of the masses, also by engaging in a mutual exchange with popular culture. These theories can then be disseminated, and refined in this process, to ever larger sections of the masses, until all can speak, because a skewed distribution of power has been evened out, and because cultural democracy has been achieved, so that all have at least some access to the means to express themselves, and to intellectual tools that enable them to assess theories and make informed decisions about them, and also to contribute actively to the

---

8 The concept of 'universal high culture' was introduced by Gellner in: Gellner, *Nations and Nationalism*. This book had a major influence upon the sociological study of nationalism. It has been recently reprinted with an interesting new introduction as: Ernest Gellner and John Breuilly, ibid. (2008).

formulation of these theories, if they choose to do so. This is what a humanist social science seeks to contribute to.

4.3 The Contribution from Popular Culture to Theory

This anthropological-sociological view of philosophy and science leads me to a *view of sociology* that is comparable to the view put forward by C. Wright Mill, which has been recently taken up and expanded upon by Michael Burawoy, while differing from both of these sociologists in important ways. One way that I differ from them is that I do not subscribe to the concept of public sociology as some kind of public advocacy of good causes, as if a sociologist had to be part C. Wright Mills and part a celebrity like George Clooney, since nowadays many actors have taken on the role of advocates of good causes.[9] A better likeness to the ideal of sociology that I propose is provided by theorists like BouHabib, who have begun applying theory to specific policy questions like the brain drain from developing countries to developed countries.[10] In this case, public sociology is social science that is directly applied to policy questions. My main concern with Wright Mill's and Burawoy's approach to public sociology is that it can be manipulated to support a glamorous but empty version of sociology. Arguably, this is based upon advocacy of good causes by individuals whose main qualification is being famous, which hails back to the public role that the British monarchy invented for itself during the nineteenth century, as part

9 Actress Angelina Jolie, for example, has been United Nations special envoy for refugees for years. I gained this knowledge of celebrities' role as advocates of public causes through Layla Kaylif, a British-Emirati singer who wanted to reach out to popular culture through song. I am perplexed by this role of celebrities for two reasons. Firstly, it seems incongruous to me that very wealthy individuals wearing Prada, just to mention one famous item of conspicuous consumption, take on public causes aimed at improving the lives of the masses. Secondly, I believe that art should be part of politics, but should not be substituted for politics. I delve upon these points in the book on humanist social science and in the book on humanist social theory, where I discuss the inter-relationship between aesthetics and politics. For a study that conveys the sheer scale of the use of celebrities as UN Special Envoys, see: Francesco Morini, "Adapting Dynamically to Change in Diplomacy: A Comparative Look at Special Envoys in the International Arena," *The Hague Journal of Diplomacy* 13, no. 4 (2018). Recent scholarly work on celebrities as UN Special Envoys includes: Katharine A. M. Wright and Annika Bergman-Rosamond, "NATO's Strategic Narratives: Angelina Jolie and the Alliance's Celebrity and Visual Turn," *Review of International Studies* (2021).

10 I know from BouHabib that the European Union funds research into theory. Theory is seen as a useful discipline that can inform policy decisions by providing a synthesis of the social science literature and an analysis of the key questions and key concepts that are necessary to address a given social problem.

of an invention of tradition.[11] This public role has been continued to this day, for example by Lady Diana, or Lady D, her name as used in the press reflecting such fame that she was immediately recognized by her first name, or even just the initial of her name.

Another way in which I differ from Wright Mills and Burawoy is that I believe *there is no such thing as public sociology. There is only social science,* and all social science ought to have the function of contributing to the culture and politics of the masses and not just the elites, also through a mutual exchange with popular culture. Like Gramsci, I believe that this contribution ought not to be simplified or watered down, but social science should be made clear and accessible to all social groups. I also believe that this function belongs to all domains of knowledge and that philosophy is an especially important domain of knowledge, which shares this function with social science. However, many university professors today, partly because they are very specialized and confined to ivory towers with little contact with the masses, are ill-equipped to provide this contribution. I believe therefore that we need new and more innovative ways to organize culture, which include altogether different figures, including organic intellectuals who are close to the life and needs of the masses, and who are thus different both from celebrities and from university professors. Lastly, I also differ from Wright Mills in the *prospects that I attribute to the emancipation of the masses from the elites*. Wright Mills' seminal work, *The Power Elite*, showed remarkable prescience in foreseeing already in the 1950s the emergence of an establishment in the United States. However, it also contained the pessimistic view that the masses are at the mercy of powerful elites.[12] In this project I argue instead that the masses can emancipate themselves from elites, and that organic intellectuals are part of the means that are necessary to achieve this emancipation.

One way to achieve this goal is by making social science learn from popular culture, as part of the mutual exchange I suggested above. A central part of this mutual exchange is *informal observation, complemented by formal studies of popular culture*. Literary theorist Terry Eagleton has ridiculed

---

11 This historical phenomenon was described by a number of contributors in: Eric J. Hobsbawm and Terence Ranger, eds., *The Invention of Tradition*, A Canto Book (Cambridge and New York: Cambridge University Press, 1992). Aspects of this phenomenon that involved the British royal family and its display of power were more recently described in: David Cannadine, *Ornamentalism: How the British Saw Their Empire*, Oxford Paperbacks (Oxford and New York: Oxford University Press, 2002).

12 C. Wright Mills, *The Power Elite*, Galaxy Book (Oxford and New York: Oxford University Press, USA, 2000).

this, disparaging cultural studies researchers whose doctoral dissertation is written by sitting on a couch and watching many TV series.[13] I differ from Eagleton on this as well as on other points. It is useful to formulate this difference as entailing two sets of differences, regarding firstly the importance of leaning about popular culture and from popular culture, and secondly the methods to formulate theory. Learning *about* popular culture is especially important to this project, because culture is an important component of mass political mobilization, and this learning can start anywhere, and then be complemented by formal scientific observation. Learning *from* popular culture is equally important, because it is part of the humanist social science and cultural democracy that I propose. Here I want to emphasize that learning from popular culture can especially benefit from informal observation. It is useful to conceptualize formal and informal observation as lying alongside a continuum, and the difference between them being a matter of degree, not of substance. In the mutual exchange between, on the one hand, philosophy and science and, on the other hand, popular culture, formal observation is associated with the first, whereas informal association is associated with the latter.

This argument can be clarified by considering *the anthropological-sociological view of science and how it relates to qualitative studies,* which are based on a formal methodology used widely in social science. The anthropological-sociological view is associated, in Gramsci's work, with the view that there is much wisdom in common sense, especially in that part that Gramsci referred to as *buonsenso,* or good sense, but it lacks the internal coherence and the subtlety of philosophy and social science. This does not preclude the possibility of an exchange between philosophy and common sense.[14] This exchange is essentially an exchange between academic and non-academic knowledge, which are not as far apart as mainstream views of knowledge might suggest. In particular, we should not equate universities with science and the rest of society with non-scientific knowledge. As argued above, the difference between,

13 Terry Eagleton, *Literary Theory: an Introduction* (Oxford: Basil Blackwell, 1983). For Eagleton's views on criticism, see: *Criticism and Ideology: a Study in Marxist Literary Theory*, Verso Classics (London and New York: Verso, 1998). Another edition of Eagleton's book on literary theory was published in 2008.

14 For a review of Gramsci's theory of common sense and good sense, see chapter 5 in: Guido Liguori, *Sentieri Gramsciani* (Roma: Carocci, 2006). I think of common sense, and especially good sense, as a discipline, because it is a way of acquiring knowledge with the same dignity, though sometimes lacking in subtlety or breadth, as university disciplines. I addressed the importance of good sense for Gramsci in: Olsaretti, "Croce, Philosophy and Intellectuals."

on the one hand, philosophy and science and, on the other hand, popular culture, is a difference of degree. Similarly, *the difference between formal and informal observation is a difference of degree, not of substance.* Professional philosophers formulate worldviews, and scientists make observations, by going to greater lengths, and in a more formal manner, and with formal training, than anyone else, but at bottom they exercise the very same basic human faculties as everyone else, and simply follow more rigorous and systematic methods for doing so.

This is especially clear in the case of *qualitative studies, which include ethnographies, interviews, and participant observation.* Ethnographies involve systematically observing some social settings and the social phenomena within them, taking field notes, and carefully processing and labelling these notes through specialized software. Interviews follow a similar process, but use recording equipment. Participant observation involves actually participating in the social lives of different social groups, typically by living or working within them, and both taking notes and talking to their members. The formal observation associated with these qualitative studies differs from informal observation only in degree, not in substance, since these are activities that we all carry out to a greater or lesser extent, and more or less formally. Moreover, *the formal observation associated with qualitative studies presupposes informal observation.* All graduate students at the beginning of their doctoral research, and also established ethnographers at the beginning of a new research, start with research questions, and even choose their field of research, based on previous informal observation, and insights derived from informal observation. In other words, before undertaking formal observation, we always undertake some informal observation, and rely upon it as the starting point for formal observation. This informal observation can be crucially important to the success of the research, and we should not disparage observation made outside of the profession, or on the side of a professional project.

We should also not disparage observations made by non-professionals. To the contrary, *good sense and insights by non-professionals can be especially important insights.* A researcher can gain very important insights directly from participants in social processes, who might not have formal training, but have *first-hand knowledge* of ongoing social processes, and can thus have insights that, besides being as profound as those of professional researchers, are in some cases better informed. They just have to be worked out. Agents directly involved in economic, cultural, and political or military processes, such as entrepreneurs involved in these processes, no matter how small, are aware of changes in ongoing social processes long before university professors, and can even have a more realistic or more nuanced view of these processes than these professors.[15] The same is true for trends in job markets, for example. This means that social scientists should learn from good sense, whether through formal or informal observation, and then subject the insights that they gained to formal scrutiny, and elaborate upon them using a formal scientific method. *Informal observation can be very helpful also in the study of high culture, and of the interaction between high culture and popular culture*, and for this project my informal observation of university culture proved decisive. I also benefited from informal observation at companies that I worked for, and from many conversations with university professors, professionals and workers. The rest of this book works out in detail these and other insights, and proposes a general theory that seeks to make sense of aspects of popular culture, as well as university culture, and phenomena like culture wars and the withdrawal of university professors from public debate that affect us all.

4.4 The Contribution from Popular Art to Theory

The exchange just sketched out, and the importance of informal observations emphasized, can both be *applied to the study of art, including in particular popular art*. My view of the usefulness of art for social science is derived in part from Gramsci and in part from Ghosh, who used to include in the readings he assigned for history seminars also novels and short stories. Others have

15 I derive this view both from my reading of Gramsci and from my experience of qualitative studies. Szabolcs Kemeny first drew my attention to the importance of managers' knowledge of economic processes. This was part of his qualitative studies in sociology. I introduced him around 1988 to small entrepreneurs in the eye-glasses industry in Cadore, part of the Veneto region of Italy, where the industry giant Luxottica eventually emerged. Kemeny interviewed these entrepreneurs and discussed with me the functioning of this local industry. He similarly discussed with me interviews of managers in Hungary that he interviewed in the 1990s who were involved in the transition from state socialism to capitalism. It was only years later, after I started studying sociology and gained an experience of qualitative studies, that I got a clear sense that these economic agents had important knowledge of ongoing economic processes. Kemeny's work is not easily available but is very interesting. An example of his published work in English is: Szabolcs Kemeny, "Subcontracting in the Publishing Industry," *Logos* 7, no. 4 (1996). He also worked with sociologists David Stark and Ronald Breiger on a joint paper that was published in a Hungarian journal in two parts: David Stark, Szabolcs Kemeny, and Ronald Breiger, "Postsocialist Portfolios: Network Strategies in the Shadow of the State, Part I, in Hungarian," *Közgazdasági Szemle* (*Hungarian journal*) 47 (2000); "Postsocialist Portfolios: Network Strategies in the Shadow of the State, Part II, in Hungarian," *Közgazdasági Szemle* (*Hungarian journal*) 47 (2000). The English draft of this paper is: "Postsocialist Portfolios: Network Strategies in the Shadow of the State."

similarly argued that it is desirable to teach sociology through literature, and that it is even possible to derive important insights from literature.[16] There are two reasons for this. One is that literature is part of culture, and in a multidisciplinary social science that includes culture, informal observation contained in literature can contribute to social science. Another reason is that great art is defined in part by its ability to gain and to convey insights into individual behavior and society. Some writers' work is as insightful into the reasons for individual behavior, and how it fits in society, as that of ethnographers, it only conveys the insights using a poetic language and literary devices, as opposed to scientific language and the devices associated with scientific prose. This is especially clear in novels by Dostoevsky or Pirandello, both of whose work contains many insights into individual behavior and society, and were appreciated by Gramsci for this reason.[17]

It is useful to *extend this approach to popular literature, and popular art more in general*, and draw insights from it too, not just from great literature and high culture. Gramsci drew attention in particular to the importance of popular literature in shaping popular culture, and criticized the shortcomings of popular literature in Italy. I want to suggest that it is useful to extend this approach further and *include also new art forms like music videos*. These art forms are especially important to understand popular culture today, which is greatly influenced by such cultural products as music videos that are much more widely and readily circulated than novels or short stories, yet can have artistic value and can help us understand both language and culture.[18] The diversity of

16 Lewis A. Coser, *Sociology through Literature* (Englewood Cliffs, NJ: Prentice-Hall, 1972); Karen A. Hegtvedt, "Teaching Sociology of Literature through Literature," *Teaching sociology* (1991). This point has been recently taken up in an edited volume: Christofer Edling and Jens Rydgren, eds., *Sociological Insights of Great Thinkers: Sociology through Literature, Philosophy, and Science* (Santa Barbara, California, Denver, and Oxford: Praeger, 2011).

17 See entries on 'letteratura', on 'letteratura popoplare', and on Pirandello in: Liguori and Voza, *Dizionario Gramsciano*.

18 The use of films to teach about social themes that are central to a culture was introduced to me by Paola Quadrini, a teacher of Italian as a second language with knowledge of teaching both in the United States and Germany, and who is knowledgeable about Italian films, including Vittorio De Sica's, and used these films to teach Italian language and culture. This is apparently an increasingly common educational practice in foreign language courses, which complement the study of language with film and with topics drawn from cultural studies. For example, the department of French and Italian at the University of Indiana in Bloomington has professors specialized in Italian film. I find this use of film is an extension to new media of Ghosh's use of novels. I am suggesting to further extend it from film to artistic music videos. There is a multimedia company, VEVO, which is specialized in high-quality music videos and posts them on YouTube, where they have wide

formats of artistic music videos and the social themes they address is striking. I want to introduce some examples here to clarify how music videos can help us understand social themes that are central to popular culture and therefore to social science, and to counter Eagleton's disparaging comment regarding doing research by watching television series.

I want to focus in particular upon *music videos that comment on social themes*. There are videos on YouTube that are little more than slides, and hark back to the early days of multimedia, yet they can be very interesting conceptually for the view of music that they propose, as a commentary on historical events at another crucial time in American history than the 9/11 attacks, the long decade starting with events that led to the assassinations of John Fitzgerald Kennedy and Robert Kennedy, and lasting into the early 1970s.[19] This was a time that included earlier culture wars around American involvement in Vietnam, and the 'British invasion' that started in the mid-1960s and was spearheaded by the arrival of *The Beatles* and *The Rolling Stones* on the American music scene.[20] There are also videos that directly and explicitly address social

---

circulation. I refer below to some VEVO videos to illustrate the artistic quality that some music videos can achieve.

19 Lonestarsound, "The Day the Music Died – Don Mclean on Buddy Holly's Crash. YouTube video dated January 26, 2007," by audio and video producer Jim O'Neill, provides a remarkably interesting and sophisticated interpretation of the language in Don McLean's popular song 'American Pie', conveyed through visual clues regarding the significance of the poetic imagery in the song's lyrics. This is a view of poetic imagery in popular song that might have justified the award of the Nobel prize for literature to Bob Dylan in 2016. I derive knowledge of important details of the American culture of the time from the personal recollections of elderly Americans I had the opportunity to speak to, from the music of the time, including Bob Dylan and the Rolling Stones, and from the literature of the time, including novels like Philip Roth's *Portnoy's Complaint*. This novel, in my interpretation, depicts the excesses of the sexual revolution that only some music stars engaged in, but the novel seems perceptive in its depiction of everyday settings. One might debate how perceptive is the depiction, which seems to me stereotypical, of the relationship between the young Jewish man who is the protagonist of the novel and his mother, a model Jewish-American housewife who could be the embodiment of the ideal of 'Miss American Pie'. This is probably just a literary device to inject humor in the novel, with no other artistic value. However, the novel, first published in 1969, sold millions of copies and was republished as a cheaper paperback: Philip Roth, *Portnoy's Complaint* (Toronto, New York, London: Bantam Books, 1970). It certainly had an impact on American culture. What I think is especially important, instead, is the sophisticated interpretation of imagery and the perceptive view of American history and the earlier culture wars proposed in lonestarsound's video, a reading that can arguably be extended also to such books as Roth's.

20 For an overview of the 'British Invasion' and its place vis-a-vis the American music of the time, see: James E. Perone, *Music of the Counterculture Era*, American History through Music (Greenwood Press, 2004); *Mods, Rockers, and the Music of the British Invasion*

themes. For example, there are many videos that address themes related to sex, which began to be explicitly addressed in popular culture since the 1960s' and 1970s' counterculture, and the subsequent revolution in customs. These videos can present an idealized and restrained picture of sex, in traditional settings that complement this picture, like in the video on Julian Cope's song 'China doll'.[21] Or they can present a raw and even violent picture of sex, coupled with imagery from war and fascism and nazism in particular, with high-tech gear that nods to H. G. Well's and Jules Verne's novels, like in Lady Gaga's video 'Alejandro'.[22] There are also videos that address themes related to fatherhood and married life, like in Stromae's 'Papaoutai', or 'Where are you dad', and in Vasco Rossi's 'Come nelle favole', or 'Like in Fairy Tales', as well as videos that deal with friendship, growing up and, interestingly, with the desire for a better world, by Antonello Venditti and Lorenzo Cherubini Jovanotti, just to mention two big artists on the Italian music scene.[23]

(Westport, Connecticut and London: Praeger, 2009). A general view of the origins of British pop is provided by Billy Bragg, who went from searching a career in the British Army to becoming an outspoken Marxist singer-songwriter: Billy Bragg, *Roots, Radicals and Rockers: How Skiffle Changed the World* (London: Faber & Faber, 2017). For an overview of British pop and the role of music managers in creating staged differences to increase sales, see: John McMillian, *Beatles Vs. Stones* (New York: Simon & Schuster, 2013). Andy Bennett and Jon Stratton, eds., *Britpop and the English Music Tradition*, Ashgate Popular and Folk Music Series (Abingdon, UK and New York: Ashgate Publishing Limited, 2013). Culture wars can similarly accentuate differences. It is important to remember that Bob Dylan and Don McLean were just one side of the coin, and that in the culture wars of the time there were also Christian singers like Barry McGuire, with his hit song 'Eve of Destruction' of 1965, in which there seem to be echoes of the 1962 Cuban missile crisis.

21 DANA9918, "Julian Cope – China Doll. YouTube video dated March 17, 2012." There can be a negative use of art in these videos. The lyrics of Julian Cope's song include a line that is perhaps allusive to violence, 'feel my flailing arms around your neck China doll', but the beauty of the idyllic setting and romantic motorbike getaway ride shown in the video tend to gloss over or smooth over these allusions to violence.

22 Lady Gaga, "Lady Gaga – Alejandro. YouTube video dated June 8, 2010," VEVO. Singer-songwriter Nena also addresses themes that touch upon war, although her treatment of war has changed, from '99 Luftbaloons' to 'Licht', moving away from the explicit treatment of war, towards a more abstract and more artistic treatment: Nena, "Nena | Licht [Official Music Video]. YouTube video dated May 21, 2020," Nena store. I am reminded of a history teacher in high school, Walter Hetzer, who had lived through the 1960s revolution as a student at Columbia University, and told us an anecdote about someone mixing up 'lebensraum', or living space, with 'liebensraum', or love space. Lebensraum was the Nazi codeword for the mass murder and ethnic cleansing of Jews and Slavs in Eastern Europe. Hetzer had a point about the fact that war and mass murder are no longer acceptable in speech, and that the 1968 generation distanced itself from war and violence.

23 Stromae, "Papaoutai (Clip Officiel). YouTube video dated June 6, 2013."; Vasco Rossi, "Un Mondo Migliore. VEVO video on YouTube dated October 13, 2016," Vevo; "Come Nelle

These popular music videos should be subjected to criticism, and not just be consumed without reflecting upon their symbolism. Simply as an example of the criticism that I propose in this project, I want to express my view and personal reservations about Lady Gaga's use of imagery in her artistic video 'Alejandro', of indisputably high quality, yet being used to make a mix of Catholic, with fascist or nazi, and sex, imagery seem appealing. Similarly, her video '911' mixes imagery of Catholic missions in the Americas with orientalist images that exoticize and at the same time stereotype both Christians and Muslims, including Muslim prayer, and with dramatic images from emergency services.[24] I argue in the books on the humanist theory of society and on humanist political philosophy that we should recover Croce's concept of ethical-political behavior, namely, that both political and ethical considerations are central to human behavior. I extend this concept to aesthetics, but suggest that aesthetic-political behavior ought to complement ethical-political behavior, and not be alternative to it and make unethical behavior like fascist violence, or stereotyping religious persons, whether Catholic or Muslim, seem appealing. *These popular music videos should also be subjected to scientific scrutiny.* As far as their scientific value is concerned, a review of these music videos can only provide insights that have to be subjected to formal scrutiny and detailed analysis, but a review can be a very promising place to start. For example, insights from music videos suggest that there is a different treatment of sex in Italian popular culture compared to North American popular culture, which could be an especially interesting insight to subject to formal scrutiny.[25]

Favole. VEVO video on YouTube dated March 16, 2017," Vevo. Other videos show the angst when these values are denied, for example Jovanotti's 'Kiss me again', and Antonello Venditti's 'Night before the exams': Lorenzo Jovanotti Cherubini, "Baciami Ancora. YouTube video dated January 1, 2010."; Antonello Venditti, "Vendittivevo – Notte Prima Degli Esami. VEVO video on YouTube dated November 23, 2017," Vevo. The theme of a better world appears in Vasco Rossi's 'Un mondo migliore', or 'A better world'. 'Il migliore' was also Togliatti's nickname, in Italian 'migliore' can be used to mean both 'best' and 'better'.

24 Lady Gaga, "Lady Gaga – 911 (Short Film). YouTube video dated September 18, 2020," VEVO. Lady Gaga posts new versions of her videos.

25 The following is an example of the kind of insights that can emerge from informal observation of music videos. Famous Italian-American artists like Lady Gaga and Madonna have built a huge following with raw depictions of sex in the United States and English-speaking countries more in general. Interestingly, this seems to affect magazines. A very successful American photographer, Terry Richardson, has shot photographs with models and celebrities, many of which present a very raw image of sex, including pictures that allude to humiliating sexual acts: Terry Richardson, *Portraits and Fashion, Vol. 1: Portraits* (New York: Rizzoli USA, 2015); *Portraits and Fashion, Vol. 2: Fashion* (New York: Rizzoli USA, 2015). These two volumes contain collections of Richardson's work, and the index at the end of each volume shows this work has been printed on major magazines. By

Another interesting insight could be the different treatment of the mafia in Italian culture compared to North American culture. Most hero characters in Italian cultural products that deal with the mafia are or used to be anti-mafia, whereas the converse is true of North American cultural products, which show a domesticated view of the mafia and contain many mafia characters that audiences are encouraged to identify with.[26]

---

contrast, famous Italian artists have proposed less raw, and in some cases even idealized, depictions of sex, related to family, children and community. Jovanotti is a partial exception, for example his video 'Ragazzo fortunato', in which the lyrics provide depictions of restrained and even idealized sex, whereas the video shows another, raw and overly negative, depiction of sex. This is not to suggest that Italian culture is always less raw and violent. There are subcultures that can be very different from each other. For example, there was a subculture within the Italian Army, known as 'nonnismo', in which older recruits called 'nonni', or grandpas, hazed and humiliated, sometimes brutally, new recruits. This subculture might have been a left-over from fascist times.

26 This can reach into everyday culture. There is in Canada a small group of Italian-Canadian comedians, headed by Franco Taddeo, who specialize in ethnic comedy portraying Italian-Canadians that includes mafia gags. A whole generation of Italian-American actors has built their success using mafia roles: Robert De Niro, Al Pacino, James Gandolfini, all ended up playing mafia roles. Possibly the mafia has been brought to public attention in the United States by suggestions regarding mafia involvement in the assassination of John Fitzgerald Kennedy, and has recently been made acceptable by injecting humour and an everyday feel into mafia roles, as in the Sopranos TV series. My view of the mafia is that it is as brutal as the training depicted in Stanley Kubrick's film *Full Metal Jacket*, with Vincent D'Onofrio, which was possibly behind the 2013 tragic episode at Marine Base Quantico. I want to emphasize that this is *not* a negative reflection on the US Marine Corps, which has played an important role in United States policy since the First Barbary War under Thomas Jefferson. It is just a criticism of the military leadership that subjects recruits to brutal training. I also want to emphasize that in my view there is nothing funny about the mafia, which besides being brutal, is a serious social problem, police problem, and political problem. It is also divisive. Some Italian authors have blamed the United States for helping the Neapolitan mafia, the *camorra*, and possibly *guappos*, become powerful just after the Second World War, and similar arguments have been made about the Sicilian mafia, *cosa nostra*. My view is that the reality on the ground is more complex than these suggestions that pin responsibility on just one country or another. These suggestions ignore the truly international dimension of the mafia, whose networks stretch from crime into politics, and into different countries. For a recent take on organized crime in Italy by Italian mafia researchers, see: Antonio Nicaso and Marcel Danesi, *Made Men: Mafia Culture and the Power of Symbols, Rituals, and Myth* (Lanham, Boulder, New York, and Oxford: Rowman & Littlefield Publishers, 2013); Pasquale Peluso, "The Roots of the Organized Criminal Underworld in Campania," *Sociology and Anthropology* 1, no. 2 (2013); E. Ciconte, *Storia Criminale: La Resistibile Ascesa di Mafia, 'Ndrangheta e Camorra dall'Ottocento Ai Giorni Nostri*, Universale Rubbettino (Soveria Mannelli: Rubbettino, 2019).

I want to suggest that it is *necessary for social science to understand the criminal underworld, but that it is necessary to do so without pandering to stereotypes.* There are entire subcultures that include marginal social groups who live at the boundary between behaviors and practices that are legally allowed and those that are not, and also social groups that live to the other side of this boundary. It is necessary to understand these subcultures for several reasons. One reason is that these subcultures are increasingly important within our societies. They include mafias and drug cartels that reach wide into society and have built huge crime empires. They also include an entire social category, illegal immigrants, which has been recently created by globalization, and which is exploited by the criminal underworld, sometimes shading into it, as *some* immigrants end up participating in this underworld. *It is important to understand these subcultures because they have contributed to the rise of populism.* The importance to society of the law, and of the criminal underworld that it fights, is reflected in North America in the fact that criminology is often taught alongside sociology, and conversely that sociology often ventures to study crime and behaviors and practices that are at the boundary with what is legally allowed.[27] These studies are necessary, yet sometimes they end up simply reinforcing stereotypes.

It is important to understand the criminal underworld also because it can help us to understand mainstream culture. This is because it can help us, firstly, to understand culture as a whole and, secondly, to understand our own culture. These two points are related in what can aptly be described as a relational view of culture, which I address elsewhere. In Italy a former anti-mafia judge, Gianrico Carofiglio, became a writer and author of several successful novels, now part of a television series, which show remarkable insights into, and understanding of, the criminal underworld, gained from years of handling this world. Interestingly, Carofiglio does not just deal with the criminal underworld, but also touches upon the mainstream life of Bari, the city in Apulia where he was a judge, without pandering to stereotypes that all southern Italians are *mafiosi* or prone to a life of crime. He thus provides a picture of Bari's culture as a whole, which does not reduce southern Italian culture to mafia and crime, yet

27 Already in the early 1990s there were studies on the importance of criminology as a subfield within sociology: Ronald L. Akers, "Linking Sociology and Its Specialties: the Case of Criminology," *Social Forces* 71, no. 1 (1992). Since then, there has been a growth in the United States in criminology and related sociology courses and research, and there is a perceived need that it is important to encourage and regulate this growth, as exemplified by the report: Dennis W. MacDonald et al., " Report of the ASA Task Force on Sociology and Criminology Programs," (American Sociological Association, 2010).

takes them into consideration.[28] Bari has a very old university that, although affected today by the patronage practices described in Italy as baronial practices, has also produced interesting studies of ancient Greek philosophy and Gramsci, just to mention a topic central to this project, in the work of historian Luciano Canfora.[29]

Bari is also relevant to this project because it represents *different models of development*, and is the place where the Italian state and the Italian Army are introducing organizational and technological innovations comparable to those they introduced in northern Italy, in this case involving the Pinerolo

28 I am thinking of the following novels: Gianrico Carofiglio, *Ad Occhi Chiusi*, Le Indagini dell'Avvocato Guerrieri (Palermo: Sellerio Editore, 2003); *Le Perfezioni Provvisorie*, Le Indagini dell'Avvocato Guerrieri (Palermo: Sellerio Editore, 2010). These have been respectively translated as: *A Walk in the Dark*, trans. H. Curtis, Guido Guerrieri series (London: Bitter Lemon Press, 2011); *Temporary Perfections* (New York: Rizzoli USA, 2011). Other novels in the same Guido Guerrieri series have also been translated into English: *A Fine Line*, trans. H. Curtis (London: Bitter Lemon Press, 2016); *Involuntary Witness*, trans. P. Creagh (London: Bitter Lemon Press, 2005). This is possibly a sign of an increasing interest in contemporary Italian culture within North America, visible also in the increasing demand for language courses in Italian as a second language. Some other literary works are harder to translate, like works that rely upon very specific cultural jokes, and current cultural debates, for example: Daniela Carelli, *Vado a Napoli e Poi … Muoio!* (Ravenna: SensoInverso, 2013). Carelli lives in Milan but is from Naples, and her humorous novel comments on stereotypes about Neapolitans that became common in Milan, which gave birth to a populist secessionist movement that fed on these stereotypes, the Northern League. Carelli emphasizes the need for mutual understanding between northern and southern Italy, and the former Prime Minister and tycoon from Milan, Silvio Berlusconi, was in a long-term relationship with a showgirl from Naples, Francesca Pascale. I point this out in order to emphasize that realities on the ground are far more complex than stereotypes. An example of a subtle and sympathetic commentary on Sicilian culture, part of southern Italian culture, can be found in all of Andrea Camilleri's novels of the Ispettore Montalbano series, which had great success throughout Italy. Mutual stereotyping and misunderstandings between north and south have plagued Italian culture since Count Cavour's time. Count Camillo Benso di Cavour was one of the architects of the modern Italian state. I address Cavour's place in Italian unification in chapter 6.

29 Some of Canfora's work has received international recognition and has been translated into English: Luciano Canfora, *The Vanished Library: a Wonder of the Ancient World*, trans. Martin Ryle, Hellenistic Culture and Society (Berkeley and Los Angeles: University of California Press, 1990); *Julius Caesar: the Life and Times of the People's Dictator*, trans. Kevin Windle and Marian Hill (Berkeley and Los Angeles: University of California Press, 2007). Canfora has also published important work on Gramsci from a perspective that is radically different than mine: *Spie, Urss, Antifascismo; Critica della Retorica Democratica*, Economica Laterza (Bari: Editori Laterza, 2014). For example, Canfora focuses on the spy debates that surround Gramsci, which are highly politicized, whereas I don't.

brigade and the *Soldato Sicuro*, or Safe Soldier program, which includes applying IT and networking technologies to soldiers and their vehicles.[30] Carofiglio's integration of the life of Bari in his novels is interesting both because it rejects stereotypes, and also because it helps us understand how cultural identities arise according to a relational view of culture. I argued elsewhere, building upon a growing literature in social history, that in urban culture, in which different social groups live side by side, a cultural identity is often constructed in contrast to other identities, and that high and low cultures, and cultures that live within the law or outside of it, are defined vis-à-vis each other, in relation to each other, sometimes simply by being different than the other, by being unlike the other.[31]

4.5 The Eclectic Methodology, Rhetoric, and Theory

The approach to social science just described, involving a mutual exchange with popular culture, and relying upon informal observation of popular culture, including popular art, has implications for scientific method. It is important therefore to explain the methodological implications of this approach and *define my eclectic approach to formulating theory*. In doing so, it is useful to contrast my methodology and my philosophy of science with the methodology and philosophy of science advocated by philosopher Paul Feyerabend. Although I build upon some of Feyerabend's points, I differ from him in very important ways. One way is that, while *I reject formal scientific method that proceeds always in a set pattern, like Feyerabend did*, I also reject Feyerabend's answer to this, which he characterized as methodological anarchism.[32] I propose methodological eclecticism instead, one aspect of which *is to look everywhere for insights through informal as well as formal observation, and then subject these insights to formal scrutiny* and integrate them into a formal theory

30 These units and programs of the Italian Amy are described in the webpages: Esercito Italiano, "Brigata Meccanizzata 'Pinerolo'," Italian Army website; "Forza Nec," Italian Army website; "Sistema Soldato Sicuro," Italian Army website. The Soldato Futuro program has been recently renamed Soldato Sicuro. However, despite these investments, I know from discussions with IT professionals in central Italy that central Italy and southern Italy still suffer from brain drain, whereas I believe the technical training gained in these units should be used to encourage local economies and to facilitate the transition to civilian careers of former recruits.

31 I addressed this type of cultural processes and the literature on this topic in: Olsaretti, "Urban Culture, Curiosity and the Aesthetics of Distance.."

32 Paul Feyerabend, *Against Method* (London and New York: Verso, 1993).

For example, in the next chapter I explain that I follow an axiomatic-deductive method for formulating theory that is common to much of social science. Feyerabend's mistake is to reject one extreme in scientific method, which puts such strict rules that amount to placing a straitjacket upon scientific research, and then propose another extreme, which rejects all rules. Arguably, this is part of a tendency to formulate false dichotomies that is common in universities. I address its origins and propose answers to it in the book on humanist social science.

I also share Feyerabend's view that science involves rhetoric, and I would extend this insight to all human social activities, but I reject Feyerabend's response, which is to equate science with non-scientific domains, including magic.[33] Gramsci pointed out that unfortunately science is often perceived as a higher kind of magic, and criticized the philosophers and scientists who are responsible for this perception by presenting to the public a misleading view of science, or simply by making science seem difficult to understand and inaccessible to all except the initiated few.[34] What I propose instead is an *approach that sees rhetoric as complementary to science*. The opposition between science and rhetoric arises only when rhetoric is used to make false theories accepted. This is neither the only use of rhetoric, nor the most obvious and important use of rhetoric. Instead, rhetoric is an integral part of social activities, because in all social activities we need to make our goals and reasons clear to others, and this involves rhetoric. This point applies even more clearly to collective action, which is based upon shared goals, and shared means to pursue these goals.

The view of rhetoric that I propose calls for a language that is as clear and precise as possible, without however falling into extremes. This view is based on the premise that *there is nothing as persuasive as the truth, and the main task for rhetoric is to make the truth accessible*. Therefore, this view rejects obscure language as bad rhetoric. This view of rhetoric can be applied to science in at least two useful ways, both of which support the view that rhetoric and science are complementary. In the first way, I propose that we deal with science as a type of social activity, and that we view science and rhetoric as two moments or phases of a single process of production and dissemination of scientific knowledge. In this process both moments are necessary for the process to be complete. This process always has a social dimension, whereby after formulating a theory, one has to present it to the scientific community, and then to a wider public. Rhetoric contributes to the process, which includes acceptance

33 *Farewell to Reason* (London and New York: Verso, 1987).

34 Gramsci, *Quaderni del Carcere*, 1067–68, 1459, 1937–40.

by the scientific community, and I would say also by a wider public. In the second way, I propose that we extend the concept of science itself and relate it to engineering. I argue in the book on the humanist theory of society that science and rhetoric are complementary, because engineering criteria prescribe a certain rhetorical principle. The book on the humanist theory of society then proposes an engineering explanation of the golden middle rule, as part of an Aristotelian-Ciceronian approach to formulating theory and policy that rejects all extremisms, including theoretical extremisms like Feyerabend's.

This leads me to another difference from Feyerabend, whereby we use rhetoric to make science close to a wider public, but in very different ways. I want to explain this in detail because it *illustrates what I mean by bad rhetoric and how it is incompatible with science.* Some high intellectuals joke and cultivate an eccentric public persona as a way to reach out to their audiences. Apparently, Feyerabend was amongst these intellectuals, and cultivated an eccentric public persona that included riding his motorbike to university, and on one occasion a practical joke or stunt that involved at the end of a class jumping directly onto his motorbike, which he had parked under the window of the classroom that he was lecturing in, and speeding away, much to the amusement and hilarity of the entire class.[35] This public persona matched his methodological anarchism. It is apparently shared by some other famous philosophers, including Cohen, who joke in such a manner as to bridge the gap between the high intellectual who jokes and the audience, but this can be misleading.[36] The most serious problem is that high intellectuals are often incomprehensible because of the obscure language they use. This is the problem that we need to address, squarely, without just making the high intellectuals seem more personable. The latter can be of help, but only if it complements

35 Feyerabend's eccentric public persona is famous, and it was to some extent cultivated by Feyerabend himself, even in his autobiography: Paul Feyerabend, *Killing Time: the Autobiography of Paul Feyerabend*, Science/Philosophy (Chicago: University of Chicago Press, 1995). It is commented on by scholars who work on Feyerabend: John Preston, Gonzalo Munévar, and David Lamb, eds., *The Worst Enemy of Science? Essays in Memory of Paul Feyerabend* (Oxford and New York: Oxford University Press, 2000).

36 G. A. Cohen, who used to follow the established and very impersonal practice amongst British university professors of an older generation to use first name initials, also indulged in jokes with his students and there are even videos on YouTube of his jokes posted by students, who apparently include renowned comedian Ricky Gervais. Cohen's jokes might have had a serious intent, but I still find joking by university professors for the most part not very funny nor very useful. It now makes me think about the 'joker' character of popular fiction, who is not really funny, or about Neapolitan comedian Totò, who for all his jokes cultivated a very serious public persona.

reducing the gap between high intellectuals and their audiences, and bridging the language divisions between them.

Therefore, I differ from both Feyerabend and Cohen in two important ways, both related to the fact that *I rely upon a completely different rhetoric and methodology for building theory*. As far as rhetoric is concerned, the observations that I propose regarding popular culture are not merely a nod to the need to bridge the gap between intellectuals and a wider public through jokes or quirky observations. This is a real need, but I try to address it through a clear language that makes arguments accessible. The observations that I make regarding popular culture are all aimed instead at showing the relevance of theory to culture, including popular culture. As far as the methodology for building theory is concerned, I want to suggest that *the eclectic methodology that I propose might lead to valid and useful theories*, if only we keep an open mind regarding informal observation, and combine it with a multidisciplinary approach, all of which sets me apart from both Feyerabend and Cohen. In the book on humanist social science I provide an example of how a theory of hegemony can make sense of informal observations that one might be tempted to ignore, if relying only upon a formal methodology, but which can be very useful.

4.6 The Contribution from Theory to Popular Culture

I suggested above that in the mutual exchange between, on the one hand, philosophy and social science and, on the other hand, popular culture, philosophy and social science can contribute to popular culture. One contribution they can give is by providing actual substantive theories, another is by providing a moderating influence upon culture, including good rhetoric and appropriate rhetorical genres, which help assessing the substantive theories and any policies that might be based upon them. I believe that a general theory derived using the eclectic methodology just sketched out can be very useful for popular culture, as well as for cultural democracy and ultimately for democracy as a whole. Yet my choice to spend years working on philosophy and theory, at a time of mounting social problems and alarming political phenomena like populism, might raise some eyebrows. This is also because theories are often perceived today as useless appendages to social science, and social science to be all that is needed to formulate policies. Nothing could be further from the truth. I argue throughout this project that theory is very important for formulating and assessing policies, and is therefore important for everyone in a democracy, including policymakers and citizens. The importance of theory for policy is due to both of the contributions that it can give. I address the contribution

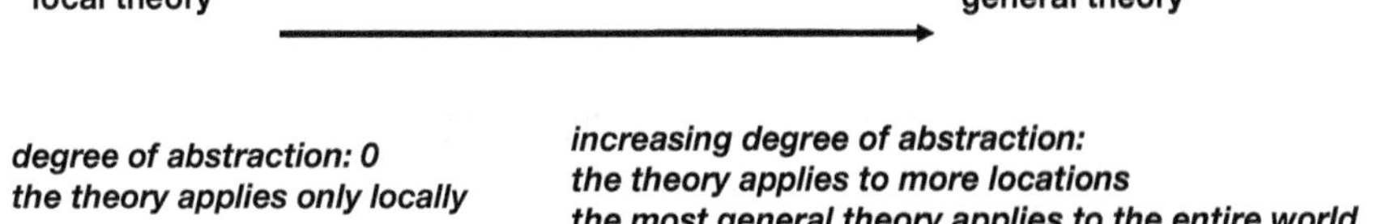

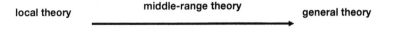

FIGURE 1 Theory alongside a continuum from local theory to general theory

through appropriate rhetorical genres and a moderating influence upon culture in the next section. Here I want to begin by discussing the usefulness of theory to policy, focusing on general theory, since it is understudied, and it is central to this book.

General theory is relevant to policy both indirectly and directly. To clarify this point it is first necessary to introduce *another preliminary definition of general theory*. I propose that we should distinguish between different types of theory and arrange them along a continuum depending upon the degree of abstraction, from local theory to general theory. I clarify this distinction in chapter 5, but to begin with it can be intuitively understood. Figure 1 depicts the continuum, as if it were a Cartesian axis: at one end of the spectrum there is local theory, which is very close to social science and empirical research; at the other end there is general theory, which is much more abstract than local theory and largely overlaps with philosophy, with the coordinate having the maximum value, representing the case of general theory that applies to the entire world, which is the most general type. In between, there is middle-range theory.

Figure 2 illustrates the additional consideration that it makes sense to refer to local-*range* theory and general-*range* theory as including ranges of values at each end of the spectrum, in addition to middle-range theory. This chapter and the entire book focus upon general-range theory, which I refer to simply as general theory. I believe all three ranges of theory are necessary, but focus upon general theory because it is arguably the most neglected of these three ranges.

The preliminary definition of theory I just proposed can help clarify the relationship between philosophy, theory, and social science traditionally understood as empirical science that informs this book. *Social science contributes empirical knowledge, which contributes to both theory and philosophy*, where theory is the crucial intermediary in this exchange, overlapping with both philosophy and social science. Typically, empirical knowledge leads to local-range theory that, when combined with other local-range theories, contributes to general theory. Another procedure is to abstract from empirical knowledge of

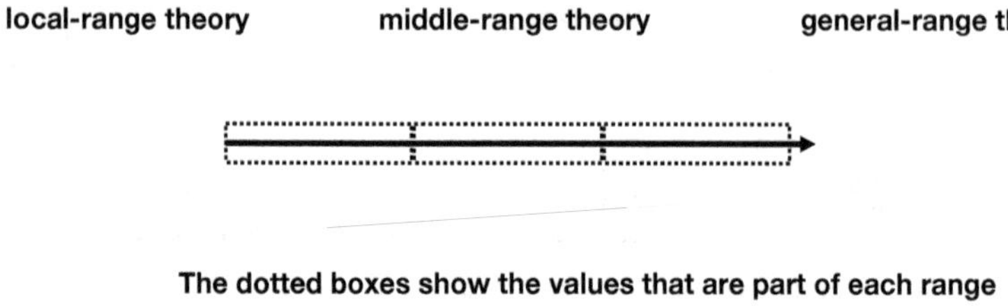

FIGURE 2 The three ranges of theory: local, middle, and general ranges

a locality and derive the most general concepts that one can derive, then refine these general concepts by checking how they apply to another locality. This approach to theory is close to Robert K. Merton's approach, in the sense that I share many of his concerns and part of his answers.[37] For example, I believe that theory exists in a mutual exchange with empirical research, and that both theory and empirical research are indispensable to social science. I also find the concept of 'theoretical work' useful, and I provide my interpretation of this concept. Lastly, I believe that an important part of social theory is the study of social structures and I combine the concept of social structure with the concept of social boundary emphasized by Tilly, and also with the study of social groups.[38] I come to share many of Merton's concerns not so much through a detailed study of Merton's work, but through my reading of Gramsci, whose work has been compared to work by sociologist Karl Mannheim and philosopher Karl Korsch, who belonged to the same generation as Gramsci and shared some of his concerns.[39] All three authors, particularly Mannheim, anticipated many themes in the sociology of knowledge, which was central to Merton's work and influenced Merton.

---

37 Robert K. Merton, *Social Theory and Social Structure*, American Studies Collection (New York: Free Press, 1968); Robert K. Merton and Piotr Sztompka, *On Social Structure and Science*, Heritage of Sociology Series (Chicago: University of Chicago Press, 1996).

38 The concept of 'opportunity structure' used by Tilly is derived from Merton. However, in this project I use the word structure to refer to something different than both Merton's and Tilly's use of the word, to mean actual structures understood as networks of individuals. I use instead the word interaction to refer to Merton's and Tilly's expression micro-macro linkages. On these concepts in Merton, see chapter 2 in: *On Social Structure and Science*. In chapter 6 I propose that there are influences between micro and meso collective action problems.

39 Harvey Goldman, "From Social Theory to the Sociology of Knowledge and Back: Karl Mannheim and the Sociology of Intellectual Knowledge," *Sociological Theory* 12, no. 3 (1994); Leonardo Salamini, "Gramsci and Marxist Sociology of Knowledge: an Analysis of Hegemony-Ideology-Knowledge," *The Sociological Quarterly* 15, no. 3 (1974).

I differ from Merton however in very important ways. Two of these ways are especially relevant here, and both are related to a *different understanding of the promise and limitations of theory in social science*. The first way is that Merton suggested severe limitations to theory that ended up promoting a marked emphasis upon empirical research in North America. I suggest that social science can benefit instead from a greater emphasis upon theory, to redress the current overemphasis upon empirical research. The second way in which I differ from Merton is that he completely rejected general theory. Merton suggested that the most that theory could achieve was to produce what he called 'theories of the middle-range'.[40] I suggest instead that there are many different types of theory that range from local-range theory to general-range theory, with middle-range theory in between. As emphasized above, the difference between local-range theory and general-range theory lies chiefly in the degree of abstraction. Local-range theory is the least abstract, since it contains concepts that apply only to a specific area, and only the concepts that are necessary to explain social phenomena in that specific area. General theory proposes the most abstract concepts, and while adhering to a sensible amount of theoretical economy, it also introduces as many causal factors as are necessary to understand as many social phenomena as possible. The theory that I propose in this book is as close to general theory as a I could get with my knowledge. It is a theory covering modern history in the West, which aspires to lay the foundations for a truly general theory with contributions from others whose knowledge extends beyond my knowledge, or fills the gaps in my knowledge.

Having defined general theory, as it applies to this project, we can address *the importance of general theory to policy*. Theory is *indirectly* important to policy through its importance for social science. I believe that a theory of society and history is necessary to social science and should be conceived of as an integral component of social science. It is necessary, for example, to address the trend towards ever increasing specialization in universities. This trend has the drawback that social science has become a very obscure enterprise for experts only, with no obvious relevance to policymakers and citizens, who have to trust the experts to a large extent and rely upon them for important decisions. The failures of neoliberalism are arguably associated with this trend towards specialization. Neoliberal economic theories promised greater economic growth

40 See chapter 3 in Merton and Sztompka, *On Social Structure and Science*. See chapters 1 and 2 in the following handbook, and ultimately the entire handbook: Peter Hedström and Peter Bearman, *The Oxford Handbook of Analytical Sociology*, Oxford Handbooks (Oxford and New York: Oxford University Press, 2011).

for everyone and instead led to the massive relocation of industry, and the impoverishment of the working class and of sections of the middle class and petite bourgeoisie. They are arguably an instance of specialized social science that has deceived some policymakers, failed citizens, and advanced only the interests of the elites, undermining the masses. This arguably led to the uneven development that affects Western countries and the rise of populism. I address the negative effects that specialization in social science has upon policy at some length in the book on humanist social sience, where I suggest that the aura of intellectuals is sometimes coupled with an obscure language, which in the case of neoliberalism and mainstream economic theory includes mathematical language. This makes it possible for some intellectuals to give the impression that they have some deep understanding of a field, and an unfathomable truth to convey, even when they do not, and to remain unaccountable, because it is very hard to pinpoint their claims, or it takes very long.

I argue in this book that theory, especially the general theory that I propose, is also *directly* important for both policymakers and citizens in a number of ways. One way is by providing broad pictures of society and history that are necessary to policy. A general theory of society and history, complementing the humanist social science that I propose, together with a humanistic education, can help policymakers and citizens with their choices without blindly relying upon the recommendations of specialized social scientists, because it helps assessing the reasons for the policy recommendations, and diverse policies. Another way in which general theory is directly important for policymakers and citizens is by providing, not just any broad picture, but a *significantly new* broad picture that can point research in new and more fruitful directions. This is the paradigm shift that I suggested in chapter 1 is necessary to overcome the shortcomings of mainstream economic theory today, including neoliberalism. I argue in chapter 5 at some length that general theory is ideally suited to achieve such a paradigm shift because it can produce new broad pictures in a manner that neither empirical work, nor theoretical work alone, can do. General theory includes extensive theoretical groundwork, which is a type of theoretical work focused on providing new and comprehensive syntheses of assumptions or axioms, the starting points of theory. The distinctive contribution of general theory is to arrange all these new assumptions into a new synthesis. This can achieve the paradigm shift and provide the significantly new theories of development and democracy. An important clarification is necessary here, namely, that this paradigm shift can be achieved, despite the apparently daunting nature of the task. Most of the important concepts that are necessary for the new broad picture can be found in different fields, and in different sub-fields within these fields. A paradigm shift is achievable because one has to re-interpret these concepts, and provide new syntheses and ultimately a new broad picture, not reinvent everything from scratch.

The direct relevance of general theory to policy can be clarified through two examples. The first example concerns the *usefulness of general theory for formulating social science questions that can inform policy*. Gellner proposed a broad theory of society that is complementary to Gramsci's theory of hegemony and that re-introduced in contemporary social theory the importance of culture. Gellner also drew attention to important changes in social structures and culture as societies transition from agrarian societies to modern industrial societies. From this vantage-point, Gellner suggested that the key question in modern European history, and by extension in the history of the West, is the replacement of aristocratic-military elites by economic elites. In the West, aristocratic-military elites are elites that prevail in agrarian society, whose status is transmitted from one generation to the next, and which are specialized in military power. Economic elites are factions of the bourgeoisie, and they grow in importance in modern industrial societies. However, and this is an important insight that I develop at length below, they never quite replaced aristocratic-military elites.

This complements a point made by Gramsci, that even in Great Britain and in Germany, where industrial development in Europe was most advanced already in the nineteenth century, aristocratic-military elites remained in power, only allowing other elites like the industrial bourgeoisie to pursue their goals to a limited extent and under the leadership of aristocratic-military elites.[41] In other words, aristocratic-military elites remained the hegemonic social group, the leading group in society. This is true even in the United States, which did not have aristocratic elites, but in which there are strong martial traditions exploited by political leaders like G. W. Bush and Donald Trump, whose demeanor is closer to that of military leaders like George Armstrong Custer and George S. Patton, than to civilian leaders. This is a problem, because aristocratic-military elites tend to be closed and not meritocratic, since their members acquire status by birth, and they tend to employ military means to achieve their goals. That is what they were trained to do, and those are the means they know how to use. By contrast, economic elites pursue economic growth, then the question for democracy is only how to ensure that this growth can benefit to the whole of society. If this view is correct, and I argue at length below that it is, then the most important goal for policymakers and citizens in a democracy is how to replace, or at least counter-balance, the

---

41 Gramsci, *Quaderni del Carcere*, 1526.

aristocratic-military elites with cultural and economic elites as the hegemonic social group. It is a goal that complements the goal introduced above of how to create organic intellectuals who are close to the masses.

The second example of the direct relevance of general theory to policy concerns the means that aristocratic-military elites have used to pursue policies. I argue in this project that *divide-and-rule tactics are historically a favorite means used by aristocratic-military elites,* whose power tends to include undermining the power of other social groups. As an example of divide-and-rule tactics, consider the following interpretation of the success of neoliberal policies. This interpretation suggests that the adoption and continued implementation of policies depends upon, not just how persuasive a theory is, but how much political support it can garner from different social groups and social movements based on their economic interests. This support can be due to short-term gains, which might then be undermined in the long term. A knowledge of past divide-and-rule tactics, together with axiomatic-deductive methods distinctive of general theory that I address in chapter 5, can lead to formulate a theory of neoliberal politics and how they affect the social bases of democracy, which I believe include both the middle class, traditionally seen as the bastion of democracy since Aristotle's time, and the working class, which has also contributed to democracy.[42] Therefore, divide-and-rule tactics that set the working class against the middle class can dramatically undermine democracy.

The following is an example of a theory of the politics of neoliberalism, which if found to be true, could be especially useful to policies that promote a more equitable development and greater democracy. Neoliberal politics first undermined the working-class through policies that encouraged the relocation of industry and initially benefited the middle class, because of the low cost of imported consumer goods. This involved splitting the working class from the middle class. These politics then began undermining the middle class, when relocation started affecting middle-class jobs like programming jobs for example, which relocated to India. This involved splitting the lower middle class whose jobs are relocating from the upper middle class, the top managers

42 Lipset has re-proposed Aristotle's argument that the middle-class is the bastion of democracy: Seymour Martin Lipset, *Political Man: the Social Bases of Politics* (Baltimore: Johns Hopkins University Press, 1981). More recently, Rueschemeyer and his collaborators have proposed that the working class is also important for democracy. These authors have undertaken a large analysis of the modern literature on social movements, in: Dietrich Rueschemeyer, Evelyn Huber Stephens, and John D. Stephens, *Capitalist Development and Democracy* (Chicago: University of Chicago Press, 1992). Lange brought this book to my attention.

relocating lower middle-class jobs and receiving high bonuses for saving companies IT expenses. Divided from the working class, the lower middle class is less likely to be able to reverse government policies encouraging relocation. Populist politics compounded this state of affairs by electing unscrupulous leaders with disgruntled working-class votes. These leaders further divided the working class from the lower middle class, for example by heightening and exploiting xenophobia, which exploited cultural divisions between the working class and the middle class. Eventually, both the working class and the lower middle class are impoverished, and neither the middle class nor the working class are able to defend their place in society.

4.7 The Contribution from Rhetoric to Popular Culture

In order for philosophy, social science and popular culture to engage in a mutual exchange, and to participate in formulating and assessing policies, it is necessary to engage in measured public debate. Philosophy and social science, also through general theory, can contribute to measured public debate in a number of ways, which include *exercising a moderating influence upon popular culture that is necessary to counter two techniques of power used by populism*, which go together: blaming scapegoats, and fostering bad rhetoric and a polarized cultural and political climate. General theory can help us respond in a democratic manner to these two techniques of power. Firstly, general theory *provides a sense of perspective,* together with well-thought-out answers that draw attention to such phenomena as recurrent features of world politics that are embroiled with globalization. I argue that these have to do with the struggle for the world that sees empires pitted against democracies, and that the camps are divided along lines that are surprising and in some ways counter-intuitive, but that they always involve imperialist elites expanding their power to other parts of the world and challenging democracies. Secondly, *general theory helps to promote good rhetoric, as opposed to bad rhetoric, which includes inflammatory rhetoric*. By contrast, good rhetoric proposes answers in such a manner as to avoid knee-jerk reactions or judgmental attitudes, focusing instead upon finding workable solutions, which is part of the moderating influence. In particular, a true theory conveyed with good rhetoric can have a moderating influence upon culture, and can point to workable solutions that avoid blaming scapegoats. I introduce at the end of this chapter the Aristotelian-Ciceronian approach to theory and policy that is part of the book on the humanist theory of society, as an example of good rhetoric.

Let us consider the first technique of power, *blaming scapegoats*. The general theory that I propose, by focusing upon past lessons, including the recurrent features of world politics, can *provide a sense of perspective that helps us avoid repeating past mistakes* especially by understanding important social phenomena that have occurred before. In the book on humanist social science I focus upon recurrent errors and I try to understand what gave rise to them. In the last 150 years there arose mass movements, by which I mean social movements with a large following, which have been manipulated through several techniques of power. This manipulation worked on the interaction between development and democracy, and it could take either of the following forms: as problems of development leading to problems of democracy or, conversely, as problems of democracy leading to problems of development. These techniques of power included blaming scapegoats, as part of broader social phenomena that include economic crises that heighten social conflict and that help movements like fascism and nazism, and today populism. For example, the 1929 financial crisis helped Mussolini and Hitler consolidate their power, also by blaming marginalized social groups and foreign countries, the working class with Socialist sympathies, Jewish communities, and the Soviet Union, while seeking protectionist measures that provided no permanent solution against the global financial crisis, which dragged on for a considerable time. The financial crisis of 2008 has had a similar effect in paving the way to power for populist leaders, who have similarly blamed scapegoats at home and abroad for problems of development, and proposed protectionist measures that similarly have not provided a permanent answer to these problems.

It is useful to put this technique of power, blaming scapegoats, in a *broader social context*. The manipulation of culture, including blaming scapegoats, is possible because of the move highlighted in chapter 2 from the hard military power of aristocratic-military elites to the soft power of cultural elites, which includes the *greater importance of culture in modern politics*. An important question to ask regarding the recurrent features just pointed out is: what are the conditions under which the above tactics or techniques of power work? The short answer is that these conditions include an increasing importance of culture. These conditions are partially described by the insight that the most important sources of power today are in the hands of professors of management like Andrea Prencipe at LUISS university in Rome, or actors like Bruno Ganz, who influence respectively the way we perceive of present and past development challenges, and the way we perceive of past challenges to democracy, rather than militaristic leaders like Mussolini and Hitler themselves.[43] As emphasized by Gramsci, political-military power is closely coupled with

43 I bring up this example, rather than the previous example of Haig and Churchill that I gave in chapter 2, since it is closer to the subject being discussed, fascism and populism,

cultural power, and cultural power is becoming increasingly important today. I add to this insight, however, that cultural power can be as brutal as political-military power, but in another guise that makes it less obviously dangerous, hiding in some cases the continuity between political-military power and cultural power. I believe that the greater role of culture in our societies is an improvement, but it is no guarantee that our democracies will not be subjected to challenges as serious as those of the past, especially if culture is in the wrong hands and is manipulated.

Let us consider now the second technique of power, *the use of bad rhetoric to create a polarized cultural and political climate and heighten social conflict.* The general theory that I propose can enable us to understand how bad rhetoric works and provide alternatives to it. Studying the bad rhetoric used by fascist, nazi, and populist leaders alike can yield important lessons that are useful to advance development and democracy. Criticizing bad rhetoric might seem redundant, since Mussolini's buffoonish posturing would be out of place today.[44] But it is important because *bad rhetoric can be damaging to democracy, especially if culture is militarized*, which is what is happening with the culture wars and the populism that builds upon them. In many ways Donald Trump's manner hails from an earlier generation of political leaders. I find it remarkable that such a long time was spent scrutinizing Trump's ties to Russia,

---

but the principle is the same. It is Andrea Prencipe, rather than a military commander like Giuseppe Cavo Dragone, the Commander in Chief of the Italian Navy, who has more power today. The latter is a modern military leader, and as such relies upon the same sources of power as Mussolini, who built his power on military and paramilitary units, but today significant power rests upon those who make plans, who are often an intellectual establishment that is unresponsive to pressures from below.

44 I have allowed myself this one deviation from measured public debate, by defining Mussolini's posturing buffoonish, because the word buffoonish describes it well in several ways, some obvious, others less so. If one watches videos of Mussolini's speeches it becomes clear that his posturing was so excessive as to be almost a caricature. Other words than buffoonish do not adequately describe it. Moreover, enough time has passed since Mussolini's days, and most Italians are detached enough from Mussolini's politics, with only a few exceptions, which are growing in number, however. Had Benito Mussolini been alive and still attempting to corrupt politics and culture, it would be more important to discuss his manners in a detached way and show what was wrong with them. I do this too in this project. I just want to point out that in popular culture macho attitudes that border on caricature can still be found, for example in Richardson's photographs of a François Sagat: Richardson, *Portraits and Fashion, Vol. 2: Fashion*, 286–288. The tight t-shirt might allude to gay sex, and implicitly stereotypes gay men. To Italians, the maroon beret and the sand-coloured boots might signify the Folgore brigade of the Italian Army, sacrificed by Mussolini in the North Africa campaign. This too makes Richardson's photographs problematic.

and so little discussing his cultural ties to fascist and nazi ideologies and the political circles in Italy and Germany that are promoting their resurgence.[45] It seems to me that Nancy Pelosi's efforts to impeach Trump for his ties to Ukraine and Russia were doomed to failure. I also find it remarkable that there is no detailed study comparing Trump to Patton, to understand the militarism that is creeping into American politics since the 9/11 attacks, through the culture wars, and through new forms of communication in the age of the internet and twitter.

Bad rhetoric can be damaging to democracy also for other reasons. *Bad rhetoric encourages short-term responses, such as angry knee-jerk reactions*, and thus undermines deliberate and sustained collective action. Patton, it should be remembered, caught public attention with his tough talk about killing Germans, rather than nazis, and then apparently ended up cooperating with a number of former nazis in reconstructing Germany, despite the fact that the horrors of nazism, including the Holocaust and the crimes of nazi doctors, were already surfacing.[46] I believe this was not despite the talk of killing Germans, but because of it. Back then, like today, *aggressive language and xenophobia were used to build quick fame through sound-bites* blaming scapegoats and promising quick solutions, which were as quickly forgotten as they had been uttered, and were replaced by other goals that served the immediate interests of the proto-populist leader using these sound-bites and of the elite of the time, like Dwight D. Eisenhower. In this context, a question to ask would be whether Trump would have done something similar to Patton and built ties to Mexico if there were real estate opportunities for investment there,

---

45 There is a resurgence of interest in Benito Mussolini and Adolf Hitler that was promoted by politicians with a different face. In Italy Silvio Berlusconi started a cultural revisionism of Fascism, initially as a critique of some communist anti-fascists, and then moved on to creating political alliances with parties that were ideologically close to fascism, like Alleanza Nazionale, and to elect politicians, like Mussolini's granddaughter Alessandra Mussolini, who are more or less openly supportive of Benito Mussolini, or who failed to distance themselves from this dictator as other politicians in Italy did. There are similarities between these politicians and Trump. In the United States this was pointed out by diplomats and financiers in the press, and by one historian: Ruth Ben-Ghiat, "Donald Trump and Benito Mussolini," *The Atlantic*, August 10th 2016. However, it seems not to have been the subject of any academic study.

46 On Patton's biography and controversial activities, see: Carlo D'Este, *Patton: A Genius for War* (New York: HarperCollins, 1996); Alan Axelrod, *Patton: a Biography*, Great Generals (New York: St. Martin's Press, 2015). For an example of the enduring popular history interest in Patton, see the Summer 2020 special issue of the magazine *WWII History*: Kevin M. Hymel, ed. *WWII History Presents: Patton's Battles*, Collector's Edition (WarfareHistoryNetwrok.com, 2020).

or particularly attractive opportunities to invest in garments or accessories factories.

There is a similarity and continuity between Patton and Trump, which can usefully be conceptualized by *extending philosopher Ludwig Wittgenstein's concept of 'family resemblance'*, which in Wittgenstein's work was a linguistic point concerning the similarities between words. The concept of family resemblance is part of Wittgenstein's philosophy of language and is related to the concept of 'language games', which I address in the book on humanist social science.[47] Here I want to anticipate that language games are a way to describe the use of words, or of numbers I would add, which relies on words being close in meaning to each other, but not quite the same. It is analogous to number games similar to mathematical series.[48] This is not to say that Patton and Trump *actually* resemble each other, as family members would, or like the Italian name Renato, literally 'born again', which is given to remember a father

47 The concept of 'family resemblance' was put forward by the later Wittgenstein: Ludwig Wittgenstein and Gertrude Elizabeth Margaret Anscombe, *Philosophical Investigations: the German Text, with a Revised English Translation* (Oxford: Basil Blackwell, 2001). This important text was first published in 1953 and then republished in 1968. I address Wittgenstein's philosophy of language and the concept of 'language game' in the book on humanist social science.

48 I find the following to be a good example of language games that use family resemblance, applied to numbers as opposed to letters. This example also raises the important point that there is a complex relationship between science and language, which I begin to address in the book on humanist social science. Language games can be involved in classifications that are not scientific. Mathematics professor Shirey taught us students at UWC Adriatic to identify mathematical series of numbers and tell them apart from a random sequence of numbers, since mathematical series are generated by a formula. A simple mathematical series is: 1, 2, 4, 8. These numbers are all powers of 2, generated by the formula 2^n, so that the numbers are generated as: 2^0, 2^1, 2^2, 2^3. This commonality by formulas is not the same thing as the similarity in the linguistic concept of family resemblance. This can involve classifying different things in one group or set, by one or more attributes that they have, and it involves similarity, not a common generating formula. For example, the following three types of explosives can all be represented by the number 67: TNT, which was invented in 1867; PENTA, a component of plastic explosives, which has an effectiveness factor of 1:66, that is, the explosive power of 1 gram of PENTA is the same as that of 66 grams of TNT, so that if they are used together, they add up to 67; detonation chord with explosive velocity of 6.7 km/s. The point here is that 67 is not a generating formula as in mathematical series, nor a scientific classification, but a linguistic classification that draws from similarities between words or numbers. In this case these are similarities regarding features that are not scientifically comparable, such as year of invention, and explosive power. 67 in this example could be simply a linguistic label that aids communication, or a memory aid, both of which are important functions of language other than scientific classification, which are additional to scientific classification.

or grandfather. It is instead to make a point regarding cultural symbolism and leaders. Not only some of the language they use has similarities, but they share an entire rhetorical genre based upon inflammatory rhetoric, which includes similar posturing, for example aggressive or mocking posturing. I argue in the book on humanist social science that the combination of language with posturing is an important point in Gramsci's theory of language. Here I want to emphasize that totalitarian and populist leaders share a type of language and posturing that does make them look alike, and that this is a problem for democracy.

Inflammatory rhetoric is a type of bad rhetoric and is a component of a rhetorical genre that is part of the recurrent tactics or techniques of power used by imperialist elites. In comparing the language of political leaders, we can focus like Wittgenstein upon specific words and show that the exact same word is used, or that a similar word is used, in speech. Or we can focus upon entire rhetorical genres. We would then see the similarity between Mussolini's and Trump's languages. These observations are not due to an anti-Republican bias on my part. Far from it. I think that Barack Obama's and Joe Biden's language and posturing shares important traits with G. W. Bush's and Trump's language and posturing, and that if a thorough study was made of their language and posturing, carefully comparing one leader to the other, it would reveal all four to be populist leaders, and all to be part of one establishment trying to reinvent itself in order to remain in power, by 'changing everything in order not to change anything'.[49] Arguably, Rudolph Giuliani re-introduced in contemporary American politics the tough language and posturing of earlier generations of leaders, or possibly even initiated it, if we focus on the novelties in this language and posturing since Custer's and Patton's days.

During this project I was reminded on a number of occasions of *the ancient pedigree of bad rhetoric and also of the new opportunities that we have to move past it.* One occasion was a few years ago, before Trump's election, when I found myself passing through Arpino, a village in central Italy that is the birthplace of ancient Rome's republican statesman and philosopher Cicero, and wondering

49 This expression was coined by Sicilian novelist Tomasi di Lampedusa: Giuseppe Tomasi di Lampedusa, *Il Gattopardo*, I Narratori di Feltrinelli (Milan: Feltrinelli, 1985). This book, first published in 1958 in Italy, went through many editions in Italy and was translated into English as: Giuseppe Tomasi di Lampedusa and Gioacchino Lanza Tomasi, *The Leopard: Revised and with New Material*, trans. Archibald Colquhoun and Guido Waldman (London: Vintage Books, 2010). This tactic or technique of power is associated with the concept of *trasformismo*, which is part of Italian political discourse. As it applies to recent politics, this technique is based on proposing or even implementing sweeping changes with a dramatic appearance that however leave the same establishment in power.

about the abuse of rhetorical arts and what it means for democracy.[50] Trump's subsequent election was another such occasion, and it reminded me that the power of rhetoric, and the threat it poses if it is in the wrong hands, has only increased with the rise of new means of communication like the internet and Twitter. Even West Point, whose graduates have experienced the brutality of war and militaristic leaders first-hand, seems to have forgotten this, as it is still home to a statue of Patton. Cicero was assassinated during the turmoil that led to the decline of the Roman republic and its replacement with the Roman empire, but compared to that time we have a vast knowledge of social science and the conditions that favor or undermine democracy, and compared to Patton's time we have a vast knowledge of the cultural bases of democracy, thanks in no small part to Gramsci. All of this makes it both more important and feasible to recover good rhetoric and a balanced approach to formulating theory and policy.

General theory, which is an integral part of the humanist social science that I propose, can help us also to *formulate alternatives to bad rhetoric*, including especially the bad rhetoric that has fueled fascism and populism alike. The Aristotelian-Ciceronian approach proposed in the book on the humanist theory of society is essentially a reformulation and justification based on general theory of the golden middle rule that was advanced in different ways by both Aristotle and Cicero. This golden middle rule rejects extremisms and can help us provide a moderating influence on culture and public debate that is especially important at a time of culture wars. The Aristotelian-Ciceronian approach can also contribute at one and the same time to formulating more balanced theory and more balanced policies. This should enable us to secure both development and democracy for a very long time, if not forever, since

50 I have also wondered about the loss of community and social ties. I explored for a year or so the new world of internet communities, also through Meetup groups like the Skeptics, Atheists and Secular Humanists Meetup group and the Casual Friends Meetup group that met in Montreal around 2016. I discovered a form of society half-way between real society and the virtual world, which was new to me, and I became aware of the use of shopping malls like the Alexis Nihon shopping mall, in a city that at the same time has many bike lanes and boutique bicycles stores like Velo s'a Coche and Velodidacte, as centers of this new social life that uses the internet and Twitter for instant communication. It exists alongside gentrifying old neighborhoods like Verdun and its Wellington street, and Notre Dame de Grace, or NDG. I ended up gaining many important insights, but I never found any community nor true social ties in this form of society. This helped me conceptualize how knowledge societies can develop, a point I discuss in the books on humanist urban and regional planning, and the book on the humanist theory of history.

not even diamonds are forever, despite what some *impresarios* might suggest.[51] It should be possible to build an alternative hegemony that includes cultural democracy and uses good rhetoric. Cultural democracy and good rhetoric can in their turn help us to leverage social structures and to encourage deliberate and sustained collective action by the masses, and thus to achieve a more equitable distribution of power and of the fruits of development. This book begins to suggest how.

51 I am referring to James Bond movies like *Never Say Never Again*, or *Diamonds are Forever*, starring Sean Connery and Kim Basinger. James Bond as a cultural icon has been the subject of academic studies, starting with Tony Bennett's book, which contributed to the emerging field of cultural studies: Tony Bennett, "James Bond in the 1980s," *Marxism Today* 27, no. 6 (1983); Tony Bennett and J. Woollacott, *Bond and Beyond: the Political Career of a Popular Hero*, Communications and Culture (Basingstoke: Macmillan Education, Limited, 1987). It is important to add criticism to these studies. In my view, one fault of the James Bond movies and the popular literature they are based on is that they are sensationalist and build upon base and raw emotions. This feature seems to me to have become worse with time. It would be interesting to make a study of the changes in the James Bond and the Bond girl characters since *Never say Never Again*, or *Diamonds are Forever*, and of the different interpretations provided by Roger Moore, Sean Connery and Pierse Brosnan, all actors who played James Bond. At the same time, the basic ingredients of Bond stories have remained the same, just increasing sensationalism, which to me is a sign of lack of cultural innovation and progress. I argue in this project that this impoverishment of popular culture is due also to economic considerations alone being applied to cultural products, and encouraging the production of cultural products just for a quick profit. For this, as well as for other reasons, there is a need for the cultural arena to be kept separate from the economic arena. If in popular fiction there had been a 001, this character would have profit and power, the two are closely related, as his first and only motives. Interestingly, intelligence officers themselves are contributing to this popular fiction. Novelist John Le Carre was apparently an intelligence officer in MI6 before becoming a writer, and Ian Fleming, the author of the James Bond novels, was apparently a naval intelligence officer. Fleming has become himself an icon and entire books have been devoted to him: Edward P. Comentale, *Ian Fleming & James Bond: the Cultural Politics of 007* (Bloomington and Indianapolis: Indiana University Press, 2005); Ben Macintyre, *For Your Eyes Only: Ian Fleming and James Bond* (London, Berlin, New York: Bloomsbury, 2009); John Pearson, *The Life of Ian Fleming* (London, Berlin, New York: Bloomsbury, 2011). Similarly, Connery served in the Royal Navy, which possibly exercises a cultural influence also through the sheer numbers of those who worked for it, and the prestige that some of them acquire. Nicholas Dew pointed out to me the continued prestige of Oxford and Cambridge Universities for all professionals to this day, and thus the continued prestige of an academic career at these institutions, but careers as writers and acting careers might be growing in importance, even in Great Britain, where tradition is very important and where many cultural products cater to the elites.

PART 3

The Methodology and the Hypotheses and Theses of the Project

∵

The Problem of Political Leadership in the Making and Development of the Nation and of the Modern State in Italy

The entire problem regarding the connection between the various political currents in the Risorgimento, that is, [the problem of their] relations with the homogeneous or subordinate social groups that existed in the various historical sections (or sectors) in the national territory can be reduced to this fundamental fact: *the moderates [Cavour's party] represented a relatively homogeneous social group, so that their leadership underwent only relatively limited oscillations* [...] *whereas the so-called Action Party [Garibaldi and Mazzini's party] did not base itself upon any historical class* [but only on volunteers from disparate social groups], and the oscillations it underwent were in the last instance influenced by moderates' interests: that is, the Action Party historically was led by the moderates: the statement attributed to Victor Emmanuel II [the Duke of Savoy and later King of Italy] to have the Action Party "in his pocket," or something of this sort, is practically correct, and not just because of the personal contacts between the King and Garibaldi, but because in fact the Action Party was directed by Cavour and the King.

Antonio Gramsci, *Prison Notebooks*, Notebook 19, Note 24, p. 2010. My emphasis.

∵

CHAPTER 5

The Theory, and the Hypotheses and Theses on Elites

This book proposes a general theory of development and democracy. It is appropriate therefore to *begin by defining theory and showing why it is important.* Theory occupies a central place in this book and also in other books that are part of this project. As sketched out in the introduction, there are three arguments and theories that run through this entire book. The three theories are: first, the meta theory, concerning the definition and importance of theory, together with the eclectic methodology I used to formulate theory; second, the theory regarding neoliberalism and the populist backlash; third, the general theory of development and democracy. This chapter focuses upon the meta theory, and at the same time it introduces some important hypotheses and theses that are part of the theory regarding neoliberalism and the populist backlash. These hypotheses and theses serve also to clarify the usefulness of the meta theory, because they show how the meta theory applies to the substantive arguments regarding neoliberalism and the populist backlash. This chapter thus provides a defense of the usefulness of theory, and of general theory in particular, by arguing and exemplifying how useful theory can be. I especially *focus on the usefulness of general theory to overcome problems of specialization.* The next three sections define the problems in knowledge that arise from academic specialization and that constitute what Gramsci called 'partial and erroneous ideologies', the main instances of which are one-sided pictures of society and history, which lead to reductive scientific models based upon these one-sided pictures. I next define the two main types of academic specialization that I seek to address, suggesting in each case the exact flaws in knowledge that they lead to. I suggest that a general theory that is not domain specific, and that is built using extensive theoretical groundwork and thoroughly scrutinizing assumptions, can help us overcome specialization and these problems in knowledge. The rest of this chapter shows that general theory can address all these problems related to specialization and is useful also to understand neoliberalism and the populist backlash.

5.1 Specialization and the Origins of One-Sidedness

It is useful to begin by clarifying what are the *problems in knowledge arising from academic specialization* that I seek to address. Specialization is a problem because most university professors today do research that is so specialized that they invariably lose sight of the forest for the trees. This means that they themselves lack, and fail to provide to others, the broad picture of society and history that I argued is very important for policymakers and citizens. In particular, this project seeks to address the *problems in knowledge associated with two types of specialization* that are very common in research today. The first type is specialization in studying different domains of human activity, each of which is the focus of a separate academic field of knowledge: the economy is studied by economics, culture by cultural studies, politics by political science, and the military by military science. The second type is specialization that arises from an exclusive focus upon empirical research, which leads to theories that are exclusively local-range theories. Each one of the next two sections considers one of these two types of specialization. Before moving on to this discussion, I want to clarify how these problems of specialization relate to one-sidedness and reductiveness, because of the importance of overcoming partial pictures.

One-sidedness and reductiveness are two very common features of partial ideologies that arise because of specialization. *One-sidedness refers to partial pictures of reality*, which are close to a worldview, but which consider only one side of the picture, as if there were self-contained economic, or cultural, or political and military processes. The first type of specialization is associated with the most common type of one-sidedness in social science, namely, considering only one of the domains of human behavior, the economic, cultural, political, or military domain, and ignoring the other ones, whereas most of us are involved in three or four of these domains, and most processes in society are affected by all four of these domains. Specialization can also lead to even narrower one-sidedness, whereby, for example, some scholars focus on studying culture alone, and furthermore consider culture only as expressed values, an example that I address below.

Reductiveness refers to *partial scientific models,* which rely only upon one-sided worldviews. It is essentially a type of *over*-simplification in scientific models. Reality is very complex, and scientific models are useful if they simplify reality by focusing upon just a small number of factors. This is what theoretical economy seeks to achieve. However, models must still be able to predict real outcomes, and this requires that they should not *over*-simply. Reductiveness has another aspect, which involves over-simplification across fields. Much of mainstream economics is reductive because it tries to model human behavior by taking into consideration economic behavior alone, and furthermore considers economic behavior only as acquisitive individualism, which entails competing with other individuals in order to maximize one's profits, neglecting the importance of team spirit, for example, which is central to productiveness. This is bad enough when applied to the economy. Over-simplification across fields arises because there is a strong tendency in social science to apply these reductive economic assumptions to other fields and reduce culture or politics, which are different, to already reductive economic views of individual behavior. Multidisciplinary approaches try to overcome one-sidedness and reductiveness.

My approach to one-sidedness and reductiveness is an extension and elaboration of *Gramsci's concern with partial and erroneous ideologies,* which include theories. Between partial and erroneous ideologies, erroneous ones pose the lesser theoretical and political difficulties. From a theoretical point of view, it is relatively easy to identify and build arguments against ideologies that are erroneous. From a political point of view, it is easier to convince audiences that an ideology is erroneous, because we are all trained to some extent to spot errors, and the concept of error is widely understood and widely recognized. By contrast, partial ideologies pose a more serious problem, both theoretically and politically. These theories are not erroneous, but *over*-simplifications of reality. What is worse, these over-simplifications are backed up by the institutional compartmentalization of knowledge in universities. Therefore, it becomes harder to spot a partial ideology. For example, a work on economics is circulated only in economics departments or on economics journals, and it is read only by economists, who share many of the same assumptions, having been trained in economics departments. This leads to a form of tunnel vision, or difficulty in thinking outside of the economics box.

As I use these concepts, *one-sidedness and reductiveness are related to partial ideologies*. One-sidedness is one type of partial ideology that focuses on only one side of a picture. Starting from one-sided pictures, theorists build reductive models, and combine several such reductive models in a faulty theory, which works some of the times, but fails at other times. Or which works initially, but fails in the long run. The sketch of a theory regarding neoliberal politics introduced in chapter 4 is a clear example of a divide-and-rule tactics that exploits one-sidedness in views of reality, and a short-term approach to development. Market deregulation and the relocation of working-class jobs provided short-term economic gains for the middle class, at the cost of political losses, because the middle class lost its ability to cooperate with the working class. These political losses can then lead to long-term economic losses, as the lower middle class is unable on its own to influence policy and prevent its jobs from being relocated too, after the relocation of working-class jobs. This divide-and-rule tactic can be encouraged by theories of development based exclusively upon economics and that make short-term predictions. One-sidedness and reductiveness can also have purely political negative effects by leading mass movements to embrace limited political goals, such as seeking cultural democracy while neglecting political-military democracy. I address these effects in the book on the humanist theory of society. Here, I want to focus on ways to overcome one-sidedness, one of which is provided by multidisciplinary approaches, which are meant precisely to overcome partial ideologies and limit the negative effects of institutional compartmentalization.

5.2 Specialization Due to Compartmentalization

One-sidedness is deeply engrained because it is based upon specialization that is sanctioned and reinforced by the institutional compartmentalization of knowledge in universities. This specialization is very hard to overcome for any individual intellectual who tries to do so. Therefore, I want to begin this chapter by addressing the first kind of specialization that is prevalent in universities today, specialization in studying different domains of human activity, whether the economy, culture, politics or the military. Gramsci's multidisciplinary approach was meant to address the problems created by this type of specialization, which requires overcoming institutional compartmentalization. Here I want to address two very important efforts to provide a multidisciplinary approach to social science. The first is closely associated with Gramsci's project, whereas the second is associated with Weber's approach to sociology. Both are important for a humanist social science. I refer to them respectively as the PPE approach, where PPE is short for philosophy, politics and economics, and the sociology approach. They show that there is a widely perceived need for a multidisciplinary approach to social science, but they fall short of overcoming all specialization. The best approach would combine the PPE and sociology approaches, together with organization that transcends the institutional compartmentalization of universities. This is the approach that I propose in this project and that I apply in my work.

The PPE approach involves combining philosophy with social science. It remarkably follows very closely Gramsci's approach to formulating a humanist social science. Building upon interpretations of the origins of Marx's thought and of modern social science, Gramsci suggested that a humanist social science would have to include three component disciplines, which should be in constant dialogue with each other. These are philosophy, which studies theoretical activity, and politics and economics, which study practical activity.[1] At around the same time when Gramsci was formulating these ideas, a new degree course was established at Oxford University called Philosophy, Politics and Economics, often referred to as PPE, showing the perceived need for, and the importance of, this approach. This degree course combining all three disciplines in one degree program still exists and, furthermore, has apparently become very successful and has conquered, as it were, nearly 200 other universities throughout the world, including universities in continental Europe and in the United States, all of which have adopted or imitated this program by combining to a greater or lesser extent studies in philosophy with studies in social sciences, particularly politics and economics.[2] There is also a scholarly journal called *Politics, Philosophy & Economics*. Clearly, the need for this kind of multidisciplinary approach is widely felt.

The *importance of combining philosophy with social science* follows from the fact that philosophy provides social science with four contributions that are indispensable to it. The first two can be called *analytical contributions to social science*. The first is clarity of definitions. This is obviously important if one adopts a method that involves *using assumptions* or axioms and deriving theory from these assumptions, which must be defined as clearly as possible. Below I define this method as the axiomatic-deductive method and in chapter 6 I give examples of it. The second contribution is deriving statements *using logic*. This too is essential to the axiomatic-deductive method, because the theses it produces are derived from assumptions using logic. These two functions of philosophy are widely taught in Great Britain, including in the PPE course, and they are associated with a tradition of philosophy called Analytic Philosophy. Recently, a tradition of sociology has emerged that is called Analytical Sociology and that adopts a similar approach, which is arguably based upon Analytic Philosophy. This approach has the undoubted merit of having emphasized the importance of clear definitions to social science.

---

1 Gramsci, *Quaderni del Carcere*, 1246–47.

2 A very thorough review of Oxford economics, the Political Economy degree, and the newer PPE degree, is provided by: Warren Young and Frederic S. Lee, *Oxford Economics and Oxford Economists* (London and New York: Palgrave Macmillan, 1993). A list of the many universities offering the degree is provided by: Wikipedia, "Philosophy, Politics and Economics." From what I know about some of the universities in the list on the Wikipedia page, they do not offer exactly the same PPE degree as Oxford University, but some combination, in their own degree courses, of philosophy with social science, and in some cases teaching of Analytic Philosophy, which is associated with British philosophical traditions. It seems to me this long list can be more accurately described as a list of universities influenced by Oxford University and in particular by the PPE approach.

However, I do not subscribe wholesale to this approach because I think that analysis, while necessary, is not sufficient. One also needs synthesis and a clear exposition or presentation that is based on good rhetoric, two other very important activities that I undertake in this project.

Philosophy can contribute also to synthesis and exposition in social science. Synthesis is essential to providing broad pictures of society and history. Synthesis too calls for clarity of definitions and logic, amongst other intellectual tools, but in this case clarity of definitions and logic are applied at a later stage in theory-building, to ensure the internal coherence of a general theory containing many theses, which involves harmonizing the theses in various ways. It also uses the strategic vision that is associated with a broad view of society and history, which requires different tools than logic. The other contribution that philosophy can give to social science is *exposition*, for example by justifying clarity of exposition and providing the tools for it, including good rhetoric. This project emphasizes the importance of clarity of exposition, which is closely associated with a dialogic tradition in Western philosophy that originated with Socratic dialogues and was continued by Renaissance humanism, in important works by Machiavelli and Guicciardini, for example.[3] The dialogic tradition sees philosophy as existing in a constant dialogue with common sense or everyday philosophy, which, as I argued in chapter 4, provides to philosophy the questions that have to be addressed and even some preliminary answers. Philosophy then clarifies and reformulates systematically these questions and preliminary answers, providing a clear and coherent exposition of the questions and the answers. These last two contributions are associated with Continental Philosophy, which is supposed to be the philosophy in most of Europe except for Great Britain. I believe instead that the dividing line between Analytic and Continental philosophy is not so geographically clear-cut. I also believe that

3 There are many studies of the importance of dialogism, and thus indirectly of dialogues, to Gramsci's theory. However, these studies usually focus exclusively on the linguistic theory known as dialogism formulated by Mikhail Bakhtin, for example: Peter Ives, *Gramsci's Politics of Language: Engaging the Bakhtin Circle and the Frankfurt School*, Cultural Spaces (Toronto: University of Toronto Press, 2004). This approach was first introduced in Italy by Frosini's supervisor: Giorgio Baratta, *Le Rose e i Quaderni: Saggio sul Pensiero di Antonio Gramsci* (Roma: Gamberetti Editrice, 2000). Bakhtin is relevant to this project also for his effort to combine humanism with concepts drawn from technology, for example in his application of the concept of 'chronotope', which he derived from physics, and which he applied to the theory of the novel. I was first introduced to key concepts in physics by an erudite physics teacher at UWC Adriatic, who also introduced us to the importance of science, including physicis, in the culture of many East European countries, including nearby Slovenia and Ljubljana University.

these different traditions are not mutually exclusive, but complementary. They are both essential to formulate a worldview, the highest kind of philosophical synthesis.

I have two *reservations about the PPE approach*. One is that PPE, as it is taught at Oxford University, relies only upon Analytic Philosophy and the first two contributions of philosophy to social science, largely ignoring the other two. The other one is that the multidisciplinary approach that it provides is incomplete from an institutional point of view, and also in terms of the domains that it covers. The PPE approach is incomplete from an institutional point of view because the universities that implemented it, starting with Oxford University, generally still have separate departments of philosophy, of politics, and of economics. Although the course is multidisciplinary, the research is still institutionally compartmentalized into different disciplines and departments. The PPE approach is also incomplete from the point of view of the domains that it covers, because some key domains that study human activity are missing from the PPE approach or are marginalized, and these missing domains are domains that are especially important for Gramsci's project to formulate a humanist social science and that are especially important today, such as the study of culture, and the study of the military, including the study of intelligence.

While emphasizing politics and economics, *Gramsci gave also important contributions to the study of culture and the military that I build upon*. Gramsci's work served as the *foundation for cultural studies and the sociological study of culture*.[4] This work emphasized such concepts as intellectuals constituting a distinct social group, defined by Gramsci as the social group that includes all those who produce and organize culture, and the related concept of hegemony, which in Gramsci's definition is political power complemented by cultural power, which is derived at least in part from intellectuals. Gramsci is also amongst the modern thinkers who initiated a very *fruitful exchange between military science and political science*, adapting many key concepts from military science to the sociological study of politics, including the key concept of force ratios, which Gramsci suggested is applicable to the balance of forces in society as much as to the military, and the concepts of vanguard and army, which are applicable respectively to small cultural or political groups that act as vanguards and the mass movements they interact with, and the concepts of war of position and war of maneuver, which Gramsci suggested can be respectively

4 Gramsci spoke negatively of sociology because he associated it exclusively with the positivist sociology of Auguste Comte and of soviet Marxists like Bukharin, whereas today there are many different non-positivist approaches within sociology that are close to Gramsci's project for a social science, although falling short of it because of academic specialization.

applied to describe a slow buildup of political support and access to power, as opposed to a rapid rise to power or seizure of power. This last distinction is especially useful to understand some aspects of the culture wars that we are living through and has been applied to them.[5]

The need to cover all domains of human activity is better addressed by *the sociology approach* to formulating a multidisciplinary social science, which is the other notable attempt to provide a multidisciplinary approach to social science. Sociology at its inception, at least in Weber's formulation, was *multidisciplinary precisely in the sense of encompassing all the main domains of human activity* and the associated academic disciplines, and even different dimensions of human activity. At one point some sociology departments brought together under one institutional roof the study of economics, culture, politics and the military. There are within sociology recognized sub-fields of economic sociology, cultural sociology, and political sociology, which includes studies of war and the military, as well as the emerging sub-field of the sociology of development. There are also more specialized sub-fields, which overlap with one or more of these sub-fields. For example, there is a specialized sub-field focused on the study of social movements and collective action, which overlaps largely with political sociology. There are also two *specialized* sub-fields, one focused on the study of nationalism, the other focused on the study of empires and multi-ethnic societies, both of which overlap with two sub-fields, namely, political sociology and cultural sociology.

Equally as important as the attempt to combine the study of all the main domains of human activity, there is in sociology, since its inception, an attempt to *study human activity by covering its two dimensions: time and space*. Most politics and economics provide a static picture of a certain political or economic phenomenon at one point in time, typically the present. Sociology at its inception sought instead to study social phenomena by taking into consideration a time or historical dimension, which shows how social phenomena change with time, and a space or geographical dimension, which shows how they vary in space. There is a sub-field within sociology, historical sociology, which focuses precisely upon understanding social phenomena in their time and space dimensions, especially in theories like Wallerstein's.

My *reservation about the sociology attempt to provide a multidisciplinary approach to social science* is that within sociology departments philosophy

---

5 Timothy Brennan, *Wars of Position: the Cultural Politics of Left and Right* (New York: Columbia University Press, 2006). Brennan was Edward Said's student, and he represents an approach to literary and cultural studies that overlaps with social science and uses Gramsci, like Said did in his work.

is not studied, theory is marginalized, and specialization is creeping in and destroying the multidisciplinary approach. *The best multidisciplinary approach would be one that combines features of both approaches*, the PPE multidisciplinary approach to social science, and the sociology approach. *The most important feature to incorporate from the PPE approach* is its emphasis on philosophy and theory as necessary to social science. One reason for their importance is spelled out below, in the discussion of the definition of theory and its contribution to social science by refining and corroborating hypotheses. Another reason follows from the uses of philosophy in social science. Philosophy provides intellectual tools such as logic, and also the worldview, which make it possible to integrate disparate disciplines concerned with the economy, culture, politics and the military into a single, coherent, broad picture of society and history. Philosophy provides or refines key concepts in such a manner as to enable us to build this coherent picture, like the idea that human beings can act both as Aristotle's *Zoon Politikon,* or political being, and also as modern economists' *Homo Oeconomicus*, or the acquisitive and calculating individual active in markets, and we are thus capable respectively of political activity and collective action, and also of economic activity and individual action in the pursuit of profit.

The most important feature to incorporate from the sociology multidisciplinary approach is that all different domains of human activity should be studied together and combined into a single, coherent, broad picture of human activity in society, that includes both time and spatial dimensions. Here I want to point out that this is the broad picture of society and history that I was referring to in chapter 2, and that only past thinkers like Gramsci and Weber have sought to provide such a picture, by combining to different extents both features, namely, to practice philosophy and theory as well as social science, and to study all the main domains and the main dimensions of human activity. In order to provide such a broad picture, one has to study past thinkers like Gramsci and Weber, and make a synthesis of the state of knowledge in social science, a task that is often neglected today, but that we should address if we want to formulate a social science that is useful to all citizens in democracies, and that can advance development and democracy for the masses and not just the elites.

5.3 Specialization Due to the Needs of Empirical Research

There is a second type of specialization in universities that is very widespread today. It is *empirical specialization, which arises from an increasing focus upon empirical research alone*. The specialization associated with empirical research is dictated in part by the needs of empirical research to gather data. Depending upon the type of data that is gathered, this specialization can lead to two more specific types of empirical specialization and the associated problems in knowledge: the first is specialization that provides local pictures of society, which arises from the needs of gathering and analyzing qualitative data; the second is specialization that provides detailed pictures of specific aspects of human activity, which arises from the needs of gathering and analyzing quantitative data. I want to review briefly these two specific types of empirical specialization and discuss the flaws that they lead to. This specialization is often in addition to the specialization that arises from the institutional compartmentalization of the study of different domains of human behavior into different academic fields. For example, within a department of political science, the study of political behavior is further narrowed down by the needs of empirical research. Let us consider each one of the needs of empirical research that lead to one of the two types of specialization.

Gathering and analyzing qualitative data leads to the fist type of empirical specialization problem, which can best be described as producing *local-range theory*, a theory based on a local picture of society that includes social mechanisms with only a small number of variables, or with specific variables, such that they explain well a specific phenomenon, but are not easily applicable elsewhere. Gathering and analyzing qualitative data, which relies upon direct observation by the researcher, typically in the form of ethnographies, leads to this empirical specialization problem and to local-range theories, because research has to be done at a specific time and place, or at a few specific times and places. The number of individuals who can be observed or interviewed is also limited. The narrow focus of qualitative studies upon a few individuals at one time and place enables researchers to observe directly how society works, including social mechanisms that can be viewed as if through a lens, which is a great advantage in furthering our understanding of society. In the case of most empirical studies, however, the resulting theory is only a local-range theory that applies to those individuals, at that time and place, and might ignore causal factors that are part of this social mechanism, but are only found elsewhere, for example. It is useful to consider instances of local-range theories in order to illustrate just how local they can be.

An instance of scholarship with this very narrow local focus, the scholarly equivalent of military targeting through a sniper's lens that allows you to see far, but only a very small area, is the 2000 study by Harvey Molotch and a number of other scholars of communities and urban planning, of two counties in

California, Santa Barbara and Ventura County, over a period of a few years.[6] This study was ambitiously and oddly titled *History repeats itself, but how?* I say oddly because the very big question asked in the title was followed instead by a local-range theory that has no apparent bearing upon history, and even less upon the question that Vico called the 'corsi e ricorsi storici', whereby history 'occurs and re-occurs' and thus repeats itself in a sense, a question that I address in the book on the humanist theory of history.[7] Another example of scholarship with this very narrow local focus is the 2007 study by Tim Clydesdale, *The First Year Out*, which focuses on the last year of high school of one school in New Jersey, and the first year of university, of a handful of students, including a few ambitious and talented African-American girls.[8] These are important studies. But their narrow focus is effectively individual history, or life-stories, and their theoretical goals are to provide an explanation of very specific, almost individual, phenomena that are their targets, as it were. The picture of society that they provide is necessarily only a local picture. If they propose any theory, this theory is only a local-range theory.

Gathering and analyzing quantitative data, as opposed to qualitative data, leads to the second type of empirical specialization problem, which can best be described as a *detailed theory* of a domain or even just one aspect of human activity, which is detailed in the sense that it goes into depth in exploring details of a picture, rather that providing a broad picture.[9] Quantitative data typically consists of socio-economic indicators such as educational attainment or income, or socio-cultural indicators such as a scale of the importance attached to family by individuals in a social group. Quantitative data can be based on the responses given to surveys by many, even thousands, of individuals, also across societies. However, despite being applicable to many localities, specialization arises from the need to ask specific questions to these individuals, questions that one has to set in advance of the data gathering. This leads

6 Harvey Luskin Molotch, William Freudenburg, and Krista E. Paulsen, "History Repeats Itself, but How? City Character, Urban Tradition, and the Accomplishment of Place," *American Sociological Review* (2000). Molotch has been carrying out research on the different fortunes of different cities or towns for a very long time. His 1987 book was republished for a 20th Anniversary Edition: John R. Logan and Harvey Luskin Molotch, *Urban Fortunes: the Political Economy of Place* (Berkeley and Los Angeles: University of California Press, 2007).

7 Giambattista Vico, *New Science* (London: Penguin, 1999). This book was reprinted already in 2000.

8 Tim Clydesdale, *The First Year Out: Understanding American Teens after High School* (Chicago: University of Chicago Press, 2008).

9 Steven Rytina's latest theory is an example of detailed theory: Rytina, *Network Persistence and the Axis of Hierarchy*. Another example is Inglehart's theory, addressed in the next paragraph.

to research that is detailed in the sense of focusing upon a specific aspect of human activity, for example by investigating how educational attainment and other socio-economic indicators are related to the importance attached to family. One can get a detailed knowledge of these social phenomena and how they relate to each other, but this knowledge is always limited by what can be asked in a survey, and by the work done before the survey in order to decide what to ask.

This problem can be illustrated by the World Values Survey, or WVS, and research done on data from this survey by political scientist Ronald Inglehart, at the University of Michigan. The WVS arguably represents the most that can be achieved by a survey: it asks nearly 300 questions from thousands of individuals throughout the world, and it is repeated at regular intervals, and updated by introducing new questions.[10] Inglehart's thorough analyses of the data provided by this survey have offered many important insights into the changes that different societies undergo in the transition to modernity.[11] However, they suffer from specialization problems that arise from a detailed picture of one aspect of human activity. Not only they focus upon culture alone, and thus on just one domain of human activity, but they also focus upon just one particular aspect of culture that can be most easily studied through a survey, namely, expressed values. They thus rely upon a disembodied view of culture that ignores some very important aspects of culture emphasized by Gramsci that I address at some length in the book on humanist social science, and the book on the humanist theory of society. One such aspect of culture is that there are implicit values associated with behavior, which can only be observed in a qualitative study, by actually observing behavior through participant observation. Another aspect is that values, whether expressed or implicit, are

10 The WVS has a website with detailed explanations of the surveys it carries out. On the latest one, see: World Values Survey, "WVS Wave 7 (2017–2020)." A very comprehensive sourcebook was published in 1998: Ronald Inglehart and Miguel Basanez, *Human Values and Beliefs: A Cross-Cultural Sourcebook* (Ann Arbor: University of Michigan Press, 1998). The WVS is hosted by the University of Michigan in Ann Arbor.

11 Inglehart, who contributed to the creation of the WVS, has published numerous books on the subject. One of the early studies is: Ronald Inglehart, *Culture Shift in Advanced Industrial Society* (Princeton and Oxford: Princeton University Press, 1990). In this book, reprinted in 2018, Inglehart introduced the idea that there is a fundamental culture shift in the transition to modernity. In other books he mapped the changes in values across cultures throughout the world, for example in: Paul R. Abramson and Ronald Inglehart, *Value Change in Global Perspective* (Ann Arbor: University of Michigan Press, 1995); Ronald Inglehart, Pippa Norris, and M. G. Norris, *Rising Tide: Gender Equality and Cultural Change around the World* (Cambridge and New York: Cambridge University Press, 2003). The first of these two books has been reprinted in 2009.

closely associated with social structures, and the combination of values and social structures is arguably very important to understand society, and collective action in particular. Therefore, the process of transition to modernity has to be studied by taking into consideration both values and social structures.

The failure of WVS studies arguably also stems from insufficient theoretical groundwork, which reinforces the disembodied view of culture just mentioned. The map by Inglehart and political scientist Christian Welzel, for example, uses this view of culture to define society, and divides the world into societies that are defined by a mix of religious and linguistic features, for example: Catholic societies, Confucian societies, Protestant societies, English-speaking societies, Latin-American societies.[12] This mix might be justified by underlying structures. For example, theoretical groundwork like the one I carried out for this book suggests that we have to consider culture together with social structures, in order to explain human activity. It is the combination of culture with social structures that explains collective action in the pursuit of goals, rather than just values. Moreover, there are very important differences that Inglehart and Welzel's classification obscures. For example, there are within Italy, which Inglehart and Welzel classify indistinctly as Catholic, very important differences in social structures that affected development and democracy in the north and south of the country, leading to very different outcomes. The differences between the north-west and the north-east of Italy are also significant. I define theoretical groundwork next. Before moving on to this task, I want to clarify an important point in order to avoid misconceptions. I am not against specialization in itself, but only against reliance upon specialists alone in social science. I believe instead that there should be the right balance in research between generalists and specialists, and between theory, qualitative research and quantitative research, all of which should complement each other and be in a constant dialogue with each other.

5.4 Theory, Theoretical Groundwork and General Theory

Before arguing in detail why this dialogue is important, it is necessary to define the following three inter-related concepts: theory, theoretical work and general theory. My *definition of theory* complements this ideal of a dialogue between theory and empirical research, and focuses upon theoretical work. I believe there is a continuum between empirical research, whether qualitative or

12 World Values Survey, "Findings and Insights, Inglehart–Welzel Cultural Map."

quantitative, and theory. Most empirical research is to some extent informed by theory and, conversely, most theory is to some extent empirically informed. Pure theory is rare and arguably not very useful. The same can be said of pure empirical research. Therefore, it is more useful to focus upon theoretical work, which is something that is common to all studies. I focus in this section upon defining theoretical work and propose that theory is simply a study in which theoretical work prevails over empirical work. I do not, however, attempt to define an exact point at which enough theoretical work is done to qualify a study as theory. This point is somewhat arbitrary, and in any case this book is well past this point and is undoubtedly theory, albeit empirically informed theory.

Another important definition that is relevant to this project, and to this book in particular, is the *definition of general theory*. I want to combine here the preliminary definitions introduced above into a single full definition. The general theory that I propose is general in three ways. One way is that it is a multidisciplinary theory, as opposed to a one-sided theory, which is a theory concerned with only one domain of human behavior and the academic field that studies this behavior. By contrast, this multidisciplinary theory encompasses not just the economy, or culture, or politics or the military, but all of these domains and ultimately the whole of society. This means that the social theory that I propose addresses how society works, which includes all domains of human activity. By contrast, economic theory or political theory address respectively how the economy works and how politics works, and are thus concerned with just one domain. The second way in which this is a general theory is that it abstracts from works focused upon specific times and places, and the associated local-range theories, which only provide local pictures. Mindless empiricism dismisses this type of general theory as 'books about books', a disparaging expression I have come across several times in seminars. This is a misrepresentation that obscures the important contributions that general theory can give. The third way in which this is a general theory is that it addresses phenomena that are widespread and last a long time, like globalization. These tend to occur in many different locations, and this geographical spread requires a theory that abstracts from all these different locations in order to provide explanations that apply to them all. I address this point in the book on the humanist theory of society, where I address the relevance of general theory to policy.

The methods that I use to formulate the general theory that I propose consist chiefly of *two important types of theoretical work*. One type involves summarizing many different books based upon empirical research, but this is best described, not as a 'book about books', but as *theoretical groundwork*, a form of theoretical work that draws general lessons by abstracting from insights provided by many empirical studies of specific times and places. This is an important contribution to social science, if it is done in such a way as to make the lessons of these studies more broadly applicable, to other times and places. It is also useful if it provides a synthesis of the local pictures from these disparate times and places, and incorporate them into a broad picture of society and history that explains social phenomena in all of these times and places. These lessons are effectively hypotheses about society, which can be submitted to empirical tests, in such a way that theoretical groundwork and empirical work complement each other. Many of the best empirical studies do this already to some extent and complement empirical work with theoretical work. This book does it in a sustained and extensive manner, in order to provide the broadest picture possible that I could produce with my knowledge.

The other type of theoretical work that I pursue in this book is *axiomatic-deductive theoretical work*. This is a type of theoretical work that builds theory using an axiomatic-deductive method. I start from axioms, which are premises about human beings and the environments we live in. In this book and in the book on humanist social science I focus especially on axioms about human beings. In the book on the humanist theory of society, I address also the environment, which is a particular type of axiom that is part of the circumstances that all subjects find themselves in. I deduce from these premises a number of statements, which are effectively consequences, and I call them theses in order to differentiate them from the hypotheses provided by theoretical groundwork. Gramsci aptly summarized the axiomatic-deductive method as the method of 'supposing that' or 'given that', which I understand to be a way of saying that, given certain starting points, certain consequences will follow.[13] The earliest fully formalized axiomatic-deductive theory in the West is Euclidean geometry. Arguably, Aristotelian philosophy was also built on an axiomatic-deductive method.

I use throughout this book the words *hypothesis and thesis*, and it is necessary to define them clearly and explain how they differ. This also serves to clarify the relationship between theoretical groundwork, general theory and social science. Following conventions that are fairly established in social science, I use the words hypothesis and thesis in the following manners. I use the word *hypothesis* to refer to a statement that can be *directly* tested by empirical tests. The main task of social science traditionally understood is testing hypotheses and thus confirming them or rejecting them, depending upon the results of the test. After carrying out the theoretical groundwork sketched out

13 Gramsci, *Quaderni del Carcere*, 1076, 1245–6.

above, one arrives at hypotheses, which can be directly tested by social science. By contrast, I use the word *thesis* to refer to a statement defined by two features. The first feature is that the statement is supported by logic, which is used in the axiomatic-deductive method to derive statements that are effectively consequences of the starting points. The second feature is that a thesis cannot be directly tested by empirical tests, however, it can be *indirectly* tested by empirical tests. Thus, depending upon the results of the empirical tests, one can *limitedly* confirm or reject the thesis. To explain fully what I mean by thesis, it is necessary to go into greater detail into these two features.

The two features that define a thesis correspond *to two different criteria: validity and usefulness*. When considering the first feature, we can *make sure that the theses are valid,* which means they are correctly derived using logic, and are logically coherent. Being valid is an important criterion for all claims of the form: given these starting points, or axioms, these consequences will follow. Being valid, however, is not the only criterion that should be applied to theses. Correctly derived theses are also *useful,* besides being valid, if they sufficiently approximate reality to be able to make predictions. This requires that theses should be indirectly supported by empirical evidence, which involves meeting at least three criteria. Firstly, the theses should start from axioms that are a close approximation of reality. These axioms can be confirmed empirically, so that the theory is indirectly supported by empirical evidence in the limited sense of starting from actually existing axioms. Secondly, the theses should use these axioms to explain phenomena that are important in society and history, for example because these phenomena are frequently occurring, which can also be confirmed empirically, by testing how often the consequences predicted by the theory are found in reality. In addition, the theses should explain important phenomena that affect many other phenomena, globalization and uneven development being especially important to this project for this reason. Thirdly, there should be empirical correlation between the axioms used and the consequences predicted, which makes the thesis plausible.

It is important to acknowledge the limitations of confirming theses indirectly, which does not *prove* theses, as directly testing hypothesis does. However, *we can do at least some direct tests,* which provide *limited* confirmation or rejection of the thesis, which is different than fully confirming or proving the thesis. Most theses are statements that describe social mechanisms, whereby the axioms lead to the consequences. These statements can be indirectly tested empirically by proving correlation, which is a statement of the form: where these axioms are found, the following consequences predicted by the theses are also found. The tests can limitedly confirm or reject the thesis, but they do not prove it, for example because a different causal mechanism leading from the axioms to the consequences might be at work than the one proposed by the theory. To prove a thesis, one would have to observe the causal mechanism that leads from the axioms to the consequences. Furthermore, one would have to observe the causal mechanism at work in many cases. It is even harder to test directly the entire theory, which includes many theses, which taken together can constitute complex mechanisms that from the axioms lead to the consequences. Entire theories are much harder, though not necessarily impossible, to confirm, which is another reason why it is important to work with other researchers in collaborative projects, each addressing one part of the theory, and each testing one part of the theory.

The two forms of theoretical work that I pursue in this book, *theoretical groundwork, and axiomatic-deductive theoretical work, can be complementary.* They are certainly complementary in the manner in which I practice them in this book, and in the next sections I want to sketch in greater detail what these two forms of theoretical work consist in, and how they complement each other. Together, they can lead to formulating the most useful general theory that one can formulate. We can conceptualize these two forms of theoretical work as if they undertook four theoretical tasks, each of which builds upon the previous one. By theoretical tasks I mean tasks that one undertakes as part of formulating theory. These four tasks are: first, critiquing past studies; second, providing a synthesis of past studies; third, formulating hypotheses; and fourth, formulating general theory and theses. The first three tasks, taken together, constitute the theoretical groundwork that is the necessary prerequisite to all social science. The fourth task involves general theory, which is often ignored today, but which is especially important for social science and also for policymakers and citizens. The overall relationship between the two forms of theoretical work can be summarized thus: a very effective way to formulate general theory is by starting with theoretical groundwork, which contributes to axiomatic-deductive theoretical work, which in in its turn provides the general theory. Thus, theoretical groundwork contributes to general theory. The relationship works also the other way, and general theory contributes to theoretical groundwork.

5.5 The Contribution from Theoretical Groundwork

Let us consider first how theoretical groundwork can contribute to general theory and to axiomatic-deductive theoretical work in particular. Here I want to focus on each one of the three tasks of theory, beginning with the first two tasks. *The first two tasks of theory*, critiquing past studies, and providing a synthesis of past studies, are especially important to axiomatic-deductive theoretical work, because they can be used to provide better assumptions, and also better social mechanisms, for example by introducing more factors in a mechanism, which then explains more cases. Providing better assumptions and social mechanisms both require *scrutinizing concepts and providing key concepts* to be used by the theory, which can become the axioms used by the theory. They can also contribute to the concepts that are part of the social mechanisms proposed by the theory, and in the second volume I refer to these concepts as intermediate concepts. There are other concepts that theoretical groundwork can improve upon, for example, a better understanding of circumstances, but I address them in the book on the humanist theory of society and the humanist theory of history. There are also meta theory concepts, such as theoretical economy, or reductiveness of the model, which contribute to formulating better theory. Scrutinizing concepts and providing key concepts, whether starting points or intermediate concepts, is an important way in which theoretical groundwork can contribute to general theory. Each of the first three tasks of theory, which are all part of theoretical groundwork, can contribute to formulating general theory both by *providing better assumptions*, and by providing better social mechanisms.

The three tasks of theory can be especially useful to provide better assumptions. The first task of theory, critiquing past studies, can be used to criticize past assumptions. For example, we can criticize the concept of *Homo Oeconomicus*, an axiom regarding human behavior. Much of mainstream economic theory, including neoliberalism, and also a growing number of sociological theories, use as axioms the behavior of human beings that is associated with the concept of *Homo Oeconomicus*. This states that human beings are motivated by acquisitive individualism, whereby human beings behave in an individualistic manner in the search for profit and do not take others into account, so that profit can be made at the expense of others, or not shared with others. Gramsci criticized this view upon theoretical grounds, drawing attention to our ability, which we all know and share to some extent, to cooperate with others in collective action with shared goals. This task of theoretical groundwork can be supported by empirical work. Bowles and Gintis and a number of other scholars have completed a large empirical study of 15 different small-scale societies, in which people live in villages and interact with a limited number of persons, typically in face-to-face interactions, and showed that individuals in these societies often take others into account and can also behave altruistically, for example by sharing profits with others.[14] Clearly, the assumptions of *Homo Oeconomicus* are not sufficient to cover all types of human behavior, and not even all the most important types.

The second task of theory, providing a *synthesis, can lead to more comprehensive assumptions by combining different assumptions*. Gramsci suggested that human beings are capable both of acquisitive individualism, as described by the concept of *Homo Oeconomicus*, and also of collaborative behavior whereby the individual acts in concert with others and takes them into account, as described for example by Aristotle's concept of *Zoon Politikon*, or political being. A synthesis of these two different assumptions can contribute to a more useful general theory, by providing to the general theory assumptions that together describe more types of human behavior and thus help avoid reductive models. Synthesis can help us provide also the relationship between the concepts, which is the beginning of a theory. In my interpretation, Gramsci suggested the following relationship: in modern societies there are separate economic and political arenas; the type of behavior described by *Homo Oeconomicus* prevails in the economic arena, whereas the type of behavior described by *Zoon Politikon* prevails in the political arena.[15] These relationships are relevant to formulating theory, by suggesting where certain mechanisms are at work: market mechanisms based upon acquisitive individualism are at work chiefly in the economy, but might be spreading to politics.

The third task of theory, *formulating hypotheses, can include hypotheses about where this synthesis of assumptions can be found*. For example, Gramsci's suggestion regarding the relationship between *Homo Oeconomicus* and *Zoon Politikon* can lead to formulating two hypotheses: in markets, which are an important part of the economy, *Homo Oeconomicus* prevails, whereas in social movement organizations and amongst activists, which are an important part of politics, *Zoon Politikon* prevails. Studies like the one of 15 small-scale societies cited above tested the hypothesis whether *Homo Oeconomicus* can be found in small-scale societies. The tests were negative, and suggested that altruistic or other-regarding behavior is frequently encountered in small-scale societies. In this project, all three tasks of theory led me to the hypothesis that in communities, altruistic behavior is also often encountered, and possibly prevails over acquisitive individualism, at least in some cases. Since altruistic behavior, by contrast to the egoistic behavior associated with acquisitive individualism, is important to collective action, community is important to collective

14 Joseph Henrich et al., "In Search of Homo Economicus: Behavioral Experiments in 15 Small-Scale Societies," *The American Economic Review* 91, no. 2 (2001).

15 This argument builds upon the arguments that I proposed in my doctoral dissertation.

action. This means that the loss of community can present a major challenge for political activity by the masses, and can undermine democracy in the long run. One could add another hypothesis: in contemporary societies, individualistic behavior is coming to prevail in the political arena too, where only the elites and small groups of activists live in communities of one kind or another and regularly participate in collective action, reducing political participation by the masses to a spectator sport.

The three tasks of theory can also be very useful to provide better social mechanisms. As an example, we can consider two very different sociological studies. *The first task of theory*, critiquing past studies, could focus on the study by Molotch cited above and the social mechanism that it proposes.[16] In my interpretation, the main contribution of this study is to suggest that the built environment, community and collective action can reinforce each other. In the county of Santa Barbara, a thriving and wealthy community was able to engage in collective action and to defend and further enhance the built environment it lived in. This acted both as a rallying symbol and also as a rallying place for the community, and in its turn contributed to collective action by the community. In the nearby Ventura county, a struggling and impoverished community was unable to engage in collective action and prevent unscrupulous entrepreneurs from building factories or motorways that degraded the built environment and split up the community. This further reduced the ability of the community to engage in collective action. Criticizing Molotch's study suggests that he ignored or failed to theorize properly an important causal factor, namely, external actors. The ability of the community to engage in collective action is undoubtedly an important factor, but its success or failure depends also upon the strength of external actors, for example the unscrupulous entrepreneurs mentioned above, the presence or lack of which is part of the circumstances that the community has to face. In some cases, such external actors are so strong that their intervention is the decisive factor.

This observation is reinforced by a different study, which shows the usefulness of *the second task of theory*, providing a synthesis of different studies. This is a very useful way to build theory that the disparaging label 'books about books' fails to appreciate. In a very different study of communities, focused upon popular neighborhoods in Paris during the second half of the nineteenth century, sociologist Roger Gould provided another account of the interaction between the built environment, community and collective action.[17] Gould suggested that

---

16 Molotch, Freudenburg, and Paulsen, "History Repeats Itself, but How? City Character, Urban Tradition, and the Accomplishment of Place."

17 Roger V. Gould, *Insurgent Identities: Class, Community, and Protest in Paris from 1848 to the Commune* (Chicago: University of Chicago Press, 1995).

Napoleon III's massive interventions on the built environment of Paris had a major impact upon collective action, since they flattened neighborhoods and constructed large boulevards, which split up popular communities, made it hard to construct barricades, and made it easy to move large numbers of troops in the center of Paris. This eventually undermined the ability of popular communities to engage in collective action, particularly revolutionary activity. The contribution of Gould's study, compared to Molotch's, was to point to the fact that external actors like the French state can have a *major* impact on community by changing its built environment. I see this type of intervention to be part of a broad category of interventions that can be described as acting upon the material bases of collective action. I argue in this project that the means of transportation and communication are a very important component of the material bases of collective action, because they influence the form and frequency of social interaction and other important factors that influence collective action, and ultimately influence social stratification itself.

The third task of theory, formulating hypotheses, can build upon a synthesis providing better social mechanisms. This synthesis would propose a model that takes all of these factors into account, namely, the built environment, community, collective action, and also external actors, like entrepreneurs and the state, for example. The theory proposed below adds even more factors, like social structures and culture. The third task of theory, formulating hypotheses, would lead to the formulation of the hypothesis that in modern societies external actors like unscrupulous entrepreneurs and the state can destroy community also by acting upon the built environment, and more in general upon the material bases of collective action, at a time when the masses would otherwise be able to act successfully against elite rule. The three tasks of theory can stop at this point, as they do in much of sociology. Alternatively, they can contribute to general theory, the fourth task, through axiomatic-deductive theoretical work. In this case, one would formulate a theory using the axioms or starting points, and including intermediate causal factors like community, to derive theses. I want to suggest that contributing to the fourth task is important, and not just for theory itself, but also for social science, because the general theory produced by the fourth task can contribute to theoretical groundwork, also by corroborating and refining hypotheses.

5.6 The Contribution from General Theory

The relationship between theoretical groundwork and general theory can work the other way, and general theory can contribute to theoretical groundwork.

As suggested above, theoretical groundwork culminates in the third task of theory, formulating hypotheses. Empirical work then tests the hypotheses. An important way in which general theory can contribute to theoretical groundwork is by corroborating and refining hypotheses, both of which are important for testing hypotheses, and thus for social science. The process addressed here, which is illustrated in Figure 3, involves *two tasks that can be carried out together: first, to formulate a thesis*, which is part of a simple theory; and second, *to test this thesis and at the same time corroborate and refine the hypothesis* that one seeks to explain. I suggested above that a thesis is useful if, in addition to being valid, it is also a sufficiently close approximation to reality, which includes criteria such as whether the axioms used by the theory actually exist, and how often they are encountered in practice. Therefore, it is important to subject all theories, including general theory, to empirical tests. Here I want to emphasize that there can be a close inter-relationship between the general theory and these empirical tests. After we formulate a thesis, we must test it, and in this task, we can also corroborate and refine the hypothesis that we started with. The entire process and both tasks are represented in Figure 3, which shows four steps: a, b, c, d.

Let us consider first the *formulation of the thesis*, which seeks to explain the hypothesis. Formulating a hypothesis and formulating a thesis, respectively the third and fourth task of theory, are represented as steps a and c in Figure 3. This Figure contrasts *two steps that are part of sociological explanation*. Step a, to formulate the hypothesis, is associated with empirical work, as it is the product either of empirical work, or of theoretical groundwork that includes critiquing empirical studies. Step c is the formulation of a thesis, which involves axiomatic-deductive theoretical work, whereby from axioms one deduces statements using logic. It is useful *to begin by clarifying the words I use in the discussion of these steps*. A causal explanation or mechanism includes many factors that are part of one or more causal chains. Some of these factors are premises, because they occur at the beginning of a mechanism. It is useful to distinguish between premises, and axioms or assumptions, depending on whether they are part of formulating a hypothesis, or formulating a thesis. Premises are the starting points that a social scientist observes in a given social mechanism, if this mechanism can be observed to start at a given point. Axioms or assumptions are the theoretical equivalent of premises, they are the most basic starting point in a theory, which cannot usefully be broken down any further, nor be explained in terms of yet more basic concepts. Therefore, axioms are assumptions, that is, starting points that we take as given.

In this book I present *theses using concepts derived systematically as part of a methodology for choosing concepts* that leads from step a, to step b, on to

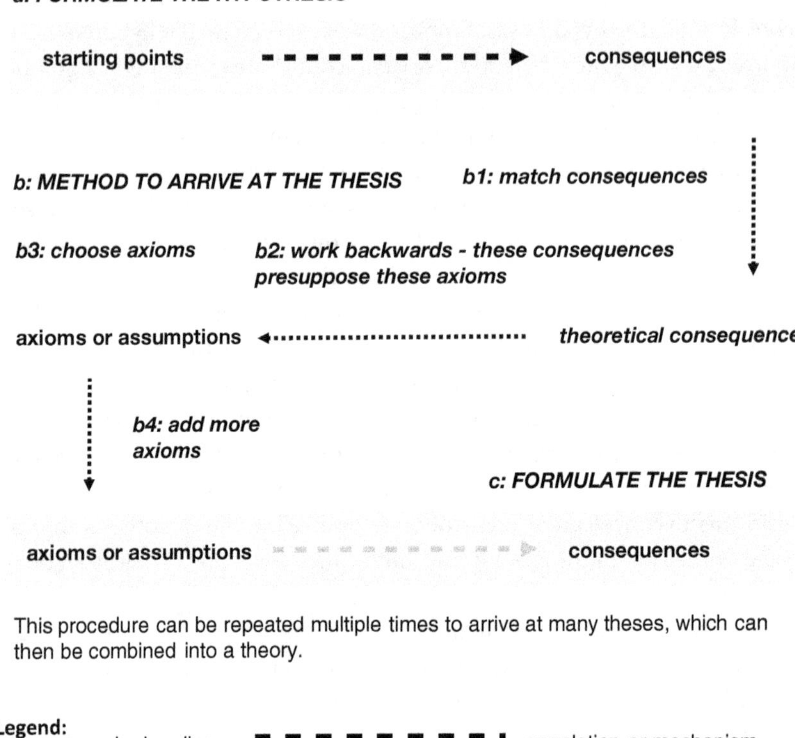

FIGURE 3 Formulating a hypothesis and a thesis that explains the hypothesis

step c. A few examples can clarify the steps involved and the usefulness of proceeding in a formal and systematic manner. As shown in step a, we can formulate a hypothesis that we later need to corroborate, which predicts that certain premises lead to certain consequences. This could be based on an observed correlation, which however might contain suggestions of a mechanism. It can be the product of empirical observation, or can be derived from theoretical groundwork. As an example of theoretical groundwork, critiquing past studies could include reviewing historical studies of early modern Europe, suggesting that there was much social conflict, together with a tendency towards imperial expansion, which led to the creation of colonial empires. This suggests the *hypothesis that much social conflict can lead to imperial expansion.* The next step is to formulate a theory with at least one thesis. This can usefully be conceptualized as entailing two steps: steps b and c in in Figure 3. Step b involves coming up with all the causal factors and all the axioms that are necessary to provide an adequate explanation. To do so, we work our way backwards in a causal chain, towards the axioms. The causal chain is not known at this point, but rather than coming up with all causal factors and axioms by some feat of imagination, we can instead proceed systematically in the following manner.

We start, in b1, by positing an abstract case that matches the consequences predicted by the hypothesis. This would be an abstract modern European society with imperial expansion. It is the case that we seek to explain. From this case, we can systematically arrive at the axioms that we need in order to explain the case, by deducing, as shown in b2, that these consequences presuppose certain axioms. Working our way backwards in a causal chain is especially useful if there are intermediate factors in a more or less long causal chain, a point that I address in the second volume. In the example given, imperial expansion presupposes social conflict. The following mechanism could have been suggested by the same historical studies: where there is much social conflict between elites and masses, the elites respond to the challenge posed by the masses by expanding their power, and this leads to imperial expansion. One can then add more causal factors, as shown in b3 and b4. Once we have all the intermediate factors and assumptions that are needed, we can finally formalize this causal mechanism, as part of step c, into a thesis, using more axioms and causal factors. The resulting explanation, step c, is represented by an arrow of a different color, because the thinking involved is different than the thinking involved in formulating the hypothesis, and it involves an abstract mechanism. An example of a thesis describing a social mechanism that is central to the theory proposed in this book is: with the expansion of markets under capitalism, the masses can, under certain circumstances, increase their power compared to the elites, which leads to much social conflict, some of which results in victories for the masses, and elites that are thus challenged respond by conquering new territories and thus try to expand their power.

We can now consider the second task, *testing the thesis, which can help us at the same time corroborate and refine the hypothesis*. This is illustrated in Figure 4. Testing the thesis involves step d, within which it is important to distinguish between four to five parts: d1 to d4-d5. Additionally, step d would have to be tested in multiple cases, to see if the mechanism applies beyond one case, and it is therefore an explanation that applies more widely than local-range theory. *Corroborating the hypothesis* can be done in the following manner. First, simply having a theory already corroborates the hypothesis by answering the question:

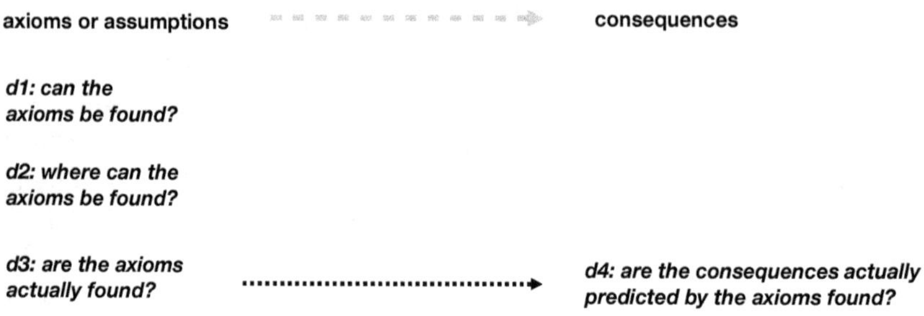

FIGURE 4 Step d: testing a thesis and corroborating and refining a hypothesis

is there a mechanism whereby from the observed starting points there follow the observed consequences? This corroborates the hypothesis simply by suggesting a valid mechanism that explains the hypothesis. This is important because, especially when there are only few cases that are not sufficient to make statistics, an observed correlation like the one between the two factors pointed out above, social conflict and imperial expansion, could be simply accidental. If we can provide a mechanism, instead, we can claim that one causal factor leads to the other. Moreover, we can do better than providing just a valid mechanism and also test whether it is a sufficiently close approximation to reality. The first and simplest test, that any theorist should carry out, is just an *estimate* as to whether the mechanism provides a plausible explanation, which starts by answering the question: can the axioms be found? This simple test, which is not a full empirical test, can involve just preliminary evidence, like the evidence that one can gather from a review of existing historical studies. In the example of a social mechanism proposed above, this would be an estimate of whether there really was an expansion of markets, which led to capitalism and social conflict.

The other parts of step d, d2 to d4, constitute an indirect empirical test of the thesis, and they can also lead to *refining the hypothesis*. Parts d2, followed by d3 and d4, involve the empirical test. This test is aided by d2, which refines the hypothesis by providing another estimate in answer to the question: *where* can we find the axioms presupposed by the consequences? This is where we can begin to carry out an *indirect empirical test*, with steps d3 and d4, which proves that both the axioms and consequences predicted by the thesis can be found at a certain location, and thus proves correlation between the axioms and the consequences. This correlation is different than the correlation between premises and consequences of the hypothesis, since the thesis proposes a more basic mechanism, which in the example of the social mechanism provided above involves the expansion of markets and capitalism, which are proposed as the explanation of social conflict. The last step, d5, is another empirical test, in this case a *direct empirical test* confirming the thesis. This test consists in observing the mechanism at work, which is possible in some specific cases. Figure 4 shows graphically what this test entails: observing the mechanism that leads from the axioms to the consequences.

In some cases, answering d2, together with additional theoretical groundwork, can also lead to *refining the thesis* itself, in the sense of suggesting a narrower or more specific thesis to be tested, linked to a geographically and historically specific place, or additional factors to take into consideration. For example, in the case of the thesis suggested above, we could distinguish between two different types of conflict: the social conflict that prevailed in Italian city-states, which led to little or no imperial expansion, and the social conflict that prevailed in north-western European proto nation-states, which led to great imperial expansion. One would then have to introduce additional factors in the mechanism that explain these differences. In a theory with many theses, carrying out a direct test for the entire theory, as in step d5, is impossible. However, in the case of an entire theory with many theses, it is possible and useful to keep the theses separate, and even to refine each thesis and differentiate between different statements that are part of the thesis, so that some theses, or parts of these theses, can be tested.

All of this is part of a *successive rounds approach to testing hypotheses and formulating theory* that combines theoretical groundwork with general theory in order to help test hypotheses by building increasingly strong arguments, with more and more evidence, which are more comprehensive, although still incomplete, and can thus be described as incremental rounds. We should not dismiss this approach. The mindless empiricism mentioned above can dismiss a book like this one, proposing hypotheses, and corroborating and refining them through theses proposed by general theory, as being far from social science because it proposes 'mere hypotheses' and not ascertained truths. It can also dismiss the ways that I have just suggested for corroborating and refining hypotheses as 'cherry picking', an expression used by some social scientists to say that one focuses on a few select cases in which it is easy to prove one's hypotheses. Far from it, putting forward hypotheses that one then corroborates and refines, is always important for social science, and becomes indispensable when one is working in a new field, or in a field that is vast. Both of these considerations apply to this project.

When working in *a new field* one is often faced with the dilemma that, at first sight, some new hypotheses might seem promising but far-fetched, and one might doubt whether they are worth further investigation. When working in *a field that is vast*, like the study of globalization, one is faced with the daunting task of where to look for the evidence of the sources of globalization, since this evidence could be anywhere around the world. This is actually not so removed from established practices in social science. In all social science research, before undertaking the empirical research, one always makes a case as to why the hypotheses are important and how they can be tested, which might include preliminary evidence that a certain place or dataset is especially relevant for testing a certain hypothesis. The importance of the successive rounds approach follows from the fact that, when one needs to test new hypotheses that are also vast, one necessarily proceeds through several rounds, and corroborates the hypotheses before proceeding to the next round, building an increasingly strong case, also by refining the hypotheses and theses, until one eventually confirms or rejects the truthfulness of the hypotheses and the usefulness of the theses.

This successive-rounds approach to testing hypotheses and formulating theses can be *conceptualized best by extending ideas and practices from the field of law*. One builds first a *prima facie* case, suggesting that at first sight, based on the evidence that is already available, it is reasonable to assume that a certain hypothesis might be true, which warrants further investigation to gather more evidence and interpret it. In the case of a large project, one would then build what might be called a *secunda facie* case, based on further evidence and more theory building. One would continue along these lines until the hypothesis and the thesis are confirmed or rejected. As part of this process, one would also refine the hypothesis and the thesis, not simply accept or reject the initial hypothesis and thesis. All of this makes the hypotheses put forward here more than 'mere hypotheses'. They are partially supported by the empirical evidence that is behind the theoretical groundwork, and they are supported by general theory proposing valid theses. I argue also that the theses are *plausibly at work in important cases*. All of this amounts to a strong case for preliminarily accepting these hypotheses and begin testing them, as part of the larger research project. This use of general theory to corroborate and refine hypotheses can best be illustrated by considering in detail, firstly, the theoretical groundwork behind this project and the hypotheses suggested by this theoretical groundwork, which is the focus of the next section, and secondly, by considering the general theory put forward in this book and how it refines and corroborates the hypotheses of the project, which is the focus of the last section of this chapter.

5.7 Theoretical Groundwork and Hypotheses on Elites

The theoretical groundwork behind this project led to the formulation of *hypotheses regarding the existence of a world-elite* and its involvement in formulating neoliberal theories and devising and implementing policies based on these theories. These hypotheses are based on theoretical groundwork, including all of the first three tasks of theory. I present here only the main points from this theoretical groundwork that are directly relevant to the hypotheses. Economist Joseph Stiglitz has suggested that there was a 'Washington consensus' over the sources of economic growth that emphasized austerity and deregulation of markets. This consensus was shared by many economists in economic institutions like the World Bank and the International Monetary Fund and it led to the imposition of economic policies emphasizing austerity and market deregulation upon developing countries that needed loans from these economic institutions.[18] Closer reflection upon Stiglitz's argument and what is arguably common knowledge in universities, suggests the following points regarding the social groups that were part of the Washington consensus.

The economists referred to by Stiglitz might be described as a *single cultural or intellectual elite*, as opposed to a number of different intellectual elites, because they shared the same profession, and also because they shared some important views regarding economic growth. Knowledge of graduate research in universities suggests that such shared views can come from having done graduate work at the same university or a few related universities, or from having been influenced by major thinkers like Milton Friedman, or both of these things. Some universities and thinkers can have a huge influence, which is what happened with neoliberalism: the department of economics at the University of Chicago, where Friedman taught, has produced a disproportionate number of Nobel prize winners, and has greatly influenced contemporary economics.[19]

18 Joseph E. Stiglitz, *Globalization and Its Discontents* (New York: W.W. Norton, 2003).

19 Robert Van Horn, Philip Mirowski, and Thomas A. Stapleford, *Building Chicago Economics: New Perspectives on the History of America's Most Powerful Economics Program*, Historical Perspectives on Modern Economics (Cambridge and New York: Cambridge University Press, 2011). This book was reprinted in 2013. Other departments at the University of Chicago have also influenced academic fields, although not as much as the economics department. I know from Renee Worringer and Karen Barkey that the department of history and the department of sociology have both produced new approaches to the history of the Ottoman empire and historical sociology. The University of Chicago as a whole has acquired an international reputation, attracting such leading scholars as Pierre Bourdieu from France. John Jacob Hartman suggested to me that Friedman had exercised great influence on American culture, not just economics, through the view that economic freedom is essentially freedom to choose amongst products or services on offer.

At least some members of this intellectual elite are likely to have ties to other elites. These would include other elites that are part of culture, because successful intellectuals, including economists, can form ties to publishing houses and media conglomerates, and it is useful to conceive of all these intellectuals as part of cultural elites that include both universities and the broader cultural arena. I address this concept in the second volume, here it is sufficient to point out that, in order to reach their audiences, intellectuals have to go through publishing houses, although today the internet is providing a new means of diffusion of ideas.

This intellectual elite is becoming very important in contemporary societies and is cooperating with non-intellectual elites, in other arenas. Some intellectuals, especially some economists, are experts in a domain of knowledge, and in the associated academic field, which is deemed immediately relevant to policies, and therefore their advice is especially sought after by policymakers. Their importance might have grown to such a point in our societies that it might be appropriate to talk of a 'rule of experts', or a new intelligentsia.[20] These experts' advice is sought both by media, in the cultural arena, and by politicians, in the political arena, and some are more or less directly involved in formulating policies from economic theories. Stiglitz himself was in the Clinton administration, despite being some sort of outsider amongst economists, at least as he presents himself.[21] Interestingly, Bill and Hillary Clinton, with Stiglitz' participation, presided over a decade of remarkable growth in the American economy that Stiglitz described as the 'roaring nineties', by analogy with the 'roaring twenties'. What is interesting about this analogy is that it suggests the nineties were also going to be followed by a depression, since the 1920s famously led to the Great Depression of 1929, as part of a boom-and-bust cycle. Stiglitz suggests this was because the state failed to provide adequate

---

Roemer has paraphrased and criticized this view of economic freedom: John E. Roemer, *Free to Lose: an Introduction to Marxist Economic Philosophy* (Cambridge, Massachusetts and London: Harvard University Press, 2009).

20 Timothy Mitchell, *Rule of Experts: Egypt, Techno-Politics, Modernity* (Berkeley and Los Angeles: University of California Press, 2002). This book focuses on Egypt. However, the importance of experts is arguably growing in the West too. Ivan Szelenyi and Larry King's book on intellectuals, which focuses on the East European concept of intelligentsia as a new class, a concept that is close to the concept of expert, shows that there is interest in this concept in the West: King and Szelényi, *Theories of the New Class: Intellectuals and Power*.

21 I am not an economist and rely on Stiglitz's account, without having researched his ties to other schools of economics. Just by denouncing the 'Washington consensus' Stiglitz appears to be an outsider: Stiglitz, *Globalization and Its Discontents*.

regulation of markets, and to avoid a boom-and-bust cycle.[22] The 1990s also saw the beginnings of the terrorist threat to the United States, with the 1993 World Trade Center bombing, which in retrospect marked this site for destruction. Whatever threat might have existed before, this new threat was of an altogether different magnitude and sophistication. It is useful to introduce at this stage how this theoretical groundwork fits into the broader project, before focusing on the hypotheses that it led me to formulate.

I expand upon Stiglitz' argument regarding the importance of the state to ensure the proper functioning of markets, within a theory that calls for a balance between state, society, and markets, and I also *add two insights to Stiglitz' call to recognize the importance of the state*. The first insight involves the role of the state to ensure the functioning of markets. I emphasize that *the proper functioning of markets requires also intellectuals and a truly independent civil society*, which is indispensable to provide adequate economic theories that learn from past mistakes. It is not just the state, but also the intellectuals who advise policymakers, who are responsible for such failures as the uneven development produced by industry relocation, or the effects of the 2008 depression, both of which were arguably related to market deregulation. It is these intellectuals who failed to learn the important lessons of the Great Depression, and who failed to find a proper balance between too much and too little regulation, swinging from one extreme to the other, from over-emphasis to under-emphasis on the state, or even complete neglect of it. I address this point in the book on humanist social science, drawing attention to the responsibilities of *some* intellectuals, and to problems of universities as a whole that include specialization, which led in some important cases to a persistent and recurrent failure to learn from past mistakes. I elaborate upon this insight within a Gramscian theory of intellectuals that is more nuanced and useful than theories of the intelligentsia as an independent class, or theories of intellectuals as invariably class-bound.[23] This theory is informed by discussions I had with economist and economic sociologist Szabolcs Kemeny, who in the 1990s, with Cornell University and Columbia University scholars, was working on the importance

22 I refer to Bill and Hillary Clinton together because they proposed themselves as a Presidential couple of equals in the White House and they arguably both participated in the economic growth of the 1990s described by Stiglitz in: *The Roaring Nineties: a New History of the World's Most Prosperous Decade*, 1st ed. (New York: W.W. Norton, 2003). Stiglitz specifically emphasizes that it was too little state regulation that caused the first signs of depression already in the early 2000s, when he was writing: ibid., 15. By contrast, Michelle Obama presented herself as a more traditional spouse in her role as First Lady.

23 Olsaretti, "Beyond Class." "Croce, Philosophy and Intellectuals." In this theory some managers are organic intellectuals because they are close to economic processes.

of managers in the transition from state socialism to capitalism in Hungary, which was picking up pace during the 1990s in the wake of the demise of the Soviet Union and the Warsaw Pact.[24] At the University of Michigan, sociologist Elaine Weiner, now at McGill University, was also working on this transition, and adding a gender perspective to it, drawing attention to the fact that in this transition both workers and women lost out, a very important argument.[25]

The second insight that I add to Stiglitz' call for recognizing the importance of the state is *how to conceptualize the cooperation between the intellectual elite and other elites*. I add to the above picture *the important concept of hegemonic bloc suggested by Gramsci*. I define this concept in detail elsewhere in this project, for the purposes of this volume it is sufficient to introduce the preliminary definition that a hegemonic bloc is a more or less well-structured alliance of diverse social groups, all of which are necessary, in different ways, in order to ensure the viability of political projects. A hegemonic bloc is led by a hegemonic social group. In the context of this argument, applying this Gramscian concept to understand neoliberalism entailed formulating a series of hypotheses that can be summarized as suggesting that *neoliberalism was made possible by a hegemonic bloc of social groups that included political, cultural, and economic elites*, more or less well coordinated. In addition, there must have *been a part of this elite, the hegemonic social group, which was able to coordinate the activities of these elites* across countries and for a long period of time, which must therefore have been a world-elite. Some of this argument follows from my reading of Stiglitz, who also suggested that the Washington consensus was shared by at least some politicians in the West. This implies that the economists might have had *ties to politicians* in countries in the West who implemented similar policies to those imposed upon developing countries. Upon

24 Kemeny and I shared a disillusionment with economics and an interest in sociology, because of the dryness of economics, and because of its failure to address concrete problems. Kemeny drew my attention to the importance of the emerging field of economic sociology, which is relatively strong at Cornell University and at Columbia University, and encouraged my interest in sociology. Kemeny worked with David Stark, the author of a study on the transition from socialism to capitalism: David Stark and Laszlo Bruszt, *Postsocialist Pathways: Transforming Politics and Property in East Central Europe*, Cambridge Studies in Comparative Politics (Cambridge and New York: Cambridge University Press, 1998). Kemeny and I also shared an interest in consulting, but he managed to extricate himself from an increasingly difficult academic job market before the 9/11 attacks and the 2008 financial crisis, a climate that has made business as hard as academic careers.

25 Elaine S. Weiner, *Market Dreams: Gender, Class, and Capitalism in the Czech Republic* (Ann Arbor: University of Michigan Press, 2010); "No (Wo) Man's Land: the Post-Socialist Purgatory of Czech Female Factory Workers," *Social Problems* 52, no. 4 (2005).

reflection, it seems likely that the intellectual elites had *ties to members of the economic elite* too or developed these ties. Neoliberal theories and policies benefited overwhelmingly owners and top managers of companies that relocated. It seems likely that these members of the economic elite would have joined the intellectual elite, and the political elite, in actually implementing or continuing and expanding these policies.

This theoretical groundwork led to the formulation of *three main hypotheses* that inform the entire project. The *first main hypothesis regards national elites,* and it can be usefully divided into smaller hypotheses, or sub-hypotheses. I put these hypotheses in bullet point form, in order to show more clearly how each statement is refined by the theory that I propose later in this chapter.

1. *There are national elites in many or even in all countries that are part of the West, and they are responsible for formulating neoliberal theories and implementing neoliberal policies.* The national elites are distinguished by the following features.
   a. The national elites are divided into economic, cultural and political-military elites, each of which derives power from a different source, respectively: the economy, culture, politics and the military.
   b. These elites however have ties to each other, or are building ties to each other, which enable them to cooperate more or less closely.
   c. Parts of these elites are consolidating into establishments, which are social groups that are closed and not affected by democratic pressures, compared to social groups that are open and recruit from below.
   d. There are already in countries that are part of the West economic, cultural, and political-military establishments.

Hypothesis 1.b, regarding the coordination between different elites, builds upon the suggestion that economists and politicians cooperated in formulating policies from economic theories. Hypotheses 1.c and 1.d, regarding establishments, were introduced because many of these elites seem capable of pursuing their own agenda independently of the needs of the masses who constitute most of the electorate in their countries, at least for a certain period of time, until the condition of the masses is so desperate that it causes a backlash, like the populist backlash that has affected many Western countries.

A *second main hypothesis* is needed to explain neoliberalism. This is a *hypothesis regarding the existence of a world-elite involved in globalization.* This hypothesis is necessary because the first hypothesis is not enough to explain the implementation of neoliberal policies. *Neoliberal policies required significant coordination across countries.* The national elites in the West were able to coordinate their activities across many countries, for example by opening up the markets of developing countries to investment from the West and at around the same time opening up markets in the West to goods produced in developing countries. This requires significant coordination between political elites in developing countries and political elites in the West. Entire countries in the developing world had to be opened up to investment from Western economic elites, laws had to be issued to facilitate this investment, and port facilities and other logistics infrastructure had to be built to enable trade flows from these countries to the West. In addition, market deregulation had to take place in the West at around the same time in order to open up Western markets to goods from developing countries, without running the risk of creating gluts that would have undermined manufacturers who relocated. Therefore, the second hypothesis is that *there must have been a social group that coordinated between the different national elites*, in order to make the implementation of neoliberal policies possible. This leads to the formulation of the second hypothesis and a number of sub- hypotheses within it.

2. *There is an emergent world-elite that coordinates between national elites to make neoliberalism possible.* The emergent world-elite is distinguished by the following features.
   a. The emergent world-elite derives its power from globalization processes that transcend countries, in such a manner that its power is not based in just one country, but in many countries around the world.
   b. It has ties to the national elites or establishments of different countries and cooperates with them.
   c. Parts of it are imperialist elites and are consolidating into an emergent imperialist world-elite, or have consolidated into an imperialist world-elite.

This second main hypothesis was the product of additional theoretical groundwork, which helps clarify some of the sub-hypotheses. The qualifier *emergent* is suggested by the consideration that, even if a world-elite does not exist already, some of the elites in the West and some of the elites in developing countries might be forming especially close ties to each other, and might be distancing themselves from their countries of origin as they participate in the process of opening up markets in many parts of the world, and in the expansion of trade flows that is part of this process. Sociologist Leslie Sklair has made a convincing case that a transnational capitalist class is emerging, which might be conceived of as an economic elite within the world-elite, and which is involved in, and derives its wealth from, economic processes that are associated with international trade flows and globalization.[26] Interestingly, Sklair emphasized that they also share a similar education, sometimes at the same leading universities and business schools. It seems likely that analogous processes are leading to the creation of a transnational political elite that serves in institutions like the United Nations, in regional blocs like the European Union, and in think tanks.[27] Lastly, there has been much discussion of the return of imperialism in the wake of the 9/11 attacks, the search for cheap oil, and a return to an expansionist policy previously associated with Western imperialism.[28] It seems possible, even likely, that parts of the emergent world-elite involved in globalization might be consolidating into an *imperialist* world-elite, if they have not done so already. This is an elite that is committed to imperialist practices to build up power, and that is active on a world stage.

The concept of hegemony is important to understand what makes a world-elite possible. I define hegemony in greater detail in chapter 6. Here I just want to emphasize that it is a type of power in which culture plays an important role. This makes it especially important for groups like the world-elite that is at the center of the second hypothesis. Power across vast distances requires that actors who are not in close contact with each other, and are not constantly communicating, should share some of the same culture, including some of the same worldview, and even theories regarding how the world works, in order to facilitate cooperation. This shared culture and worldview could be acquired from the leading universities and business schools studied by Sklair. They could also be acquired from having participated in, and from continuing to participate in, imperialist enterprises. This leads to the introduction of the *third main hypothesis*. It focuses upon establishments, rather than national elites more in general, because the establishments are unresponsive to pressures from below, and would more readily cooperate with the emergent imperialist world-elite, than with the masses in their countries.

26 Leslie Sklair, *The Transnational Capitalist Class* (Oxford: Blackwell, 2000). This book went to a second edition already in 2001.

27 Some authors have suggested that a world state is emerging: Alexander Wendt, "Why a World State Is Inevitable," *European journal of international relations* 9, no. 4 (2003). These changes would be part of the creation of a world state. I gained insights into this political elite also through Jose Manuel Bassat, at the World Bank for many years, but who had an interest in politics and international relations and discussed these topics with me.

28 David Harvey, *The New Imperialism* (Oxford and New York: Oxford University Press, 2003). Other authors who have dealt with the return of imperialism in the wake of the 9/11 attacks include Arrighi and Mann. I address their work in the second volume.

3. *The emergent imperialist world-elite exercises a form of hegemonic leadership over the establishments of different countries that includes sharing the same culture and worldview.* The power of this emergent imperialist world-elite is distinguished by the following features.
   a. The emergent imperialist world-elite and the establishments of different countries are scattered over vast territories, but they share the same views regarding economic growth, and development more in general, which enables cooperation amongst them.
   b. They also share the same imperialist worldview that gives them a sense of superiority and entitlement compared to the masses and that predisposes them to pursue development in ways that exclusively benefit them, or even that benefit them at the expense of the masses.
   c. The emergent imperialist world-elite cooperates with establishments to gain acceptance for policies that benefit them most of all, rather than imposing them by coercion.
   d. It is these elites, the imperialist world-elite and the establishments, who are responsible for neoliberalism, market deregulation policies, and the relocation of industry.

5.8 General Theory and Theses on Elites and Masses

The general theory proposed in this book can contribute to corroborating and refining these three main hypotheses. This is important. Hypotheses 1, 2 and 3 might seem promising, but still far-fetched. Could there really be a single imperialist world-elite whose power is based in many countries, potentially straddling the globe? Critics might try to dismiss this as a conspiracy theory, rather than a theory of history. But there are sound reasons to take the above hypotheses seriously. In this section, I show how the theses put forward in the second volume contribute to *corroborating hypotheses 2 and 3*. They corroborate these hypotheses by suggesting a plausible mechanism from European history that explains the emergence of imperialist world-elites out of a combination of social conflict and interstate conflict. Imperialist world-elites in Europe would have emerged because of this mechanism. The theses also contribute to *refining hypotheses 2 and 3*, by suggesting that an imperialist world-elite emerged in the past. This was the imperialist world-elite that built the British empire. The theses thus serve both to corroborate and also to refine the hypotheses. The study of the British empire, which is based on evidence that is already available, can be used to build a *prima facie* case to accept the hypothesis that there might be an imperialist world-elite, because such an elite emerged in the past.

The theses can also be used to refine hypothesis 2, which can help us begin testing it, by focusing initially upon just one time and place: nineteenth-century Great Britain. In the next chapter I add Italy as another interesting case. The theses also help refine hypothesis 3, by suggesting that the British imperialist world-elite that emerged in the past exercised hegemony over other elites who participated in empire-building. This point is taken up in chapter 6, which presents additional theoretical groundwork focused on hegemony, and refines hypothesis 1. It also introduces hypothesis 4, regarding the use of hegemony in empire-building and its ties to collective action. The next chapter also argues that Italy provides an especially interesting case of a national elite that consolidated into an early establishment.

The theses put forward in this book suggest *a social mechanism that led to imperial expansion in some European states and the creation of a world-elite.* This mechanism is based upon the twin concepts of intensive power and extensive power proposed by sociologist Michael Mann. I differ from Mann in many important ways, but this distinction, and how it applies to European history, is very important, and I re-interpret it and expand upon it throughout this project.[29] In my interpretation, intensive power is power that is concentrated geographically, which means it is concentrated in one geographical area, typically a city and nearby areas, in which the population enjoys high average income, a measure of economic power. Extensive power by contrast is dispersed geographically, and it originally was derived from vast rural areas in which the population is especially polarized between an elite with high income and vast power, and masses with low income and little or no power. These concepts are useful to propose a social mechanism explaining the emergence of world-elites out of a combination of social conflict between elites and masses with interstate conflict. This combination leads to territorial expansion and the creation of empires, in other words, to *imperialist tendencies in modern European history and the creation of world-elites.* The modern history of Europe, and by extension of the West, is actually distinguished by two tendencies that together explain its imperial expansion. These tendencies, rather

---

29 Three important ways in which I differ from Mann are: firstly, I propose a theory which uses fewer variables than his theory; secondly, I take an analytical approach and I define the variables more carefully, thinking both about the exact meaning of each concept and also about how each concept relates to reality, and specifically how useful it is to describe an aspect of reality; thirdly, I take an engineering approach to many of the concepts and I combine them in a single theory. I discuss Mann's concept of 'organizational outflanking' in the book on the humanist theory of society, which also clarifies each of these three important ways in which I differ from Mann.

than ideology alone, explain imperialism, including the return of imperialism in the wake of the 9/11 attacks. They both concern the balance of power. I introduce here two theses that the axiomatic-deductive theoretical work for this book led me to formulate, theses XI and XII. These are part of the outline of a general theory that I propose in the second volume, however, they are intelligible on their own, without the earlier theses, and they are most relevant to the discussion here.

Thesis XI concerns social conflict and the balance of power between social groups within one state, or the balance of power within society. It suggests a social mechanism that explains the first tendency towards expansion.

XI. *In modern Europe there was competition between two forms of power, the intensive power distinctive of democracies and the extensive power distinctive of empires. There was no decisive victory between these forms of power, but a dynamic balance of power that kept changing.*

- a. *This balance of power was internal to states* and consisted in a dynamic balance of power between social groups within the state, whereby if some groups increased their power, so did the other groups.
- b. *The balance of power between social groups overlapped with the balance between intensive and extensive forms of power*. It was distinguished by the following features.
  - i. Democracies achieved a breakthrough in developing intensive power and raising wealth in cities, where population was concentrated, and proved a match for feudal lords.
  - ii. Feudal lords, and later imperialist elites, reacted by further extending their power, typically in areas that were poorer and less densely populated and were thus easier to conquer, but they developed this extensive power to the point that they could fight back against democracies and conquer some of them.
  - iii. This social conflict led to a first tendency towards state expansion. This is because there was no fixed balance of power between the intensive and extensive forms of power, but a tendency whereby each form tried to outgrow the other, leading to both economic growth and imperial expansion.

Thesis XII builds upon this last point and concerns the balance of power between states and interstate conflict. It suggests a social mechanism that explains the second tendency towards expansion.

XII. *In modern Europe there emerged a number of powerful states of a new kind for Europe, namely, proto nation-states.* These were *England, France, Spain, with the Netherlands and Portugal as intermediate cases. There was no decisive victory nor permanent peace amongst these states, or between these states and other states, but a dynamic balance of power that kept changing.*

a. *This balance of power was external to states* and consisted in a dynamic balance of power between states, whereby if one state increased its power, so did the other states.

b. *The balance of power between these states kept changing slowly* through a mix of external and internal factors. It was distinguished by the following features.

   i. There was, post 1648, a relatively stable balance of power between states, whereby major wars within Europe were rare compared to the previous two centuries.

   ii. The proto nation-states concentrated in expanding outwards, in areas outside Europe, by a mix of trade and conquest, expanding extensive power.

   iii. The net effect was that European proto nation-states engaged in a sustained outward expansion, and then occasional very destructive wars in Europe when expansion altered the balance of power between states.

   iv. Some of these proto nation-states also developed the internal economy to a great extent, and this led to more of the competition highlighted in thesis XI and thus even more expansion, especially within one state, England, which went through a historically unprecedented expansion.

These two theses, together with additional theoretical groundwork, can be used to *corroborate* hypothesis 2. This is thanks to the fact that these two theses propose a mechanism that explains how a world-elite can emerge. They also serve to direct additional theoretical groundwork and build a *prima facie* case for considering the British empire and its elites as an early instance of an imperialist world-elite. The following paragraphs summarize the additional theoretical groundwork.

The British empire was the largest empire in modern history, therefore it was the most powerful empire in terms of sheer conquests. This empire also built vast trading networks around the world, therefore it drove an early form of globalization.[30] Interestingly, in this process, it pioneered free trade and an

30 There have been several studies of the global dimension of European colonial empires and their ties to trade flows that spanned the world: David B. Abernethy, *The Dynamics of Global Dominance: European Overseas Empires, 1415–1980* (New Haven and London: Yale

earlier economic liberalism, referred to as free-trade liberalism, that neoliberalism is partly modelled on. Most importantly, this was part of a new form of imperialism that progressively emerged during the course of the early modern era, *circa* 1500–1800, and shortly afterwards, which slowly but drastically changed the balance of power amongst European states. During that period, the British aristocratic-military elite that built the British empire became an imperialist world-elite that elaborated a significantly new type of imperialism, which it refined from around 1800 onwards, and which made the British empire the largest and most powerful of all European colonial empires, such that this elite was active on a truly world stage.[31] Other elites and their empires survived only by becoming clients of the British aristocratic-military elite and its empire. Such was the case with some elites in the Mughal empire in India, which was conquered by the British aristocratic-military elite, who retained

University Press, 2000); Timothy H. Parsons, *The Rule of Empires: Those Who Built Them, Those Who Endured Them, and Why They Always Fall* (Oxford and New York: Oxford University Press, 2010); *The Second British Empire: In the Crucible of the Twentieth Century*, Critical Issues in World and International History (Lanham, Boulder, New York, and Oxford: Rowman & Littlefield Publishers, 2014). These authors also suggest that, because of their sheer size, these empires were doomed to fall sooner or later. Parsons especially portrays the Second British Empire as weak, also because of the contradictions it was caught in, officially fostering democracy at home, yet committed to conquest and military rule abroad. I disagree with this assessment and I provide arguments against it in the second volume.

31 Historian Christopher Bayly is amongst those who argued that around this time a Second British Empire was built, which replaced the First British Empire brought to an end by the American Revolutionary War. The turning point in this process and the social bases of this Second British Empire are described in: Christopher Alan Bayly, *Imperial Meridian: the British Empire and the World, 1780–1830*, Studies in Modern History (London: Longman, 1989). This book was republished in 2016. The cultural changes that occurred around this time in the imperialism associated with the British empire are described in: D. Graham Burnett, *Masters of All They Surveyed: Exploration, Geography, and a British El Dorado* (Chicago: University of Chicago Press, 2001). Others have emphasized continuities in the scientific culture of the Atlantic world: James Delbourgo, *Collecting the World: Hans Sloane and the Origins of the British Museum* (Cambridge, Massachusetts and London: Belknap Press of Harvard University Press, 2019); James Delbourgo and Nicholas Dew, eds., *Science and Empire in the Atlantic World*, New Directions in American History (New York and London: Routledge, 2008). It is important to remember that Canada continued to be a British dominion and is to this day closely associated with British culture and the British monarchy. It had great strategic importance for the British aristocratic-military elite, both because of its location, and because it was a source of raw materials for British industry. Arguing that there were important changes associated with the Second British Empire does not necessarily rule out all continuities. Additionally, the Atlantic system itself was changed: Wim Klooster, *Revolutions in the Atlantic World: A Comparative History* (New York: New York University Press, 2009).

some local elites in the administration that they built. Such was the case also with the Portuguese aristocratic-military elite and its colonial empire, and also to some extent with the Dutch and French aristocratic-military elites and their colonial empires. All became allies in a subordinate position, and thus clients, of the British aristocratic-military elite.[32]

The two theses and the additional theoretical groundwork enable us to *refine hypotheses 2 and 3* by suggesting that, in order to test and eventually prove or reject these hypotheses, a promising place to start is with research on the British empire and its centers of power. Here I reformulate hypotheses 2 and 3, using a very similar format with the same number and order of sub-hypotheses, and I call the reformulated hypotheses 2′ and 3′. One would refine hypothesis 2 in the following manner and then test it.

2′. *The British aristocratic-military elite that built the British empire became an early world-elite.* This early world-elite was distinguished by the following features.
   a. It derived its power from an early process of globalization that it encouraged by building trade networks around the world that involved many different countries.
   b. It ruled to a greater or lesser extent through local elites that cooperated with it.
   c. In this process of expansion, this world-elite became an *imperialist* world-elite distinguished by a worldview with racial overtones, such as Rudyard Kipling's 'white man's burden', which justified conquest in the name of bringing civilization to other parts of the world, somehow seen as lacking civilization.

I argue below that this ideology was, and to some extent still is, part of the culture of the British aristocratic-military elite, and of the Piedmontese elite that built the modern Italian state, and that I refer to as the Piedmontese national elite. This ideology, combined with favorable social organization and structures, contributed to the imperial expansion of countries in modern European

32 On Indian society, including Indian elites, see: Christopher Alan Bayly, *Indian Society and the Making of the British Empire* (Cambridge and New York: Cambridge University Press, 1987). On the Portuguese empire and its inability to survive as an independent entity because of competition with Great Britain, which reached a peak during the Napoleonic wars, see: Jorge M. Pedreira, "From Growth to Collapse: Portugal, Brazil, and the Breakdown of the Old Colonial System (1760–1830)," *Hispanic American Historical Review* 80, no. 4 (2000). On the comparative history of empires, see: Christopher Alan Bayly and Dirk H. Kolff, eds., *Two Colonial Empires: Comparative Essays on the History of India and Indonesia in the Nineteenth Century*, Comparative Studies in Overseas History (Dordrecht: Springer Netherlands, 2012).

history and the creation of a world-elite. This ideology still surfaces from time to time, if only in tactless behavior like that shown by British Prime Minister Boris Johnson, then Foreign Secretary, who began reciting Kipling's poetry at an official function in a former colony, in which the Rohingya genocide was under way.[33] The theses could lead us to refine and thus help us test the third hypothesis too.

3'. *The British imperialist world-elite exercised a hegemonic leadership over other elites also through cultural leadership and its ability to justify its rule through ideologies*. The power of this early imperialist world-elite was distinguished by the following features.
   a. The British imperialist world-elite and the other European imperialist elites that became its clients shared similar views regarding economic growth, and development more in general.
   b. The British imperialist world-elite and other European elites, and some of the elites of the countries they conquered, shared a sense of superiority and entitlement compared to the masses of these countries that predisposed them to extract wealth from the masses rather than create wealth and share it with the masses.
   c. The British imperialist world-elite cooperated with parts of the cultural elite in Great Britain to gain acceptance for policies that benefited them most of all, rather than imposing them by coercion, because it faced strong opposition within Great Britain.

---

33 Boris Johnson tactlessly muttered lines from Rudyard Kipling's poem 'The Road to Mandalay', at a public gathering in Burma: Robert Booth, "Boris Johnson Caught on Camera Reciting Kipling in Myanmar Temple," The Guardian. European imperialism, including British imperialism and Italian imperialism, stirred ethnic divisions and led to violence in many former European colonies. European imperialists showed equal disregard for the lives of working-class people in their countries. Rudyard Kipling is also the author of the poem 'The White Man's Burden: the United States and the Philippine Islands' inciting the United States to colonize the Philippines. I believe that Kipling and other European imperialists called for the use of working-class people, and other countries' troops, the United States, as expendables for their military enterprises, also by presenting imperial conquests as an adventure with a good purpose, and attractive to European working classes, and beneficial to the populations of conquered countries. I am convinced that if Haig or Cadorna, the commander of Italian troops at the beginning of Italy's involvement in the First World War, had to lead the assaults against German or Austrian fortified positions from the front, rather than the rear, they would not have ordered the assaults. Imperial conquests were typically less costly for European armies than First World War battles, but they were neither adventures, nor beneficial for conquered peoples. I provide a critique of Lange's argument regarding these beneficial effects in the second volume.

d. It is these elites, including the imperialist world-elite and parts of the cultural elites in Great Britain, which developed the academic discipline of economics and free-trade liberalism.

We can also introduce an additional sub-hypothesis that, if proven correct, would contribute to corroborating and refining also hypothesis 1, besides hypotheses 2 and 3. This hypothesis suggests that something similar to the flooding of markets with cheap goods produced abroad that has occurred in our time has happened before, and that it was similarly justified through ideologies.

e. These ideologies, combined with political-military means, helped the British aristocratic-military elite exercise hegemony within Great Britain and gain acceptance of politics that favored it. They justified an early opening of markets, which flooded Great Britain with cheap agricultural products at the time of the repeal of the Corn Laws, and with cheap textiles produced abroad like calico prints imported by the East India Company, both of which became the object of prolonged political and economic struggles in Great Britain.

The next chapter corroborates and refines hypothesis 1, focusing specifically upon hypotheses regarding hegemony and collective action that explain why some elites turn into establishments that are not affected by democratic pressures, and are able to implement policies with little or no regard for the masses in their countries.

CHAPTER 6

Case Studies and Hypotheses on Hegemony and Collective Action

This chapter presents theoretical groundwork on two case studies, elites in Great Britain and elites in Italy, and the different types of hegemony that they built, which serves to formulate *hypotheses regarding hegemony and collective action*. The theory that I propose in this book focuses on the concepts of hegemony and collective action, and argues that they affect development and democracy. It is appropriate therefore to *define in greater detail what I mean by hegemony* and address its importance to democracy and development. The preliminary definition of hegemony introduced above emphasizes that it is power that has a large cultural component. Here I want to add that *hegemony concerns leadership that includes a large cultural and consensual component.* Hegemonic leadership is leadership that exercises influence through culture, which is used to gain the consent of those who participate in a polity, or of the allies of that polity. Hegemony can be of various types, not all of which are compatible with democracy. For example, as pointed out above, culture can be manipulated and abused to gain consent in a manner that is anti-democratic and that leads to pursuing anti-democratic goals. Fascism and nazism and soviet communism are instances of this manipulation and abuse of culture. This chapter seeks to explain two different types of hegemony and suggests that they arise from features of social groups and society, all of which affect the ability to engage in collective action. This chapter also suggests that some elites enjoy such a marked collective action advantage over the masses that they can dictate their own terms, largely ignoring democratic pressures in a given society. This chapter also introduces the concept of meso collective action, that is, collective action that occurs on a meso scale of social interaction and involves entire social groups. The collective action advantage of elites can exploit and compound meso collective action problems that affect other social groups.

6.1 Historical Case Studies to Understand Contemporary Cases

This chapter uses the methodology outlined in the previous chapter and presents theoretical groundwork on past elites. Historical case studies can be a very important way to formulate theory. Two points clarify the importance of historical case studies to the substantive arguments of this book. The first point is that *past cases of imperialist world-elites and their empires are a very useful way to formulate hypotheses and theory.* This is for example because there is far more work about the British aristocratic-military elite and its empire than there is about contemporary world-elites and contemporary empires. Additionally, cases from the recent past can be especially useful to understand contemporary cases, both because of similarities across short time spans, an approach associated with historical studies, and because of possible continuities between these cases and contemporary cases, an approach associated with historical sociology. Historical sociology was pioneered by Weber, and is represented today by Wallerstein and Mann, whose work I address in the second volume. One continuity it emphasizes is continuity in social structures. Another is continuity in tendencies like those described by theses XI and XII. The fact that the new imperialism in the wake of the 9/11 attacks still comes from the West suggests that there might be some such continuity. Therefore, historical case studies, and in particular focusing on the British aristocratic-military elite, is especially useful because it enables us to build a better theory much more quickly, then test it and see whether it applies to the recent past and also to contemporary cases.

The second point that I want to clarify is that *case studies are especially useful for corroborating and refining hypotheses,* which serves to test these hypotheses through the successive rounds approach. If the refined hypotheses 2′, and 3′ put forward in chapter 5 regarding the British imperialist world-elite and the British empire were proven to be correct, this would help testing hypotheses 2 and 3. This is because, in the case of complex hypotheses that apply to a relatively small number of cases, one would seek to prove the hypothesis first in one case, then in a few other cases, then in all cases, as part of the successive rounds approach. *Choosing the case to test first can be especially useful to the successive rounds approach.* For example, focusing on the case of the British imperialist world-elite and the British empire is not cherry picking, but testing the hypothesis in the most important case. This is the case showing that a world-elite existed in the past, corroborating hypothesis 2. It is more efficient than testing hypotheses 1 and 3 first. This is because corroborating hypothesis 2 also helps corroborate hypothesis 3. If a world-elite existed in the past, it cannot have acted alone, but it must have had ties to elites in other countries. This follows from the observation that the means of transportation and communication were much slower than today, and national elites necessarily had great leeway in administering their territories, therefore there must have been some shared culture or worldview that enabled coordination. This corroborates hypothesis 3 and suggests that institutions that educated administrators of far-flung places would be a promising place to begin testing hypothesis 3. Testing hypothesis 3 thus refined can also help test hypothesis 1, because knowing who the world-elite was might help identify cases that are especially relevant to test hypothesis 1. In particular, the centers of power of the world-elite might yield pointers to the national elites in Europe, and to the national elites in the colonies, who cooperated with the British imperialist world-elite. It would therefore suggest where we have to start testing hypothesis 1, following the successive rounds approach, case by case, until we prove that hypothesis 1 was true in sufficiently many cases.

In this chapter, besides refining hypotheses, I also undertake theoretical groundwork that serves to formulate theses, a task that I carry out in the second volume. Here I want to emphasize that *case studies of hegemony and collective action are especially important to formulate theses regarding democracy and development.* This can be clarified by a few simple considerations. Hegemony is crucially important for *democracy*, because although not all hegemonic leadership is democratic, all democratic leadership is hegemonic. This follows from the fact that in a democracy those in positions of power ought to win the consent of the masses and thus ought to participate in the cultural life of the polity, without however subordinating this cultural life to their own ends. Hegemony is crucially important for *development* because it is inextricably tied to collective action, and through collective action it affects what kind of development is pursued. This follows from hypothesis 1 and sub-hypotheses c and d, which suggest that the establishments of countries in the West were capable of pursuing their own political and economic agendas for a long time, without being affected by democratic pressures, and continued pursuing these agendas regardless of the disastrous effects they had on the masses, all of which suggests that they had some kind of advantage in terms of collective action.

Hegemony was arguably part of the collective action advantage of elites over the masses enabling national elites to implement neoliberal policies. Hegemony contributed to this advantage in two ways: firstly, by gaining consent to a policy; and secondly, by contributing to processes of domination, whereby a relatively small elite, made cohesive by hegemony, is able to dominate vast masses that by contrast are divided by cultural differences, which lead to collective action problems that the cohesive elite can compound. In the next section I sketch the usefulness of case studies to theory, and to a theory of hegemony in particular. I then introduce Gramsci's theory of hegemony and contrast it with that of elite theorists. Lastly, I focus on the two case studies, namely, the British imperialist world-elite, and the Piedmontese national elite, which represent two different uses of hegemony. The first used hegemony chiefly to gain consent, whereas the second used hegemony chiefly to exercise domination.

6.2 The Use of Case Studies to Understand Hegemony

In this chapter I also propose my interpretation of *important aspects of Gramsci's theory of hegemony* and relate them to collective action. Gramsci emphasized that *a hegemonic social group exercises hegemonic leadership over allied social groups and domination over other groups.*[1] Political theorist Joseph Femia has suggested that Gramsci implicitly made also another important distinction, between *integral and minimal hegemony*, respectively referring to hegemony that encompasses most of society, and to hegemony that encompasses just a few relatively small social groups.[2] These distinctions are important to the two case studies that I use in order to formulate hypotheses and theses: the British aristocratic-military elite who built the British empire, and the north-Italian, to be precise Piedmontese, elite who built the modern Italian state. The usefulness of focusing on these elites in order to understand hegemony stems from two insights. The first insight is that the British aristocratic-military elite became an imperialist world-elite and it built ties to other elites, both in Great Britain and abroad, and is an instance of integral hegemony. Its use of culture is especially interesting theoretically to understand consent. The second insight is that the Piedmontese national elite is instead an instance of minimal hegemony. Culture was still important for the internal cohesion of this elite, but domination of the masses in Italy played a greater part in its power. Its use of mechanisms of cooptation and defection to undermine collective action by the masses is especially interesting theoretically. Both types of hegemony, whether for gaining consent, or for enabling domination, were to some extent at work in both cases. But one type of hegemony clearly prevailed in each case, and this makes it useful to formulate theory.

This is one of the reasons why I focus on case studies, namely, that they can be especially useful to formulate theory. There are two main reasons why case studies are especially useful to formulate theory. The first is that *case studies can help us formulate explanations of social phenomena by providing social mechanisms*. This is because of the in-depth knowledge one can gain in a case study. In addition, some case studies are especially fruitful for formulating

1 Gramsci, *Quaderni del Carcere*, 2010–11.

2 Joseph V. Femia, *Gramsci's Political Thought: Hegemony, Consciousness, and the Revolutionary Process* (Oxford: Clarendon press, 1987), Revision of thesis – Oxford University, 1979, 46–47.

explanations involving mechanisms. Charles Darwin's theory of evolution was formulated thanks to such a fruitful case study, which illustrates this point very clearly. It was formulated based on long studies of past theories, bits of evidence that Darwin gathered around the world, and evidence and a breakthrough he had thanks to his work on the Galapagos Islands, which turned out to be an especially clear case of evolutionary mechanisms at work, for those who knew how to read these mechanisms thanks to extensive reading and other evidence.[3] The same considerations apply to social science. A detailed description of the use of case studies in social science is provided by Lange, who has highlighted the importance of case studies in order to understand mechanisms and also to contribute to formulating theory.[4] Lange builds upon a tradition of sociological thought initiated by Weber, which suggests that case studies are an important tool in comparative and historical methods for social science.

This is the second reason why case studies are especially useful to formulate theory. As discussed by Lange, *case studies can be very fruitful in a comparative context, when two or more cases are studied together*, for example because they allow us to focus on a causal factor, or a part of a mechanism, that is present in one case but not in the other, and thus can help us find out how important that single factor or part of the mechanism is, within the overall mechanism. *The comparison can be made between cases that are very similar*. The British empire could be compared to other European empires it competed with, the French empire and the Spanish empire, for example. *The comparison can also be made between different cases*, as I do in this chapter, by contrasting the British imperialist world-elite and the Piedmontese national elite. This helps us to construct models that are different, by contrasting a type of hegemony that emphasizes consent, with another type that emphasizes domination, in order to bring out the different effects that they have on society, for example. Lastly, *comparisons*

3 This view of Darwin's theory, widely accepted, is criticized in: Frank J. Sulloway, "Darwin and the Galapagos," *Biological Journal of the Linnean Society* 21, no. 1–2 (1984). Sulloway criticized this view by emphasizing that Darwin formulated his theory of evolution long after leaving the Galapagos islands. Sulloway's argument rejects the view that Darwin had a eureka moment on the Galapagos islands but it does not diminish the argument that the information Darwin gathered on the Galapagos Islands was important. It could have generated a eureka moment later, as Darwin revised his notes, or it could have contributed to formulating the theory through a later long period of reflection without a eureka moment. Either way, it would have been an important case study for the theory.

4 Matthew Lange, *Comparative-Historical Methods* (London, Thousand Oaks, New Delhi, Singapore: Sage, 2012). Lange also provides a detailed discussion of various case studies at the end of his book on the British empire: *Lineages of Despotism and Development*.

can be made also between cases across historical periods, for example between the British imperialist world-elite and the imperialist world-elite of today.

In this chapter I use case studies to understand social mechanisms. The two mechanisms that I address are especially *important to understand why elites are winning today* in the struggle to steer globalization in one direction rather than another: the first is the mechanism whereby hegemony contributes to the strength in collective action of a world-elite; the second is the mechanism whereby a national elite can undermine collective action by the masses. Before focusing on these mechanisms, it is useful to address important theories. The next two sections address Gramsci's theory of hegemony, and Gramsci's criticism of a group of theorists known as elite theorists. After introducing Gramsci's theory of hegemony, and in introducing Gramsci's criticism of elite theorists, I address the concepts of meso collection action and meso collective action problems, which are part of the mechanism whereby elites exercise domination. I then focus on the two case studies and introduce additional considerations regarding collective action. The two mechanisms that I address in this chapter are also *important to understand forms of power that might emerge* in the future. I especially want to draw attention to the fact that forms of power that emphasize a combination of consent and domination can emerge and would pose a serious threat to democracy. In the second volume I suggest that this is a threat because it could put an end to development and democracy.

6.3 Gramsci's Theory of Hegemony and Collective Action

The theory of hegemony that I propose in this book is based largely upon my interpretation of *Gramsci's theory of hegemony*. I elaborate Gramsci's theory of hegemony in new directions that have been neglected by most discussions of his theory. In particular, only very few authors writing in English have characterized Gramsci's theory of hegemony as a theory of power.[5] I argue that Gramsci's theory of hegemony is best characterized as *a theory of power that emphasizes the importance of deliberate and sustained collective action*. This theory emphasizes political-military power, which is based on collective action. It was in part a response to the shortcomings of focusing on economics alone. Marx's theory can be summarized as arguing that economic power is decisive in history, and therefore the states that advance economic power the

5 Steven Lukes, *Power: a Radical View*, Studies in Sociology (London and New York: Palgrave Macmillan, 2004). This is a second edition with two more chapters than the 1974 edition. The second edition shows the growing interest in the study of power within sociology.

most, which includes advancing the economic conditions of the masses, will eventually triumph, and this will lead to a new society of perpetual growth.[6] This interpretation of arguments in Marx's later work has been put forward most convincingly and forcefully in Cohen's book on Marx's theory of history. Cohen claimed he was proposing a theory that was different than the theory put forward by Althusser.[7] But he ended up proposing just another variant of the same misconception that history occurs without deliberate human intervention, focusing upon forces that are seen to be beyond human control. The theory that I propose emphasizes instead deliberate and sustained collective action, and thus goal-oriented human activity, which under certain circumstances can steer even vast phenomena like globalization in a different direction.

The theory of power that I propose here, building upon Gramsci, diverges radically also from another argument that is put forward in Cohen's work. Gramsci emphasized the point that economic power is decisive only in the last instance.[8] *What immediately decides success or failure in social conflict of any kind is political-military power*. This is in part dependent upon the

6 Gellner's description of industrial society defines it as a society of perpetual growth. This explains the rise of nationalism in modern times, because of the requirement for a culture accommodating continuous growth and the associated mobility: Gellner, *Nations and Nationalism*.

7 Cohen, *Karl Marx's Theory of History*. This book was assigned reading at Oxford University for students of Modern History who took the course on the history of social and political thought in the early 1990s. It was reprinted in 2000 as: *Karl Marx's Theory of History: a Defence* (Oxford: Clarendon Press, 2000). It was also reprinted by Princeton University Press in 2001. The late 1970s saw a number of important new studies, and 1978 was some sort of *annus mirabilis*. Edward Said published his landmark book on Western views of the Orient that gave new meaning to the concept of orientalism: Edward W. Said, *Orientalism* (New York: Pantheon Books, 1978). Interestingly, sociologist Bryan Turner published a much less well-known study of orientalism that is however important for the modernism against postmodernism debate: Bryan S. Turner, *Marx and the End of Orientalism* (London and New York: Routledge, 1978). Charles Tilly wrote a book that started the modern study of revolutions: Charles Tilly, *From Mobilization to Revolution* (London: Random House, 1978). Less well-known but no less interesting, Rytina worked with other sociologists at suggesting new directions for the modern study of social movements: Bruce Fireman et al., "Encounters with Unjust Authority," in *CRSO Working Paper #167* (Center for Research on Social Organization, University of Michigan, 1978). This was published as a book in 1982. Tilly's book might have been originally a CRSO working paper too. Lastly, Max Weber's *work* on economy and society was re-published in English, showing a renewal of interest in important questions addressed by sociology at its inception: Max Weber, Guenther Roth, and Claus Wittich, eds., *Economy and Society: an Outline of Interpretive Sociology* (Berkeley and Los Angeles: University of California Press, 1978).

8 Cohen, *Karl Marx's Theory of History*.

previous economic power that a society has achieved, but it is also relatively independent. This claim regards *a single state*. For example, for any given level of economic power, there might be a range of different possible levels of political-military power. This could be simply because a state spends a greater or lesser percentage of the national GDP on the military. The claim that political-military power is immediately decisive can then be split into two parts. Political-military power is *decisive* because if a state is conquered this can stunt development in the economy and culture too, or can put an end to democracy. It is *immediately* decisive because at any one point in interstate conflict a state can win by quickly raising political-military power. Economic power is important too, but it requires more time to be raised. This claim applies also to *states that are part of a system*, since it is conceivable that a state or group of states that have greatly developed economic power, but failed to develop political-military power, can be taken over by other states that have developed political-military power to a greater extent. This is arguably what happed to Italian city-states towards the end of the Renaissance, a suggestion made by Gramsci that I expand upon in this project.

Gramsci's theory also drew attention to the *importance of cultural power* in history. The combination of cultural power with political-military power is one of the reasons why Gramsci's theory is referred to as a theory of hegemony. The concept of hegemony originated in ancient Greece, where it was used to refer to leadership over other states that was obtained by spontaneous adherence, rather than conquest.[9] Gramsci's contribution was to apply this concept to social groups. What is less well-known is that Gramsci argued that *a hegemonic social group ought to combine political-military power with cultural power and also with economic power*. Gramsci's theory of hegemony thus presupposed the multidisciplinary approach to social science sketched out in the previous chapter.

In this theory, *cultural power is important to political-military power for two main reasons*. One reason is that political-military power is largely based upon collective action, and it is therefore reliant upon what could be called the *cultural foundations of collective action*: a shared worldview; a shared set of goals, and a plan on how to achieve these goals. Therefore, a social group needs to be able to formulate its own philosophy and theory in order to be able to engage in deliberate and sustained collective action. This requires cultural power. The other reason is *that cultural power exercised in a democratic manner enables*

9 Richard Ned Lebow and Robert Kelly, "Thucydides and Hegemony: Athens and the United States," *Review of International Studies* 27, no. 4 (2001).

achieving greater political-military power. This is because consent is important both for the collective action of a social group, and to form class alliances and to coordinate collective action with other social groups. Democracies are likely to prevail because the greatest political-military power is achieved by obtaining the consent of those that one leads, not by domination, and by extending one's power base by forming alliances with other social groups and obtaining their consent too, not by conquest. This entails that *cultural power has to be built and exercised in an inclusive and expansive manner,* by taking into consideration the values and aspirations of other social groups. Furthermore, cultural power should be in addition, not in alternative, to economic power, which similarly entails that the economy should be developed in an expansive and inclusive manner, which is another part of the activities of a hegemonic social group involved in integral hegemony. An *expansive hegemony* entails that the leadership seeks the spontaneous consent, and to advance the interests, of more and more social groups. Gramsci thus argued that we should consider as hegemonic social groups only those groups that increase the total economic power and that also advance the interests, including the economic interests, of all the social groups that they lead, and not just their own interests.

In this context, it is important to emphasize the *difference between Gramsci's concept of hegemonic social group and the elites involved in neoliberalism*. I want to begin elaborating here a typology of hegemony, as part of the argument that, in addition to building an inclusive and expansive as opposed to a minimal hegemony, social groups striving for democracy have to build a relatively permanent, as opposed to a temporary hegemony, and that this permanent hegemony has to be inclusive and also expansive. Let us consider first the *difference between permanent and temporary hegemony*. The elites involved in neoliberalism certainly used cultural power to persuade policymakers in many countries to embrace neoliberalism and implement policies based upon it. To some extent, these elites managed to convince also parts of the masses to embrace neoliberalism. This was only a temporary hegemony however, for example because as argued above the middle class later lost out. Thus the elites achieved consent only temporarily, leading to the populist backlash. Moreover, the elites built a *false integral hegemony that was not truly inclusive, nor expansive*. It is perhaps best described by the Latin expression *panem et circenses*, or bread and circuses. The elites involved in neoliberalism used cultural power in order to advance their own economic power and their own political-military power only. Trickle-down economics, for example, is not truly inclusive and expansive for the masses, because the masses see their share of total wealth grow less than the elites', or even stagnate, so that the masses see their relative position in society worsen, as the elites get richer than them. Lastly, the elites in Western countries seem to be moving towards especially dangerous combinations of consent coupled with domination. Behind the appearance of integral hegemony, there is increasingly the harsh reality of domination. Arguably, the elites involved in neoliberalism are more and more practicing towards the masses divide-and-rule tactics, which are a tool of domination, not of hegemony.

6.4 Gramsci's Theory and Criticism of Elite Theorists

The minimal hegemony exercised by the Piedmontese national elite is interesting especially because, despite its very narrow social base, this elite was able to dominate the masses in Italy. It was able to do so by hampering collective action by the masses, in particular, by compounding collective action problems. As used in this book, the expression *collective action* refers to any action that involves many individuals, including groups of individuals acting within institutions, or several social groups, or several states.[10] The expression *collective action problem* refers to any problem that arises in participating in collective action. It is associated mainly with social phenomena first described by

10 It is fairly common in the sociological literature on social movements to include also organizations and the ties between organizations and institutions in the study of social movements. Some studies have focused on organizations and provided an interesting view of movements within organizations. Mary Fainsod Katzenstein introduced the idea that groups of individuals within institutions can be studied as a type of social movement. Katzenstein's whole approach is informed by one driving concern, to answer questions like where have all the activists gone? or where is the women's movement now?, no doubt to show that work to advance women's rights continues. Katzenstein pointed to the fact that women within institutions were continuing the struggle of the women's movement, even after the women's movement seemed to have petered out or lost its mass component: Mary Fainsod Katzenstein, "Feminism within American Institutions: Unobtrusive Mobilization in the 1980s," *Signs: Journal of Women in Culture and Society* 16, no. 1 (1990). Katzenstein has expanded upon this approach in a number of other studies: *Faithful and Fearless: Moving Feminist Protest inside the Church and Military* (Princeton and Oxford: Princeton University Press, 1998); "Protest Moves inside Institutions," in *Women, Gender, and Politics: a Reader*, ed. Mona Lena Krook and Sara Childs (Oxford and New York: Oxford University Press, 2010). Katzenstein has also contributed to a comparative approach to social movements that involves comparing European and United States social movements: Mary Fainsod Katzenstein and Carol McClurg Mueller, eds., *The Women's Movements of the United States and Western Europe: Consciousness, Political Opportunity, and Public Policy*, Women in the Political Economy (Philadelphia: Temple University Press, 1992).

economist Mancur Olson, and with responses to Olson's work.[11] This work gave rise to a whole literature that focuses upon *micro phenomena associated with collective action problems like defection or free riding*. These are problems that are central to social movements, which have to deal with the recruitment and ongoing participation of individual members in the social movement, some of whom might be less committed than others and defect, and some of whom might take credit for work done by others and thus free ride. As emphasized by Olson, others yet might not even participate in the movement, and free ride by benefiting from the achievements of a movement, for example by accessing public goods made available by the efforts of others, without contributing to these efforts. Analogous problems arise amongst organizations and social groups, not just individuals. This suggests that there is also a meso scale at which collective action problems occur.

Collective action problems are difficult to deal with but have solutions. For example, *forums* like the World Social Forum can help overcome some of these problems by encouraging many activists from different social movement organizations to come together and discuss and agree to common goals and common means to pursue these goals. *Meetings* like the G8 or the G20 serve the same function for states. *Institutions* can also serve to solve collective action problems, for example by enforcing a certain level of commitment to pre-agreed goals, short of which one is removed from the organization or even barred from the movement. There is a whole other type of *collective action problems that are associated with micro, meso and macro collective action*. Their interaction can either help or compound micro collective action problems. Some of the problems include meso collective action problems that are specifically related to the interaction amongst organizations and social groups, and how this interaction is affected by social stratification and social structures. They include a series of questions linked to IC, which are necessary for coordination amongst those who engage in collective action in the pursuit of shared goals. This book focuses upon meso and macro collective action, and specific types of collective action problems that are associated with meso and macro collective action.

Let us begin by focusing upon *meso collective action problems*. I progressively became aware of this type of collective action problems as significant and in need of investigation as a result of theoretical groundwork for this

---

11 Mancur Olson's work was first published in 1965 and 1971. It is by now a classic and has recently been re-published: Mancur Olson, *The Logic of Collective Action*, Harvard Economic Studies (Cambridge, Massachusetts and London: Harvard University Press, 2009).

project. There were two directions of research in this theoretical groundwork that converged upon this type of collective action problems. The first direction of research involved scrutinizing theories regarding the interaction between elites and masses. This is addressed in this chapter. The second direction of research involved scrutinizing the failures of past theories and how they affected the social movements and states that relied upon these theories. This is addressed in the book on humanist social science. A central part of the groundwork scrutinizing the interaction between elites and masses involved focusing on collective action and the suggestion made by the elite theorists that elites enjoy what can aptly be described as a *collective action advantage* compared to the masses. This consists essentially in the fact that elites are less affected by collective action problems, and are more capable to engage in collective action, than the masses. In addition, they are able to increase this advantage by compounding the collective action problems of the masses.

There were at the beginning of the twentieth century in Italy a number of social scientists who worked on these questions, who have been referred to as *elite theorists*, both because they were interested in the study of elites, and because they could be said to have formed a lose school of thought.[12] Their work was recently rediscovered. Gramsci is sometimes misleadingly associated with the elite theorists because he addressed the same questions and also addressed their theories. This association is at least partly due to the fact that Gramsci's theory has applications well beyond the political parties that he participated in, and is relevant to anyone who wants to understand power and democracy, which can lead to conflating Gramsci with the elite theorists as being all democratic elitists.[13] I disagree with this argument, because there are also *very important differences between the elite theorists and Gramsci.* An important difference is that they were elitists, whereas Gramsci was not. He was simply interested in formulating a theory of elites. Another important difference is that Gramsci began integrating his theory of elites within a theory of

---

12 Stuart Hughes's book on the history of social and political thought devoted to these theorists an entire chapter. This 1958 book was reprinted in 1977 and most recently as: H. Stuart Hughes and Stanley Hoffman, *Consciousness and Society* (London and New York: Routledge, 2017). These theorists were also associated with fascism. Femia has led a recent low-key revival of interest in these thinkers: Joseph V. Femia, *The Machiavellian Legacy: Essays in Italian Political Thought* (New York: St. Martin's Press, 1998). I came to appreciate the importance of these thinkers as a teaching assistant in a course on political sociology taught by Lange, who drew attention especially to Michels's work, and through discussions with Lange.

13 Femia and Finocchiaro conflate Gramsci with the elite theorists in: Femia, *The Machiavellian Legacy*; Finocchiaro, *Beyond Right and Left.*

history that was completely different than those of the elite theorists'.[14] Both these points stand out if we compare Gramsci to economist Vilfredo Pareto, the most famous amongst the elite theorists, at least outside Italy, who essentially argued that elites were genetically superior to the masses, and that this was the reason why they ruled over the masses. Gramsci did not share this racist view and aimed instead to create an elite drawn from the masses and accountable to the masses, and ultimately to raise the masses to the intellectual level of the elites. Gramsci also proposed an altogether different theory of history than Pareto's, which would help achieve these goals.[15]

Gramsci took more seriously, but still criticized, the views of other elite theorists than Pareto. Political scientist Gaetano Mosca first argued that there was a distinctive political elite that he called a 'political class', which was self-perpetuating and not affected by democratic pressures, or pressured from below. It was arguably a predecessor of contemporary establishments. Gramsci also drew attention to the complementary process of cooptation of the leadership of new social forces that was occurring in Italy at around the same time, which shielded existing elites from democratic pressures. This tactic was known as *trasformismo,* and it involves occupying a center position in the political spectrum, which enables coopting different sides of the political spectrum, from the left or right, to the center.[16] This was an instance of defection. Michels, the student of Weber's who moved to Italy, made an important study of the leadership of the Social Democratic Party in Germany, in which he showed that this leadership was not affected by democratic pressures from below within

14 Pareto's treatise on sociology applied a natural science model to social science. So did Robert Michels's work. Lange referred to Michels' theory regarding oligarchical tendencies as the 'iron law of oligarchy', whereby democracy within organizations is always replaced by oligarchy, implying it was a tendency that could not be overcome. Gramsci thought instead that all sociological laws were only tendential laws.

15 Many authors discuss Pareto's ties to fascism and sometimes touch upon his essentially racist views and amoral machiavellianism. Surprisingly, some authors are rekindling interest in Pareto despite all of this: Joseph V. Femia, *Pareto and Political Theory*, Routledge Studies in Social and Political Thought (London and New York: Routledge, 2006). Today, themes central to Pareto's racist views, and in a sense a critique of these views, are being discussed by: Andrea Sangiovanni, *Humanity without Dignity* (Cambridge, Massachusetts and London: Harvard University Press, 2017).

16 *Trasformismo* is chiefly associated with occupying a center position. In my interpretation, the center position is important to *trasformismo*, but only in conjunction with processes of cooptation and defection, which I address in the next section. In Italian politics the center position was politically useful to some elites because from this center position one can exercise leadership over both right and left, including by forming coalitions with either right or left, and including cooptation, more or less openly, of leaders on either right or left.

the party, from the party base, and that they had been coopted by the national elite.[17] This too is an instance of cooptation. The importance of Gramsci's work, compared to the elite theorists' work, is that he took seriously the problems that they highlighted, but sought to formulate a theory that pointed to the root causes of these problems, and that also suggested ways to overcome these problems. Gramsci's analysis of collective action problems focused on the case of Italy, and in particular on the collective action problems that beset mass movements during the Risorgimento, the process of national unification in Italy. Interestingly, Germany went through a similar process of national unification at around the same time. It is useful to begin however by focusing upon the case of the British aristocratic-military elite, because it marks a stark contrast to the case of the elites involved in Italian national unification.

6.5 The British Elite and Its Use of Culture for Consent

Understanding the sources of power of the British aristocratic-military elite can serve to understand processes of formation of world-elites, and what makes world-elites successful, including winning the consent of other social groups. I focus in particular upon a further hypothesis that complements the hypotheses 3 and 3′ that were put forward in chapter 5. These two hypotheses suggested that hegemonic leadership is especially important to world-elites whose members are scattered over vast territories, or we could add, who have to deal with a strong internal opposition and thus emphasize consent over coercion. I want to introduce here first a fourth hypothesis, hypothesis 4, then show how a case study focused upon the British aristocratic-military elite can serve to corroborate this hypothesis and refine it, putting forward a refined hypothesis 4′. I have suggested above that culture should be conceived of in relation to social structures, not as if it existed in a disembodied state. The fourth hypothesis emphasizes that culture depends also upon organization and focuses upon the organizational means that are available to elites to exercise their hegemonic leadership.

4. *Elites that exercise hegemonic leadership do so thanks to organizational means*. The following are features of these organizational means that contribute to hegemonic leadership.

17 Robert Michels, *Political Parties: a Sociological Study of the Oligarchical Tendencies of Modern Democracies*, Political Science (New York: Free Press, 1968). There is also a 2016 reprint of the 1962 edition.

a. Cultural institutions are important to formulate a shared worldview and culture and to educate members of the hegemonic social group and allied social groups in this worldview and culture.
b. Humanistic studies that provide a broad picture of society and history are important to this worldview and culture.
c. Education of new generations that provides long-term continuity in policies and a build-up of knowledge from one generation to the next is also important.

A case study focused on the British aristocratic-military elite can show that these organizational means were actually used in the British case, thus corroborating hypothesis 4, and also help us refine this hypothesis. In particular, since case studies help us conceptualize social mechanisms, they can introduce refinements to these social mechanisms. The following discussion shows how focusing on this case can lead us to refine hypothesis 4 and propose a social mechanism to begin to explain hegemonic power.

4' The British aristocratic-military elite that built the British empire was able to exercise hegemonic leadership thanks to organizational means.

We can then delve into the sub-hypotheses that are part of this hypothesis and provide *prima facie* cases for these sub-hypotheses. One factor that stands out in the success of the British aristocratic-military elite is that it developed early on an appreciation of the importance of culture and cultural institutions, a key factor of hegemony. This appreciation of culture is shown by the fact that *the British aristocratic-military elite put a premium on the education of its members, and developed elite institutions for this education*, so much so that it might not be an exaggeration to say that the centers of power of the British empire were in its cultural institutions. Oxford University and Cambridge University in England, and St Andrews University in Scotland, where all places where the aristocracy and other upper classes educated their members.[18]

a. Cultural institutions like elite universities played an important role in the formation of the British imperialist world-elite, bringing together

18 St Andrews University is important because a British identity was fashioned around the combination of English with Scottish, Irish and Welsh identities. Linda Colley discusses British identity as being inclusive in: Linda Colley, *Britons: Forging the Nation, 1707–1837*, Nota Bene (New Haven and London: Yale University Press, 2005). Scottish elites were coopted into, and some fully participated in, British imperial enterprises. Scottish merchants and entrepreneurs were often involved in these enterprises. James McGill, the founder of McGill University, was a Scottish businessman who became very wealthy in Canada.

disparate members of the upper classes into one elite through a shared culture and worldview.

This sub-hypothesis suggests that in the emergent world-elite too cultural institutions might have an important role to play in fashioning a single imperialist world-elite out of disparate elites. Therefore, the study of these cultural institutions might give an important contribution to our understanding of world-elites.

A case study focused on the British aristocratic-military elite can also suggest *which specific parts of the culture and education of world-elites made it successful.* This enables us to refine the claim regarding the importance of a strategic vision and focus upon domains and academic fields that are especially important for this vision. Some specific degree courses at the elite universities just mentioned became associated with political-military power and empire-building. At one point, the degree courses at Oxford University in Classics, in Modern History, in Modern History and Modern Languages, served to educate British elites involved in empire-building.[19] More recently, the course in Philosophy, Politics and Economics partly supplanted them in the education of administrators destined to work in Great Britain and abroad. This can lead to the refinement of the second sub-hypothesis of hypothesis 4.

b. Amongst humanistic studies, historical studies and language studies have played an especially important part in the education of the British aristocratic-military elite, and in its success.

This too might be relevant to understand what makes world-elites successful. *Language studies* and linguistic ability are obviously important to every elite that is active on a world stage, because on this stage it interacts with many different social groups speaking different languages. *Historical studies* are equally important, though perhaps less obviously so. They arguably contribute to an *historical memory*, understood as a trait of cultures that cultivate historical studies. Cultures that have an historical memory have a sense of their place in history, the tasks that they accomplished, what made them successful, and what other tasks are necessary to consolidate this success. It is part of the strategic vision associated with broad pictures of society and history that I argued is important to formulate and pursue successful policies, which in order to be successful need, amongst other things, to be integrated into medium and long-term plans. Every world-elite, and I argue like Gramsci every social group

---

19 Richard Symonds, *Oxford and Empire: the Last Lost Cause?* (Oxford: Clarendon Press, 1991); Phiroze Vasunia, *The Classics and Colonial India*, Classical Presences (Oxford and New York: Oxford University Press, 2013).

that wants to drive social change to its advantage, has had, or needs to have, a historical memory.

The British aristocratic-military elite and its culture exercised an enduring influence upon the whole of British culture. This is an aspect of its integral hegemony. There was a remarkable continuity with the tradition of historical and language studies *of the British aristocratic-military elite*, when other universities and new courses were started in Great Britain to make higher education more widely available. The University of London was started with the foundation of University College London, which was meant to be a center for the education of middle classes largely excluded from Oxford and Cambridge Universities. But London University too was eventually coopted into imperial enterprises, and this is the point that I want to draw attention to here. The School of Oriental and African Studies, where languages spoken through much of Asia and Africa are taught, is the forerunner of modern area studies, and is one of the largest such institutions in Western countries. It was started and expanded also in order to educate administrators of colonies scattered throughout Asia and Africa.[20] The most important institute of technology in Great Britain is part of the University of London and is significantly called Imperial College, a testament to the importance of science and technology in empire-building, as a base both of economic power and political-military power. Of course, London also has vocational education colleges like Ealing, Hammersmith and West London College, which teach trades, now a university in its own right, just like Edinburgh, in Scotland, has Heriot-Watt University. They both contributed to the industrial revolution and to British industrial power.

Another continuity with the traditions of the British aristocratic-military elite consists in this feature: the School of Advanced Studies of the University of London, the most prestigious institution of learning within London University, only has institutes that focus either on area studies, Latin American studies for

20 Rosalind Hampton, a professor of African Studies and education, who is officially an activist, that is, someone openly and vocally engaged in progressive causes, and thus with a great and direct knowledge of these causes, first drew my attention to the importance of area studies. However, I associate area studies, unlike her, with racist and imperialist enterprises. This was the origin of area studies, which at their inception were meant to educate European men who would be involved in administering far-flung colonies, in the languages and cultures of these colonies. Undoubtedly, in the right hands, area studies can have an emancipatory potential. But in the wrong hands, they can be used to undermine the masses, also by leading each country or ethnic group to pursue its own separate goals. My view is that there should be constant dialogue amongst activists engaged in progressive causes in different countries, and also between university professors and activists, in order to prevent divide-and-rule tactics.

example, or the study of classics, which focuses on ancient Greek and ancient Roman history only, or the study of history more in general. It also includes the Warburg Institute, a world-level institution for the study of art, which includes studies in the history of art. It is instructive to contrast this institutional arrangement with other European universities. While studies of languages, history and art are part of a Western humanistic education, they were especially strong in Great Britain. Universities in other countries, for example, gave equal prestige to sciences and engineering. The University of Bern, in Switzerland, has within itself the Albert Einstein Center for Fundamental Physics and centers for applied sciences, as well as a faculty of humanities focused on the study of history and languages. One might object that Bern and Switzerland more in general are not representative of European history, because they were not affected by major upheavals such as fascism, nazism or soviet communism, and more recently the War on Terror in the wake of the 9/11 attacks and the emergence of ISIS. Yet Swiss-German culture has close ties to German and central-European culture, and the University of Bern is similar in its mix of subjects to the University of Bologna, for example, which offers a similar mix of studies of science with studies of history and languages.

The enduring influence of the British aristocratic-military elite stretched beyond cultural institutions and university education and reached also into British popular culture. Imperial College is where one of the founders of modern science fiction, H. G. Wells, studied biology, and through him it influenced British culture.[21] Although officially describing himself as a socialist, and despite running for election in the Labour Party but never quite making it to such a high place as Westminster, Wells was close to Churchill, a free-trade liberal turned conservative politician. Wells had a huge success in book sales, exercising an enduring influence on the perception of science and technology in British popular culture. There are similarities between Churchill's political trajectory and that of Tony Blair, who became one of the longest serving Prime Ministers of Great Britain by making the Labour Party close to conservative interests and sensibilities. Blair also bridged the political divide across the Atlantic, by building a strong working relationship with G. W. Bush. Literary theorist David Lodge, for many years at the University of Birmingham, one of the red brick universities,

21 H. G. Wells' famous novel *The War of the Worlds* showed remarkable foresight in anticipating the devastating effects that pandemics like the Spanish flue pandemic of 1918 could have, and the apocalyptic potential of biological weapons, thus anticipating the impact of the Avian Flu pandemic and the COVID pandemic. Wells also foresaw the growing importance that aviation could have in war and the threat that it could pose even to the United States, thus anticipating the military importance of Russian Strategic Aviation.

and also in the Russell Group, has provided a brilliant, humorous and insightful account of Wells' life that makes Wells look more like a dashing character and seducer like Burt Lancaster, and thus more of a popular figure, than the image of writers that one might have.[22] I believe this explains how he could influence British popular culture so deeply, thanks to the first-hand knowledge he had acquired of it through the working-class jobs he had before becoming a writer. I have argued elsewhere that British popular culture was in some ways as distant as foreign cultures from the viewpoint of British elites, who sometimes got a kick by 'going native' and dressing up in the traditional costumes of different ethnic groups, in a practice that was partly masquerade and partly camouflage.[23] Arguably, Wells understood British popular culture even better than these elites understood foreign cultures, or than the many anthropologists who studied cultures in far-flung corners of the earth[24]

The tradition of historical studies of the British aristocratic-military elite has exercised an *enduring influence beyond British institutions and British culture, even in the United States*, which fought the British aristocratic-military elite to win its independence and secure its democracy. Leading British historians like Davide Cannadine, Linda Colley, and Niall Ferguson, all hail from the British

---

22 David Lodge, *A Man of Parts* (New York: Vintage, 2011). Red brick universities is an expression that was used to denote non-elite universities. The University of Birmingham and the University of Warwick might be thought of as red brick universities. These universities could still produce important innovations. The University of Birmingham, for example, played an important role in the emergence of cultural studies. As the quality of education in Great Britain has increased, the elite universities have formed the Russell Group, which includes Cambridge University, Oxford University, Imperial College, University College London, and 20 other universities that aspire to become leaders in research and education in Great Britain.

23 I discuss this dressing up and its relation to disguises in masquerades in: Olsaretti, "Urban Culture, Curiosity and the Aesthetics of Distance." The most famous representatives of this masquerade culture abroad were Lady Esther Stanhope and Lord Byron.

24 I want to emphasize that this is in no way a judgement on British culture, just on some individual British aristocrats, particularly the higher members of the aristocratic-military elite. I also do *not* seek to portray an undifferentiated British 'other'. Working-class British culture is a world apart from upper-class British culture. This British working-class culture is more at home in the United States. It would be interesting to compare the integration in North American cultures of immigrants from Great Britain, with the integration of immigrants from Italy, and find out what is the relative percentage of success stories amongst these two groups of migrants. In popular culture, actors Robert De Niro and Sylvester Stallone, in politics Fiorello La Guardia, Nancy Pelosi and Mario Cuomo, in law Antonin Scalia, just to name a few, show that at least some Italians could adapt to American culture and succeed spectacularly within it. I am sure there are more British equivalent stories, including perhaps success stories of British working-class immigrants, but they are not as visible because they more easily or even completely blend into American culture.

tradition of historical studies and are influencing teaching and research in history in the United States. So does Anderson, who teaches at The University of California in Los Angeles, or UCLA.[25] Ferguson has even become a media personality of sorts, commenting amongst other things on the return of imperialism in the wake of the 9/11 attacks.[26] The influence of British elites and their institutions of learning across the Atlantic is not a recent phenomenon, but a phenomenon rooted in the past. Princeton University and Yale University in the United States are to some extent modeled on Oxford University. Columbia University and New York University arguably resemble University College London in more ways than one, and have attracted notable scholars from Great Britain like Gilsenan and sociologist Steven Luke, whose work I address in this project, besides educating such pop icons as Lady Gaga.

There are other instances of universities as centers of power that continue the tradition of the British aristocratic-military elite. The influence of this elite to some extent merges with that of analogous elites that it has influenced in the United States, and both of these traditions contributed to the prestige of English-language education. For example, there are many British cultural influences over *all Ivy League universities in the United States, including Brown University and Dartmouth College,* which are perhaps the less well-known amongst the Ivy League universities and the least obvious examples, and even

25 Cannadine and Colley teach at Princeton University, Ferguson taught at Harvard University, but arguably the whole of the Ivy League has been influenced by British intellectual traditions: Brown University, Columbia University, Cornell University, Dartmouth College, and Yale University. Universities like UCLA are carving out a name for themselves also thanks to centers of excellence like the Center for Social Theory and Comparative History, where Anderson and Mann teach.

26 Niall Ferguson, "The Empire Slinks Back," (New York Times, 2003). Interestingly, Ferguson has adopted colloquialisms and a jocular manner in the press, for example commenting in the New York Times article just cited: 'Let me come clean. I am a fully paid-up member of the neoimperialist gang', a choice of words that I find inappropriate, since neoimperialism is a problem that has cost thousands of American lives, and even more lives in Arab countries, and 'gang' evokes the 'Gang of Four', which cost millions of lives in China, or gangs involved in robberies, or ganging up, none of which is even remotely funny. This is not political correctness on my part. I want to emphasize instead that words have specific meanings, and that Ferguson's choice of words, coming from a native speaker of English, identifies a specific mindset. I also and most importantly think that, while it is necessary for intellectuals to avoid specialized language and to engage with popular culture, joking is inappropriate, at least joking of this kind. I address specialist language and inappropriate language by university professors in the book on humanist social science , specifically the use of the words 'assholes' and 'bullshit' in academic texts. In some cases, philosophy and social science glaringly fail to exercise a moderating influence, and embrace instead the worst of mud-slinging that takes place in popular culture during culture wars.

over Liberal Arts colleges like Middlebury College, or Williams College, which are most readily associated with American, rather than British, educational traditions.[27] It is an interesting question to what extent these traditions have influenced universities that are not in any obvious ways associated with elites, such as the City University of New York, or CUNY, and the State University of New York, or SUNY, with their many campuses, or Syracuse University. I know from Abisaab, who as a historian was trained at SUNY Binghamton, that SUNY cultivates a strong postgraduate program in historical studies, with the same postgraduate courses format, and every bit as challenging, as history courses at Ivy League universities. Binghamton is also where Wallerstein went on to start The Fernand Braudel Center for the Study of Economies, Historical Systems, and Civilizations, which was an important and innovative center for historical sociology, and World Systems Theory in particular. Arguably, reaching wider audiences means that these institutions and the courses they design are closer to the lives of New Yorkers and more in touch with ongoing trends in arts and communications, if not in history.

It would be interesting to study whether the 9/11 attacks had an impact on these educational traditions, since *these educational traditions are increasingly exported to other countries*. Georgetown University, a Jesuit university in Washington DC, now has a Qatar campus. Most strikingly, NYU has degree-granting campuses in Abu Dhabi, and Shanghai, as well as a presence in many other cities, including Florence, Paris, and Berlin. NYU also had a campus in Singapore, but was possibly forced to leave it.[28] There is also an earlier tradition of English-language education exported to other countries in the world by missionaries, a subject addressed by historian Paul Sedra amongst others. These were the origins of two notable cultural institutions in the Middle East, the American University of Beirut, or AUB, and the American University in Cairo, or AUC.[29] But missionaries were also associated with European trade

---

27 Eminent McGill scholars spoke to me positively about Dartmouth College and other New England colleges. I gained through these scholars an appreciation of the fact that there are important cultural similarities and ties between eastern Canada and New England, which includes the states Connecticut, Maine, Massachusetts, New Hampshire, Rhode Island, and Vermont. Some of these similarities are purely cultural, dating to the common colonial heritage, which was both British and French. Other similarities arise from a similar climate and geographic location.

28 On NYU campuses and centers abroad, see: New York University, "Studying Abroad."; "NYU Abu Dhabi."; "NYU Shaghai." On the controversies regarding the Singapore campus, see: Wikipedia, "New York University."

29 Sedra's work was published as: Paul Sedra, *From Mission to Modernity: Evangelicals, Reformers and Education in Nineteenth Century Egypt* (London and New York: I. B. Tauris, 2011). Other recent work on missionaries in the Middle East shows a revival of interest

and conquest, and sometimes with the struggles triggered by European trade and conquest, as described by Elizabeth Elbourne for South Africa, although they sometimes established Churches like the Anglican Church in South African, which has become an integral part of South African culture through such figures as Desmond Tutu.[30] Missionaries and a Western education were also revered by at least some groups, which were perceptively given a literary representation by novelist Arundathi Roy amongst others.[31] In other countries yet, like Iceland, American educational traditions are being exported through the world of research, which is English-speaking and dominated by American, besides British, cultural institutions. Moreover, in the case of Nordic countries like Iceland, local scholars and institutions take a leading role in the export of American educational traditions. Scholars educated at the University of Iceland, like historian Magnus Bernhardsson, have done important work

in the topic: Mehmet Ali Dogan and Heather J. Sharkey, eds., *American Missionaries and the Middle East: Foundational Encounters* (Salt Lake City: University of Utah Press, 2011); Ussama Makdisi, *Artillery of Heaven: American Missionaries and the Failed Conversion of the Middle East*, The United States in the World (Ithaca and London: Cornell University Press, 2011). On the history of AUB and AUC and American universities more in general, and their place in the modern history of the Middle East, see: Faith M. Hanna, *An American Mission: the Role of the American University of Beirut* (Boston: Alphabet Press, 1979); Betty S. Anderson, *The American University of Beirut: Arab Nationalism and Liberal Education* (Austin: University of Texas Press, 2011); Ted Purinton and Jennifer Skaggs, *American Universities Abroad: the Leadership of Independent Transnational Higher Education Institutions* (Cairo and New York: American University in Cairo Press, 2017); John Waterbury, *Missions Impossible: Higher Education and Policymaking in the Arab World* (Cairo and New York: American University in Cairo Press, 2020).

30 Elizabeth Elbourne, *Blood Ground: Colonialism, Missions, and the Contest for Christianity in the Cape Colony and Britain, 1799–1853*, Mcgill-Queen's Studies in the History of Religion (Montreal & Kingston, London, Ithaca: McGill-Queen's University Press, 2002). In this book Elbourne emphasizes that missionaries were at least some of the time caught up in bitter social struggles like struggles over land.

31 Arundathi Roy, *The God of Small Things: a Novel* (Toronto: Vintage Canada, 1997). I am thinking of the revered and unattainable character father Mulligan in this novel, and of the Reverend E. John Ipe character. Historian Wilson Chacko Jacob has made an insightful study of the types of Western masculinity that included working out, which became models even for some figures associated with Egyptian nationalism: Wilson Chacko Jacob, *Working out Egypt: Effendi Masculinity and Subject Formation in Colonial Modernity, 1870–1940* (Durham and London: Duke University Press, 2011). Laila Parsons has portrayed other figures associated with Arab nationalism that arguably represented a somewhat different model of masculinity: Parsons, *The Commander: Fawzi Al-Qawuqji and the Fight for Arab Independence 1914–1948*.

on modern Iraq and teach in the United States, but take part in promoting research at the University of Iceland.[32]

These traditions have also been exported to Eastern Europe, where they were meant to participate in the transition from state socialism to capitalism. *The Central European University*, or CEU, founded thanks to Wall Street investor and philanthropist George Soros, has brought these traditions and English-language education to the heart of Eastern Europe, and is devoted to educating a new elite in favor of markets. It has attracted eminent scholars like Gellner, and political scientist turned Canadian politician Michael Ignatieff, both with family ties to Eastern Europe, who might thus have been drawn to the region, which attracted also economists and economic sociologists trained in the United States and McKinsey & Company, the management consulting company, who are a truly global company that are aptly described as strategic consultants, another sign of the influence of intellectual traditions from English-speaking countries, in this case management traditions, upon Eastern Europe. Remarkably, the CEU has had the misfortune of being pushed out of Prague, in the Czech Republic, where it was first located, and then from Budapest, in Hungary, now operating out of Vienna, in Austria, but still with some presence in Hungary. An interesting question is whether this amounts to a rejection of the intellectual traditions that the CEU promotes, or if it is just due to personal disagreements with one politician or another.

This influence is not limited to English-language institutions or historical studies alone, but directly or indirectly has reached other countries, and *exercised an enduring influence in Spain*, for example. The Catholic Church still has great prestige in Spain and some of its leading academic institutions are part of the Catholic Church, but even this bastion of tradition is being influenced by the managerial approach to education that was first introduced in the shake-up of British higher education in the post-Thatcher era. This, in addition to the tradition of historical studies that was perhaps more readily incorporated in

32 Bernhardsson's work on Iraq was published as: Magnus Torkell Bernhardsson, *Reclaiming a Plundered Past: Archaeology and Nation Building in Modern Iraq* (Austin: University of Texas Press, 2013). Bernhardsson worked also on the theme of the Apocalypse: Abbas Amanat and Magnus Thorkell Bernhardsson, eds., *Imagining the End: Visions of Apocalypse from the Ancient Middle East to Modern America* (London and New York: I. B. Tauris, 2001). On this theme, see also: John R. Hall, *Apocalypse: from Antiquity to the Empire of Modernity* (Cambridge, UK and Malden, Massachusetts: Polity, 2013). This author's name is not a typo, John R. Hall is a professor of sociology at the University of California in Davis, not to be confused with John A. Hall, the professor of sociology at McGill University, an easy mistake to make in bibliographic references. John A. Hall and Hillary Clinton both took their knowledge of North America and educational expertise back to Great Britain.

Spanish culture since Spain had its own analogous tradition, is creating leading world-class institutions with the same strategic vision that I described for McGill University. These institutions too might have benefited from not having been drawn into bitterly divisive culture wars before and after the 9/11 attacks. Such is the case with Deusto University, a Jesuit university in Bilbao that is reaching far beyond the Catholic Church to recruit scholars and students.[33] The Opus Dei, a personal prelature of the Catholic Church, which is essentially a network of clergymen and laymen built around one or more high-ranking clergymen, has succeeded in creating in Barcelona one of the top business schools in the world, IESE, which attracts scholars and students from the around the world.[34] All of this is exemplified also by the increasingly international make-up of cities like Barcelona, with a large cosmopolitan population, including a large Italian population and Italian elementary, middle and high schools.

The above discussion helps refine the third sub-hypothesis that is part of hypothesis 4′. *The British imperialist world-elite might be more than just another case study of the importance of education across generations.* It might be the most important case study to understand imperialism in the West. This is because it might be seen as having *left a legacy to later world-elites*, that anyone with sufficient historical memory could capitalize on. This leads to reformulating the last sub-hypothesis that is part of hypothesis 4.

---

33 I gained through Dolores and Fabio Frosini an appreciation of the prestige and importance of Deusto University, and the modern managerial approach that has relaunched this university and made it into an institution with a reputation and a reach far beyond Spain, to the entire Spanish-speaking Latin America.

34 I gained an understanding of IESE's importance through non-Spanish professors and students at IESE, who found the managerial education of IESE complemented their advanced IT studies. These profiles of professionals show the extent to which Spanish universities, including Catholic universities, are becoming involved in the global flows of skilled workforce described in: AnnaLee Saxenian, *The New Argonauts: Regional Advantage in a Global Economy* (Cambridge, Massachusetts and London: Harvard University Press, 2007). I address IT and its impact on society in other books that are part of this project, and I address Smart City technologies in the books on urban and regional planning. Interestingly, there are efforts to create in Barcelona a high-tech district and to make Barcelona a leader in Smart City technologies. Barcelona is remarkable also for the striking mixes of cultures, and of old and new, that coexist within it. In the old neighborhood of Gracia in Barcelona there is a John Lennon square, with an IT company called Main Memory, an interesting mix of history, with counterculture dating to the time of the 'British Invasion', and modern IT, in a quiet and family-oriented part of the neighborhood that seems a world apart from modern culture wars, the War on Terror, and the ISIS threat. There are also quaint squares like Diamond Square, a jewel tucked in an old neighborhood, with museum-like displays that highlight tragic episodes from Spain's recent past.

c. The British aristocratic-military elite might have left to later elites the learning and knowledge of how to build extensive power, or even specific techniques of power, that they perfected over centuries. This knowledge might have been handed down to later elites in Great Britain and elites from around the world who were educated in Great Britain. It might also have been handed down to elite cultural institutions based on the model of British elite institutions.

I address some of these techniques of power in this book and in the book on humanist social science, which address also the significance of Machiavelli's *Prince* and of machiavellian politics. These still have resonance in popular culture through such figures as actors Guy Ritchie and Jason Statham, who has brought to the screen or interpreted machiavellian characters, and in the United States Sylvester Stallone, Arnold Schwarzenegger, and Danny DeVito. I argue the techniques are important to understand the threat that an imperialist world-elite might pose one day, if not today, in order to press home the point that neither development nor democracy can be taken for granted. The failures of neoliberalism certainly have taught us that development cannot be taken for granted. We should not take democracy for granted either. One of the reasons is that elites enjoyed a collective action advantage over the masses, and might be expanding this advantage.

6.6 The Piedmontese Elite and Its Collective Action Advantage

The case study focused on the Piedmontese national elite is especially useful to understand both the collective action advantage of elites, and elites' ability to dominate the masses. This is especially important to understand the source of power of the elites engaged in neoliberalism. Hypothesis 1 suggested one reason for this advantage, which is that national elites, although divided into political-military, cultural and economic elites, are to some extent unified by ties between these different elites. The implication is that these ties enable collective action. Here I want to highlight how the theoretical groundwork sketched in this chapter helps refine and corroborate hypothesis 1, and also contributes to explaining one instance of social conflict with a marked collective action advantage of the elites over the masses. This theoretical groundwork suggests that, *if we want to corroborate and eventually prove hypothesis 1, a promising place to start is by studying the processes of unification of Italy and Germany* and the emergence of national elites and the consolidation of these national elites into establishments that took place at that time and shortly after. This refines hypothesis 1 in two different ways. One way is by pointing to a specific country, Italy is the focus of this section, and to specific social groups, which were involved in an earlier instance of the creation of a national elite that consolidated into an establishment. Needless to say, one would not stop after having studied one case, but would go on to study other cases. Studying this one case can serve to show that this process has occurred in history and thus corroborates hypothesis 1, by suggesting that national elites that consolidate into establishments can emerge and did emerge in the past. The other way in which this theoretical groundwork refines hypothesis 1 is by focusing on a particular type of power, political-military power, because this is arguably the immediately decisive type of power. These refined hypotheses can be more easily tested and can thus serve to confirm the theory.

Italy and Germany constitute interesting case studies to understand processes of formation of national elites that consolidate into establishments. Arguably, Mosca was drawing attention, already by the early twentieth century, to the fact that a political elite had emerged in Italy that had consolidated into a political establishment. Michels was similarly drawing attention to the fact that the Social Democratic Party leadership and the national leadership in Germany were becoming part of a single political elite that was consolidating into a political establishment. These political elites interacted with other elites. The unification of both Italy and Germany was driven by a political-military elite that took the initiative in unifying several different states. Both Italy and Germany went through a period of economic growth after unification, Germany more than Italy, suggesting that there was some coordination between the political-military elite and the economic elite or elites. The process of Italian unification is especially interesting for the study of collective action problems, because there was a clear competition between two different movements that sought to steer this process in different directions. There was an elite movement led by count Cavour, the Prime Minister of the duchy of Savoy, a northern Italian state centered on Piedmont, which sought to create a unified Italy as a kingdom of Italy under aristocratic-military rule. There was also a mass movement led by popular figures Giuseppe Mazzini and Giuseppe Garibaldi, which sought to create a unified Italy as an Italian republic under a popular leadership. This movement is especially important to the arguments of this book, because its use of volunteers presaged the use of volunteers by Muslim fundamentalists that has come to the fore in the wake of the 9/11 attacks and the War on Terror.[35] This movement is especially important also

35 Mazzini and Garibaldi also illustrate a point analogous to that regarding elite power made in chapter 2. There has been a shift towards cultural power, and pop icons like singer-songwriter Jovanotti, who is close to politician Walter Veltroni, have considerable

because in its fight with Cavour and the elites, the latter won, and a unified Italy was created as a kingdom of Italy. How they won holds important lessons for anyone who is faced with elite power.

The following are two refined versions of hypothesis 1. The first refined version, hypothesis 1′, draws attention to the fact that the case of Italy bears important similarities to the more general case that is part of hypothesis 1 presented in chapter 5. Thus, focusing on Italy as a case study can help us formulate a refined version of hypothesis 1.

1′. *The Piedmontese national elite that drove the process of national unification in Italy became an early instance of a national elite, which emerged out of a process that brought together several elites.* This early national elite was distinguished by the following features.
   a. The national elite included economic, cultural, and political-military elites, respectively landowners, secular intellectuals and an aristocratic-military elite.
   b. These elites cooperated thanks to count Cavour's leadership, which was enabled in part by the ties between Cavour and other individuals in key positions within the elite.

---

influence over the young and not so young in central and southern Italy. But other elites still hold similar power to Garibaldi's. Garibaldi's military exploits in southern and central Italy in the mid-1800s were military operations by a member of a military elite. It would be very interesting to compare Garibaldi's use of volunteers to the use made by fascists and nazis of volunteers. Mussolini seized power in Italy using a corps of volunteer fighters. There was in Germany too widespread use of *Freikorps*, volunteer fighters, and the SA and SS might have been based on *Freikorps* precedents and possibly on the precedent set by Mussolini. This is *not* to say that Mussolini and fascist war crimes, or Heydrich and the Holocaust, were rooted in Italian or German culture, only that leaders like Mussolini and Heydrich steered a social phenomenon, undoubtedly violent and deeply problematic to start with, in monstrous directions. In my view, Mazzini was the ideologue of these types of movements, and behind his republican rhetoric, he embraced an essentially authoritarian view of society. Mazzini is known for a treatise on *The Duties of Man*. While undoubtedly all citizens have both rights and duties, at the time when Mazzini was writing the duties far surpassed the rights, and his choice to emphasize duties reveals an authoritarian approach to republican ideals, more from the viewpoint of the elites than the masses. A similar argument on Mazzini was put forward in: Simon Levis Sullam, *Giuseppe Mazzini and the Origins of Fascism*, Italian and Italian American Studies (London and New York: Palgrave Macmillan, 2015). Mazzini was also a journalist. It might be interesting to study to what extent Mazzini's ideals and activities inspired such newspapers as the Quebecois newspaper *Le Devoir*, and how they compare to the authoritarianism of fundamentalist clerics in the Muslim world. These fundamentalists are infamously associated with the 9/11 attacks and terrorism, which reinforce a similar mindset that existed in the West, and arguably still exists, even amongst ostensibly anticlerical thinkers.

c. During the course of the nineteenth century, and until the early twentieth century, these elites consolidated into establishments.

Gramsci's study of the process of national unification in Italy, and of the reasons for elite success, also draws attention to general reasons for elite success that have to do with generic features of social groups and how these features relate to social stratification and social structures. In brief, the elites were capable of forming a *hegemonic bloc consisting of several allied social groups* that were capable of acting cohesively and at the same time prevent the emergence of a unified popular bloc that could challenge it. This argument can lead to further refining hypothesis 1′.

The second refined version of hypothesis 1 is a general hypothesis regarding collective action and a number of related sub-hypotheses, all of which focus on the *sources of the elites' collective action advantage*. The national elite that created a unified Italian state steered the process of national unification in a direction favorable to themselves thanks to the fact that they were better able to engage in collective action than the masses. The following is a summary of Gramsci's argument regarding this elite and its role in the *Risorgimento*.[36] I number it as 1″ because, although pointing to a general mechanism, it is part of a case study that further refines hypothesis 1′, by explaining the collective action advantage of elites using more basic factors than those introduced in 1′, so that each of these more basic factors can be tested separately.

1″. *The Piedmontese national elite that drove the process of national unification in Italy was able to do so thanks to the fact that* they *enjoyed a collective action advantage*. This collective action advantage was derived from the following features of this elite social group, actually several elites initially, which were progressively unified.

a. The elites were more socially homogenous than the masses. They also shared a more coherent ideology than the ideology of the masses.

b. The elites had better political-military organization than the masses, and this was partly thanks to the better leadership provided by Cavour compared to Garibaldi and Mazzini.

c. All of this made the elites into a relatively cohesive bloc of social groups, compared to the disparate social groups that were part of the masses, which was unresponsive to pressures from below.

We can add another sub-hypothesis to hypothesis 1, in order to emphasize that the elite constituted a hegemonic bloc kept together in part by its ideology.

36 This argument is set out in Notebook 19 of: Gramsci, *Quaderni del Carcere*.

d. This bloc can be described as a hegemonic bloc because its power was partly based upon a coherent ideology, and also because it was able to pursue economic development, even though only a limited development.

This hegemonic bloc was small compared to the masses, and it pursued a limited economic development that benefited it over and above the masses. It was an instance of minimal hegemony, therefore, and yet it could use other mechanisms of power than consent when faced with the masses. In the Risorgimento the minimal hegemony of the elites that coalesced around the Piedmontese national elite was complemented by *domination,* which was made possible by undermining collective action by the masses. This was part of a process whereby, if a national elite is formed early, and is unified into a hegemonic bloc, and is thus cohesive, it can maintain and even expand its collective action advantage by compounding the collective action problems faced by the masses. This raises the issue of timing in historical events, because the elite has to become cohesive before the masses. I address this question in the book on the humanist theory of history. Here I want to focus on the fact that in order to understand how a cohesive elite bloc can maintain and even expand its collective action advantage requires that we conceptualize a meso category of collective action problems, because cooptation presupposes the existence of other social groups that are better organized and can launch cooptation.

6.7 Meso Collective Action Problems, Cooptation, and Defection

There are *three components in the social mechanism involved in domination* that Gramsci drew attention to. The central component of domination is the existence of meso collective action problems, which is implicit in Gramsci's discussion that led to the refined hypothesis 1″. Together with two additional components that are also part of this mechanism, it leads to the elite's collective action advantage. The first additional component involves the *interaction between micro and meso collective action problems*, that is, between the micro problems that are most often studied by the literature on collective action problems, and the meso type of collective action problems studied here. This can be intuitively understood if we consider the circumstances faced by social groups, which include social conflict. *The second additional component is social conflict.* Together, these two components contribute to the following social mechanism. A social group in a hypothetical setting in which it exists outside of social conflict already faces issues of defection and free-riding, due simply to the inclinations of some individuals, which can negatively affect the entire group. These are the micro collective action problems studied most often in the literature on collective action. In reality, most social groups exist in circumstances involving social conflict with other groups, and some exist in circumstances involving heightened social conflict. Therefore, most social groups, in addition to having to deal with the micro collective action problems arising from individuals' inclinations, are also negatively affected by the groups they face, and the incentives and disincentives these other groups can create. This is part of the meso collection action problems. One of the ways this can compound micro collective action problems is if other social groups reinforce problems of defection by cooptation.

It is useful to begin by defining micro and meso collective action problems and sketching their interactions. *Micro collective action problems* are related, amongst other things, to the difficulty in creating a cohesive group and in getting it to engage in collective action, because some individuals who form the base might defect. After a certain number of defections, the cohesiveness of the group is undermined, and the group might even cease to exist. Here I want to draw attention to a micro-type of collective action problem that was central to Gramsci's study of the Risorgimento and of *trasformismo*. This micro-type of problem is *defection of the leadership*. As can be imagined, defection can be even more damaging for a social group if those who defect are the leadership. In such a case, a small number of defections can have very negative consequences for the group. Moreover, defection of the leadership can reinforce ongoing processes of defection of the base, with disastrous consequences for a social group, which might effectively cease to exist. These micro problems related to defection can also be reinforced by meso collective action problems, and both micro and meso collective action problems affecting the masses can be compounded by an elite made cohesive by hegemony. Gramsci started from the assumption that for the masses to win concessions from the elite they would have to be able to exploit their greater numbers and engage in mass collective action. But to do so they needed organization, and organization is difficult to achieve when the masses are divided into many different groups and, moreover, are faced with the better organized elites. This points to the importance of meso collective action problems.

Meso collective action problems are related to features of social groups that are part of a society and thus exist on a meso scale. These features are: first, the number, type, and relative position of social groups in a society; second, the existence, or lack thereof, of mechanisms to coordinate the activities of different social groups; third, features of each group such as its cohesiveness, and the number and type of organizations associated with the social group. All these features can give rise to a number of *collective action problems related to coordination of different social groups*. Here I want to begin addressing meso collective action problems by focusing on their importance to understand defection, and also on the importance of a comparative and historical perspective. The *comparative perspective* involves focusing on the elites compared to masses, since both are very important for understanding collective action by the other. Put simply, in a collective action advantage what matters is not the absolute level of organization of the elite, but whether they are better organized than the masses, which is what decides the outcome of social conflict between elites and masses. The *historical perspective* involves studying the different processes that affect elite and masses through time, since the timing of these different processes is also very important. Let us consider the simplest case, involving social conflict that is fairly clear-cut between elites and masses, and the efforts to create two hegemonic blocs, one based upon the elites, the other based upon the masses. A hegemonic bloc is one way in which disparate social groups can cooperate. If the elites, initially divided, succeed in creating a cohesive hegemonic bloc before the masses, the elites can compound the collective action problems that beset the masses and make sure that the masses never move past their state of inferiority in terms of collective action. This can reach a point where the cohesive elite can completely dominate the masses.

In order to understand how the elites can compound collective action problems that beset the masses, it is useful to introduce *three important insights, which relate to the cohesiveness and leadership of social groups*. The first is the *importance of cooptation*, which was central to Mosca's and Michel's theories. In social conflict between elites and masses, cooptation and defection can go together, and cooptation can be used by the elite to encourage defection amongst the masses, thus compounding the collective action problems which affect the masses. The second insight is that there can be a *combination of cooptation of base and of leadership*, that is, a combination of cooptation of large numbers of individuals within a movement, with cooptation of small numbers of the leadership of the movement. These two types of cooptation can reinforce each other in social conflict, with disastrous or even devastating consequences for a social movement. This leads to a third insight, that cohesiveness and leadership in social groups are very important and that there are *distinctive meso collective action problems of various kinds*, all of which are related to features of a social group in comparison to other social groups. Gramsci drew attention to two such meso collective action problems from Italian history: the collective action problem associated with volunteers, and the one associated with subaltern social groups.

Gramsci formulated the *problem of volunteers* out of his analysis of Italian history. Volunteers might work entirely for another social group and might be conceived of as a *phenomenon related to mass defection*, encouraged by social features like the disaggregation of an entire social group, especially if this social group is faced with an opponent that is a cohesive social group. Gramsci observed that compared to other countries at around the same time, collective action by the masses in Italy was distinguished by two features. One feature was described by Gramsci as the problem of volunteers.[37] This was closely associated with a second feature, described by Gramsci as lack of participation by entire social groups in collective action in Italy. Compared to Germany, for example, Italy did not have a large grass-root workers movement until later.[38] This was in part because industrialization proceeded more slowly in Italy. Significantly, however, compared to France, Italy did not have a large grass-root peasants movement in the countryside either, even though the peasantry in Italy was severely affected by economic change.[39] What distinguished the process of national unification in Italy was the participation of relatively large numbers of volunteers, drawn from one or more social groups. These two features, *participation of volunteers, and lack of participation by entire social*

37 Not much has been written on Gramsci's discussion of the question of volunteers in Italian history, which Gramsci saw as a problem. Yet it is an important question to understand both Italian history and Gramsci's work. For the main points regarding volunteers in Gramsci's work, see the entries 'volontari' and 'volontarismo' in: Liguori and Voza, *Dizionario Gramsciano*.

38 This is a point that was central to philosopher Antonio Labriola's work, and also to Gramsci's work. Gramsci sought to address the point that in the 1920s Italy's working class was still relatively small compared to the total population and was concentrated in the north of the country. Steenson's volume provides contemporary views of these different working class movements: Gary P. Steenson, *After Marx, before Lenin: Marxism and Socialist Working-Class Parties in Europe, 1884–1914* (Pittsburgh: University of Pittsburgh Press, 1991). Della Porta focuses on later differences, in the 1960s and 1970s: Donatella Della Porta, *Social Movements, Political Violence, and the State: A Comparative Analysis of Italy and Germany* (Cambridge and New York: Cambridge University Press, 2006). Mann focuses on differences in consciousness and organization amongst the working classes of Western countries: Michael Mann, *Consciousness and Action among the Western Working Class*, Studies in Sociology (Basingstoke: Macmillan, 1973).

39 The peasantry played an important role in revolutions in some countries, as highlighted by Theda Skocpol, who drew attention to the fact that the peasantry played an important role in the revolutions in France, Russia and China. Skocpol's 1979 classic has been recently republished: Theda Skocpol, *States and Social Revolutions: A Comparative Analysis of France, Russia, and China*, Canto Classics (Cambridge and New York: Cambridge University Press, 2015). Gramsci drew attention to the fact that the peasantry in Italy instead took part in counter-revolutions, and the revolutions that took place could be characterized as passive revolutions. I address this point and provide a typology of revolutions in the book on the humanist theory of history. On Gramsci's views of the working class, the peasantry, and revolutions in Italy, see the many contributions in: John A. Davis, ed. *Gramsci and Italy's Passive Revolution* (New York and London: Routledge, 2014).

groups, interact and can reinforce each other through the interaction of micro and meso collective action problems. Where a social group loses cohesiveness and undergoes disaggregation, mass political mobilization can involve large numbers of individuals, but not the entire social group. In the second volume I address also the interaction of macro and meso collective action problems. Germany did have fairly large numbers of volunteers, who joined *Freikorps*, but these did not take part in national unification. German national unification took the form of an interstate war, arguably because of particular conditions relating to interstate conflict, which I describe below as a type of macro collective action.

Gramsci formulated the *problem of subaltern social groups* also out of his analysis of Italian history. Subaltern social groups too might work entirely for another social group and might be conceived of as a *phenomenon related to defection of low-ranking leadership*. Subaltern social groups are groups that lack initiative in driving social change, and are subject instead to the initiative of other groups. In this sense, they are like subaltern officers in an army, they take part in activity through a leadership role, but do not make plans.[40] They implement plans made by higher-ranking officers. I argue in this project that one of the reasons for this lack of initiative is that subaltern social groups lack the ability to form a hegemonic bloc, which is tied to lack of cultural power. Another reason is that, while they take part in C3I, and know how to use the means of C3I, they lack control of C3I, which is tied to lack of political-military organization and difficulty or even inability to acquire this organization, as well as lack of the economic means that are necessary to acquire political-military organization. They are thus subject to the initiative of social groups that control C3I and whose organizations they join. These two meso collective action problems, *the problem of volunteers, and the problem of subaltern social groups, interact and can reinforce each other*. The problem of volunteers

40 The references made by Gramsci in the Prison Notebooks to subaltern social groups are of two kinds. There are references that describe subaltern social groups as groups trying to build their own hegemony: Gramsci, *Quaderni del Carcere*, 1860–63. There are also references to subaltern social groups that describe them instead as largely or completely dominated by other groups, the hegemonic social groups: ibid., 2283. Either way, subaltern social groups do not have initiative in driving social change. I believe the best explanation of this difference is by analogy with low-ranking officers and military levies respectively. I was puzzled by the fact that the *Dizionario Gramsciano*, arguably the most authoritative summary of Italian scholarship on Gramsci's language, does not discuss the relation between the concept of 'subalterni' or 'gruppi sociali subalterni' and 'ufficiali subalterni', or subaltern officers. See entry for 'subalterno, subalterni' in: Liguori and Voza, *Dizionario Gramsciano*.

refers to the lack of cohesiveness of a social group. The problem of subaltern social groups refers to the organization that these social groups can provide, although they do not control this organization themselves, only the elites do. It is intuitive that the presence of one of these problems reinforces the other. If the elite can make use of subaltern social groups, they can take advantage of disaggregated social groups and recruit and use volunteers from these social groups to create large irregular forces, and even private armies.

We can now address *the manner in which the elite can use cooptation to reinforce defection through a combination of consent and coercion*, to create incentives and disincentives. Gramsci's work on the Risorgimento, and on the domination of the masses in Italy by the Piedmontese national elite, thanks to its collective action advantage, offers also insights into the *role of culture in cooptation and defection.* Culture plays a role in cooptation and defection by aiding both consent and coercion, albeit in different ways. Consent and coercion can be used by the elites in order to encourage defection and at the same time discourage commitment to the cause of the masses.[41] They can work as two sides of the same coin, as a mutually reinforcing pair of incentives and disincentives. These are incentives to one course of action, and disincentives to the opposite course of action. This combination entails the following narrowing of choices: if you engage in collective action and are successful, either you can defect, or you are killed. This combination of consent and coercion can have disastrous effects by depriving the masses of leadership and of subaltern officers, condemning them to remain in a condition of inferiority so that they are completely dominated by the elite and provide volunteers to military operations by the elite. Culture plays a role in all of these mechanisms, whether they involve consent or coercion.

In order to *understand the role of culture in social mechanisms involving cooptation and defection*, it is useful to distinguish between defection of the base and defection of the elite. As far as *defection of the base* is concerned, this can be illustrated by the problem of volunteers, which is a phenomenon related to mass defection of a social group, in which there is an important component of cooptation that uses culture. Culture could be manipulated to obtain the *temporary consent of volunteers,* which encourages the temporary rallying of volunteers to a cause that undermines their social groups or country. In some

41 The idea that coercion and consent go together, which is present already in Gramsci, is central to Hall's work: Hall, *Coercion and Consent: Studies on the Modern State*. For recent work on the two concepts of coercion and consent in Gramsci, see: Richard Howson and Kylie Smith, *Hegemony: Studies in Consensus and Coercion*, Routledge Studies in Social and Political Thought (New York and London: Routledge, 2008).

cases, culture can be used also to achieve spontaneous adhesion to a cause that the volunteers do not realize runs against the interests of their social groups, or even against their own interests. Garibaldi famously sailed from Genoa to Sicily with a thousand volunteers, but the aspect of Garibaldi's conquest of southern Italy through volunteers that deserves more attention is that it mobilized many thousands of additional volunteers in the south, and stoked insurrections.[42] To do so, Garibaldi and other leaders must have been able to use culture to rally large numbers of volunteers to their cause, and possibly to manipulate information to suggest to these volunteers and to the masses in southern Italy that their conditions would improve. By the time the volunteers realized Garibaldi's goals, and they were dismissed with no improvement to their lot, southern Italy had already been conquered.

I want to clarify here that I am not against the unification of Italy, which on the contrary was a historically necessary process that enabled independence, and later the political-military, cultural, and economic development of Italy. What I am criticizing is the manner in which this historical process took place, because it was steered in a direction that favored the elites over and above the masses, and because it incorporated a large part of Italy within the unified state in a condition of inferiority. All of this had enduring consequences for development and democracy, an argument that I develop in the book on humanist social theory. Here I want to focus upon the role that defection played in this process. As far as *defection of the leadership* is concerned, it too can have dramatic consequences, and arguably played an important part in the manner in which the Piedmontese national elite was able to steer the process of national unification in a direction that favored it over and above the masses, and also over and above other elites in Italy. The defection of popular leadership can be encouraged either by cooptation or by coercion.

Two figures show how this worked in Italy during the Risorgimento. In the first case, *culture can be manipulated to affect perceptions, like legitimizing a defection*. Garibaldi gave a decisive contribution to the process of national

42 Recent historiography just touches upon this subject, pointing out that there was social unrest in the Risorgimento: Silavana Patriarca and Lucy Riall, *The Risorgimento Revisited: Nationalism and Culture in Nineteenth-Century Italy* (London and New York: Palgrave Macmillan, 2011); Lucy Riall, *Sicily and the Unification of Italy: Liberal Policy and Local Power, 1859–1866* (Oxford: Clarendon Press, 1998); *The Italian Risorgimento: State, Society and National Unification*, Historical Connections (New York and London: Routledge, 2002). Recently, Enrico Dal Lago has begun addressing more explicitly social unrest, and introduced a comparison between southern Italy and the American South: Enrico Dal Lago, *Civil War and Agrarian Unrest* (Cambridge and New York: Cambridge University Press, 2018).

unification in Italy and the creation of a unified Italy as a kingdom of Italy. The many thousands of volunteers who rallied to Garibaldi's camp, and the insurrections stoked by Garibaldi, suggest that discontent and the search for a better life played a role in gaining Garibaldi mass support, which was encouraged by the perception that Garibaldi was a republican leader committed to ending aristocratic rule, and thus enabled Garibaldi to march north from Sicily all the way to Naples and conquer the whole of southern Italy. After Garibaldi's victory, Victor Emmanuel II, the Duke of Savoy, met him near Naples, ostensibly to prevent Garibaldi from marching on Rome, which would have caused an international reaction. In a brief encounter, Garibaldi handed over the whole of southern Italy to Victor Emmanuel II, without anything other than desultory concessions from the royal camp, thus effectively defecting to the royal camp.[43] Garibaldi continued to be perceived as a republican leader even after this defection, which must have required considerable ability to manipulate perceptions and culture.

In the second case, *culture can be manipulated to legitimize repression and even the killing of leadership that does not defect*. This illustrates also the difficulty in creating leadership from below, from subaltern social groups. Garibaldi's fate was significantly different than the fate of Davide Lazzaretti's, and their differences serve to illustrate the role of culture in cooptation and defection. In this case violence can be used to force defection, and even to kill those who are undeterred and still do not defect in the face of threats, but culture is also important. Lazzaretti was a man from humble origins who had started a religious movement that received the support of thousands in search of a better life shortly after Garibaldi's conquest of the south and national unification.[44]

43 Rosario Villari pointed already in the 1980s to the fact that Garibaldi's image was put to highly political uses: Rosario Villari, "La Prefigurazione Politica del Giudizio Storico Su Garibaldi," *Studi Storici* 23, no. 2 (1982). The 2010 issue of the journal *Modern Italy* contains contributions that revisit Garibaldi's image, no longer unquestionably seen as a popular hero: Mark Seymour, "Introduction: Perspectives on Garibaldi and Italian Unity," *Modern Italy* 15, no. 4 (2010). It would be interesting to make a study comparing the imagery regarding the encounter between Victor Emmanuel II and Garibaldi that prevailed within the royal camp or the conservatives, and the imagery that prevailed in the republican camp. Garibaldi is associated in Italian popular culture with the expression 'I obey', which he is said to have uttered to Victor Emmanuel II upon handing over southern Italy. In particular, it would be interesting to study the overlap between this imagery and Mazzini's imagery of duties. Both Garibaldi and Mazzini, despite their alleged differences, seem to have shared a worldview that still saw the masses as subordinate to the elites, and their flawed leadership arguably contributed to this subordination.

44 Gramsci discusses Davide Lazzaretti at the beginning of Notebook 25: Gramsci, *Quaderni del Carcere*, 2279–83. I believe that, in Gramsci's work, Davide Lazzaretti was the social equivalent of a subaltern officer, and the poor and disenfranchised people who looked up

When this movement reached such dimensions that it could pose a threat to elite interests, Lazzaretti was killed by the Royal Italian Army. This was possible in part also because of the cultural isolation of the individuals drawn from the masses who followed Lazzaretti, and of Lazzaretti himself, who could be killed without raising concerns in the press nor public outrage.[45] There were similar episodes during the conquest of southern Italy by Garibaldi.

6.8 General Theory and Theses on the Origins of Democracy

I want to introduce here three theses that formalize the arguments of this chapter and illustrate both the axiomatic-deductive method and its practical usefulness. In particular, this serves to illustrate the contribution of the theoretical groundwork introduced in this chapter to the general theory that I sketch in the second volume. They also serve to show the usefulness of this general theory to corroborate and refine hypotheses. Let us consider first the contribution of the theoretical groundwork in this chapter to the general theory. The following theses concern the most basic factors of collective action out of which the collective action advantage of elites arises, and how these basic factors change over time, leading to changes in the collective action advantage of elites compared to the masses. The three theses that I propose below all formalize the insights into the sources of the elites' collective action advantage that follow from the theoretical groundwork above. They all include a meso scale of human activity that is involved in collective action problems by entire social groups. Here too the theses are numbered according to their place in the finished outline of a general theory, which is presented in the second volume.

Thesis VIII formalizes the insight derived from Gramsci's theory that democracy depends upon the balance of power in society, and that collective action was involved in this balance of power. As pointed out by Tarrow and Tilly, democracy was the product of a democratization process that involved contention between elites and masses, and collective action. *Thesis VIII breaks down the*

to him where either subaltern social groups, or more likely they were groups completely dominated by the elites.

45 On Lazzaretti, see: Antonello Mattone, "Messianesimo e Sovversivismo. Le Note Gramsciane su Davide Lazzaretti," *Studi Storici* 22, no. 2 (1981). On Gramsci's views of Lazzaretti in contrast to the concept of subaltern social groups put forward by the Subaltern Studies Group, see: Marcus Green, "Gramsci Cannot Speak: Presentations and Interpretations of Gramsci's Concept of the Subaltern," *Rethinking Marxism* 14, no. 3 (2002).

balance of power into more basic factors, notably the balance of forces, which concerns the sheer size of forces that can be fielded. The balance of power is derived from the balance of forces. It also depends upon other factors, such as the length of time that a force can be mobilized for, but to begin formulating a theory, the balance of forces is an obviously important factor to start with. The masses could only achieve durable gains when the balance of forces in the political-military arena shifted in their favor. The balance of forces in society, therefore, is one of the social conditions for democracy.

VIII. *The social conditions for democracy in the political-military arena depend upon the following factors.*
   a. *The balance of forces between social groups in society, which affects the distribution of political-military power.* A group that is powerful, if it is faced by an even more powerful group, will not achieve democracy.
   b. *The balance of forces between social groups in society depends upon the ability to engage in collective action* of different social groups, and it is the difference in this ability from one social group to another, or collective action advantage, that matters to democracy.
   c. *The collective action advantage of the elite can be very different between one type of society and another*, in particular between agrarian-artisanal society and capitalist society.
      i. *In agrarian-artisanal society the elites enjoy a marked collective action advantage* over the masses that is very hard to undo, except in cities.
      ii. *In capitalist society the elites see their collective action advantage reduced* and a long period of social conflict starts in which there can be both victories and reversals for democracy.

The next two theses explain how the collective action advantage of the elites arises and is challenged, leading to social conflict.

Thesis IX *explains the sources of the elite's collective action advantage in agrarian-artisanal society.* This thesis breaks down the balance of forces in society into even more basic factors that affect collective action, namely, social boundaries and social structures or networks. It formalizes, in particular, insights regarding meso collective action, which suggest that meso collective action problems arise from the number of social groups that one has to coordinate. *The elites are divided into fewer social groups than the masses, because there are fewer boundaries amongst the elites*, which means they are less affected by meso collective action problems, and they can more easily form a hegemonic bloc, which requires political-military organization capable of providing C3I capabilities, whether C2 or IC.

IX. *The elites in agrarian-artisanal society enjoy a marked collective action advantage over the masses* because of the following organization and social structures that act on a meso scale.
  a. *Social organization,* which includes the number and relative position in the hierarchy of power of social groups. This is affected by culture and social boundaries, both of which affect the number and relative position of different social groups in the hierarchy of power.
    i. Social boundaries amongst the elites are fewer, are porous, and are less affected by geographical distance, enabling the elites to engage in collective action even across large distances.
    ii. Social boundaries amongst the masses are more numerous, are stronger, and are more affected by geographical distance, making it harder for the masses to engage in collective action because they are divided into many communities.
  b. *Political-military organization,* which includes networks of individuals and networks of organizations like social movement organizations and political parties, can reinforce the effects of social organization by providing, or failing to provide, IC and C2 capabilities.
    i. Social networks across the elites can be of the same form as the above stratification, and are such as to endow them with C2 capabilities that enable them to coordinate their forces across large distances, and also with IC capabilities that enable them to identify which community amongst the masses poses the greatest threat.
    ii. Social networks across the masses, from one community to another, are non-existent or weak or do not stretch very far.

Thesis X summarizes transition organizational problems that arise when the social organization described by the previous thesis changes from the social organization of agrarian-artisanal society to that of capitalist society. It formalizes the intuitive point that *a large social group with more individuals within it needs also more political-military organization,* for example more subalterns, in order to engage in collective action.

X. *The elites in capitalist society see their collective action advantage reduced because of changes in social boundaries* that make mass political mobilization possible and that favor collective action by the masses on a large scale.

a. There is however a *tradeoff between social organization and political-military organization*. A favorable social organization to the masses, a social organization with fewer boundaries, requires also greater political-military organization and the accompanying IC and C2 capabilities, which arise from networks that take time and resources to build.

b. This tradeoff creates a *window of opportunity for the elites*. At least initially, the masses lack the required political-military organization to make use of the changes in social boundaries, and this offsets their advantage in numbers. The elites can take advantage of this offset to enable them to expand their extensive power before the masses build sufficient political-military organization and intensive power and could challenge elite rule.

Let us consider now the contribution that general theory, in the form of the three theses introduced above, can give to social science by corroborating and refining hypotheses. This can help clarify the practical uses of axiomatic-deductive theory. In the case of Italy, thesis IX can serve to corroborate and refine hypotheses put forward earlier regarding the sources of elites' collective action advantage, in particular hypothesis 1″ above. This hypothesis made three statements regarding the sources of the collective action advantage of the Piedmontese national elite compared to the masses in Italy, which enabled this elite to drive the process of national unification to its advantage. Hypothesis 1″ suggests that the elite enjoyed a collective action advantage compared to the masses, thanks to a number of features of the elite's organization. The following hypothesis is a refines version of hypothesis 1″ that goes into detail to describe the features of the Piedmontese national elite that gave it a collective action advantage, based upon concepts that are part of thesis IX, particularly boundaries and social structures or networks.

1‴. *The Piedmontese national elite that drove the process of national unification in Italy was able to do so thanks to the fact that* they *enjoyed a collective action advantage*. This collective action advantage was derived from the following features of the organization of this elite, actually several elites initially that were progressively unified, compared to the masses.

The sub-hypotheses a to c are corroborated and refined in the following manner.

a. *The elites were more socially homogenous than the masses.* This hypothesis can be refined as:

i. The three elites within Piedmont, the aristocratic-military elite, the cultural elite, and the economic elite, were more unified than the masses within Piedmont.
ii. The Piedmontese national elite had ties, through personal networks, to elites in other parts of Italy, and this made the resulting elites more unified by alliances than the masses within Italy as a whole.

b. *The elites shared a more coherent ideology than the ideology of the masses.* This hypothesis can be refined as:
   i. The Piedmontese national elite and other elites in Italy shared a common language, which could have been either literary Italian, which before unification was spoken by 1 to 2 % of the population, or French, the language of diplomacy.
   ii. There was a common ideology justifying elite power in terms of the right of kings, which was being replaced by a common ideology justifying elite power in terms of natural law and improving the realm.

c. *The elites had better political-military organization than the masses, and part of this was thanks to the better leadership provided by Cavour compared to Garibaldi and Mazzini.* This hypothesis can be refined as:
   i. There were actual diplomatic ties and informal military alliances, for example with other states in the Italian peninsula that held plebiscites to unite with the newly formed Italy.
   ii. There were sources of intelligence in states that were conquered, like the kingdom of Naples. These sources could be the survivors of the Pisacane expedition, which was similar to Garibaldi's expedition, but took place a few years earlier and failed. Or they could be sources of intelligence through networks that reached into the kingdom of Naples.

As can be easily seen, introducing the concepts of social boundaries and social structures or networks, greatly helped to refine the sub-hypotheses. These sub-hypotheses can be more easily tested, and we can begin proving the theory by the successive rounds approach. The book on humanist social theory provides philosophical and theoretical arguments that support the theses introduced in this chapter.

Conclusions

The forthcoming second volume[1] will provide a broad outline of a general theory of development and democracy that includes all of the above theses organized in a coherent whole. In order to pave the way for this theory, I want to draw here some preliminary conclusions and highlight some of the *new directions for research* opened up by the arguments presented in this volume. There are three such new directions, which can be pursued alongside each other. The first involves testing the key hypothesis of this book, regarding the existence of an imperialist world-elite. The second involves exploring what effects could such an imperialist world-elite have. The third involves formulating alternatives to neoliberalism and the populist backlash. Needless to say, hypotheses need to be proven, which requires empirically testing the hypotheses, including the hypothesis regarding the existence of an imperialist world-elite at the zenith of power of the British empire. Starting with this hypothesis could help us further corroborate and refine the key hypothesis regarding the current existence of an imperialist world-elite. The theses proposed in this book, however, have already served to corroborate this key hypothesis by suggesting that, given certain starting points, a world-elite can emerge and did emerge in the past. The theses proposed in this book also suggested a mechanism that explains the power of aristocratic-military elites in European history and how they could have maintained this power despite the profound changes in social organization that affected Western countries in modern history. Aristocratic-military elites might have survived by expanding their collective action advantage and driving globalization in a manner that benefited them at the expense of the masses.

The *first new direction for research* is to test the key hypothesis of this book and related hypotheses. Therefore, I want to begin these preliminary conclusions by suggesting which hypotheses I think it is important to test first, as well as by pointing to the hypotheses to test next. I argued above that the key to the success of neoliberalism is the *existence of a world-elite, and within it of an imperialist world-elite*, which might be emerging and consolidating its power, if it has not done so already. The most promising place to start testing this hypothesis is by testing the related hypothesis that *there existed an earlier world-elite, which emerged from the British aristocratic-military elite that built*

1 The second volume, forthcoming with Brill, is tentatively titled: *The Struggle for Development and Democracy: a General Theory*.

the British empire. Testing this hypothesis first would help us test the hypothesis that a world-elite emerged in the past. This is an especially important test because the imperialist world-elite of today, if it exists, could have ties to the British aristocratic-military elite that built the British empire, and understanding the British aristocratic-military elite could help us understand the world-elite of today. These ties are likely to include *a humanistic education, and an education related to arts and communications more in general.* They are also likely to include *an historical memory associated with elite universities that also influenced popular culture*, and even the counterculture of the 1960s symbolized by the Beatles, since it was through elite universities that the British aristocratic-military elite built its power. I want to recall next the key points regarding this elite and its sources of power, and centers of power, because these points might help test the above hypotheses.

It is useful to begin by recalling *key points regarding the identity and importance of the British aristocratic-military elite*. As emphasized in chapters 2 and 3, where I introduced arguments regarding this elite, and in chapters 5 and 6, in discussing the hypotheses and theses regarding the British case study, the British aristocratic-military elite exercised hegemony over other elites throughout the world, and culture was thus very important to its power. In addition, it cultivated an historical memory that likely included the knowledge of how to build extensive power, or even specific techniques of power, which can be used to advance imperialism instead of democracy. The possibility that there might be ties between the British aristocratic-military elite and the contemporary world-elite that might be emerging is not so far-fetched. It is important to remember that the British empire only ceased officially to exist in the period 1950s-70s. This is within living memory. Moreover, people who lived through those times are still amongst us, and it is not unthinkable that, in addition to having left to later elites a historical memory and the knowledge of how to build an empire, the British aristocratic-military elite might have left also personnel resources and other resources. This is because the British aristocratic-military elite that built the British empire, the largest in European history, was the most powerful imperialist elite to emerge in the history of the West, and it would have had vast resources at its disposal. It was able to continue expanding for a very long time and was the European imperialist elite that expanded the most, becoming an early imperialist world-elite with a truly global presence.

Centers of power scattered around the world are likely the most promising places to start looking for evidence of the activities of this world-elite and what made it successful, driving imperialism on a scale even greater than the post-9/11 imperialism we have witnessed in our time. To understand the extensive power of this world-elite, and its reach around the world, it is not the centers of power in Great Britain that are most important, but the centers of power directly involved in imperialism. Aristocratic-military elites based their power first and foremost upon political-military power. This power in its turn was based upon a combination of culture and social structures that enabled these elites to exercise hegemony. This power might have survived under a new form. As argued in the last chapter, the balance of power in the political-military arena has not changed radically with the emergence of capitalist society, because aristocratic-military elites have a significant command and control, or C2, advantage, and intelligence and communications, or IC, advantage compared to the masses, and a time window to expand their power.

One center of power that could provide evidence about the activities of the British imperialist world-elite could be in Canada and in particular in Montreal, which is the seat of the oldest university in the country, and was promoted by the British aristocratic-military elite as an example of good government to legitimize its rule, after the independence and growth in power of the United States, and after a desire for autonomy re-surfaced amongst the mostly French-speaking population. This good government continued through the Quiet Revolution and interventions to promote public transportation and the built environment of Montreal. It also continued through an immigration policy that deliberately encouraged multiculturalism, which is strikingly visible in Montreal's Little Italy, and which marks such a stark contrast to the policy pursued by the Piedmontese national elite and later Italian elites, who strongly centralized Italian culture and universities, at the same time as they encouraged migration to the north of the country, where all industry and technology research was based, and to some extent are still based. *Another center of power, of a different kind of power, could be in strategically important locations in the Caribbean.* I include the Caribbean because this is where the British aristocratic-military elite built economic power bases including plantations that made the individual owners extremely wealthy at the cost of untold human suffering, as well as unofficial military bases like Port Royal, which it used to target Spanish galleons. The British aristocratic-military elite were not unique in this, and the Caribbean includes islands associated with other empires, like Cuba, most famously, but also Haiti, and the Dominican Republic, besides British colonies like Jamaica, Barbados, and Bermuda. Similarly, other cities in Canada than Montreal could be especially important to find evidence of the activities of the British imperialist world-elite, including Toronto, in Ontario, and Vancouver, Victoria, and Whistler, in British Columbia. Vancouver is arguably another striking example of multiculturalism, as its China Town is one of the largest in North America.

The theory does not stand or fall with tests in the centers of power of the British imperialist world-elite and its C2 and IC means. There could be *other ways to test the hypothesis that an imperialist world-elite existed in the past*. An especially important center of power with evidence of the existence of an earlier imperialist world-elite could be in Spain. The largest empire in European history before the British empire was *the Spanish empire*. Arguably, it underwent a reaction similar to that of the British empire, and an analogous undermining of democracy in the wake of empire-building, but earlier. It could still however hold important lessons. Barcelona, a city that pioneered capitalism in Spain, and arguably drove both development and democracy, was decisively supplanted by Madrid after the latter's success in creating a unified Spanish state and in quickly building a huge overseas empire. Barcelona was thus reduced to a secondary and subordinate position compared to Madrid, and both were ruled by an aristocratic-military elite who lived in Madrid and who got rich from the spoils of the Spanish empire. Therefore, Spain would be another place to test the hypotheses regarding the existence of a world-elite in the past, whether the first test in the centers of power of the British aristocratic-military elite was successful or not. Spain could also provide additional interesting material for the theory. Why did Barcelona not drive the process of national unification in Spain and went into decline, taking a second seat compared to Madrid? Can this be explained by mechanisms similar to those that explain the decline of Italian city-states, and later of southern Italy?

The second new direction for research that I think it is important to pursue involves exploring a more far-fetched hypothesis through further theoretical groundwork. This hypothesis suggests that *the imperialist world-elite could actually put an end to development and democracy* if it acquired detailed knowledge of the techniques of power that were successful in the past. These could be repeated and made all the more successful by current and emerging technological means that enable operations on a global scale, which could be used to coordinate disparate processes, affecting the economy, culture, politics and the military. How could anyone actually do that? The outline of a theory provided in the second volume suggests that this is possible and provides explanations including the social mechanisms that would be involved in this loss of democracy. I want to point out here how this outline applies to our own day, to give a sense both of the applications that the theory has, and also of the theoretical task that is involved in applying the theory to our own day. The following are *scenarios based upon the theory* that suggest just how the imperialist world-elite could put an end to development and democracy. The second volume explores the conditions under which the imperialist world-elite might be able to bring about these scenarios. These scenarios are based on the negative impacts that could follow from the problem of different standards at home and abroad, and the problem of private armies. These scenarios are not wild speculations, but are derived from the theory, and answer problems addressed in current affairs publications focused on defense and security. They too would have to be tested, like the hypotheses that I have proposed, by *carefully observing* whether such scenarios do start emerging.

The problem of *different standards accorded to military and intelligence operations at home and abroad* might have originated in the British empire and survives today in the division of powers of some intelligence agencies, which have different roles whereby they can operate only at home or only abroad, as is the case with the British agencies MI5 and MI6, or Italian agencies AISI and AISE, or Israeli agencies Shin Beth and Mossad. The following scenarios *suggest how this problem could worsen, by giving rise to absolutist organizations*. A serious problem would emerge if one agency like the CIA, which is not restricted to operations only at home or abroad, took control of all operations, exercising large discretion at home and abroad and in many theaters, because of perceived threats from violent social movements, for example. Such an agency would be once more in the position of European absolutist rulers, whose power was not subject to defined roles and a division of powers, and was thus absolute. Similar abuses of power could take place even in countries in which there is the division between home and foreign operations. In a climate in which there are strong perceived threats, an agency like MI5 could start carrying out *many* operations abroad to protect expatriates, and an agency like MI6 could start carrying out *many* operations on home soil against foreign agents in Great Britain, and this could lead, not to one absolutist agency, but to two such agencies.

The same could happen with Italian agencies like AISI and AISE, the successors of SISDE, a civilian agency, and SISMI, a military agency. SISDE and SISMI were officially disbanded because of irregularities, like other Italian agencies before them since the end of the Second World War. This is yet another sign of the enduring power of the aristocratic-military elite or elites in Italy, which are not answerable even to the Italian Parliament, let alone foreign Parliaments, and have always acted at the border between what is legal and what is not. Benito Mussolini openly showed contempt for Parliament and due process, and took over the Italian Parliament also through the creation of such secret police as the Fascist OVRA, similar to the Nazi Abwehr and the Francoist Brigada Politico-Social. The recent irregularities of SISDE and SISMI show what is arguably a continuity from those times, and possibly since the Risorgimento, to our times. Perhaps the same could happen in Israel, where the perceived threat from violent social movements is even higher, and Mossad could start encroaching upon Shin Beth and the Israeli Parliament.

The different standards accorded to military and intelligence operations at home and abroad could be compounded by the second problem, *the problem of private armies*, which are arising once again due to a growing reliance upon contractors, and a continued reliance upon irregular forces and volunteers. The return to *private armies relying upon contractors* is a real possibility. Blackwater, now re-branded as Academi, has been consolidated into a fairly large military contractor that provides military services to the CIA. Contractors in the United States already form a very substantial part of the Intelligence Community. Private armies could grow even larger if they tapped into opportunities around the world. An elite like the British aristocratic-military elite could conceivably fund not two agencies, but many more, MI1 to MI20, or even MI30. Today, multiple military headquarters can be assigned the same units, for planning specific operations, and with such duplication and private armies of military planners, the agencies could conceivably be even more. Similarly, the British aristocratic-military elite could fund, not just one dashing and photogenic 007 film-screen agent, but ten thousand actual top agents, 001 to 10,000, and hundreds of thousands of other agents, who in keeping with the importance of the monarchy in Great Britain could all be King's Men.

An elite like the Piedmontese aristocratic-military elite could similarly fund a massive expansion, using cheap labour provided by Italians struggling to find jobs in a country large parts of which are still suffering from underdevelopment. The technologies that already exist, and that are fast evolving, could compound these developments. One day, if not today, the advances in computing and Artificial Intelligence, or AI, could make possible an even greater expansion and the creation of more MIs, all manned largely or even exclusively by AI systems, using cheap military labour as boots on the ground. An agency like the British agency Defence Intelligence, or DI, that is above the British MI agencies, could bring other agencies under its control thanks to the vast expansion in computing power and means of communication. These are already capable of coordinating vast armies across the world. On a smaller scale, an agency like the CIA, the only independent agency in the United States Intelligence Community, could bring under its control other agencies like the DIA and NSA. Modern changes in infrastructure and the means of transportation and communication are making IC and C2 possible on a truly global scale to anyone with the required knowledge of cyber operations, which use the internet.

The return to *private armies made up of irregular forces* is another real possibility. Mexico has been fighting for years against the drug cartels in what is effectively a war, with thousands of deaths. These cartels have built large irregular forces that are effectively private armies outside the control of the state. They are like modern privateers for all intents and purposes. With the growing sophistication and wide availability of means of communication, anyone with the ability to coordinate such forces could wield significant power. There were news reports that Raqqa, at one point the capital of ISIS in Syria, had a multitude of internet connections that enabled communications and recruitment across the world. The fate of destabilized countries could easily be under threat. The whole Levant today is destabilized, and in war-thorn areas, or areas of uncertain international status, irregular forces can plan their expansion and launch their operations without their systems being subjected to any oversight. Israel and Jordan are the only two countries with stable economies and societies in the area. Syria is still thorn by war, Lebanon and Iraq are still suffering from the legacy of a past ridden by civil war and violent social movements. So are the Palestinian Territories and the Gaza Strip.

In such a scenario, *the fate of small countries and independentist provinces* could also be under threat. There are already corporations whose revenues are greater than the national products of small countries. Private security companies and private cyber security companies who work for agencies like the CIA could easily hire contractors and become themselves like agencies. The Tech Big Five, namely, Amazon, Apple, Facebook, Google, Microsoft, already have vast expertise in cyber security, and it is sensible to ask what would be the effects if they became full-blown non-state agencies. WhatsApp provides hard to decrypt messaging with cutting-edge cyber technology to anyone who downloads their app, and Cyber Ark provides advanced cyber communications to any company that can buy them. If a province like Quebec built its own agency, it would be no match for such non-state agencies, or for a powerful and independent agency like the CIA, or for large private armies controlled by an aristocratic-military elite, all of which could easily take it over and use it as a base. Perhaps not even Canada as a whole would be a match. Perhaps not even the United States would be a match, if one day Canada, Mexico, the Caribbean, all became bases for operations against the United States.

I want to emphasize that the points I am making are *in favor of private enterprise and not against it.* In the second volume I address and begin to elaborate in new directions the argument introduced by Trigilia that development is the product of the right balance between markets, society, and the state. Here I want to anticipate key parts of this argument. Private enterprise is indispensable to the economy, and in a different way to culture too. Some of the problems that I am highlighting actually follow from *lack of private enterprise.* When there are only a few gigantic enterprises in a field, like the Tech

Big Five, and market entry costs are very high, this limits private enterprise and poses a threat to development and also to democracy, because if such an enterprise fails, the state has to step in, either to rescue the enterprise, or to prop up markets. The economy suffers and the state has to foot the bill for bad decisions taken by private individuals that it has no control over. Lack of private enterprise is affecting culture too. In this case the problem of lack of private enterprise is compounded by *misplaced motives*. A few large enterprises dominate the market for publishing. In addition to the same problems just mentioned for economic enterprises, large cultural enterprises also bring a profit motive to culture that does not belong to it. Truth should be the first motive of those active in cultural enterprises, followed by the goal to enrich the culture and knowledge of a country and all individuals within it. The search for personal monetary rewards that is associated with acquisitive individualism should come after these other motives and never be a replacement for them. Otherwise, there is a danger that one would write or produce whatever sells the most and whatever minimizes one's risks, rather than what is true or what enriches one's culture. Risk averseness has been identified as a factor behind the production of very similar films that seem to follow templates by some *big* Hollywood studios, which wield as much power as the DIA, the next biggest agency in the United States after the CIA.

The same problems that affect culture also affect politics and the military. In this case *private enterprise is misplaced, the profit motive is misplaced, and there is also the danger of a rapid loss of democracy* in the political-military arena that could rapidly affect other arenas. Weber famously described the modern state as the organization that has the monopoly of legitimate violence over a territory. Arguably, the state is a natural monopoly, because the control of violence lends itself to be centralized and needs to be carefully regulated in order to minimize social conflict and interstate conflict and the staggering costs they have. Small private armies have been accepted as providers of services to the state in the name of greater efficiency, but this has the potential of bringing to an end the state monopoly of legitimate violence, and lead to destabilizing effects. In the political-military arena, it is necessary to put national security way above personal monetary rewards. It is also necessary to put the public good above one's own personal gains. Politicians who blame scapegoats and divert attention from real problems can endanger national security, and can contribute to loss of democracy, through a coup d'etat by unscrupulous military leaders, or to loss of independence. This is because the same considerations pointed out above for large economic or cultural enterprises apply to the military. If a military contractor became large, or if a foreign elite established ties to many small military contractors, which started carrying out illegal operations on behalf of higher-paying clients, following a profit motive, one could not really treat them like a private enterprise and fire them at will. Who would disarm them? Additionally, the theory sketched out in this book suggests that the effects of violence are deep and long-lasting, and the same applies to failures in security. If a private company fails, the economy suffers, but one can rebuild. If an army unit like the US Army III Corp started obeying unscrupulous military leaders, or if NORAD, which monitors and defends the airspace throughout North America, fails to do its job, it could lead to loss of democracy in the country they are supposed to protect, or massive destruction with disastrous consequences, which would take decades or even centuries to undo. Needless to say, having one large organization like the Pentagon take charge of all national security requires that its functioning be very carefully monitored. This is because, like NORAD, the Pentagon covers the entire United States, and inefficiencies or failures in such an organization could lead to massive destruction.

The third new direction for research that I propose is to *begin formulating alternatives to neoliberalism and the populist backlash.* In this context, I also want to emphasize that the points I am making are not aimed at painting sinister apocalyptic scenarios or fueling conspiracy theories. To the contrary, they are aimed at preventing the above scenarios from arising, or growing to the point that they are beyond control, which requires formulating valid alternatives to current problems. This leads me to return to an important point made by Gramsci, which is stated in the quote at the beginning of Part I, and which I addressed in chapter 2. This is the point that there is a *struggle for objectivity*, and that this struggle is related both to partial ideologies and to globalization. Gramsci wrote that 'there is a struggle for objectivity, and this struggle is the same as the struggle for the cultural unification of humankind'. This association between the struggle for objectivity and globalization is a very important insight that begins to make sense if we relate it to the above discussion regarding the expansion of elite power. The unification of humankind is taking place in the form of a process of globalization that is largely or even entirely driven by elites who expand their power in response to challenges from below. Elites drive this process to their own exclusive advantage, shaping globalization in a way that favors them at the expense of the masses. They are able to do so also because of their ability to formulate theories, which is part of hegemony. In hegemony by elites, theories are important because they legitimize the form of globalization chosen by the elites. They also provide elites with the ability to formulate and pursue plans, including long-term plans. It is necessary to change this process, and to do so we need an alternative plan for development and democracy, and a plan needs a theory. The problem that we need to address next is how to formulate such a theory. Formulating valid theories might start with the work of one or a few individuals but proceeding any further requires action on a larger scale than what an individual or a few individuals can achieve. In the first part of this volume, I emphasized the importance of collaborative projects. Here I want to emphasize that this action involves working on democracy, and this leads me to address the importance of democracy for development.

In order to re-start development in the West we need to work on securing democracy first. *It is necessary first of all to secure democracy within the political-military arena.* Of the two reasons that I suggested why theories are important to hegemony, namely, legitimizing a choice, and formulating plans that enable deliberate and sustained collective action, the second is arguably the most important, at least at this conjuncture in history. Marx pointed out sarcastically that the criticism of arms defeats the arms of criticism. There are times when this is true. I believe that the most important reason why neoliberalism was adopted and pursued for such a long time was not so much that it was persuasive, but because elites had political-military power largely or even entirely on their side. Elites with vast political-military power can impose the model of development that they prefer regardless of theoretical arguments. However, because of long-term effects, it is always also necessary to subject politics to ethical considerations, which have to be debated through the arms of criticism, or politics itself will suffer.

This is perhaps obvious in the case of fast developing countries like Brazil, India, China and Russia, which took decades to recover from colonial exploitation and the past dictatorial regimes that followed it. They are still to some extent subject to dictatorial regimes. But it might be true just as much in the West, where elites in the past exploited various combinations of coercion and consent. Moreover, as suggested above, these elites exploited their greater political-military organization to maintain their collective action advantage and continue expanding their power. There might be an economic component to this process. When exploitation was prevented at home, European aristocratic-military elites found ways to continue it and even expand it abroad. The flooding of markets with cheap goods produced abroad might be a way to regain both the economic and political-military power that they had lost at home. This could strengthen the power of elites even more. Therefore, in order to be able to formulate true theories and make measured arguments regarding policies, it is necessary first to secure democracy and begin redressing the balance of political-military power in society.

It is necessary at the same time to secure democracy also within the cultural arena. Unlike the later Marx, we should not abandon the arms of criticism for the criticism of arms. There are many valid reasons not to do so. An especially important one is related to the need to overcome partial ideologies. As it applies to this book, which is concerned with theory, it is necessary to put an end to the tendency to move from one one-sided or partial theory to another, without finding a synthesis and proper balance, which has undermined mass movements in the West for the past 150 years. Socialism-Marxism led to totalitarianism through several routes, an important one of which has to do with recurrent cycles in the world system. Recurrent cycles that are observable in much of the recent history of the West include knee-jerk reactions that encourage swings from one extreme to another. Just like free-trade liberalism and the red scare from the Soviet Union fed the fascist backlash in Italy, neoliberalism and the terrorist scare from Muslim fundamentalists fed the populist backlash we are living through today, in both cases by creating a reservoir of discontent that fueled knee-jerk reactions. To avoid past mistakes, and to avoid this tendency to swing from one one-sided theory to another, from one extreme to another, we need to work on securing the social conditions for objectivity in social science. Arguably, these conditions have been ensured in natural science, but are still largely lacking in social science.

The social conditions for objectivity in social science include cultural democracy. Without cultural democracy it is exceedingly hard to formulate valid alternatives, and also to disseminate these alternatives, and subject them to a measured public debate. Without cultural democracy we will also be condemned to repeat past mistakes. Worse still, we might be at the mercy of the whims of populist leaders whose position changes at a moments' notice without being backed by long-term plans nor a theory. Taken on their own, their pronouncements might seem just full of sound and fury and signifying nothing. But when put in a long-term perspective, they acquire meaning. Mussolini's posturing might seem absurd today, but it was one and the same thing as his coup d'état in Italy, because both arose from the end of measured public debate in Italy. Successive governments in Italy after the Second World War that seemed to have restored democracy ended up leading to a spiral of bad government and what is described in Italian political discourse as the fall of the First Republic, in the early 1990s. The optimism at around that time was followed by the rise of populism, less violent than fascism, but arguably more insidious. Populism today has many faces, some friendlier than others, but no less dangerous. We are still lacking a balanced synthesis between different theories, we are still operating within the same framework that encouraged veering from over-reliance upon the state, to complete rejection of the state, in favor of markets alone. Or from over-reliance upon reason, understood reductively as a cold and calculating faculty, to complete rejection of reason, in favor of strong emotions or reassuring faces. This too is a knee-jerk reaction that has a fascist precedent.

I want to end these preliminary conclusions with a note of *optimism on what science, including social science, can achieve*. I believe it is possible to understand and thus to stop the cycles in the world system that have led to fascism and populism. I believe we can still turn the tables on the rising imperialist tide and secure greater development and democracy for all. Unlike apologists of imperialist gangs, elitists of various stripes, and those who have abandoned reason to appeal to emotions alone, I remain optimistic at heart that the main goal of the numerous mass movements of the past, which was to secure a better future with longer and happier lives for everyone, is still within our reach. In all these years, I have often found comfort in an expression that Gramsci adopted as a motto, which is 'to be a pessimist by the intellect, and an optimist by the will'. I still do. As it applies to this book and the humanist social science that I seek to contribute to, if we coolly prepare for the worst, we can achieve far better outcomes. This should include making available to everyone, and not just the elites, advanced technologies and scientific knowledge that increase productivity and life expectancy to far higher levels, which most of us, with the scientific knowledge that is part of mainstream culture, do not even dream of. This could relaunch the American Dream in the United States and open up similar dreams throughout the world, including Italy and all countries that have suffered from underdevelopment in the modern world system, and that deserve a future as bright as their past.

Bibliography

Abdelal, Rawi. "Dignity, Inequality, and the Populist Backlash: Lessons from America and Europe for a Sustainable Globalization." In *Harvard Business School Working Paper 20–123*, 2020.

Abernethy, David B. *The Dynamics of Global Dominance: European Overseas Empires, 1415–1980.* New Haven and London: Yale University Press, 2000.

Abisaab, Malek. *Militant Women of a Fragile Nation.* Middle East Studies Beyond Dominant Paradigms. Syracuse: Syracuse University Press, 2010.

Abisaab, Malek. "The So-Called Arab Spring, Islamism and the Dilemma of the Arab Left: 1970–2012." *R/evolutions: Global Trends & Regional Issues.* 4, no. 1 (2016): 38–59.

Abisaab, Malek. ""Unruly" Factory Women in Lebanon: Contesting French Colonialism and the National State, 1940–1946." *Journal of Women's History.* 16, no. 3 (2004): 55–82.

Abisaab, Rula Jordi, and Malek Abisaab. *The Shi'ites of Lebanon: Modernism, Communism, and Hizbullah's Islamists.* Middle East Studies Beyond Dominant Paradigms. Syracuse: Syracuse University Press, 2014.

Abramson, Paul R., and Ronald Inglehart. *Value Change in Global Perspective.* Ann Arbor: University of Michigan Press, 1995.

Akers, Ronald L. "Linking Sociology and Its Specialties: the Case of Criminology." *Social Forces.* 71, no. 1 (1992): 1–16.

Alsanea, Rajaa. *Girls of Riyadh.* Translated by Rajaa Alsanea and Marilyn Booth. London: Penguin, 2007.

Althusser, Luis. *For Marx.* Radical Thinkers. London and New York: Verso, 2010.

Althusser, Luis. *Pour Marx.* Collection Théorie. Paris: François Maspero, 1965.

Amanat, Abbas, and Magnus Thorkell Bernhardsson, eds. *Imagining the End: Visions of Apocalypse from the Ancient Middle East to Modern America.* London and New York: I. B. Tauris, 2001.

Ancelovici, Marcos. "In Search of Lost Radicalism: The Hot Autumn of 2010 and the Transformation of Labor Contention in France." *French Politics, Culture & Society.* 29, no. 3 (2011): 121–140.

Ancelovici, Marcos. "Occupy Montreal and the Politics of Horizontalism." In *Street Politics in the Age of Austerity: from the Indignados to Occupy*, edited by Marcos Ancelovici, Pascale Dufour and Heloise Nez. Amsterdam: Amsterdam University Press, 2016.

Ancelovici, Marcos. "Organizing against Globalization: the Case of Attac in France." *Politics & Society.* 30, no. 3 (2002): 427–463.

Anderson, Betty S. *The American University of Beirut: Arab Nationalism and Liberal Education.* Austin: University of Texas Press, 2011.

Anderson, Perry. *Arguments within English Marxism.* London: New Left Books, 1980.

Anderson, Perry. *Considerations on Western Marxism.* London: New Left Books, 1976.

Anderson, Perry, and E. Terrén. *Teoría, Política e Historia: un Debate con E. P. Thompson.* Teoria. Mexico City: Siglo XXI, 1985.

Arrighi, Giovanni. "The Three Hegemonies of Historical Capitalism." In *Gramsci, Historical Materialism and International Relations*, edited by Stephen Gill. Cambridge and New York: Cambridge University Press, 1993.

Arrighi, Giovanni, Terence K. Hopkins, and Immanuel Maurice Wallerstein. *Antisystemic Movements.* London and New York: Verso, 2012.

Avineri, Shlomo. *Karl Marx: Philosophy and Revolution.* Jewish Lives. New Haven and London: Yale University Press, 2019.

Avineri, Shlomo. *The Social and Political Thought of Karl Marx.* Cambridge Studies in the History and Theory of Politics. Cambridge and New York: Cambridge University Press, 1968.

Axelrod, Alan. *Patton: A Biography.* Great Generals. New York: St. Martin's Press, 2015.

Baller, Silja, Soumitra Dutta, and Bruno Lanvin. "The Global Information Technology Report, 2016." World Economic Forum in collaboration with INSEAD and the Cornell University Johnson School of Management, http://www3.weforum.org/docs/GITR2016/WEF_GITR_Full_Report.pdf, accessed April 9, 2021.

Bar-On, Tamir. "'Islamofascism': Four Competing Discourses on the Islamism-Fascism Comparison." *Fascism.* 7, no. 2 (2018): 241–274.

Baratta, Giorgio. *Le Rose e i Quaderni: Saggio sul Pensiero di Antonio Gramsci.* Roma: Gamberetti Editrice, 2000.

Bartolini, Francesco. *La Terza Italia: Reinventare la Nazione alla Fine del Novecento.* Studi Storici Carocci. Roma: Carocci editore, 2015.

Bayly, Christopher Alan. *Imperial Meridian: the British Empire and the World, 1780–1830.* Studies in Modern History. London: Longman, 1989.

Bayly, Christopher Alan. *Indian Society and the Making of the British Empire.* Cambridge and New York: Cambridge University Press, 1987.

Bayly, Christopher Alan, and Dirk H. Kolff, eds. *Two Colonial Empires: Comparative Essays on the History of India and Indonesia in the Nineteenth Century*, Comparative Studies in Overseas History. Dordrecht: Springer Netherlands, 2012.

Ben-Ghiat, Ruth. "Donald Trump and Benito Mussolini." *The Atlantic*, August 10th 2016.

Bendix, Reinhard, and Guenther Roth. *Max Weber: an Intellectual Portrait.* Berkeley and Los Angeles: University of California Press, 1977.

Bennett, Andy, and Jon Stratton, eds. *Britpop and the English Music Tradition*, Ashgate Popular and Folk Music Series. Abingdon, UK and New York: Ashgate Publishing Limited, 2013.

Bennett, Tony. "James Bond in the 1980s." *Marxism Today.* 27, no. 6 (1983): 39.

Bennett, Tony, and J. Woollacott. *Bond and Beyond: the Political Career of a Popular Hero.* Communications and Culture. Basingstoke: Macmillan Education, Limited, 1987.

Bernhardsson, Magnus Torkell. *Reclaiming a Plundered Past: Archaeology and Nation Building in Modern Iraq.* Austin: University of Texas Press, 2013.

Blumenberg, Werner, and Gareth Stedman Jones. *Karl Marx: an Illustrated Biography.* Translated by Douglas Scott. London and New York: Verso, 2000.

Boles, John B. *Jefferson: Architect of American Liberty.* New York: Basic Books, 2017.

Booth, Marilyn. *Classes of Ladies of Cloistered Spaces: Writing Feminist History through Biography in Fin-de-Siecle Egypt.* Edinburgh: Edinburgh University Press, 2015.

Booth, Marilyn. *May Her Likes Be Multiplied: Biography and Gender Politics in Egypt.* Berkeley and Los Angeles: University of California Press, 2001.

Booth, Marilyn. "'May Her Likes Be Multiplied': 'Famous Women' Biography and Gendered Prescription in Egypt, 1892–1935." *Signs: Journal of Women in Culture and Society.* 22, no. 4 (1997): 827–890.

Booth, Marilyn. *Migrating Texts: Circulating Translations around the Ottoman Mediterranean.* Edinburgh Studies on the Ottoman Empire. Edinburgh: Edinburgh University Press, 2019.

Booth, Marilyn. "'The Muslim Woman' as Celebrity Author and the Politics of Translating Arabic: Girls of Riyadh Go on the Road." *Journal of Middle East Women's Studies.* 6, no. 3 (2010): 149–182.

Booth, Marilyn. "On Translation and Madness." *Translation Review.* 65, no. 1 (2003): 47–53.

Booth, Marilyn. "Three's a Crowd: the Translator-Author-Publisher and the Engineering of Girls of Riyadh for an Anglophone Readership." In *Translating Women: Different Voices and New Horizons*, edited by Luise von Flotow and Farzaneh Farahzad. London and New York: Routledge, 2017.

Booth, Marilyn. "Translator V. Author (2007) Girls of Riyadh Go to New York." *Translation Studies.* 1, no. 2 (2008): 197–211.

Booth, Marilyn. "Un/Safe/Ly at Home: Narratives of Sexual Coercion in 1920s Egypt." *Gender & History.* 16, no. 3 (2004): 744–768.

Booth, Marilyn. "The World of Obituaries: Gender across Cultures and over Time." *Biography.* 26, no. 3 (2003): 453–456.

Booth, Robert. "Boris Johnson Caught on Camera Reciting Kipling in Myanmar Temple." The Guardian, https://www.theguardian.com/politics/2017/sep/30/boris-johnson-caught-on-camera-reciting-kipling-in-myanmar-temple, accessed September 30, 2017.

Boothman, Derek. "Gramsci, Croce e la Scienza." In *Gramsci e l'Italia. Atti del Convegno Internazionale di Urbino. 24 – 25 Gennaio 1992*, edited by Ruggero Giacomini, Domenico Losurdo and Michele Martelli. Napoli: La Città del Sole, 1994.

Boothman, Derek. "Islam in Gramsci's Journalism and the Prison Notebooks: the Shifting Patterns of Hegemony." *Historical Materialism.* 20, no. 4 (2012): 115–40.

Boothman, Derek. *Traducibilità e Processi Traduttivi: un Caso: A. Gramsci Linguista.* S.T.A.R.: Studi sulla Traduzione. Perugia: Guerra Edizioni, 2004.

Bourdieu, Pierre. *Distinction: a Social Critique of the Judgement of Taste.* Translated by Richard Nice. Cambridge, Massachusetts and London: Harvard University Press, 1984.

Bowles, Samuel, and Herbert Gintis. *A Cooperative Species: Human Reciprocity and Its Evolution.* Princeton and Oxford: Princeton University Press, 2011.

Bowles, Samuel, and Herbert Gintis. "Social Preferences, Homo Oeconomicus and *Zoon Politikon.*" In *The Oxford Handbook of Contextual Political Analysis*, edited by Robert E. Goodin and Charles Tilly. Oxford and New York: Oxford University Press, 2006.

Bragg, Billy. *Roots, Radicals and Rockers: How Skiffle Changed the World.* London: Faber & Faber, 2017.

Braudel, Fernand. *The Mediterranean and the Mediterranean World in the Age of Philip II, Vol. 1.* Translated by Sian Reynolds. New York: Harper & Row, 1972.

Braudel, Fernand. *The Mediterranean and the Mediterranean World in the Age of Philip II, Vol.* 2. Translated by Sian Reynolds. New York: Harper & Row, 1973.

Braudel, Fernand. *The Perspective of the World: Civilization & Capitalism, 15th – 18th Century Vol. 3.* Translated by Sian Reynolds. 1st ed. New York: Harper & Row, 1984.

Braudel, Fernand. *The Structure of Everyday Life: Civilization and Capitalism, 15th-18th Century, Vol. 1.* Translated by Sian Reynolds. New York: Harper & Row, 1981.

Braudel, Fernand. *The Wheels of Commerce: Civilization & Capitalism 15th-18th Century, Vol.* 2. Translated by Sian Reynolds. New York: Harper & Row, 1982.

Brennan, Timothy. *Wars of Position: the Cultural Politics of Left and Right.* New York: Columbia University Press, 2006.

Burnett, D. Graham. *Masters of All They Surveyed: Exploration, Geography, and a British El Dorado.* Chicago: University of Chicago Press, 2001.

Burstein, Andrew. *Democracy's Muse: How Thomas Jefferson Became an FDR Liberal, a Reagan Republican, and a Tea Party Fanatic, All the While Being Dead.* Charlottesville, Virginia: University of Virginia Press, 2015.

Burstein, Andrew. *Jefferson's Secrets: Death and Desire at Monticello.* New York: Basic Books, 2006.

Buttigieg, Joseph Anthony. "After Gramsci." *The Journal of the Midwest Modern Language Association.* 24, no. 1 (1991): 87–99.

Buttigieg, Joseph Anthony. "The Contemporary Discourse on Civil Society: a Gramscian Critique." *boundary* 2.32, no. 1 (2005): 33–52.

Buttigieg, Joseph Anthony. "Gramsci on Civil Society." *boundary* 2.22, no. 3 (March 1, 2005 1995): 1–32.

Buttigieg, Joseph Anthony. "The Prison Notebooks: Antonio Gramsci's Work in Progress." *Rethinking Marxism.* 18, no. 1 (2006): 37–42.

Buttigieg, Joseph Anthony. "Reading Gramsci Now." In *Perspectives on Gramsci: Politics, Culture and Social Theory*, edited by Joseph Francese. London and New York: Routledge, 2009.

Canfora, Luciano. *Critica della Retorica Democratica.* Economica Laterza. Bari: Editori Laterza, 2014.

Canfora, Luciano. *Julius Caesar: the Life and Times of the People's Dictator.* Translated by Kevin Windle and Marian Hill. Berkeley and Los Angeles: University of California Press, 2007.

Canfora, Luciano. *Spie, URSS, Antifascismo: Gramsci, 1926–1937.* Roma: Salerno, 2012.

Canfora, Luciano. *The Vanished Library: A Wonder of the Ancient World.* Translated by Martin Ryle. Hellenistic Culture and Society. Berkeley and Los Angeles: University of California Press, 1990.

Cannadine, David. *Ornamentalism: How the British Saw Their Empire.* Oxford Paperbacks. Oxford and New York: Oxford University Press, 2002.

Carelli, Daniela. *Vado a Napoli e Poi ... Muoio!* Ravenna: SensoInverso, 2013.

Carlucci, Alessandro. *Gramsci and Languages: Unification, Diversity, Hegemony.* Chicago: Haymarket Books, 2014.

Carofiglio, Gianrico. *Ad Occhi Chiusi.* Le Indagini dell'Avvocato Guerrieri. Palermo: Sellerio Editore, 2003.

Carofiglio, Gianrico. *A Fine Line.* Translated by H. Curtis. London: Bitter Lemon Press, 2016.

Carofiglio, Gianrico. *Involuntary Witness.* Translated by P. Creagh. London: Bitter Lemon Press, 2005.

Carofiglio, Gianrico. *Le Perfezioni Provvisorie.* Le Indagini dell'Avvocato Guerrieri. Palermo: Sellerio Editore, 2010.

Carofiglio, Gianrico. *Temporary Perfections.* New York: Rizzoli USA, 2011.

Carofiglio, Gianrico. *A Walk in the Dark.* Translated by H. Curtis. Guido Guerrieri. London: Bitter Lemon Press, 2011.

Carrier, James G., ed. *Occidentalism: Images of the West.* Oxford: Clarendon Press, 1995.

Carrier, James G. "Occidentalism: the World Turned Upside-Down." *American ethnologist.* 19, no. 2 (1992): 195–212.

Chase-Dunn, Christopher, and Peter Grimes. "World-Systems Analysis." *Annual review of sociology.* (1995): 387–417.

Cherubini, Lorenzo Jovanotti. "Baciami Ancora. YouTube video dated January 1, 2010." accessed August 9, 2020.

Chester, Norman. *Economics, Politics and Social Studies in Oxford, 1900–85.* London and New York: Palgrave Macmillan, 1986.

Childers, Joseph W. "Of Prison Notebooks and the Restoration of an Archive." *Rethinking Marxism.* 18, no. 1 (2006/01/01 2006): 9–14.

Chomsky, Noam. *Requiem for the American Dream: the 10 Principles of Concentration of Wealth & Power.* New York: Seven Stories Press, 2017.

Chomsky, Noam. *Who Rules the World?* New York: Henry Holt and Company, 2016.

Chomsky, Noam. *World Orders, Old and New.* New York: Columbia University Press, 1996.

Ciconte, E. *Storia Criminale: La Resistibile Ascesa di Mafia, 'Ndrangheta e Camorra dall'Ottocento ai Giorni Nostri.* Universale Rubbettino. Soveria Mannelli: Rubbettino, 2019.

Clark, Christopher, and Wolfram Kaiser. *Culture Wars: Secular-Catholic Conflict in Nineteenth-Century Europe.* Cambridge and New York: Cambridge University Press, 2003.

Clydesdale, Tim. *The First Year Out: Understanding American Teens after High School.* Chicago: University of Chicago Press, 2008.

Coakley, Thomas P. *C3I: Issues of Command and Control.* Washington, DC: National Defense Uniiversity, 1991.

Cohen, Gerald Allan. *History, Labour, and Freedom: themes from Marx.* Oxford: Clarendon Press, 1988.

Cohen, Gerald Allan. *Karl Marx's Theory of History: a Defence.* Princeton Paperbacks. Princeton and Oxford: Princeton University Press, 1978.

Cohen, Gerald Allan. *Karl Marx's Theory of History: a Defence.* Oxford: Clarendon Press, 2000.

Cohen, Gerald Allan. *Karl Marx's Theory of History: a Defence.* Princeton Paperbacks. Princeton and Oxford: Princeton University Press, 2001.

Colley, Linda. *Britons: Forging the Nation, 1707–1837.* Nota Bene. New Haven and London: Yale University Press, 2005.

Colli, Andrea, and Michelangelo Vasta. *Forms of Enterprise in 20th Century Italy: Boundaries, Structures and Strategies.* Cheltenham UK and Northampton USA: Edward Elgar, 2010.

Comentale, Edward P. *Ian Fleming & James Bond: the Cultural Politics of 007.* Bloomington and Indianapolis: Indiana University Press, 2005.

Coser, Lewis A. *Sociology through Literature.* Englewood Cliffs, NJ: Prentice-Hall, 1972.

Cospito, Giuseppe. *Il Ritmo del Pensiero: per una Lettura Diacronica dei "Quaderni del Carcere" di Gramsci.* Napoli: Bibliopolis, 2011.

Crehan, Kate. *Gramsci, Culture and Anthropology.* Berkeley and Los Angeles: University of California Press, 2002.

Crehan, Kate. *Gramsci's Common Sense: Inequality and Its Narratives.* Durham and London: Duke University Press, 2016.

Crehan, Kate. "Gramsci's Concept of Common Sense: a Useful Concept for Anthropologists?." *Journal of Modern Italian Studies.* 16, no. 2 (2011): 273–87.

Crouch, Colin, Patrick Le Galès, Carlo Trigilia, and Helmut Voelzkow. *Local Production Systems in Europe: Rise or Demise?* Oxford and New York: Oxford University Press, 2001.

D'Este, Carlo. *Patton: a Genius for War.* New York: HarperCollins, 1996.

D'Orsi, Angelo. *Egemonie.* Napoli: Libreria Dante & Descartes, 2008.

D'Orsi, Angelo. "Piero Sraffa e la 'Cultura Positiva': la Formazione Torinese." *Il Pensiero Economico Italiano.* 8, no. 1 (2000): 105–144.

Dal Lago, Enrico. *Civil War and Agrarian Unrest.* Cambridge and New York: Cambridge University Press, 2018.

DANA9918. "Julian Cope – China Doll. YouTube video dated March 17, 2012." accessed August 9, 2020.

Davidson, Alastair. *Antonio Gramsci: Towards an Intellectual Biography.* Atlantic Highlands, N.J.: Humanities Press, 1977.

Davidson, Alastair. "The Uses and Abuses of Gramsci." *Thesis Eleven.* no. 95 (2008): 68–94.

Davis, John A., ed. *Gramsci and Italy's Passive Revolution.* New York and London: Routledge, 2014.

Dawson, Andrew. "Political Violence in Consolidated Democracies: the Development and Institutionalization of Partisan Violence in Late Colonial Jamaica (1938–62)." *Social science history.*40, no. 2 (2016): 185–218.

Dawson, Andrew. "The Social Determinants of the Rule of Law: a Comparison of Jamaica and Barbados." *World Development.* 45 (2013): 314–324.

de Tocqueville, Alexis, and Sanford Kessler. *Democracy in America (Abridged).* Translated by Stephen D. Grant. Hackett Classics Series. Indianapolis and Cambridge: Hackett Publisher, 2001.

de Tocqueville, Alexis, John Stone, and Stephen Mennell. *Alexis de Tocqueville on Democracy, Revolution, and Society.* Heritage of Sociology Series. Chicago: University of Chicago Press, 1982.

Delbourgo, James. *Collecting the World: Hans Sloane and the Origins of the British Museum.* Cambridge, Massachusetts and London: Belknap Press of Harvard University Press, 2019.

Delbourgo, James, and Nicholas Dew, eds. *Science and Empire in the Atlantic World,* New Directions in American History. New York and London: Routledge, 2008.

Della Porta, Donatella. *Social Movements, Political Violence, and the State: a Comparative Analysis of Italy and Germany.* Cambridge and New York: Cambridge University Press, 2006.

di Lampedusa, Giuseppe Tomasi. *Il Gattopardo.* I Narratori di Feltrinelli. Milan: Feltrinelli, 1985.

di Lampedusa, Giuseppe Tomasi, and Gioacchino Lanza Tomasi. *The Leopard: Revised and with New Material.* Translated by Archibald Colquhoun and Guido Waldman. London: Vintage Books, 2010.

Diamond, Jared. *Collapse: How Societies Choose to Fail or Succeed: Revised Edition.* London: Penguin, 2011.

Dogan, Mehmet Ali, and Heather J. Sharkey, eds. *American Missionaries and the Middle East: Foundational Encounters*. Salt Lake City: University of Utah Press, 2011.

DuBois, Lindsay. "Gramsci's Common Sense: Inequality and Its Narratives by Kate Crehan." *Anthropologica*. 62, no. 1 (2020): 201–202.

Dutta, Soumitra, and Irene Mia. "The Global Information Technology Report, 2010–2011." World Economic Forum in collaboration with INSEAD, http://reports.weforum.org/wp-content/pdf/gitr-2011/wef-gitr-2010–2011.pdf, accessed April 9, 2021.

Eagleton, Terry. *Criticism and Ideology: a Study in Marxist Literary Theory*. Verso Classics. London and New York: Verso, 1998.

Eagleton, Terry. *Literary Theory: an Introduction*. Oxford: Basil Blackwell, 1983.

Edling, Christofer, and Jens Rydgren, eds. *Sociological Insights of Great Thinkers: Sociology through Literature, Philosophy, and Science*. Santa Barbara, California, Denver, and Oxford: Praeger, 2011.

Elbourne, Elizabeth. *Blood Ground: Colonialism, Missions, and the Contest for Christianity in the Cape Colony and Britain, 1799–1853*. Mcgill-Queen's Studies in the History of Religion. Montreal & Kingston, London, Ithaca: McGill-Queen's University Press, 2002.

Elster, Jon. *Explaining Social Behavior: More Nuts and Bolts for the Social Sciences*. Revised edition ed. Cambridge and New York: Cambridge University Press, 2015.

Elster, Jon. *Nuts and Bolts for the Social Sciences*. Cambridge and New York: Cambridge University Press, 1989.

Esercito Italiano. "Brigata Aeromobile 'Friuli'." Italian Army website, http://www.esercito.difesa.it/organizzazione/capo-di-sme/Comando-Forze-Operative-Nord/Divisione-Vittorio-Veneto/Brigata-Aeromobile-Friuli, accessed August 13, 2020.

Esercito Italiano. "Brigata Meccanizzata 'Pinerolo'." Italian Army website, http://www.esercito.difesa.it/organizzazione/capo-di-sme/Comando-Forze-Operative-Sud/Divisione-Acqui/Brigata-Meccanizzata-Pinerolo, accessed August 13, 2020.

Esercito Italiano. "Forza Nec." Italian Army website, http://www.esercito.difesa.it/organizzazione/capo-di-sme/Comando-Forze-Operative-Sud/Divisione-Acqui/Brigata-Meccanizzata-Pinerolo/Pagine/Forza-NEC.aspx, accessed August 13, 2020.

Esercito Italiano. "Il Comando Forze Operative Nord (Comfop Nord). La Storia." Italian Army website, http://www.esercito.difesa.it/organizzazione/capo-di-sme/Comando-Forze-Operative-Nord/Pagine/la-storia.aspx, accessed April 3, 2021.

Esercito Italiano. "Rapporto Esercito 2011." Italian Army website, http://www.esercito.difesa.it/Rapporto-Esercito/Documents/Rapporto-Esercito-2011.pdf, accessed April 3, 2021.

Esercito Italiano. "Sistema Soldato Sicuro." Italian Army website, http://www.esercito.difesa.it/equipaggiamenti/sistema-soldato-sicuro/Pagine/default.aspx, accessed August 13, 2020.

Evans, Peter B. "Collective Capabilities, Culture, and Amartya Sen's Development as Freedom." *Studies in comparative international development.* 37, no. 2 (2002): 54–60.

Evans, Peter B. *Embedded Autonomy: States and Industrial Transformation.* Princeton and Oxford: Princeton University Press, 1995.

Fabian, Johannes. *Time and the Other: How Anthropology Makes Its Object.* New York: Columbia University Press, 1983.

Femia, Joseph V. *Gramsci's Political Thought: Hegemony, Consciousness, and the Revolutionary Process.* Oxford: Clarendon press, 1987. Revision of thesis (Ph.D.) – Oxford University, 1979.

Femia, Joseph V. *The Machiavellian Legacy: Essays in Italian Political Thought.* New York: St. Martin's Press, 1998.

Femia, Joseph V. *Pareto and Political Theory.* Routledge Studies in Social and Political Thought. London and New York: Routledge, 2006.

Femia, Joseph V. "Western Marxism." In *Twentieth-Century Marxism: a Global Introduction*, edited by Daryl Glaser and David M. Walker. London and New York: Routledge, 2007.

Ferguson, Niall. *Civilization: the West and the Rest.* London: Penguin, 2011.

Ferguson, Niall. "The Empire Slinks Back." New York Times, 2003.

Feyerabend, Paul. *Against Method.* London and New York: Verso, 1993.

Feyerabend, Paul. *Farewell to Reason.* London and New York: Verso, 1987.

Feyerabend, Paul. *Killing Time: the Autobiography of Paul Feyerabend.* Science/ Philosophy. Chicago: University of Chicago Press, 1995.

Filippini, Michele. *Una Politica di Massa: Antonio Gramsci e la Rivoluzione della Società.* Roma: Carocci, 2015.

Filippini, Michele. *Using Gramsci: a New Approach.* Translated by Patrick J. Barr. London: Pluto, 2017.

Finocchiaro, Maurice A. *Beyond Right and Left: Democratic Elitism in Mosca and Gramsci.* New Haven and London: Yale University Press, 1999.

Fiori, Giuseppe, and Tom Nairn. *Antonio Gramsci: Life of a Revolutionary.* Verso Modern Classics. London and New York: Verso, 1990.

Fireman, Bruce, William A. Gamson, Steve Rytina, and Bruce Taylor. "Encounters with Unjust Authority." In *CRSO Working Paper #167*: Center for Research on Social Organization, University of Michigan, 1978.

Fondazione Gramsci. "Edizione Nazionale Scritti Antonio Gramsci." https://www.fondazionegramsci.org/edizione-nazionale-scritti-antonio-gramsci/, accessed September 22, 2020.

Fontana, Benedetto. "Gramsci on Politics and State." *Journal of Classical Sociology.* 2, no. 2 (2002): 157–178.

Fontana, Benedetto. "Hegemony and Power in Gramsci." In *Hegemony: Studies in Consensus and Coercion*, edited by Richard Howson and Kylie Smith. London and New York: Routledge, 2008.

Fontana, Benedetto. "Logos and Kratos: Gramsci and the Ancients on Hegemony." *Journal of the History of Ideas.* 61, no. 2 (2000): 305–326.

Fontana, Benedetto. "State and Society: the Concept of Hegemony in Gramsci." In *Hegemony and Power: Consensus and Coercion in Contemporary Politics*, edited by Mark Haugaard and Howard H. Lentner. Lanham: Lexington Books, 2006.

Francioni, Gianni. "Gramsci Tra Croce e Bukharin: sulla Struttura dei *Quaderni* 10 e 11." *Critica Marxista.* 25, no. 6 (1987): 19–45.

Frosini, Fabio. "Egemonia Dopo Gramsci." *Materialismo Storico.* 2, no. 1 (2017): 5–13.

Frosini, Fabio. "Filosofia della Praxis." In *Le Parole di Gramsci: per un Lessico dei Quaderni del Carcere*, edited by Fabio Frosini and Guido Liguori. Roma: Carocci, 2004.

Frosini, Fabio. *Gramsci e la Filosofia: Saggio sui Quaderni del Carcere.* Roma: Carocci, 2003.

Frosini, Fabio. "Gramsci in Translation: Egemonia e Rivoluzione Passiva nell'Europa di Oggi." *Materialismo Storico.* no. 1 (2019): 43–54.

Frosini, Fabio. "Il 'Ritorno a Marx' nei *Quaderni del Carcere* (1930)." In *Marx e Gramsci: Memoria e Attualità*, edited by Giuseppe Prestipino and Marina Paladini Musitelli. Roma: Manifestolibri, 2001.

Frosini, Fabio. "Il Neoidealismo Italiano e l'Elaborazione della Filosofia della Praxis." In *Gramsci nel Suo Tempo*, edited by Francesco Giasi. Roma: Carocci, 2008.

Frosini, Fabio. "L'Egemonia Dopo Gramsci# 2: Storia, Politica e Teoria (Urbino 2018)." *Materialismo Storico.* VII, no. 2 (2019): 5–8.

Frosini, Fabio. *La Religione dell'Uomo Moderno: Politica e Verità nei Quaderni del Carcere di Antonio Gramsci.* Roma: Carocci, 2010.

Frosini, Fabio. "Note sul Programma di Lavoro sugli 'Intellettuali Italiani' Alla Luce della Nuova Edizione Critica." *Studi Storici.* 52, no. 4 (2011): 905–24.

Frosini, Fabio. "¿ Qué Es la "Crisis de Hegemonía"?: Apuntes Sobre Historia, Revolución Y Visibilidad en Gramsci." *Las Torres de Lucca: revista internacional de filosofía política.* 6, no. 11 (2017): 45–71.

Frosini, Fabio. "Realtà, Scrittura, Metodo: Considerazioni Preliminari a una Nuova Lettura dei "Quaderni del Carcere."" In *Gramsci Tra Filologia e Storiografia*, edited by Giuseppe Cospito. Napoli: Bibliopolis, 2010.

Frosini, Fabio. "Riforma e Rinascimento." In *Le Parole di Gramsci: per un Lessico dei Quaderni del Carcere* edited by Fabio Frosini and Guido Liguori. Roma: Carocci, 2004.

Gambino, Richard. *Vendetta: a True Story of the Worst Lynching in America, the Mass Murder of Italian-Americans in New Orleans in 1891, the Vicious Motivations Behind It, and the Tragic Repercussions That Linger to This Day.* Garden City, New York: Doubleday, 1977.

Gamson, William A., Bruce Fireman, and Steven Rytina. *Encounters with Unjust Authority.* Dorsey Series in Sociology. Belmont, CA: Dorsey Press, 1982.

Gellner, Ernest. *Nationalism.* Master Minds Series. London: Phoenix, 1998.

Gellner, Ernest. *Nations and Nationalism.* Cornell Paperbacks. Ithaca, New York: Cornell University Press, 1983.

Gellner, Ernest, and John Breuilly. *Nations and Nationalism.* Cornell Paperbacks. Ithaca, New York: Cornell University Press, 2008.

George, Jim, and Kim Huynh. *The Culture Wars: Australian and American Politics in the 21st Century.* London and New York: Palgrave Macmillan, 2009.

Germino, Dante. *Antonio Gramsci: Architect of a New Politics.* Political Traditions in Foreign Policy Series. Baton Rouge and London: Lousiana State University Press, 1990.

Ghosh, Peter. "Gramscian Hegemony: an Absolutely Historicist Approach." *History of European Ideas.* 27 (2001): 1–43.

Ghosh, Peter. *Max Weber and the Protestant Ethic: Twin Histories.* paperback ed. Oxford and New York: Oxford University Press, 2017.

Giannetti, Renato, ed. *Nel Mito di Prometeo. L'Innovazione Tecnologica dalla Rivoluzione Industriale ad Oggi. Temi, Inventori e Protagonisti dall'Ottocento al Duemila.* Firenze: Ponte alle Grazie, 1996.

Giannetti, Renato, and Michelangelo Vasta. *Evolution of Italian Enterprises in the 20th Century.* Contributions to Economics. Heidelberg and New York: Physica-Verlag HD, 2009.

Gintis, Herbert. *The Bounds of Reason: Game Theory and the Unification of the Behavioral Sciences – Revised Edition.* Princeton and Oxford: Princeton University Press, 2009.

Gintis, Herbert. *Individuality and Entanglement: the Moral and Material Bases of Social Life.* Princeton and Oxford: Princeton University Press, 2016.

Giugni, Marco, Doug McAdam, and Charles Tilly, eds. *From Contention to Democracy,* G – Reference, Information and Interdisciplinary Subjects Series. Lanham, Boulder, New York, and Oxford: Rowman & Littlefield Publishers, 1998.

Gocek, Fatma Muge. *Rise of the Bourgeoisie, Demise of Empire: Ottoman Westernization and Social Change.* Oxford and New York: Oxford University Press, 1996.

Goffman, Daniel. *The Ottoman Empire and Early Modern Europe.* New Approaches to European History. Cambridge and New York: Cambridge University Press, 2002.

Goldman, Harvey. "From Social Theory to the Sociology of Knowledge and Back: Karl Mannheim and the Sociology of Intellectual Knowledge." *Sociological Theory.* 12, no. 3 (1994): 266–278.

Gomez-Barris, Macarena. *Beyond the Pink Tide: Art and Political Undercurrents in the Americas.* American Studies Now: Critical Histories of the Present. Berkeley and Los Angeles: University of California Press, 2018.

Gould, Roger V. *Insurgent Identities: Class, Community, and Protest in Paris from 1848 to the Commune.* Chicago: University of Chicago Press, 1995.

Gouldner, Alvin Ward. *Against Fragmentation: the Origins of Marxism and the Sociology of Intellectuals.* Oxford and New York: Oxford University Press, 1985.

Gouldner, Alvin Ward. *The Coming Crisis in Western Sociology.* New York: Basic Books, 1970.

Gouldner, Alvin Ward. *The Future of Intellectuals and the Rise of the New Class.* Critical Social Studies. Basingstoke: Macmillan, 1979.

Gramsci, Antonio. *La Questione Meridionale.* Roma: Editori Riuniti, 1974.

Gramsci, Antonio. *Letters from Prison, Vol. I.* Translated by Raymond Rosenthal. Edited by Frank Rosengarten. Vol. 1, New York: Columbia University Press, 1994. 1965.

Gramsci, Antonio. *Letters from Prison, Vol. II.* Translated by Raymond Rosenthal. The Complete and Definitive Edition of Gramsci's Prison Letters. Edited by Frank Rosengarten. II vols. Vol. II, New York: Columbia University Press, 1994.

Gramsci, Antonio. *Prison Notebooks.* Translated by Joseph Buttigieg. 3 vols. Vol. 1, New York: Columbia University Press, 1992.

Gramsci, Antonio. *Prison Notebooks.* Translated by Joseph Buttigieg. 3 vols. Vol. 2, New York: Columbia University Press, 1996.

Gramsci, Antonio. *Prison Notebooks.* Translated by Joseph Buttigieg. 3 vols. Vol. 3, New York: Columbia University Press, 2007.

Gramsci, Antonio. *Quaderni del Carcere.* Edited by Valentino Gerratana. 4 vols. Torino: Einaudi, 2007.

Gramsci, Antonio. *Selections from Cultural Writings Paperback – Oct. 1 1991.* Translated by William Boelhower. Cambridge, Massachusetts and London: Harvard University Press, 1991.

Gran, Peter. *Beyond Eurocentrism: a New View of Modern World History.* Syracuse: Syracuse University Press, 1996.

Green, Marcus. "Gramsci Cannot Speak: Presentations and Interpretations of Gramsci's Concept of the Subaltern." *Rethinking Marxism.* 14, no. 3 (2002): 1–24.

Gualtieri, Sarah. *Arab Routes: Pathways to Syrian California.* Stanford Studies in Comparative Race and Ethnicity. Stanford, California: Stanford University Press, 2019.

Gualtieri, Sarah. *Between Arab and White: Race and Ethnicity in the Early Syrian American Diaspora.* American Crossroads. Berkeley and Los Angeles: University of California Press, 2009.

Habermas, Jurgen. *The Theory of Communicative Action, Vol. 1: Reason and the Rationalization of Society.* Translated by Thomas McCarthy. Boston: Beacon Press, 1984.

Habermas, Jurgen. *The Theory of Communicative Action, Vol. 2: Lifeworld and System, a Critique of Functionalist Reason.* Translated by Thomas McCarthy. Boston: Beacon Press, 1984.

Hall, John Anthony. *Coercion and Consent: Studies on the Modern State.* Cambridge, UK and Malden, Massachusetts: Polity Press, 1994.

Hall, John Anthony. *Ernest Gellner: an Intellectual Biography.* London and New York: Verso, 2014.

Hall, John Anthony. "Gellner and Habermas on Epistemology and Politics or Need We Feel Disenchanted?." *Philosophy of the Social Sciences.* 12, no. 4 (1982): 387–407.

Hall, John Anthony. "Globalization and Nationalism." *Thesis Eleven.* 63, no. 1 (2000): 63–79.

Hall, John Anthony. *The Importance of Being Civil: the Struggle for Political Decency.* Princeton and Oxford: Princeton University Press, 2013.

Hall, John Anthony. *International Orders.* Cambridge, UK and Malden, Massachusetts: Polity Press, 1996.

Hall, John Anthony. "Nationalisms: Classified and Explained." *Daedalus.* 122, no. 3 (1993): 1–28.

Hall, John Anthony. *Powers and Liberties: the Causes and Consequences of the Rise of the West.* Berkeley and Los Angeles: University of California Press, 1986.

Hall, John Anthony. *The Sociology of Literature.* London: Longman, 1979.

Hall, John Anthony, ed. *The State of the Nation: Ernest Gellner and the Theory of Nationalism.* Cambridge and New York: Cambridge University Press, 1998.

Hall, John Anthony, and Charles Lindholm. *Is America Breaking Apart?* Princeton and Oxford: Princeton University Press, 2001.

Hall, John Anthony, and Sinisa Malesevic. *Nationalism and War.* Cambridge and New York: Cambridge University Press, 2013.

Hall, John R. *Apocalypse: from Antiquity to the Empire of Modernity.* Cambridge, UK and Malden, Massachusetts: Polity, 2013.

Hallaq, Wael B. *Authority, Continuity and Change in Islamic Law.* Cambridge and New York: Cambridge University Press, 2001.

Hallaq, Wael B. *A History of Islamic Legal Theories: an Introduction to Sunni Usul Al-Fiqh.* Cambridge and New York: Cambridge University Press, 1997.

Hallaq, Wael B. *The Impossible State: Islam, Politics, and Modernity's Moral Predicament.* New York: Columbia University Press, 2012.

Hallaq, Wael B. *Restating Orientalism: a Critique of Modern Knowledge.* New York: Columbia University Press, 2018.

Hanna, Faith M. *An American Mission: the Role of the American University of Beirut.* Boston: Alphabet Press, 1979.

Hanson, Victor David. *The Father of Us All: War and History, Ancient and Modern.* The Group on Military History and Contemporary Conflict, the Hoover Institution, Stanford University. London, Berlin, New York: Bloomsbury, 2010.

Hanson, Victor David. *Why the West Has Won: Carnage and Culture from Salamis to Vietnam.* London: Faber & Faber, 2001.

Harris, J. Paul. *Douglas Haig and the First World War.* Cambridge Military Histories. Cambridge and New York: Cambridge University Press, 2008.

Hartman, Michelle, and Alessandro Olsaretti. "'The First Boat and the First Oar': Inventions of Lebanon in the Writings of Michel Chiha.." *Radical History Review.* no. 86 (2003): 37–65.

Harvey, David. *The New Imperialism.* Oxford and New York: Oxford University Press, 2003.

Hedstrom, Peter, and Peter Bearman. *Social Mechanisms: an Analytical Approach to Social Theory.* Cambridge and New York: Cambridge University Press, 1998.

Hedström, Peter, and Peter Bearman. *The Oxford Handbook of Analytical Sociology.* Oxford Handbooks. Oxford and New York: Oxford University Press, 2011.

Hegtvedt, Karen A. "Teaching Sociology of Literature through Literature." *Teaching sociology.* (1991): 1–12.

Henrich, Joseph, Robert Boyd, Samuel Bowles, Colin Camerer, Ernst Fehr, Herbert Gintis, and Richard McElreath. "In Search of Homo Economicus: Behavioral Experiments in 15 Small-Scale Societies." *The American Economic Review.* 91, no. 2 (2001): 73–78.

Hibbert, Christopher. *Garibaldi and His Enemies: the Clash of Arms and Personalities in the Making of Italy.* London: Longman, 1965.

Hitchens, Christopher. *Thomas Jefferson: Author of America.* Eminent Lives. New York, London, Toronto: Harper Perennial, 2009.

Hobsbawm, Eric J., and Terence Ranger, eds. *The Invention of Tradition,* A Canto Book. Cambridge and New York: Cambridge University Press, 1992.

Holland, John H. *Signals and Boundaries: Building Blocks for Complex Adaptive Systems.* Cambridge, Massachusetts: MIT Press, 2012.

Holley, Darrell, and Winston Churchill. *Churchill's Literary Allusions: an Index to the Education of a Soldier, Statesman, and Litterateur.* Jefferson, North Carolina: McFarland, 1987.

Homans, Peter, and James S. Hans. *Symbolic Loss: the Ambiguity of Mourning and Memory at Century's End.* Studies in Religion and Culture. Charlottesville, Virginia: University Press of Virginia, 2000.

Howson, Richard, and Kylie Smith. *Hegemony: Studies in Consensus and Coercion.* Routledge Studies in Social and Political Thought. New York and London: Routledge, 2008.

Hughes, H. Stuart, and Stanley Hoffman. *Consciousness and Society.* London and New York: Routledge, 2017.

Hunter, James Davison. *Culture Wars: the Struggle to Control the Family, Art, Education, Law, and Politics in America.* New York: Basic Books, 1992.

Huntington, Samuel P. *The Clash of Civilizations and the Remaking of World Order.* London: Penguin, 1997.

Hymel, Kevin M., ed. *WWII History Presents: Patton's Battles.* Collector's Edition: WarfareHistoryNetwrok.com, 2020.

Inglehart, Ronald. *Culture Shift in Advanced Industrial Society.* Princeton and Oxford: Princeton University Press, 1990.

Inglehart, Ronald, and Miguel Basanez. *Human Values and Beliefs: a Cross-Cultural Sourcebook.* Ann Arbor: University of Michigan Press, 1998.

Inglehart, Ronald, Pippa Norris, and M. G. Norris. *Rising Tide: Gender Equality and Cultural Change around the World.* Cambridge and New York: Cambridge University Press, 2003.

International Student Services (ISS) at McGill. "About International Student Services (ISS)." Office of International Student Services, https://www.mcgill.ca/internationalstudents/issoffice, accessed August 12, 2020.

International Student Services (ISS) at McGill. "International Student Body: Mcgill's International Student Body." Office of International Student Services, https://www.mcgill.ca/internationalstudents/issoffice/international-mcgill, accessed August 12, 2020.

Ives, Peter. *Gramsci's Politics of Language: Engaging the Bakhtin Circle and the Frankfurt School.* Cultural Spaces. Toronto: University of Toronto Press, 2004.

Ives, Peter. "The Mammoth Task of Translating Gramsci." *Rethinking Marxism.* 18, no. 1 (2006/01/01 2006): 15–22.

Jacob, Wilson Chacko. *Working out Egypt: Effendi Masculinity and Subject Formation in Colonial Modernity, 1870–1940.* Durham and London: Duke University Press, 2011.

Jacobitti, Edmund E. "From Vico's Common Sense to Gramsci's Hegemony." In *Vico and Marx: Affinities and Contrasts*, edited by Giorgio Tagliacozzo. Basingstoke: Macmillan, 1983.

Jacobitti, Edmund E. "Hegemony before Gramsci: the Case of Benedetto Croce." *Journal of Modern History.* 52 (March 1980 1980): 66–84.

Jacobitti, Edmund E. "The Religious Vision of Antonio Gramsci or the Italian Origins of Hegemony as Found in Croce, Cuoco, Machiavelli, and the Church." *Italian Quarterly.* no. 97–98 (1984): 101–31.

Jacobitti, Edmund E. *Revolutionary Humanism and Historicism in Modern Italy.* New Haven and London: Yale University Press, 1981.

Jones, Gareth Stedman. *Karl Marx: Greatness and Illusion.* London: Penguin, 2016.

Judson, Jen. "Prototypes for Marine Corps' New Amphibious Combat Vehicle Coming Together." Marine Corps Times, https://www.marinecorpstimes.com/news/your-marine-corps/2016/06/20/prototypes-for-marine-corps-new-amphibious-combat-vehicle-coming-together/, accessed June 20, 2016.

Karpat, Kemal H. *An Inquiry into the Social Foundations of Nationalism in the Ottoman State: from Social Estates to Classes, from Millets to Nations.* Center of International Studies, Princeton University, 1973.

Karpat, Kemal H. *The Politicization of Islam: Reconstructing Identity, State, Faith, and Community in the Late Ottoman State.* Studies in Middle Eastern History. Oxford and New York: Oxford University Press, 2001.

Karpat, Kemal H. "The Transformation of the Ottoman State, 1789–1908." *International Journal of Middle East Studies.*3, no. 3 (1972): 243–281.

Katzenstein, Mary Fainsod. *Faithful and Fearless: Moving Feminist Protest inside the Church and Military.* Princeton and Oxford: Princeton University Press, 1998.

Katzenstein, Mary Fainsod. "Feminism within American Institutions: Unobtrusive Mobilization in the 1980s." *Signs: Journal of Women in Culture and Society.*16, no. 1 (1990): 27–54.

Katzenstein, Mary Fainsod. "Protest Moves inside Institutions." In *Women, Gender, and Politics: A Reader*, edited by Mona Lena Krook and Sara Childs, 47–53. Oxford and New York: Oxford University Press, 2010.

Katzenstein, Mary Fainsod, and Carol McClurg Mueller, eds. *The Women's Movements of the United States and Western Europe: Consciousness, Political Opportunity, and Public Policy*, Women in the Political Economy. Philadelphia: Temple University Press, 1992.

Katzenstein, Peter J., ed. *The Culture of National Security: Norms and Identity in World Politics.* Edited by The Committee on International Peace and Security of the Social Science Research Council. New York: Columbia University Press, 1996.

Kemeny, Szabolcs. "Subcontracting in the Publishing Industry." *Logos.*7, no. 4 (1996): 289–292.

King, Larry P., and Ivan Szelényi. *Theories of the New Class: Intellectuals and Power.* Contradictions. Minneapolis, Minnesota: University of Minnesota Press, 2004.

Klooster, Wim. *Revolutions in the Atlantic World: a Comparative History.* New York: New York University Press, 2009.

Kratke, Michael R., and Peter D. Thomas as translator. "Antonio Gramsci's Contribution to a Critical Economics." *Historical Materialism.*19, no. 3 (2011): 63–105.

Kuhn, Thomas S., and Ian Hacking. *The Structure of Scientific Revolutions.* Fourth edition. ed. Chicago: The University of Chicago Press, 2012.

Laborde, Cecile. *Liberalism's Religion.* Cambridge, Massachusetts and London: Harvard University Press, 2017.

Laclau, Ernesto, and Chantal Mouffe. *Hegemony and Socialist Strategy: Towards a Radical Democratic Politics.* London and New York: Verso, 2001.

Lady Gaga. "Lady Gaga – 911 (Short Film). YouTube video dated September 18, 2020." VEVO, accessed January 20, 2020.

Lady Gaga. "Lady Gaga – Alejandro. YouTube video dated June 8, 2010." VEVO, accessed August 9, 2020.

Lakoff, George. *Don't Think of an Elephant!: Know Your Values and Frame the Debate.* Scribe Short Books. Melbourne and Carlton North, Australia: Scribe, 2005.

Landsvirkjun. "International Data Connectivity in Iceland: A White Paper." Landsvirkjun, the National Power Company of Iceland, https://static1.squarespace.com/static/5e787305a6309f320f7f3e1c/t/5e81cf27e8e5be5d58f4b114/1585565483336/international-data-connectivity-in-iceland-a-white-paper.pdf, accessed April 9, 2016.

Lange, Matthew. *Comparative-Historical Methods.* London, Thousand Oaks, New Delhi, Singapore: Sage, 2012.

Lange, Matthew. *Killing Others: a Natural History of Ethnic Violence.* Ithaca, New York: Cornell University Press, 2017.

Lange, Matthew. *Lineages of Despotism and Development: British Colonialism and State Power.* Chicago: University of Chicago Press, 2009.

Lebow, Richard Ned, and Robert Kelly. "Thucydides and Hegemony: Athens and the United States." *Review of International Studies.* 27, no. 4 (2001): 593–609.

Lehmann, Karl. *Thomas Jefferson, American Humanist.* Charlottesville, Virginia: University Press of Virginia, 1985.

Levi-Strauss, Claude. *The Savage Mind.* Translated by D. Weightman and J. Weightman. Nature of Human Society. Chicago: University of Chicago Press, 1966.

Levine, Andrew. *A Future for Marxism?: Althusser, the Analytical Turn and the Revival of Socialist Theory.* London: Pluto, 2003.

Lewis, Bernard. "License to Kill-Usama Bin Ladin's Declaration of Jihad." *Foreign Affairs.* 77 (1998): 14.

Lewis, Bernard. *What Went Wrong?: Western Impact and Middle Eastern Response.* Oxford and New York: Oxford University Press, 2002.

Liguori, Guido. *Gramsci Conteso: Storia di un Dibattito, 1922–1996.* Roma: Editori riuniti, 1996.

Liguori, Guido. *Sentieri Gramsciani.* Roma: Carocci, 2006.

Liguori, Guido, and Pasquale Voza, eds. *Dizionario Gramsciano: 1926–1937.* Roma: Carocci, 2009.

Lindholm, Charles, and Jose Pedro Zuquete. *The Struggle for the World: Liberation Movements for the 21st Century.* Stanford, California: Stanford University Press, 2010.

Lipset, Seymour Martin. *Political Man: the Social Bases of Politics.* Baltimore: Johns Hopkins University Press, 1981.

Llorente, Renzo. *The Political Theory of Che Guevara.* Lanham, Boulder, New York, and Oxford: Rowman & Littlefield International, 2018.

Lo Piparo, Franco. *I Due Carceri di Gramsci: la Prigione Fascista e il Labirinto Comunista.* Saggine. Roma: Donzelli, 2012.

Lodge, David. *A Man of Parts.* New York: Vintage, 2011.

Logan, John R., and Harvey Luskin Molotch. *Urban Fortunes: the Political Economy of Place.* Berkeley and Los Angeles: University of California Press, 2007.

Lombroso, Cesare. *Criminal Man.* Translated by Nciole Hahn Rafter and Mary Gibson. Durham and London: Duke University Press, 2006.

Lombroso, Cesare. "Genius and Insanity." In *The Man of Genius.* London: Charles Scribner's Sons, 1895.

Lombroso, Cesare, and Guglielmo Ferrero. *Criminal Woman, the Prostitute, and the Normal Woman.* Translated by Nciole Hahn Rafter and Mary Gibson. Durham and London: Duke University Press, 2004.

Lonestarsound. "The Day the Music Died – Don Mclean on Buddy Holly's Crash. YouTube video dated January 26, 2007." accessed August 22, 2020.

Lukes, Steven. *Power: a Radical View.* Studies in Sociology. London and New York: Palgrave Macmillan, 2004.

Lussu, Emilio. *Un Anno sull'Altipiano.* Torino: Einaudi, 2014.

Macciocchi, Maria Antonietta. *Per Gramsci.* Bologna: Il Mulino, 1974.

MacDonald, Dennis W., Steve E. Barkan, Kimberly J. Cook, Sally T. Hillsman, Heath C. Hoffmann, Jodie Michelle, Michael A. Lewis, Marc Riedel, Prabha Unnithan, Margaret Weigers Vitullo, and Saundra D. Westervelt. " Report of the ASA Task Force on Sociology and Criminology Programs." American Sociological Association, 2010.

Macintyre, Ben. *For Your Eyes Only: Ian Fleming and James Bond.* London, Berlin, New York: Bloomsbury, 2009.

Makdisi, Ussama. *Artillery of Heaven: American Missionaries and the Failed Conversion of the Middle East.* The United States in the World. Ithaca and London: Cornell University Press, 2011.

Mamdouh, Alia. *The Loved Ones: a Modern Arabic Novel.* Translated by Marilyn Booth. Women Writing the Middle East. Cairo: The American University in Cairo Press, 2006.

Mani, Lata, and Ruth Frankenberg. "The Challenge of Orientalism." *Economy and Society.* 14, no. 2 (1985): 174–192.

Mann, Michael. *Consciousness and Action among the Western Working Class.* Studies in Sociology. Basingstoke: Macmillan, 1973.

Mann, Michael. *The Sources of Social Power, Vol. 1: a History of Power from the Beginning to AD 1760.* Cambridge and New York: Cambridge University Press, 2012.

Mann, Michael. *The Sources of Social Power, Vol. 2: the Rise of Classes and Nation-States, 1760–1914.* The Sources of Social Power. Cambridge and New York: Cambridge University Press, 2012.

Mann, Michael. *The Sources of Social Power, Vol. 3: Global Empires and Revolution, 1890–1945.* Cambridge and New York: Cambridge University Press, 2012.

Mann, Michael. *The Sources of Social Power, Vol. 4: Globalizations, 1945–2011.* Cambridge and New York: Cambridge University Press, 2012.

Martin, James. *Antonio Gramsci: Contemporary Applications.* London and New York: Routledge, 2002.

Martínez, Maria Elena. *Genealogical Fictions: Limpieza de Sangre, Religion, and Gender in Colonial Mexico.* Cultural Memory in the Present Series. Stanford, California: Stanford University Press, 2008.

Mattone, Antonello. "Messianesimo e Sovversivismo. Le Note Gramsciane su Davide Lazzaretti." *Studi Storici.* 22, no. 2 (1981): 371–385.

McCullough, David. *John Adams.* New York: Simon & Schuster, 2001.

McLellan, David. *Karl Marx: a Biography.* 4th ed. London and New York: Palgrave Macmillan, 2006.

McMillian, John. *Beatles vs. Stones.* New York: Simon & Schuster, 2013.

Merton, Robert K. *Social Theory and Social Structure.* American Studies Collection. New York: Free Press, 1968.

Merton, Robert K., and Piotr Sztompka. *On Social Structure and Science.* Heritage of Sociology Series. Chicago: University of Chicago Press, 1996.

Meryon, Charles Lewis, and Hester Stanhope. *The Additional Memoirs of Lady Hester Stanhope: an Unpublished Historical Account for the Years 1819–1820.* Sussex Academic Press, 2017.

Meryon, Charles Lewis, and Hester Stanhope. *Memoirs of the Lady Hester Stanhope: As Related by Herself in Conversations with Her Physician.* Cambridge Library Collection – Travel, Middle East and Asia Minor. Cambridge and New York: Cambridge University Press, 2012.

Meyer, David S., and Sidney Tarrow, eds. *The Social Movement Society: Contentious Politics for a New Century*, People, Passions, and Power. Lanham, Boulder, New York, and Oxford: Rowman & Littlefield Publishers, 1997.

Michels, Robert. *Political Parties: a Sociological Study of the Oligarchical Tendencies of Modern Democracies.* Political Science. New York: Free Press, 1968.

Mills, C. Wright. *The Power Elite.* Galaxy Book. Oxford and New York: Oxford University Press, USA, 2000.

Mitchell, Timothy. *Rule of Experts: Egypt, Techno-Politics, Modernity.* Berkeley and Los Angeles: University of California Press, 2002.

Molotch, Harvey Luskin, William Freudenburg, and Krista E. Paulsen. "History Repeats Itself, but How? City Character, Urban Tradition, and the Accomplishment of Place." *American Sociological Review.* (2000): 791–823.

Moore, Barrington Jr. *Social Origins of Dictatorship and Democracy: Lord and Peasant in the Making of the Modern World.* Boston: Beacon Press, 2015.

Mora, George. "One Hundred Years from Lombroso's First Essay Genius and Insanity." *American Journal of Psychiatry.* 121, no. 6 (1964): 562–571.

Morini, Francesco. "Adapting Dynamically to Change in Diplomacy: a Comparative Look at Special Envoys in the International Arena." *The Hague Journal of Diplomacy.* 13, no. 4 (2018): 545–571.

Morris, Rosalind. *Can the Subaltern Speak?: Reflections on the History of an Idea.* New York: Columbia University Press, 2010.

Muller, Jan-Werner. *A Dangerous Mind: Carl Schmitt in Post-War European Thought.* New Haven and London: Yale University Press, 2003.

Muller, Jan-Werner. *What Is Populism?* Philadelphia: University of Pennsylvania Press, 2016.

Musto, Marcello. *The Last Years of Karl Marx: an Intellectual Biography.* Translated by Patrick Camiller. Stanford, California: Stanford University Press, 2020.

Musto, Marcello. *The Marx Revival: Key Concepts and New Critical Interpretations.* Cambridge and New York: Cambridge University Press, 2020.

Natoli, Aldo. "Gramsci in Carcere, il Partito, il Comintern." *Belfagor.*43, no. 2 (1988): 167–188.

Natoli, Claudio. "Gramsci in Carcere: le Campagne per la Liberazione, il Partito, L'internazionale (1932–1933)." *Studi storici.*36, no. 2 (1995): 295–352.

Nazaruk, Maja Alexandra. "Coevalness and the Self-Immolating Woman: Anthropology's Objects." *Global Journal of Anthropology Research.* 4 (2017): 1–7.

Nena. "Nena | Licht [Official Music Video]. YouTube video dated May 21, 2020." Nena store, accessed August 9, 2020.

New York University. "Nyu Abu Dhabi." https://www.nyu.edu/abu-dhabi.html, accessed April 9, 2021.

New York University. "Nyu Shaghai." https://www.nyu.edu/shanghai.html, accessed April 9, 2021.

New York University. "Studying Abroad." https://www.nyu.edu/academics/studying-abroad.html, accessed April 9, 2021.

Nicaso, Antonio, and Marcel Danesi. *Made Men: Mafia Culture and the Power of Symbols, Rituals, and Myth.* Lanham, Boulder, New York, and Oxford: Rowman & Littlefield Publishers, 2013.

Ning, Wang. "Orientalism Versus Occidentalism?." *New Literary History.*28, no. 1 (1997): 57–67.

Nolan, James L., ed. *The American Culture Wars: Current Contests and Future Prospects.* Charlottesville, Virginia: University Press of Virginia, 1996.

Nussbaum, Martha C. *Women and Human Development: the Capabilities Approach.* The Seeley Lectures. Cambridge and New York: Cambridge University Press, 2000.

Olsaretti, Alessandro. "Beyond Class: the Many Facets of Gramsci's Theory of Intellectuals." *Journal of Classical Sociology.* 14, no. 4 (2014): 363–81.

Olsaretti, Alessandro. "Croce, Philosophy and Intellectuals: Three Aspects of Gramsci's Theory of Hegemony." *Critical Sociology.* 42, no. 3 (2016): 337–355.

Olsaretti, Alessandro. "From the Return to Labriola to the Anti-Croce: Philosophy, Praxis and Human Nature in Gramsci's *Prison Notebooks.*" *Historical Materialism.* 24, no. 4 (2016): 193–220.

Olsaretti, Alessandro. "Political Dynamics in the Rise of Fakhr Al-Din, 1590–1633: Crusade, Trade, and State Formation Along the Levantine Coast." *The International History Review.* 30, no. 4 (2008): 709–740.

Olsaretti, Alessandro. "Urban Culture, Curiosity and the Aesthetics of Distance: the Representation of Picturesque Carnivals in Early Victorian Travelogues to the Levant." *Social History.* 32, no. 3 (2007): 247–270.

Olson, Mancur. *The Logic of Collective Action.* Harvard Economic Studies. Cambridge, Massachusetts and London: Harvard University Press, 2009.

Orr, George E. *Combat Operations C3I: Fundamentals and Interactions.* Montgomery, Alabama: Airpower Research Institute, Air University Press, 1983.

Paggi, Leonardo. *Le Strategie del Potere in Gramsci.* Roma: Editori Riuniti, 1984.

Palla, Marco. "Il Gramsci Abbandonato." *Belfagor.* 41, no. 5 (1986): 581–586.

Parsons, Laila. *The Commander: Fawzi Al-Qawuqji and the Fight for Arab Independence 1914–1948.* London: Saqi, 2017.

Parsons, Laila. *The Druze between Palestine and Israel 1947–49.* St Anthony's Series. London and New York: Palgrave Macmillan, 2000.

Parsons, Timothy H. *The Rule of Empires: Those Who Built Them, Those Who Endured Them, and Why They Always Fall.* Oxford and New York: Oxford University Press, 2010.

Parsons, Timothy H. *The Second British Empire: in the Crucible of the Twentieth Century.* Critical Issues in World and International History. Lanham, Boulder, New York, and Oxford: Rowman & Littlefield Publishers, 2014.

Patriarca, Silavana, and Lucy Riall. *The Risorgimento Revisited: Nationalism and Culture in Nineteenth-Century Italy.* London and New York: Palgrave Macmillan, 2011.

Pearson, John. *The Life of Ian Fleming.* London, Berlin, New York: Bloomsbury, 2011.

Pedreira, Jorge M. "From Growth to Collapse: Portugal, Brazil, and the Breakdown of the Old Colonial System (1760–1830)." *Hispanic American Historical Review.* 80, no. 4 (2000): 839–864.

Peluso, Pasquale. "The Roots of the Organized Criminal Underworld in Campania." *Sociology and Anthropology.* 1, no. 2 (2013): 118–134.

Perone, James E. *Mods, Rockers, and the Music of the British Invasion.* Westport, Connecticut and London: Praeger, 2009.

Perone, James E. *Music of the Counterculture Era.* American History through Music. Greenwood Press, 2004.

Peterson, Merrill D. *Thomas Jefferson and the New Nation: a Biography.* A Galaxy Book. Oxford and New York: Oxford University Press, USA, 1975.

Piketty, Thomas. *Capital in the Twenty-First Century.* Translated by Arthur Goldhammer. Cambridge, Massachusetts and London: Harvard University Press, 2017.

Poggi, Gianfranco. *Forms of Power.* Cambridge, UK and Malden, Massachusetts: Polity Press, 2001.

Poggi, Gianfranco. *The State: Its Nature, Development and Prospects.* Cambridge, UK and Malden, Massachusetts: Polity Press, 1990.

Pons, Silvio. "L' 'Affare Gramsci-Togliatti' a Mosca (1938–1941)." *Studi storici.*45, no. 1 (2004): 83–117.

Potier, Jean-Pierre. *Piero Sraffa: Unorthodox Economist (1898–1983).* London and New York: Routledge, 1991.

Preston, John, Gonzalo Munévar, and David Lamb, eds. *The Worst Enemy of Science? Essays in Memory of Paul Feyerabend.* Oxford and New York: Oxford University Press, 2000.

Przeworski, Adam, Michael E. Alvarez, Jose Antonio Cheibub, and Fernando Limongi. *Democracy and Development: Political Institutions and Well-Being in the World, 1950–1990.* Cambridge Studies in the Theory of Democracy. Cambridge and New York: Cambridge University Press, 2000.

Purinton, Ted, and Jennifer Skaggs. *American Universities Abroad: the Leadership of Independent Transnational Higher Education Institutions.* [in English] Cairo and New York: American University in Cairo Press, 2017.

Putnam, Robert D. *Bowling Alone: the Collapse and Revival of American Community.* A Touchstone Book. New York: Simon & Schuster, 2000.

Putnam, Robert D., Robert Leonardi, and Raffaella Y. Nanetti. *Making Democracy Work: Civic Traditions in Modern Italy.* Princeton and Oxford: Princeton University Press, 1994.

Riach, Graham. *An Analysis of Gayatri Chakravorty Spivak's Can the Subaltern Speak?* The Macat Library. London and New York: Routledge, 2017.

Riall, Lucy. *Garibaldi: Invention of a Hero.* New Haven and London: Yale University Press, 2008.

Riall, Lucy. "Hero, Saint or Revolutionary? Nineteenth-Century Politics and the Cult of Garibaldi." *Modern Italy.* 3, no. 2 (1998): 191–204.

Riall, Lucy. *The Italian Risorgimento: State, Society and National Unification.* Historical Connections. New York and London: Routledge, 2002.

Riall, Lucy. *Sicily and the Unification of Italy: Liberal Policy and Local Power, 1859–1866.* Oxford: Clarendon Press, 1998.

Riall, Lucy. "Travel, Migration, Exile: Garibaldi's Global Fame." *Modern Italy.* 19, no. 1 (2014): 41–52.

Richardson, Terry. *Portraits and Fashion, Vol. 1: Portraits.* New York: Rizzoli USA, 2015.

Richardson, Terry. *Portraits and Fashion, Vol. 2: Fashion.* New York: Rizzoli USA, 2015.

Roberts, Andrew. *Churchill: Walking with Destiny.* London: Penguin, 2018.

Roemer, John E. *Free to Lose: an Introduction to Marxist Economic Philosophy.* Cambridge, Massachusetts and London: Harvard University Press, 2009.

Roncaglia, Alessandro. *The Age of Fragmentation: a History of Contemporary Economic Thought.* Translated by Alessandro Roncaglia. Cambridge and New York: Cambridge University Press, 2019.

Roncaglia, Alessandro. *The Wealth of Ideas: a History of Economic Thought.* Translated by R. N. Lebow. Cambridge and New York: Cambridge University Press, 2005.

Ross, Ronald J. *The Failure of Bismarck's Kulturkampf: Catholicism and State Power in Imperial Germany, 1871–1887.* Washington, DC: Catholic University of America Press, 2000.

Rossi, Angelo. *Gramsci da Eretico a Icona: Storia di 'un Cazzotto nell'Occhio.'* Prima Pagina. Napoli: Guida, 2010.

Rossi, Angelo, and Giuseppe Vacca. *Gramsci tra Mussolini e Stalin.* Le Terre. Roma: Fazi, 2007.

Rossi, Vasco. "Come nelle Favole. VEVO video on YouTube dated March 16, 2017." Vevo, accessed August 9, 2020.

Rossi, Vasco. "Un Mondo Migliore. VEVO video on YouTube dated October 13, 2016." Vevo, accessed.

Roth, Philip. *Portnoy's Complaint.* Toronto, New York, London: Bantam Books, 1970.

Rousseau, Stephanie, and Anahi Morales Hudon. *Indigenous Women's Movements in Latin America: Gender and Ethnicity in Peru, Mexico, and Bolivia.* Crossing Boundaries of Gender and Politics in the Global South. London and New York: Palgrave Macmillan, 2016.

Roy, Arundathi. *The God of Small Things: a Novel.* Toronto: Vintage Canada, 1997.

Ruccio, David F. "Unfinished Business: Gramsci's Prison Notebooks." *Rethinking Marxism.*18, no. 1 (2006/01/01 2006): 1–7.

Rueschemeyer, Dietrich. *Power and the Division of Labour.* Social and Political Theory from Polity Press. Cambridge, UK and Malden, Massachusetts: Polity, 1986.

Rueschemeyer, Dietrich. *Usable Theory: Analytic Tools for Social and Political Research.* Princeton and Oxford: Princeton University Press, 2009.

Rueschemeyer, Dietrich, Evelyn Huber Stephens, and John D. Stephens. *Capitalist Development and Democracy.* Chicago: University of Chicago Press, 1992.

Rytina, Steven. "Is Occupational Mobility Declining in the US?." *Social Forces.* 78, no. 4 (2000): 1227–1276.

Rytina, Steven. *Network Persistence and the Axis of Hierarchy: How Orderly Stratification Is Implicit in Sticky Struggles.* London and New York: Anthem Press, 2020.

Rytina, Steven. "Scaling the Intergenerational Continuity of Occupation: Is Occupational Inheritance Ascriptive after All?." *American Journal of Sociology.* 97, no. 6 (1992): 1658–1688.

Sabetti, Filippo. *The Search for Good Government: Understanding the Paradox of Italian Democracy.* Montreal & Kingston, London, Ithaca: McGill-Queen's University Press, 2000.

Sabetti, Filippo. *Village Politics and the Mafia in Sicily.* Montreal & Kingston, London, Ithaca: McGill-Queen's University Press, 2002.

Safire, William. "Islamofascism." *New York Times*, October 1st 2006.

Said, Edward W. *Orientalism.* New York: Pantheon Books, 1978.

Said, Edward W. *Orientalism.* Vintage Books, 1994.

Salamini, Leonardo. "Gramsci and Marxist Sociology of Knowledge: an Analysis of Hegemony-Ideology-Knowledge." *The Sociological Quarterly.* 15, no. 3 (1974): 359–380.

Sangiovanni, Andrea. *Humanity without Dignity.* Cambridge, Massachusetts and London: Harvard University Press, 2017.

Santucci, Antonio. *Antonio Gramsci, 1981–1937.* Tutto e Subito. Palermo: Sellerio, 2005.

Saxenian, AnnaLee. *The New Argonauts: Regional Advantage in a Global Economy.* Cambridge, Massachusetts and London: Harvard University Press, 2007.

Saxenian, AnnaLee. *Regional Advantage: Culture and Competition in Silicon Valley and Route 128, with a New Preface by the Author.* Cambridge, Massachusetts and London: Harvard University Press, 1996.

Sedra, Paul. *From Mission to Modernity: Evangelicals, Reformers and Education in Nineteenth Century Egypt.* London and New York: I. B. Tauris, 2011.

Sen, Amartya. *Development as Freedom.* Oxford and New York: Oxford University Press, 2001.

Seymour, Mark. "Introduction: Perspectives on Garibaldi and Italian Unity." *Modern Italy.* 15, no. 4 (2010): 395–399.

Shor, Ira. *Culture Wars: School and Society in the Conservative Restoration.* Chicago: University of Chicago Press, 1992.

Sica, Alan. *Max Weber and the New Century.* New Brunswick USA, London: Transaction Publishers, 2004.

Sica, Alan, and Stephen Turner, eds. *The Disobedient Generation: Social Theorists in the Sixties.* Chicago: University of Chicago Press, 2005.

Skar, Rolf. "Why and How Svalbard Got the Fibre." *Telektronikk.*3 (2004).

Sklair, Leslie. *The Transnational Capitalist Class.* Oxford: Blackwell, 2000.

Skocpol, Theda. *States and Social Revolutions: a Comparative Analysis of France, Russia, and China.* Canto Classics. Cambridge and New York: Cambridge University Press, 2015.

Skyttner, Lars. *General Systems Theory: an Introduction.* Information Systems Series. Basingstoke: Macmillan, 1996.

Skyttner, Lars. *General Systems Theory: Ideas & Applications.* Singapore and London: World Scientific, 2001.

Smith, Denis Mack. *Garibaldi: A Great Life in Brief.* Great Lives Observed. Englewood Cliffs, New Jersey: Prentice-Hall, 1969.

Sopranzetti, Claudio. "Gramsci's Common Sense: Inequality and Its Narratives by Kate Crehan." *Anthropological Quarterly.*90, no. 4 (2017): 1277–1282.

Spanos, William V. "Cuvier's Little Bone: Joseph Buttigieg's English Edition of Antonio Gramsci's Prison Notebooks." *Rethinking Marxism.*18, no. 1 (2006/01/01 2006): 23–36.

Spivak, Gayatri Chakravorty. "Can the Subaltern Speak?." In *Marxism and the Interpretation of Culture*, edited by Cary Nelson and Lawrence Grossberg, 271–313. Basingstoke: Macmillan, 1988.

Spruyt, Hendrik. *The Sovereign State and Its Competitors: an Analysis of Systems Change.* Princeton Studies in International History and Politics. Princeton and Oxford: Princeton University Press, 1994.

St Clair, William, and Roderick Beaton. *That Greece Might Still Be Free: the Philhellenes in the War of Independence.* Cambridge: Open Book Publishers, 2008.

Stark, David, and Laszlo Bruszt. *Postsocialist Pathways: Transforming Politics and Property in East Central Europe.* Cambridge Studies in Comparative Politics. Cambridge and New York: Cambridge University Press, 1998.

Stark, David, Szabolcs Kemeny, and Ronald Breiger. "Postsocialist Portfolios: Network Strategies in the Shadow of the State." http://www.u.arizona.edu/~breiger/Portfol ios.pdf, accessed February 2, 2021.

Stark, David, Szabolcs Kemeny, and Ronald Breiger. "Postsocialist Portfolios: Network Strategies in the Shadow of the State, Part I, in Hungarian." *Közgazdasági Szemle (Hungarian journal).*47 (2000): 393–405.

Stark, David, Szabolcs Kemeny, and Ronald Breiger. "Postsocialist Portfolios: Network Strategies in the Shadow of the State, Part II, in Hungarian." *Közgazdasági Szemle (Hungarian journal).* 47 (2000): 430–445.

Steenson, Gary P. *After Marx, before Lenin: Marxism and Socialist Working-Class Parties in Europe, 1884–1914.* Pittsburgh: University of Pittsburgh Press, 1991.

Stiglitz, Joseph E. *Globalization and Its Discontents.* [in English] New York: W.W. Norton, 2003.

Stiglitz, Joseph E. *The Roaring Nineties: a New History of the World's Most Prosperous Decade.* 1st ed. New York: W.W. Norton, 2003.

Straw, Will. "Cultural Scenes." *Loisir et société/Society and Leisure.*27, no. 2 (2004): 411–422.

Straw, Will. "Some Things a Scene Might Be: Postface." *Cultural studies.* 29, no. 3 (2015): 476–485.

Stray, C. *Oxford Classics: Teaching and Learning 1800–2000.* London, Berlin, New York: Bloomsbury, 2013.

Stromae. "Papaoutai (Clip Officiel). YouTube video dated June 6, 2013." accessed August 9, 2020.

Sullam, Simon Levis. *Giuseppe Mazzini and the Origins of Fascism.* Italian and Italian American Studies. London and New York: Palgrave Macmillan, 2015.

Sulloway, Frank J. "Darwin and the Galapagos." *Biological Journal of the Linnean Society.* 21, no. 1–2 (1984): 29–59.

Symonds, Richard. *Oxford and Empire: the Last Lost Cause?* Oxford: Clarendon Press, 1991.

Terraine, John. *Douglas Haig: the Educated Soldier.* London: Cassell, 2005.

Thomas, Peter D. *The Gramscian Moment: Philosophy, Hegemony and Marxism.* Leiden and Boston: Brill, 2009.

Thomas, Peter D. "Hegemony, Passive Revolution and the Modern Prince." *Thesis Eleven.* 117, no. 1 (2013): 20–39.

Thomas, Peter D. "Toward the Modern Prince." In *Gramsci in the World*, edited by Roberto M. Dainotto and Fredric Jameson. Durham and London: Duke University Press, 2020.

Tilly, Charles. *Contentious Performances.* Cambridge Studies in Contentious Politics. Cambridge and New York: Cambridge University Press, 2008.

Tilly, Charles. *Democracy.* Cambridge and New York: Cambridge University Press, 2007.

Tilly, Charles. *From Mobilization to Revolution.* London: Random House, 1978.

Trigilia, Carlo. *Economic Sociology: State, Market, and Society in Modern Capitalism.* Oxford: Blackwell, 2008.

Trigilia, Carlo. *Sviluppo Locale: un Progetto per l'Italia.* Saggi Tascabili Laterza. Bari: Laterza, 2005.

Turner, Bryan S. *Marx and the End of Orientalism.* London and New York: Routledge, 1978.

Urbinati, Nadia. "From the Periphery of Modernity: Antonio Gramsci's Theory of Subordination and Hegemony." *Political Theory.* 26, no. 3 (1998): 370–91.

Urbinati, Nadia. "L'Individuo Democratico tra Tocqueville, Gramsci e Dewey." In *Gramsci e il Novecento*, edited by Giuseppe Vacca. Roma: Carocci, 1999.

Van den Berg, Axel. *The Immanent Utopia: from Marxism on the State to the State of Marxism.* Princeton and Oxford: Princeton University Press, 1988.

Van den Berg, Axel. *The Immanent Utopia: from Marxism on the State to the State of Marxism.* London and New York: Routledge, 2018.

Van Horn, Robert, Philip Mirowski, and Thomas A. Stapleford. *Building Chicago Economics: New Perspectives on the History of America's Most Powerful Economics Program.* Historical Perspectives on Modern Economics. Cambridge and New York: Cambridge University Press, 2011.

Vasunia, Phiroze. *The Classics and Colonial India.* Classical Presences. Oxford and New York: Oxford University Press, 2013.

Venditti, Antonello. "Vendittivevo – Notte Prima degli Esami. VEVO video on YouTube dated November 23, 2017." Vevo, accessed August 9, 2020.

Venn, Couze. *Occidentalism: Modernity and Subjectivity.* Published in Association with Theory, Culture & Society. London, Thousand Oaks, New Delhi: SAGE Publications, 2000.

Vico, Giambattista. *New Science.* London: Penguin, 1999.

Villari, Rosario. "La Prefigurazione Politica del Giudizio Storico su Garibaldi." *Studi Storici.*23, no. 2 (1982): 261–266.

Walker, Guy H., Neville A. Stanton, Paul M. Salmon, and Daniel P. Jenkins. "A Review of Sociotechnical Systems Theory: a Classic Concept for New Command and Control Paradigms." *Theoretical issues in ergonomics science.* 9, no. 6 (2008): 479–499.

Wallerstein, Immanuel. "World-Systems Analysis." In *Social Theory Today*, edited by Anthony Giddens and Jonathan H. Turner. Stanford: Stanford University Press, 1987.

Wallerstein, Immanuel Maurice. *Historical Capitalism with Capitalist Civilization.* London and New York: Verso, 1995.

Wallerstein, Immanuel Maurice. *The Modern World-System, Vol. I: Capitalist Agriculture and the Origins of the European World-Economy in the Sixteenth Century.* Modern World-System. Berkeley and Los Angeles: University of California Press, 2011.

Wallerstein, Immanuel Maurice. *The Modern World-System, Vol. II: Mercantilism and the Consolidation of the European World-Economy, 1600–1750.* Modern World-System. Berkeley and Los Angeles: University of California Press, 2011.

Wallerstein, Immanuel Maurice. *The Modern World-System, Vol. III: the Second Era of Great Expansion of the Capitalist World-Economy, 1730s–1840s, with a New Prologue.* Modern World-System. Berkeley and Los Angeles: University of California Press, 2011.

Wallerstein, Immanuel Maurice. *The Modern World-System, Vol. IV: Centrist Liberalism Triumphant, 1789–1914.* Modern World-System. Berkeley and Los Angeles: University of California Press, 2011.

Wallerstein, Immanuel Maurice. *The Modern World-System: Capitalist Agriculture and the Origins of the European World-Economy in the Sixteeth Century.* Studies in Social Discontinuity. New York: Academic Press, 1976.

Waterbury, John. *Missions Impossible: Higher Education and Policymaking in the Arab World.* Cairo and New York: American University in Cairo Press, 2020.

Weber, Marianne. *Max Weber: a Biography.* New York and London: Routledge, 2017.

Weber, Max, Hans Heinrich Gerth, C. Wright Mills, and Bryan S. Turner. *From Max Weber: Essays in Sociology.* London and New York: Routledge, 1991.

Weber, Max, Guenther Roth, and Claus Wittich, eds. *Economy and Society: an Outline of Interpretive Sociology.* Berkeley and Los Angeles: University of California Press, 1978.

Weiner, Elaine S. *Market Dreams: Gender, Class, and Capitalism in the Czech Republic.* Ann Arbor: University of Michigan Press, 2010.

Weiner, Elaine S. "No (Wo) Man's Land: the Post-Socialist Purgatory of Czech Female Factory Workers." *Social problems.*52, no. 4 (2005): 572–592.

Weinstock, Daniel. "Occupy, Indignados, Et Le Printemps Érable: Vers un Agenda de Recherche." *McGill Law Journal/Revue de droit de McGill.* 58, no. 2 (2012): 243–262.

Weinstock, Daniel. "The Political Philosophy of the" Printemps Érable."" *Theory & Event.*15, no. 3 (2012).

Wendt, Alexander. "Why a World State Is Inevitable." *European journal of international relations.* 9, no. 4 (2003): 491–542.

Wikipedia. "3rd Army Corps (Italy)." https://en.wikipedia.org/wiki/3rd_Army_Corps_(Italy), accessed April 3, 2021.

Wikipedia. "5th Army Corps (Italy)." https://en.wikipedia.org/wiki/5th_Army_Corps_(Italy), accessed April 3, 2021.

Wikipedia. "Division "Vittorio Veneto."" https://en.wikipedia.org/wiki/Division_%22Vittorio_Veneto%22, accessed April 3, 2021.

Wikipedia. "Mechanized Brigade "Mantova."" https://en.wikipedia.org/wiki/Mechanized_Brigade_%22Mantova%22, accessed April 3, 2021.

Wikipedia. "New York University." https://en.wikipedia.org/wiki/New_York_University, accessed April 9, 2021.

Wikipedia. "Philosophy, Politics and Economics." https://en.wikipedia.org/wiki/Philosophy,_politics_and_economics, accessed September 1, 2020.

Wikipedia. "Svalbard Undersea Cable System." https://en.wikipedia.org/wiki/Svalbard_Undersea_Cable_System, accessed April 9, 2021.

Wittgenstein, Ludwig, and Gertrude Elizabeth Margaret Anscombe. *Philosophical Investigations: the German Text, with a Revised English Translation.* Oxford: Basil Blackwell, 2001.

World Economic Forum, Global Internet of Things Council, and Pricewaterhouse Coopers. "State of the Connected World: Insight Report." http://www3.weforum.org/docs/WEF_The_State_of_the_Connected_World_2020.pd, accessed April 9, 2021.

World Values Survey. "Findings and Insights, Inglehart–Welzel Cultural Map." http://www.worldvaluessurvey.org/WVSContents.jsp?CMSID=Findings, accessed August 29, 2020.

World Values Survey. "WVS Wave 7 (2017–2020)." http://www.worldvaluessurvey.org/WVSDocumentationWV7.jsp, accessed August 13, 2020.

Worringer, Renee. *A Short History of the Ottoman Empire.* Toronto: University of Toronto Press, 2020.

Worringer, Renee, Andras Hamori, and Bernard Lewis, eds. *The Islamic Middle East and Japan: Perceptions, Aspirations, and the Birth of Intra-Asian Modernity.* Princeton: Markus Wiener Publishers, 2007.

Wright, Katharine A. M., and Annika Bergman-Rosamond. "NATO's Strategic Narratives: Angelina Jolie and the Alliance's Celebrity and Visual Turn." *Review of International Studies.* (2021).

Wright, Terence R. *The Religion of Humanity: the Impact of Comtean Positivism on Victorian Britain.* Cambridge and New York: Cambridge University Press, 2008.

Wuthnow, Robert. *Communities of Discourse: Ideology and Social Structure in the Reformation, the Enlightenment, and European Socialism.* Cambridge, Massachusetts and London: Harvard University Press, 1989.

Young, Warren, and Frederic S. Lee. *Oxford Economics and Oxford Economists.* London and New York: Palgrave Macmillan, 1993.

Index

CPSIA information can be obtained
at www.ICGtesting.com
Printed in the USA
JSHW050858271222
35400JS00003B/3